Other titles available from Broccoli Books

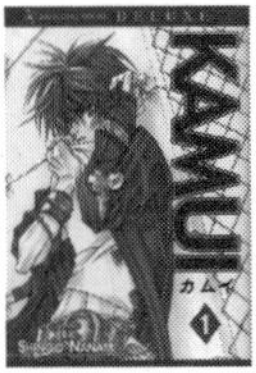
KAMUI

KAMUI

Infused with the spirit of an ancient sword, young Atsuma must leave his village to reclaim the stolen sacred spirit Okikurumi. His quest leads him to NOA, an organization of gifted youths similarly empowered by spirits, which may hold the key to Okikurumi. It is up to Atsuma to save the world before Okikurumi can be turned into a weapon of destruction.

Story & Art by Shingo Nanami

Suggested Retail Price: $9.99 each

Volume 1 Coming Fall 2005!

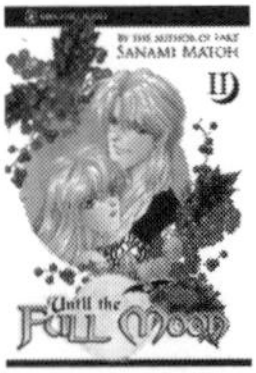
SANAMI MATOH
Until the
FULL MOON

Until the Full Moon

Marlo is half vampire, half werewolf with a problem. On nights when the full moon shines, Marlo undergoes a mysterious transformation... he turns into a girl.

Story & Art by Sanami Matoh

Suggested Retail Price: $9.99 each

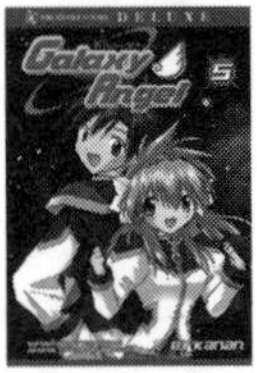
Galaxy Angel

Galaxy Angel

The Angel Troupe has one mission; they must protect Prince Shiva, the sole survivor of the royal family decimated by a coup d'état. Milfeulle, Ranpha, Mint, Forte, and Vanilla each possess special gifts, making them ideal for the job at hand. Takuto finds himself leading the mission, getting caught between the five unique Angels.

Story & Art by Kanan

Suggested Retail Price: $9.99 each

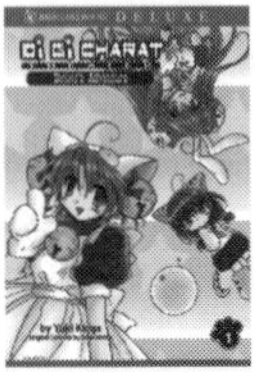
Di Gi Charat

Di Gi Charat Theater – Dejiko's Adventure

Dejiko has destroyed the Gamers retail store! Now it's up to her and the rest of the gang as they search for the secret treasure that will save Gamers.

Story & Art by Yuki Kiriga

Suggested Retail Price: $9.99 each

Volumes 2-3 Coming Soon!

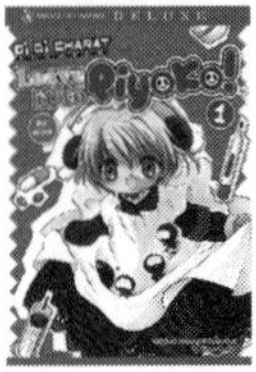
Piyoko!

Di Gi Charat Theater – Leave it to Piyoko!

Follow the daily adventures of the Black Gema Gema Gang, as they continue their road to evil.

Story & Art by Hina.

Suggested Retail Price: $9.99 each

Volume 2 Coming Soon!

For more information about Broccoli Books titles,
check out **bro-usa.com!**

AQUARIAN AGE

JUVENILE ORION ①

オリオンの少年 ™

by Sakurako Gokurakuin
Original Concept by BROCCOLI • Marekatsu Nakai

™ brought to you by
BROCCOLI BOOKS
A DIVISION OF BROCCOLI INTERNATIONAL USA

Aquarian Age™ – Juvenile Orion Volume 1

English Adaptation Staff
Translation: Rie Hagihara
English Adaptation: Stephanie Sheh
Clean-Up: Tim Law
Touch-Up & Lettering: Chris McDougall
Cover & Graphic Supervision: Chris McDougall

Editor: Satsuki Yamashita
Sales Manager: Ardith D. Santiago
Managing Editor: Shizuki Yamashita
Publisher: Hideki Uchino

Email: editor@broccolibooks.com
Website: www.bro-usa.com

A BROCCOLI BOOKS Manga
Broccoli Books is a division of Broccoli International USA, Inc.
P.O. Box 66078 Los Angeles, CA 90066

ISBN-13: 978-1-9324-8009-2
ISBN-10: 1-9324-8009-9

Published by Broccoli International USA, Inc.
Fourth printing, August 2005
First printing, December 2003

All illustrations by Sakurako Gokurakuin.

ANIME GAMERS

BROCCOLI INTERNATIONAL USA
www.bro-usa.com

10 9 8 7 6 5 4
Printed in the United States

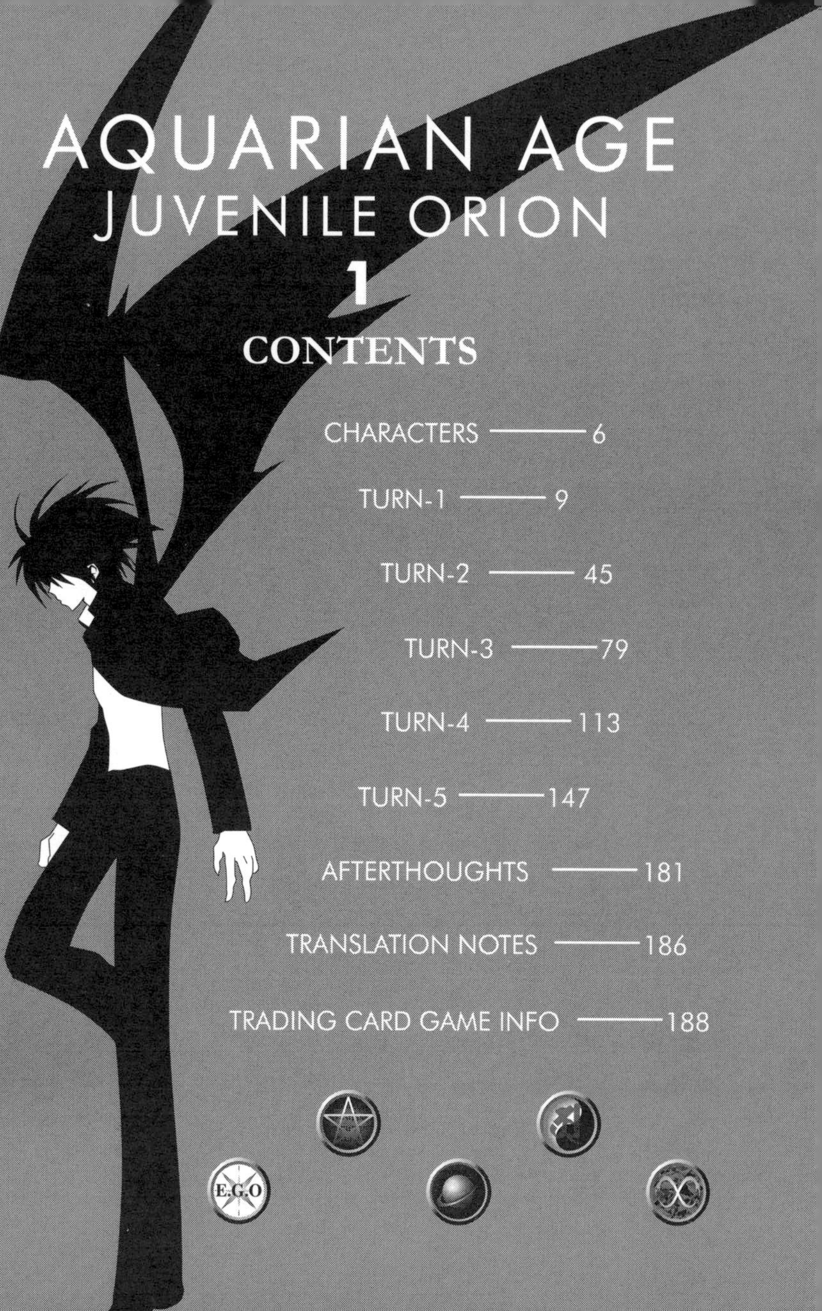

AQUARIAN AGE JUVENILE ORION 1

CONTENTS

JUVENILE ORION
CHARACTERS

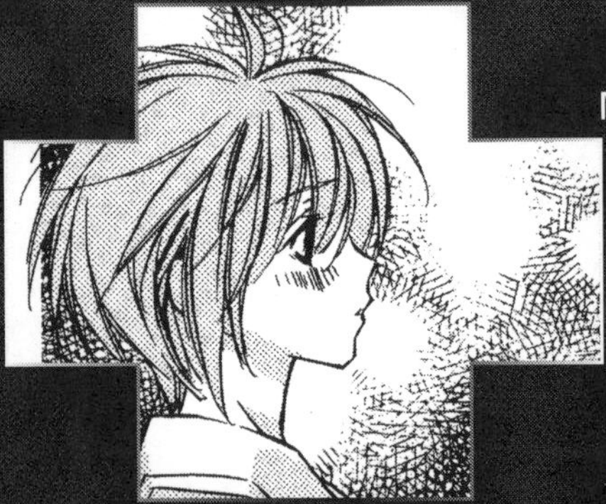

MANA KIRIHARA
Birthday May 5
Age 16
Blood Type A
Height 5'2"
Weight 99 lbs

KANAME KUSAKABE
Birthday December 7
Age 16
Blood Type O
Height 5'7"
Weight 117 lbs

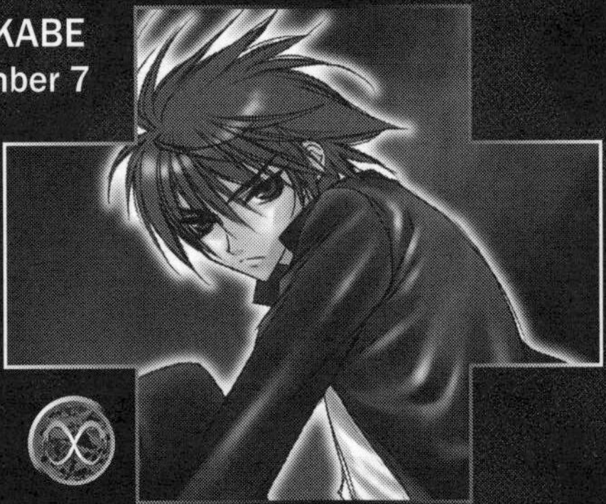

NAOYA ITSUKI
Birthday July 21
Age 17
Blood Type B
Height 5'7"
Weight 126 lbs

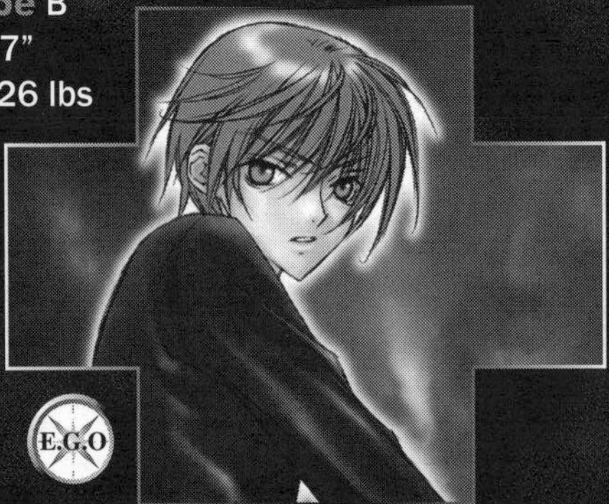
E.G.O

anuary 18

O

lbs

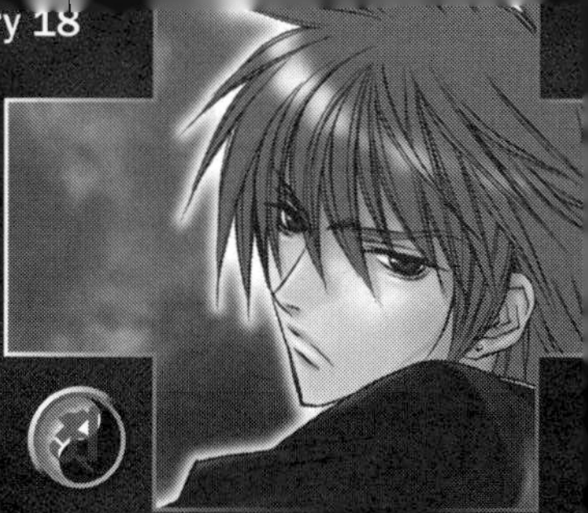

TSUKASA AMOU

Birthday March 10

Age 16

Blood Type A

Height 5'5"

Weight 95 lbs

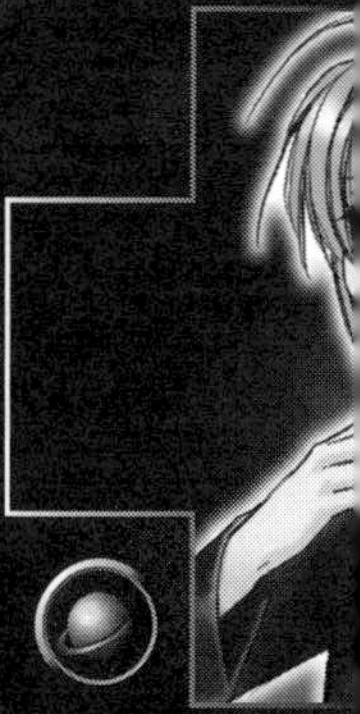

NAKAURA

pril 28

AB

lbs

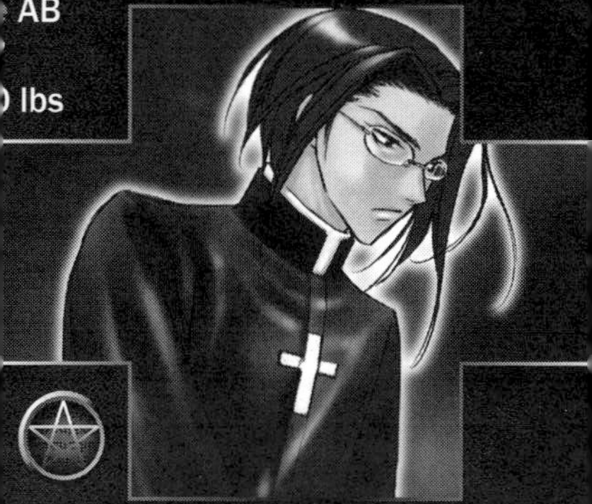

ENILE ORION

HARACT

turn. 1

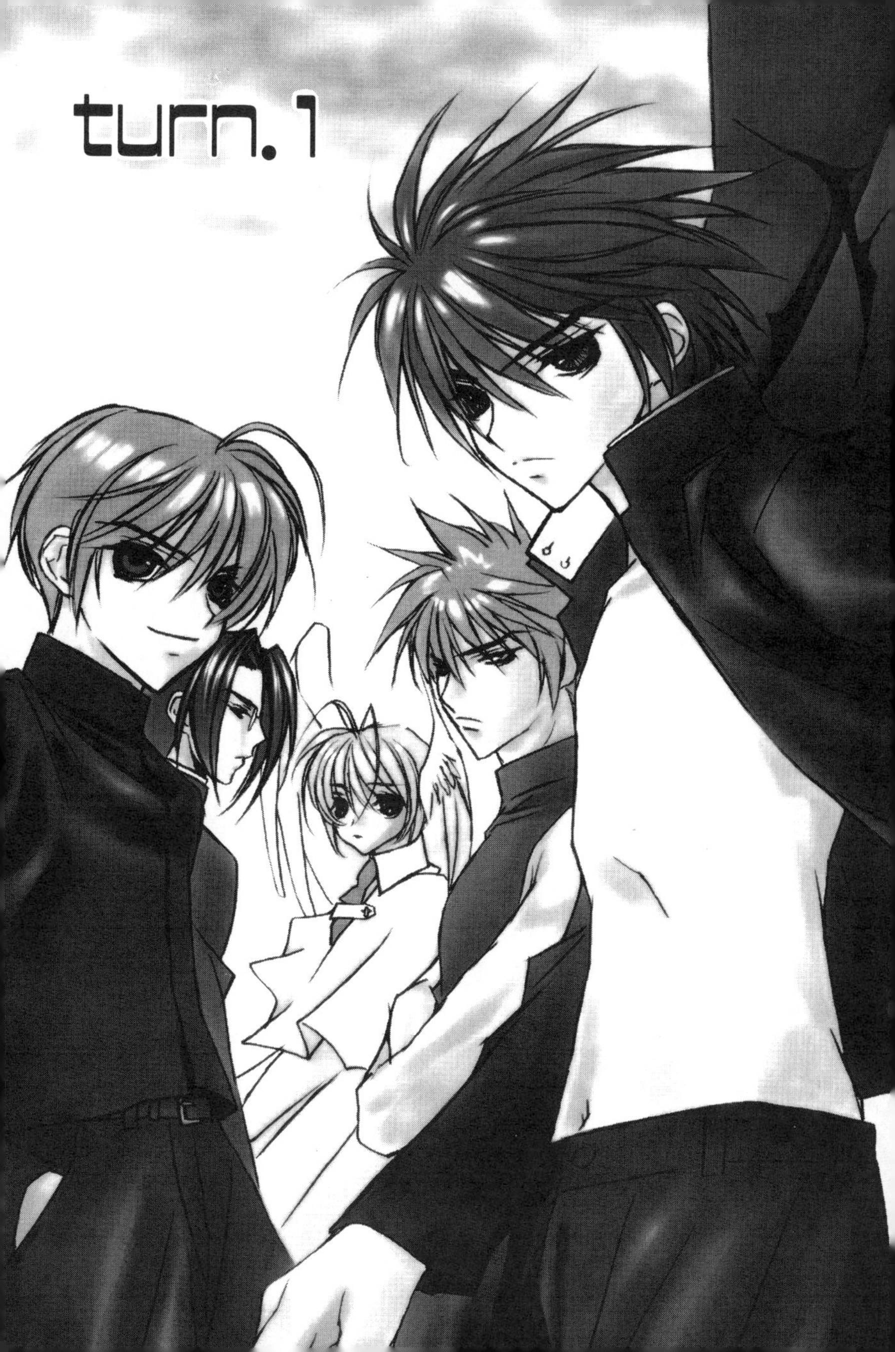

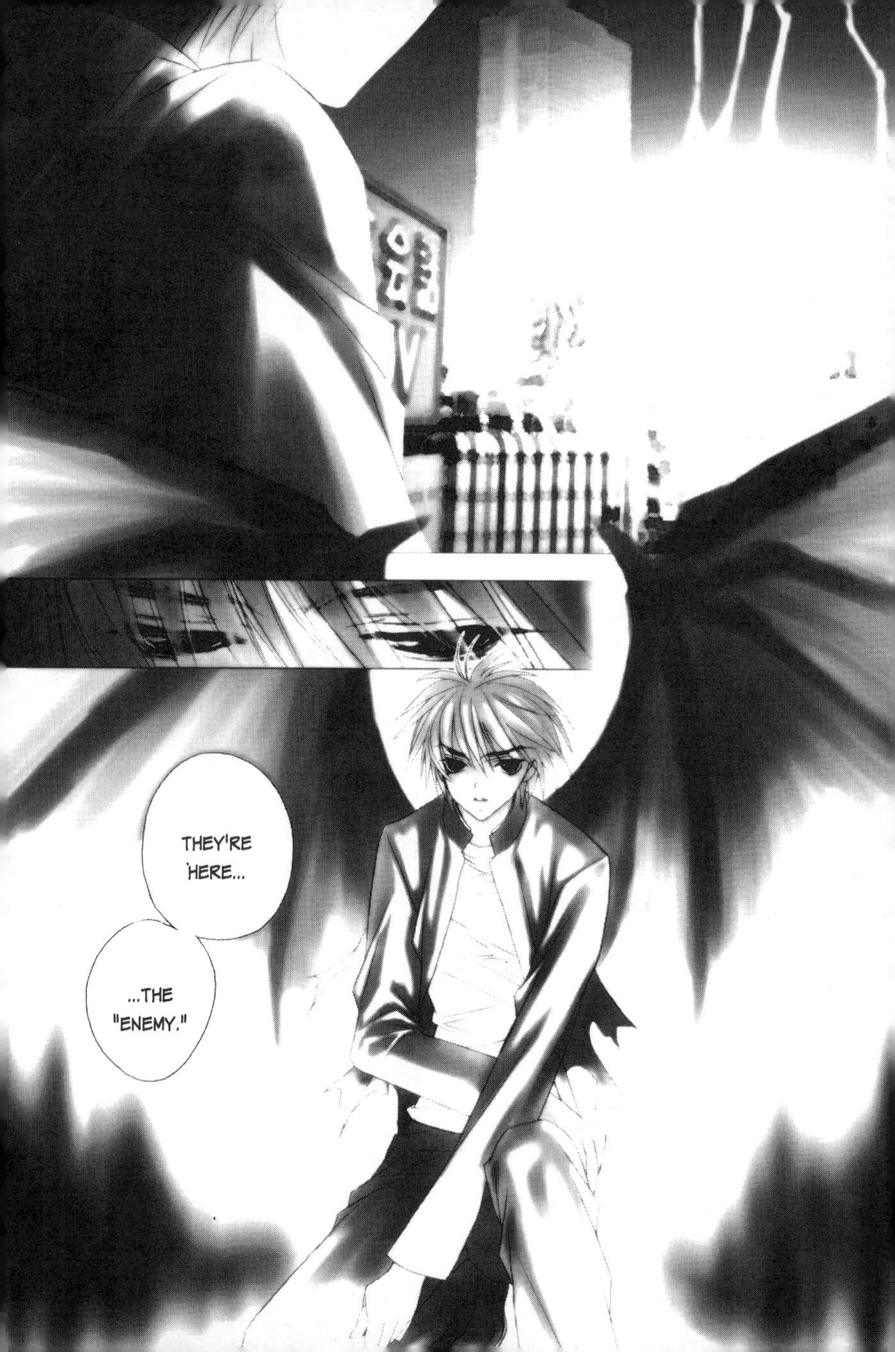
THEY'RE HERE...
...THE "ENEMY."

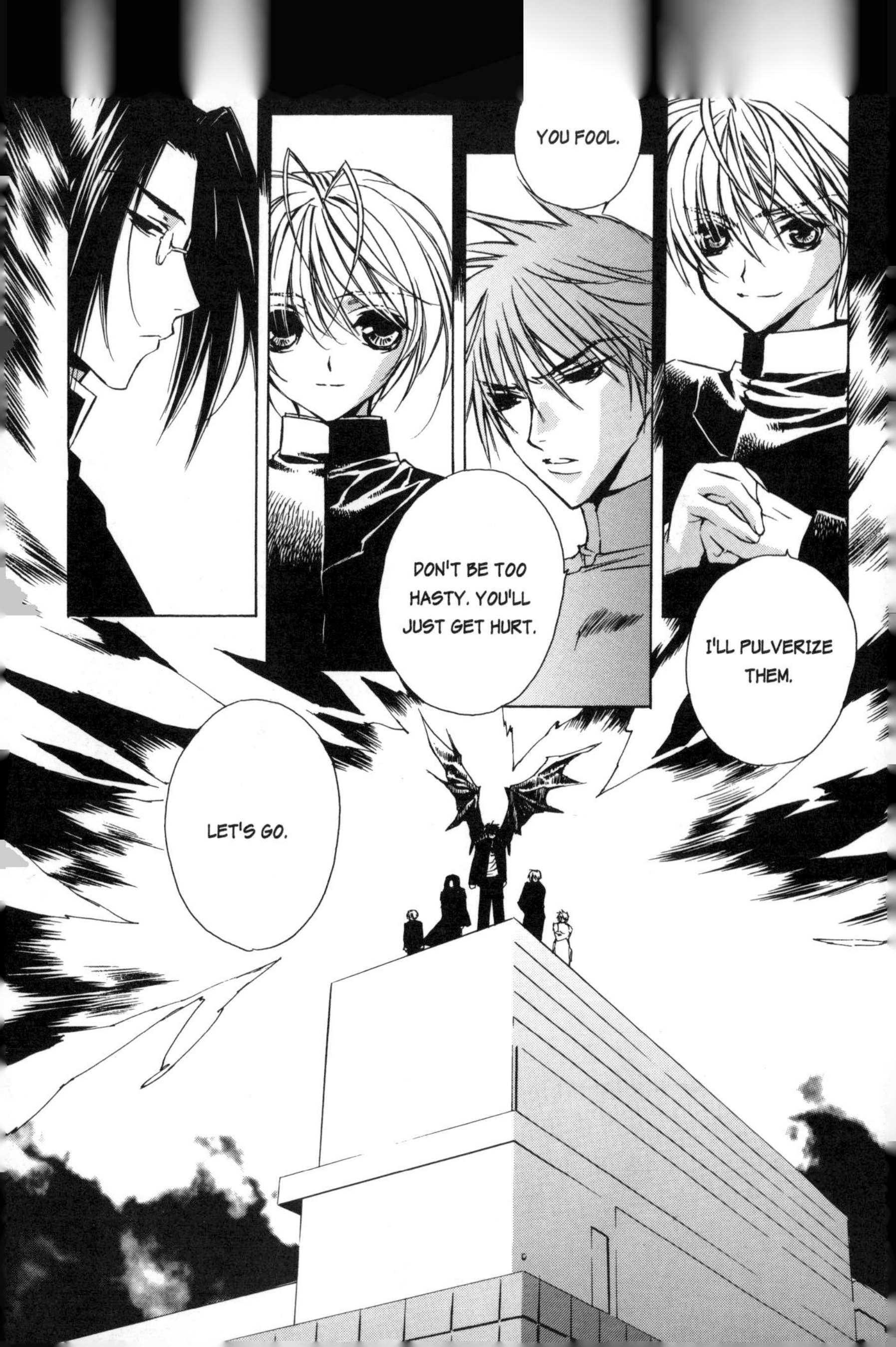
I'LL PULVERIZE THEM.
YOU FOOL.
DON'T BE TOO HASTY. YOU'LL JUST GET HURT.
LET'S GO.

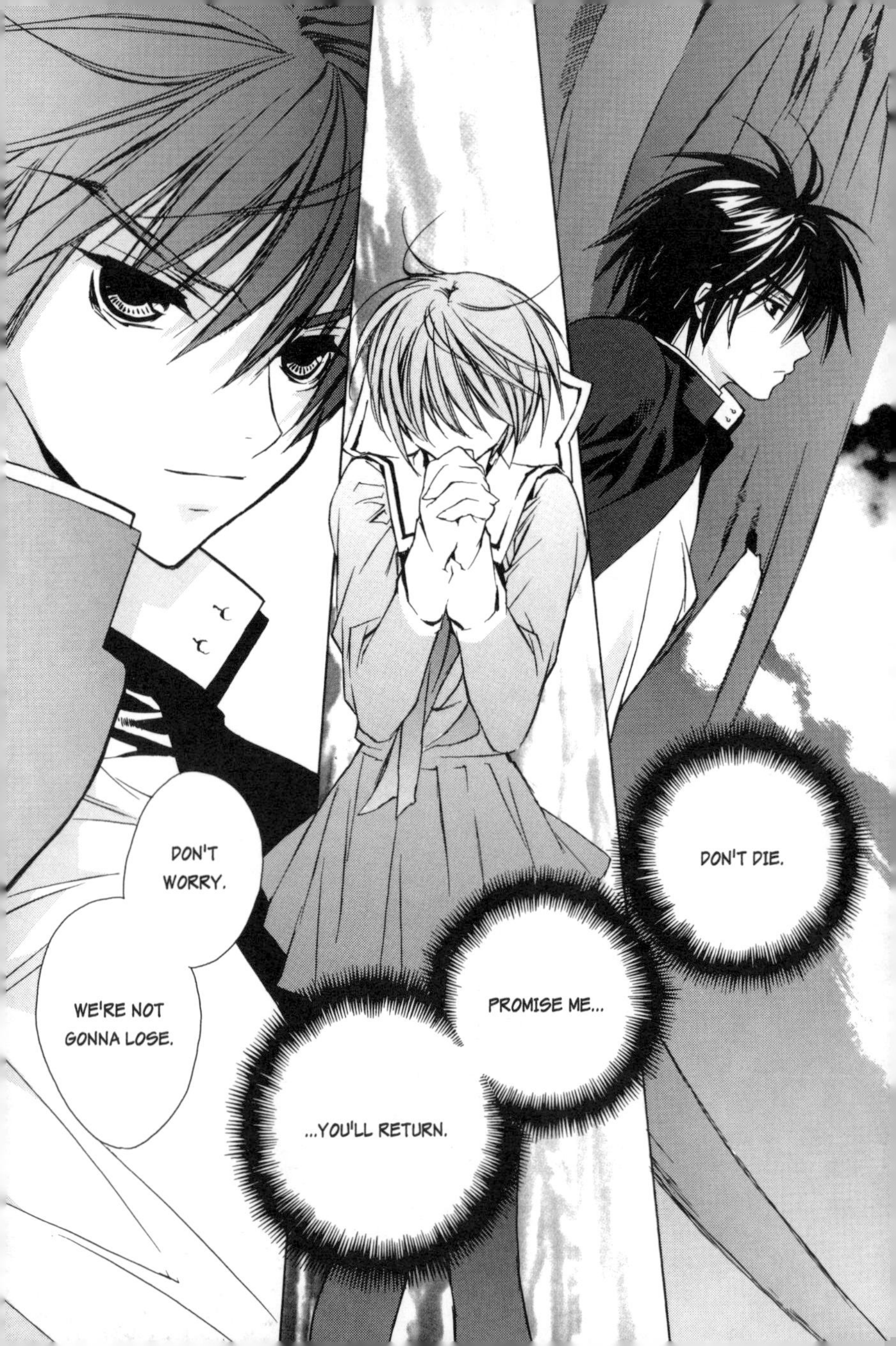
DON'T DIE.
PROMISE ME...
...YOU'LL RETURN.
DON'T WORRY.
WE'RE NOT GONNA LOSE.

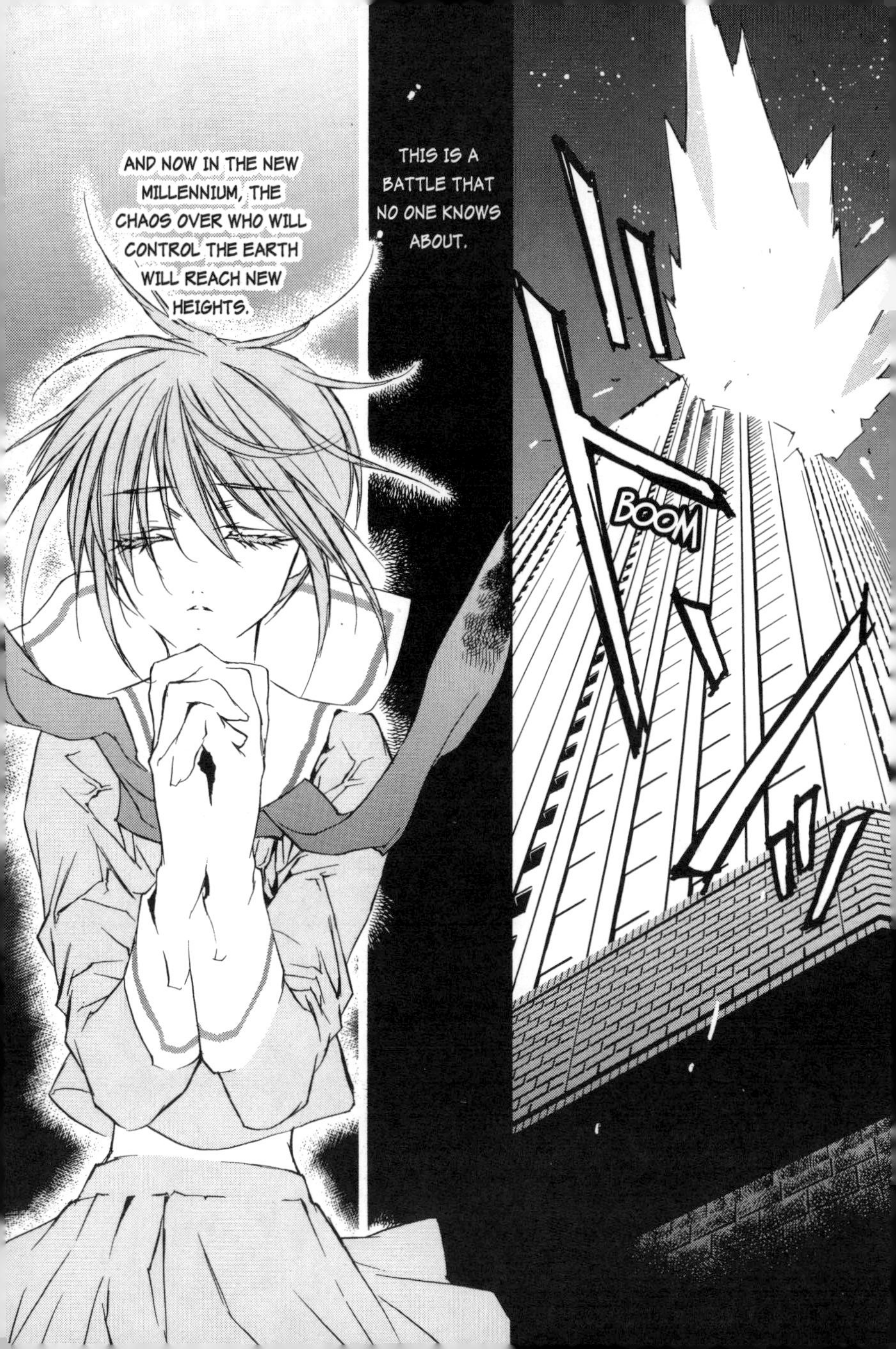
BOOM
THIS IS A BATTLE THAT NO ONE KNOWS ABOUT.
AND NOW IN THE NEW MILLENNIUM, THE CHAOS OVER WHO WILL CONTROL THE EARTH WILL REACH NEW HEIGHTS.

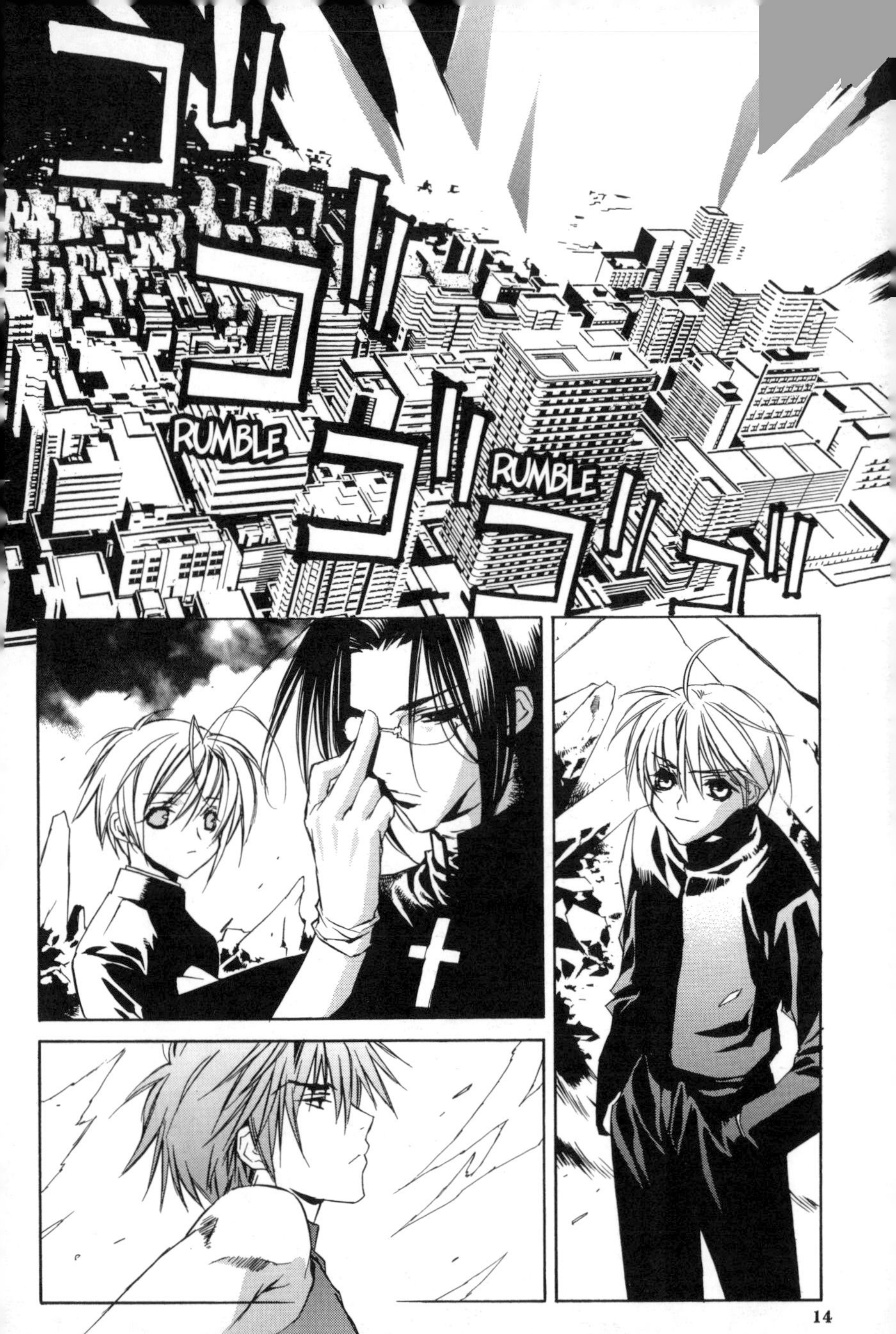
RUMBLE
RUMBLE

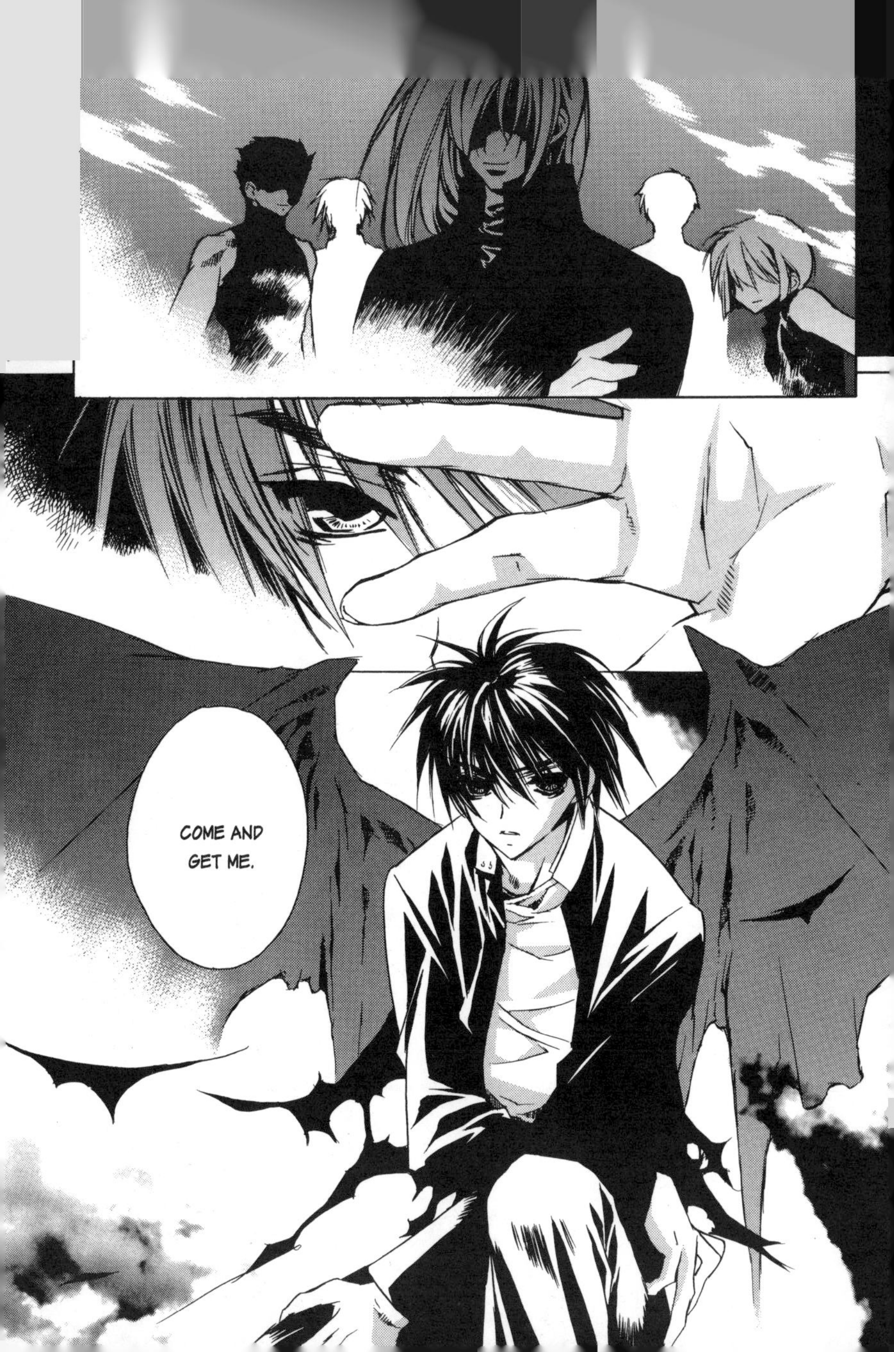
COME AND GET ME.

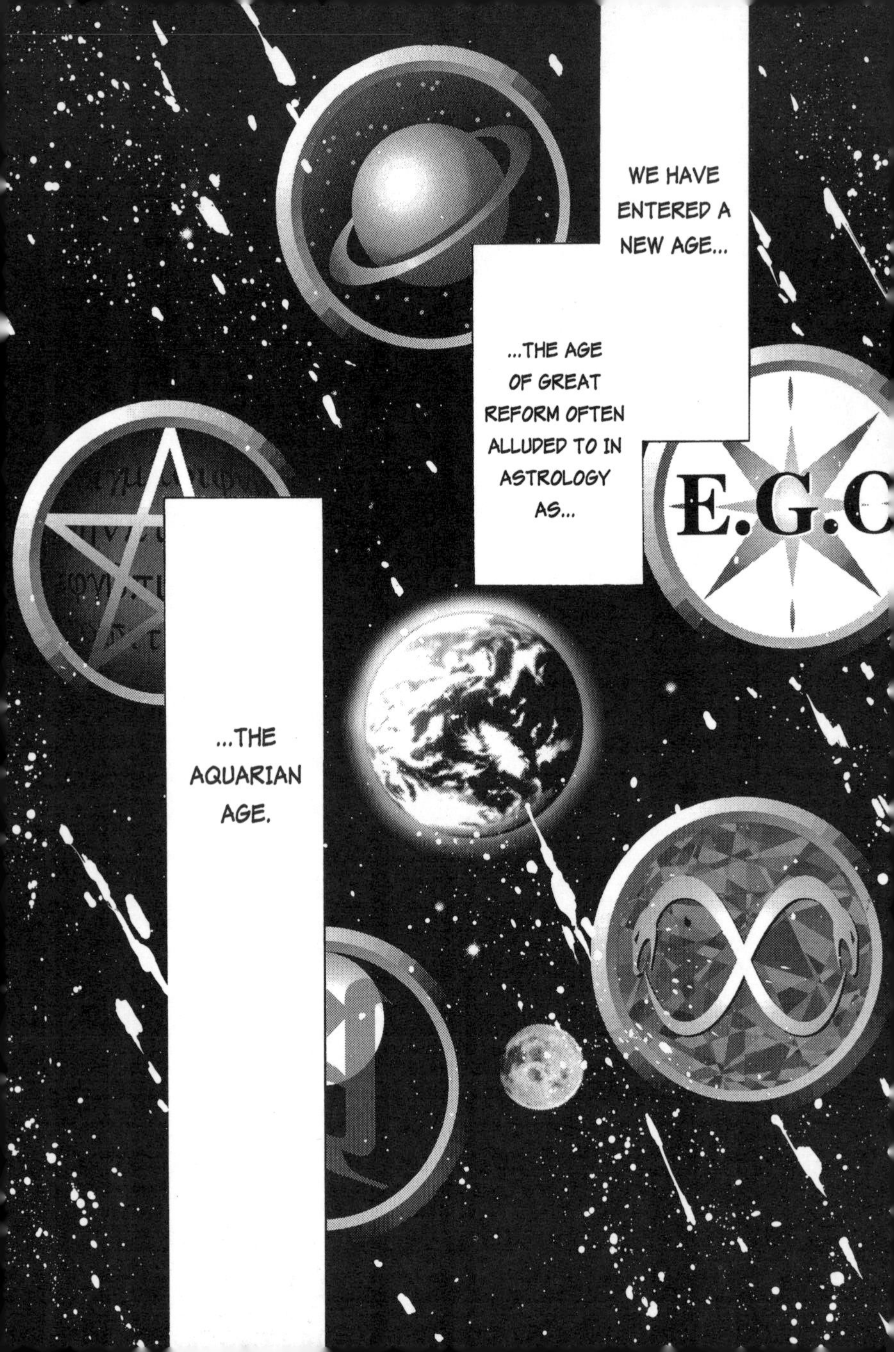
WE HAVE ENTERED A NEW AGE...
...THE AGE OF GREAT REFORM OFTEN ALLUDED TO IN ASTROLOGY AS...
...THE AQUARIAN AGE.

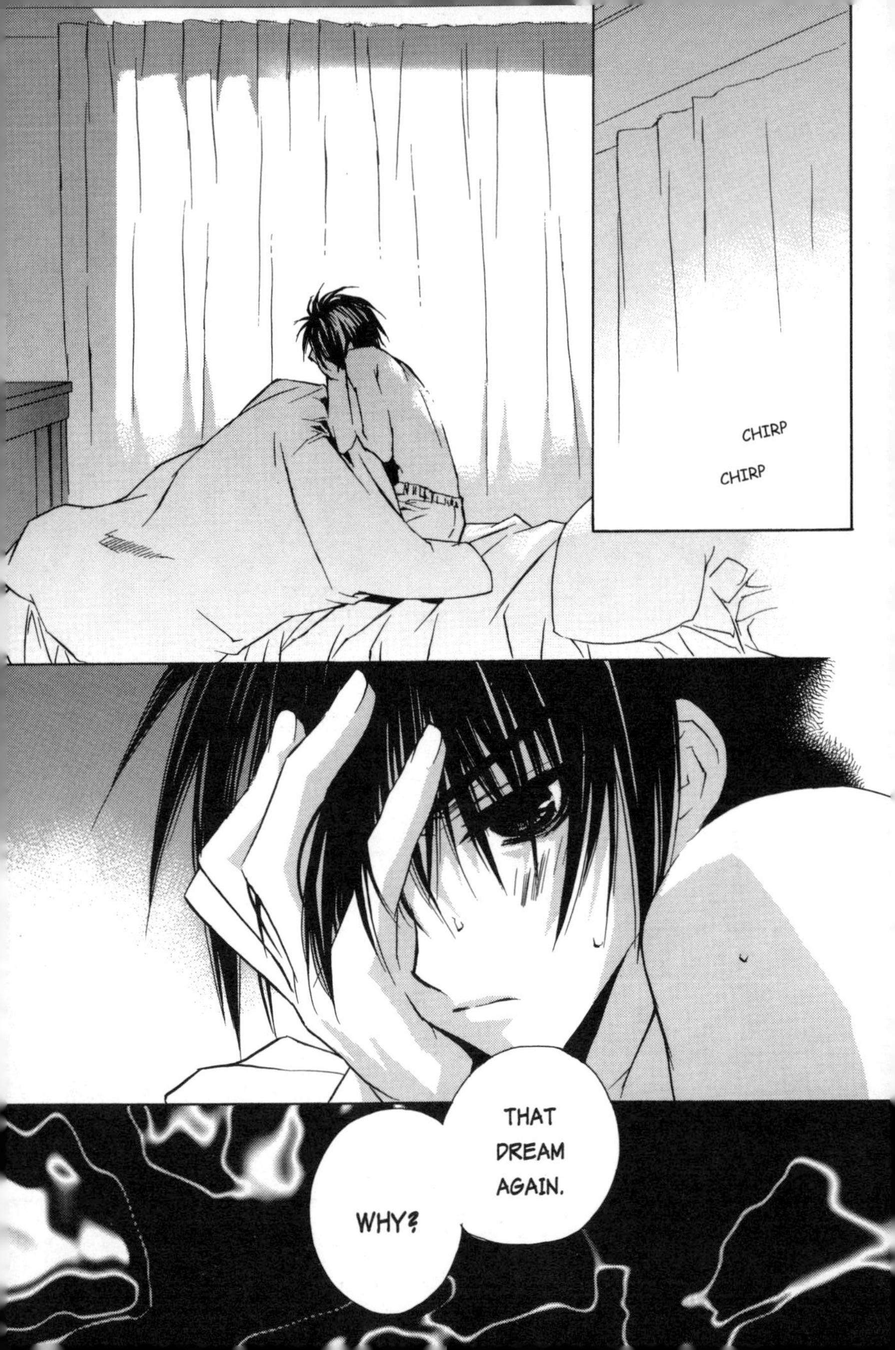
CHIRP
CHIRP
THAT DREAM AGAIN.
WHY?

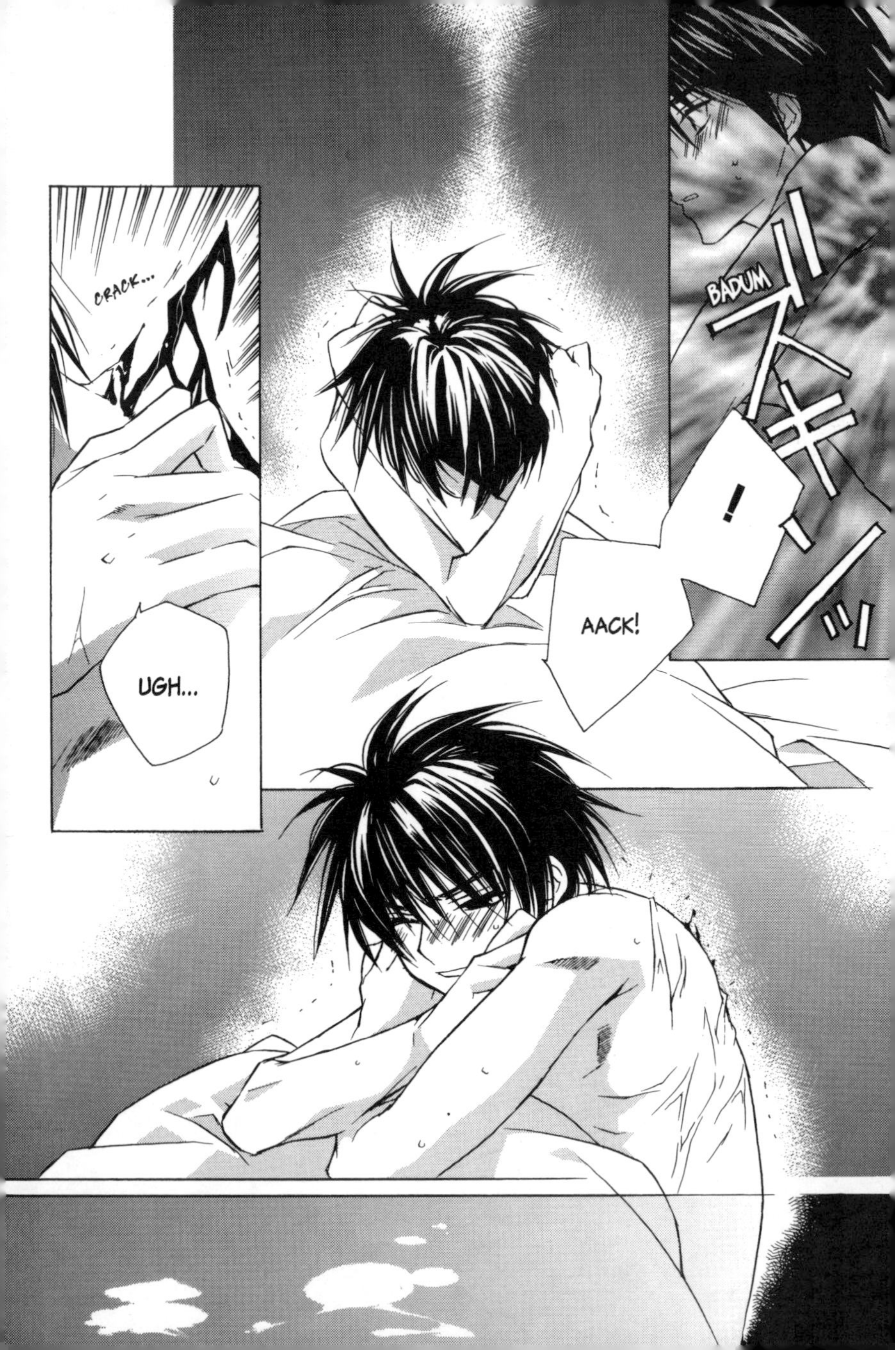
BADUM
ドキーッ
!
AACK!
CRACK...
UGH...

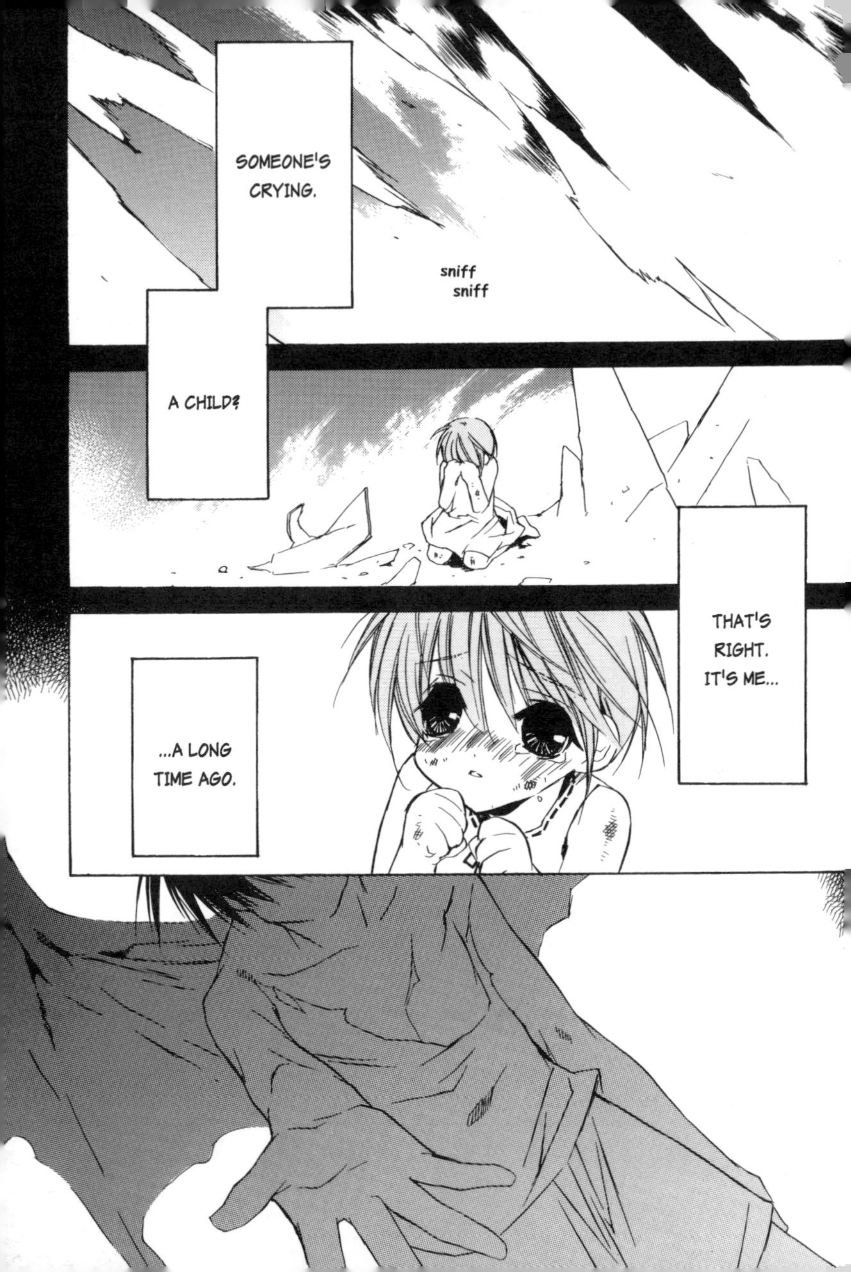
SOMEONE'S CRYING.
sniff sniff
A CHILD?
THAT'S RIGHT. IT'S ME...
...A LONG TIME AGO.

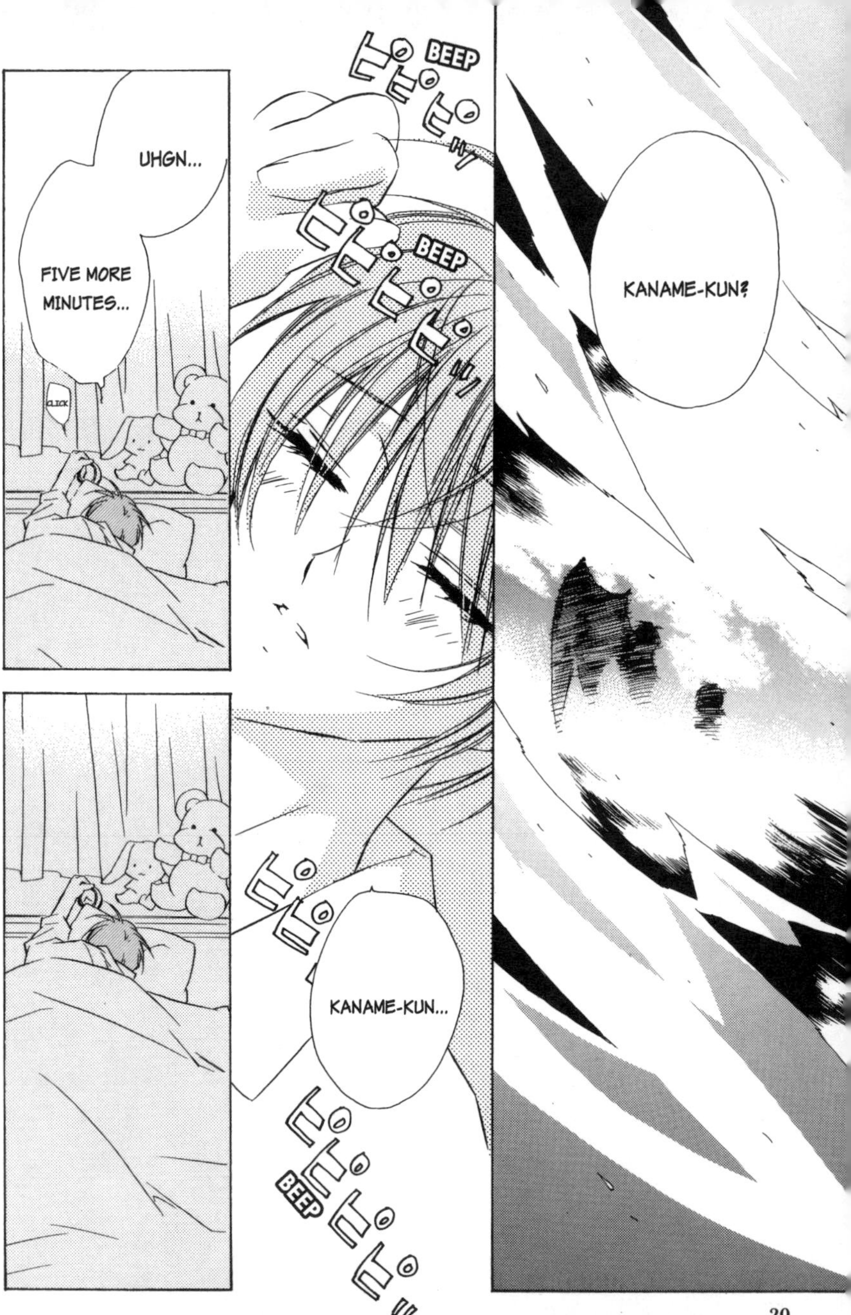
KANAME-KUN?
BEEP
BEEP
KANAME-KUN...
BEEP
UHGN...
FIVE MORE MINUTES...
CLICK

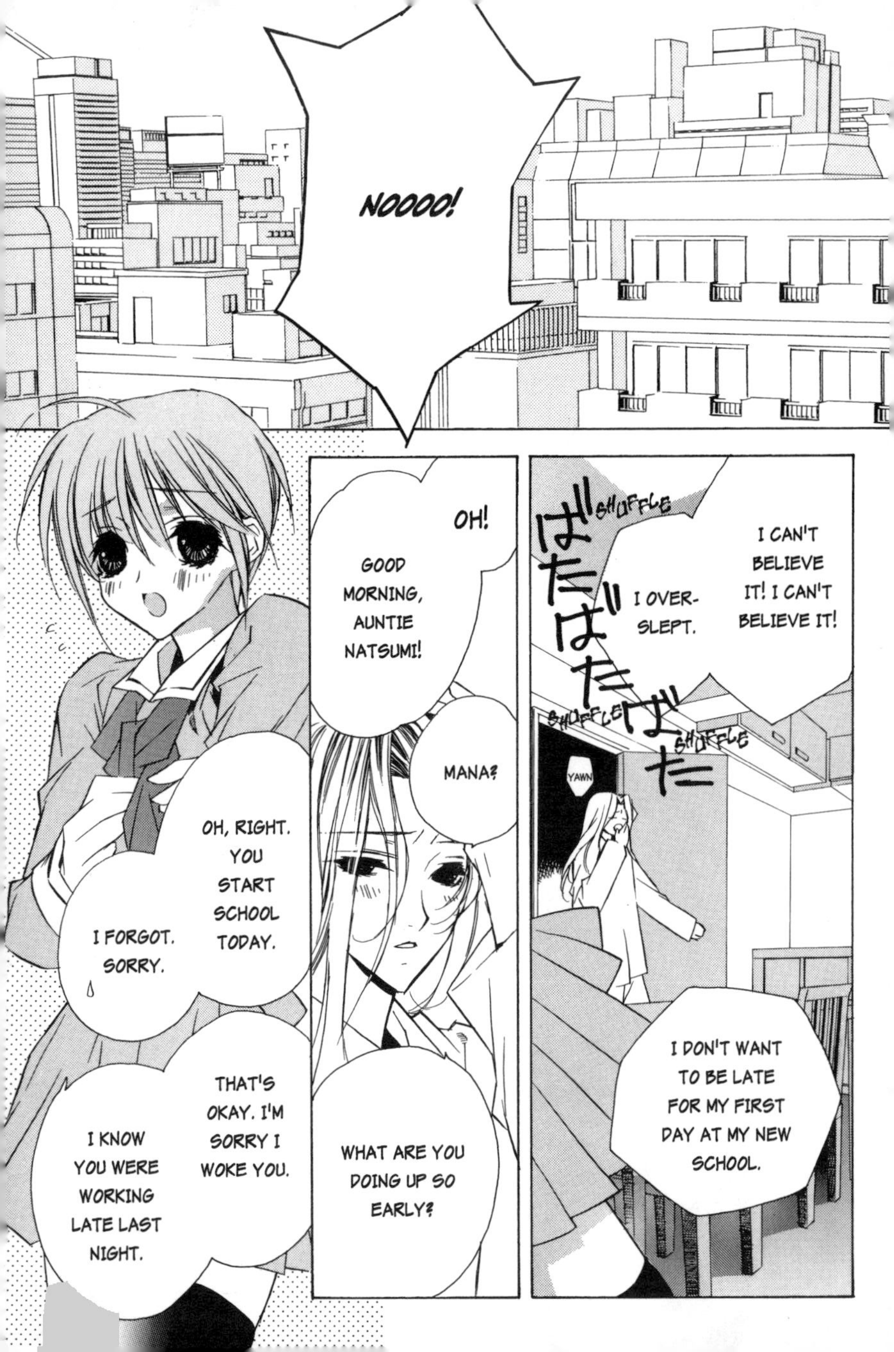
NOOOO!
ばたばた
ばた
SHUFFLE
SHUFFLE
SHUFFLE
I CAN'T BELIEVE IT! I CAN'T BELIEVE IT!
I OVER-SLEPT.
YAWN
I DON'T WANT TO BE LATE FOR MY FIRST DAY AT MY NEW SCHOOL.
OH!
GOOD MORNING, AUNTIE NATSUMI!
MANA?
WHAT ARE YOU DOING UP SO EARLY?
OH, RIGHT. YOU START SCHOOL TODAY.
I FORGOT. SORRY.
THAT'S OKAY. I'M SORRY I WOKE YOU.
I KNOW YOU WERE WORKING LATE LAST NIGHT.

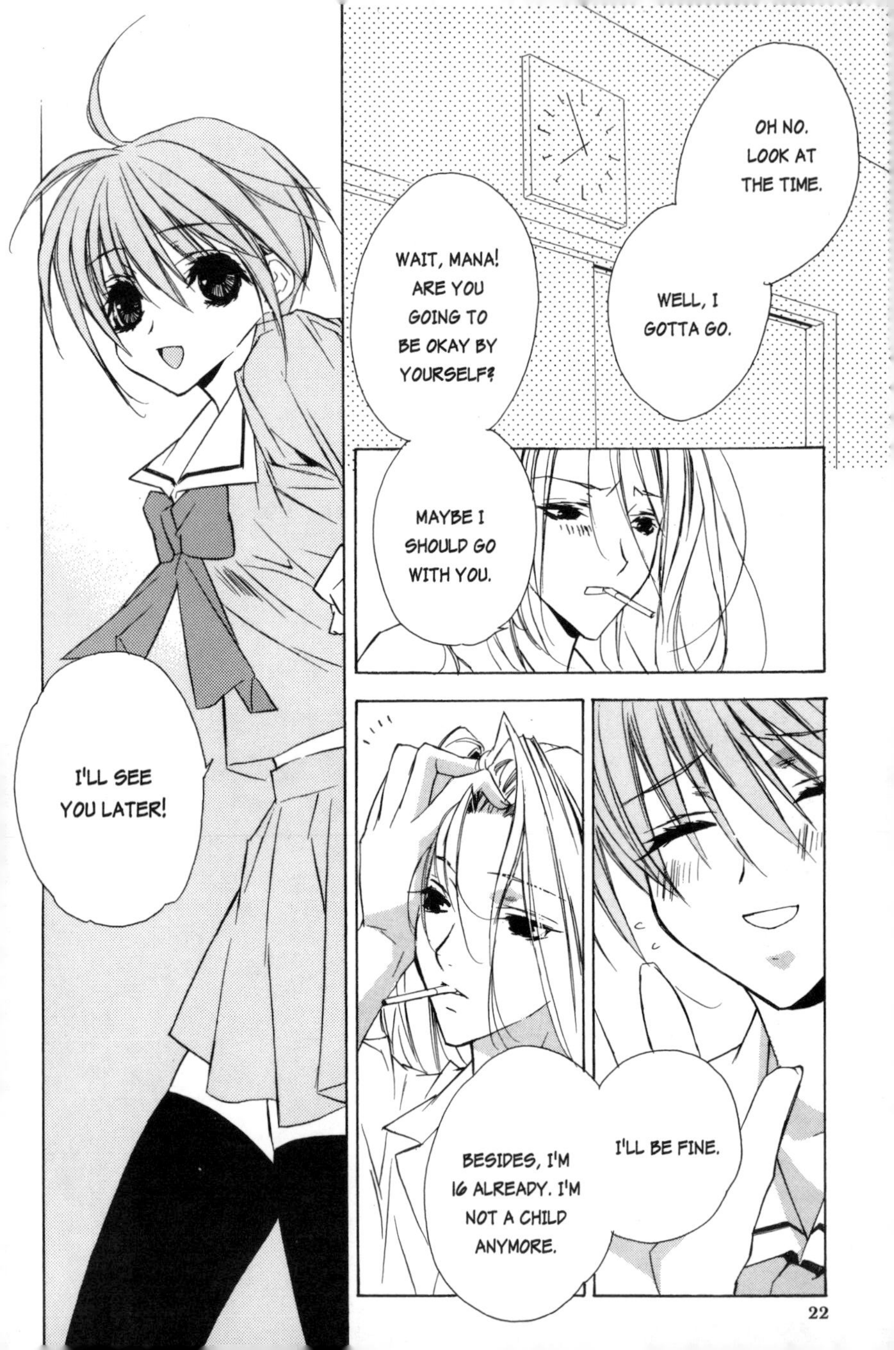
OH NO. LOOK AT THE TIME.
WELL, I GOTTA GO.
WAIT, MANA! ARE YOU GOING TO BE OKAY BY YOURSELF?
MAYBE I SHOULD GO WITH YOU.
I'LL BE FINE.
BESIDES, I'M 16 ALREADY. I'M NOT A CHILD ANYMORE.
I'LL SEE YOU LATER!

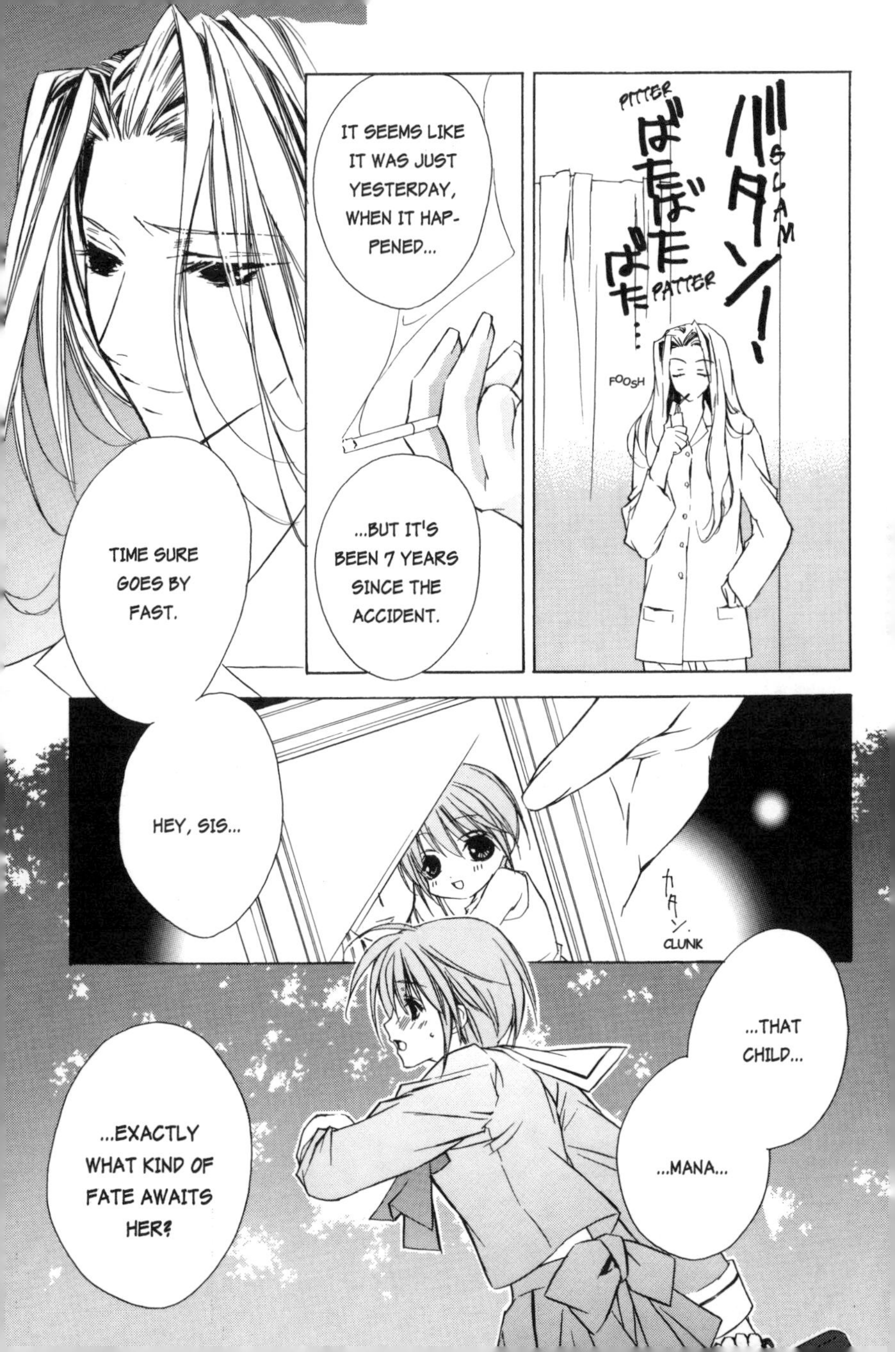
バタン！
SLAM
ぱたぱたぱた…
PITTER PATTER
FOOSH
IT SEEMS LIKE IT WAS JUST YESTERDAY, WHEN IT HAP-PENED...
...BUT IT'S BEEN 7 YEARS SINCE THE ACCIDENT.
TIME SURE GOES BY FAST.
カタン.
CLUNK
HEY, SIS...
...THAT CHILD...
...MANA...
...EXACTLY WHAT KIND OF FATE AWAITS HER?

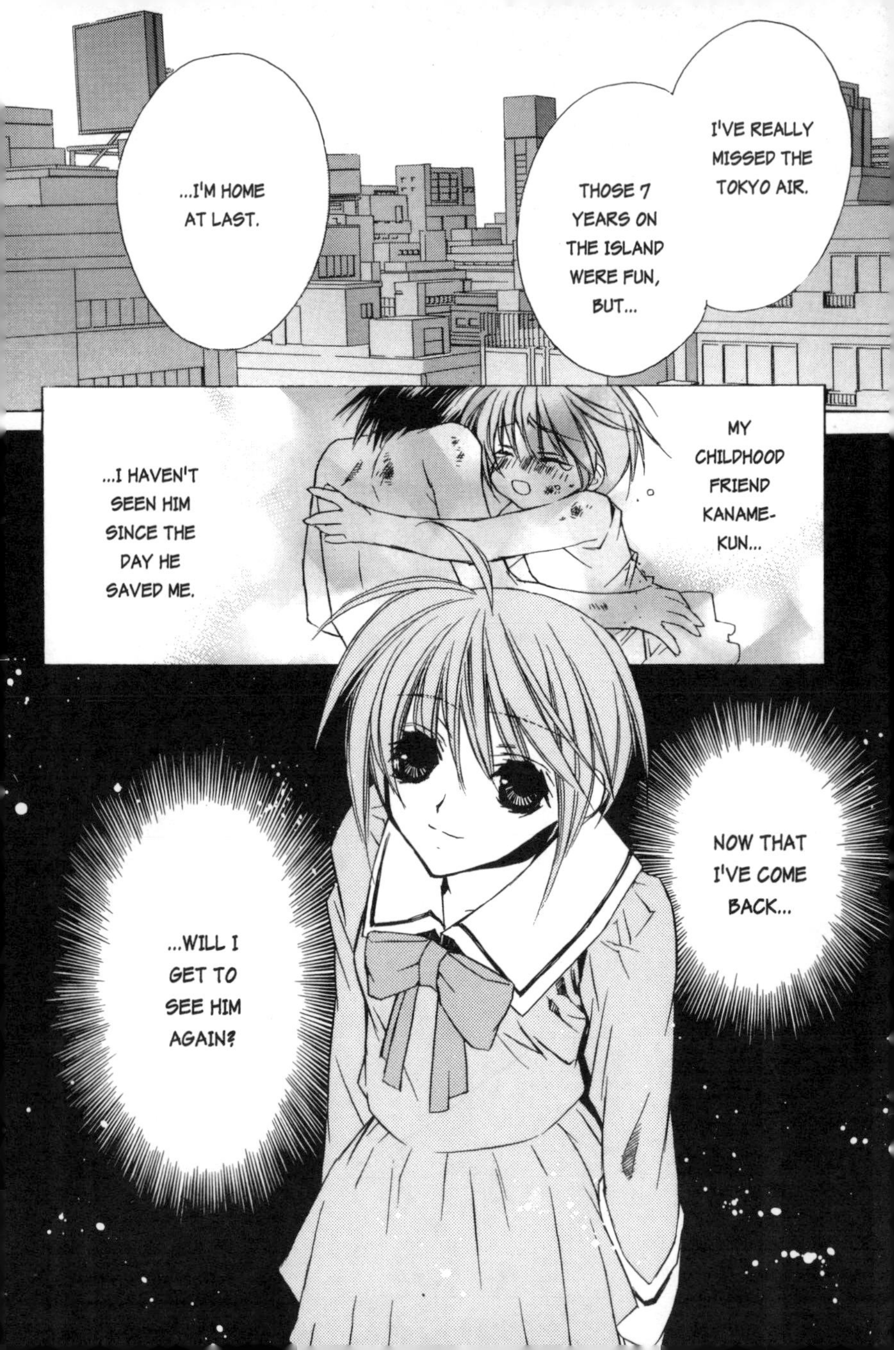
I'VE REALLY MISSED THE TOKYO AIR.
THOSE 7 YEARS ON THE ISLAND WERE FUN, BUT...
...I'M HOME AT LAST.
MY CHILDHOOD FRIEND KANAME-KUN...
...I HAVEN'T SEEN HIM SINCE THE DAY HE SAVED ME.
NOW THAT I'VE COME BACK...
...WILL I GET TO SEE HIM AGAIN?

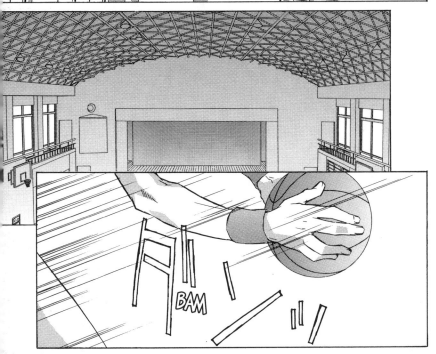

BAM

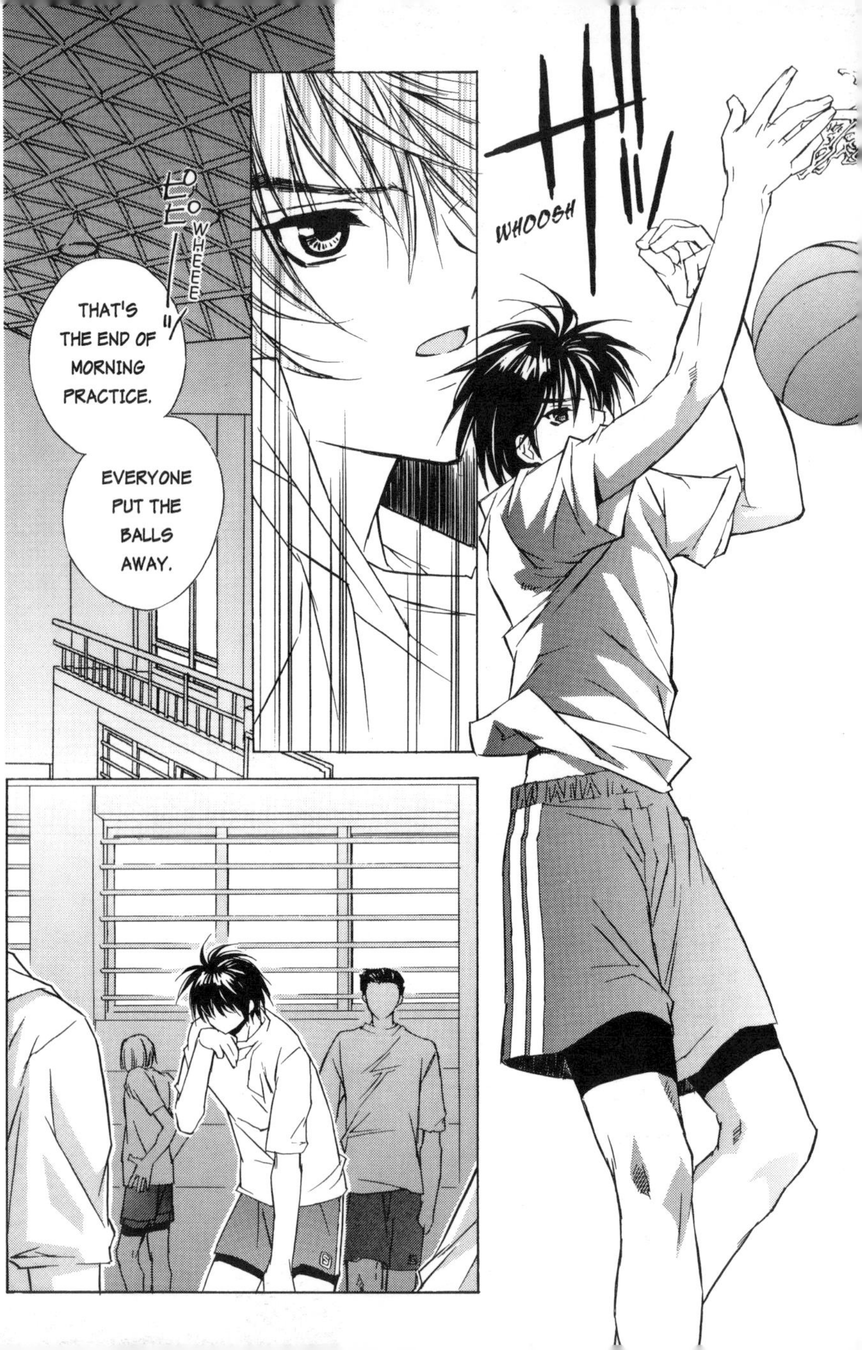
WHOOSH
WHEEEE
THAT'S THE END OF MORNING PRACTICE.
EVERYONE PUT THE BALLS AWAY.

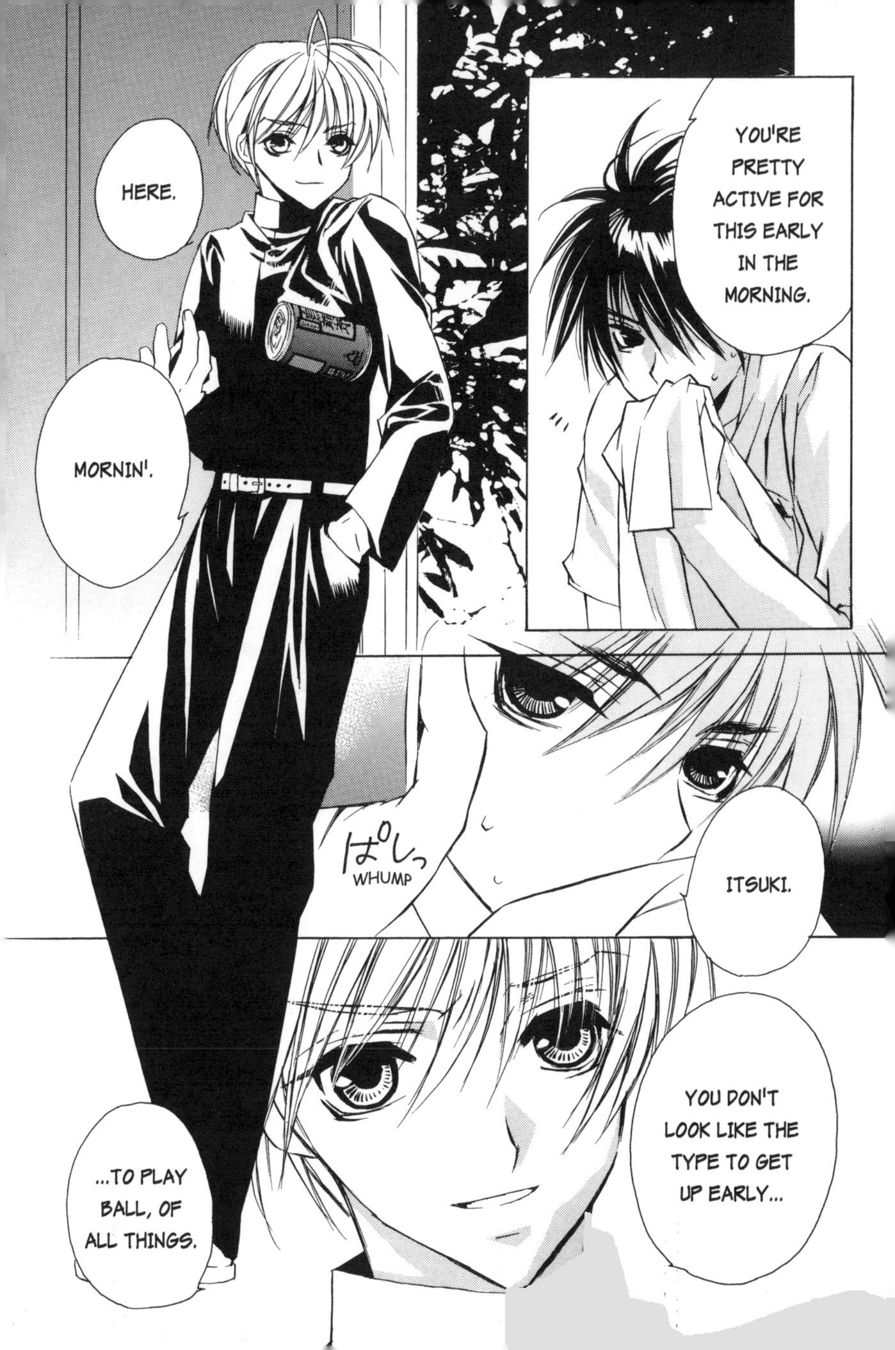
MORNIN'.
YOU'RE PRETTY ACTIVE FOR THIS EARLY IN THE MORNING.
HERE.
ぱしっ
WHUMP
ITSUKI.
YOU DON'T LOOK LIKE THE TYPE TO GET UP EARLY...
...TO PLAY BALL, OF ALL THINGS.

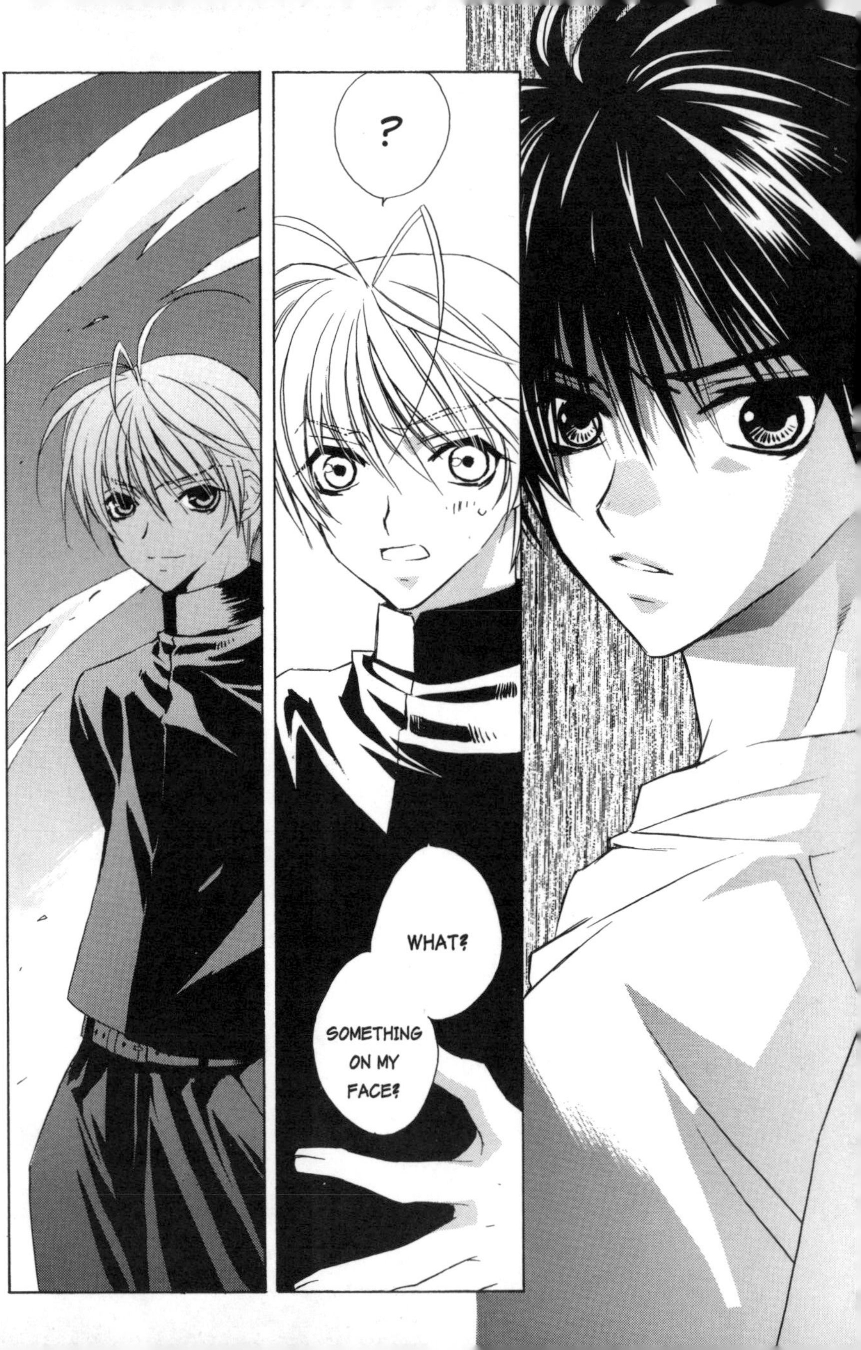
?
WHAT?
SOMETHING ON MY FACE?

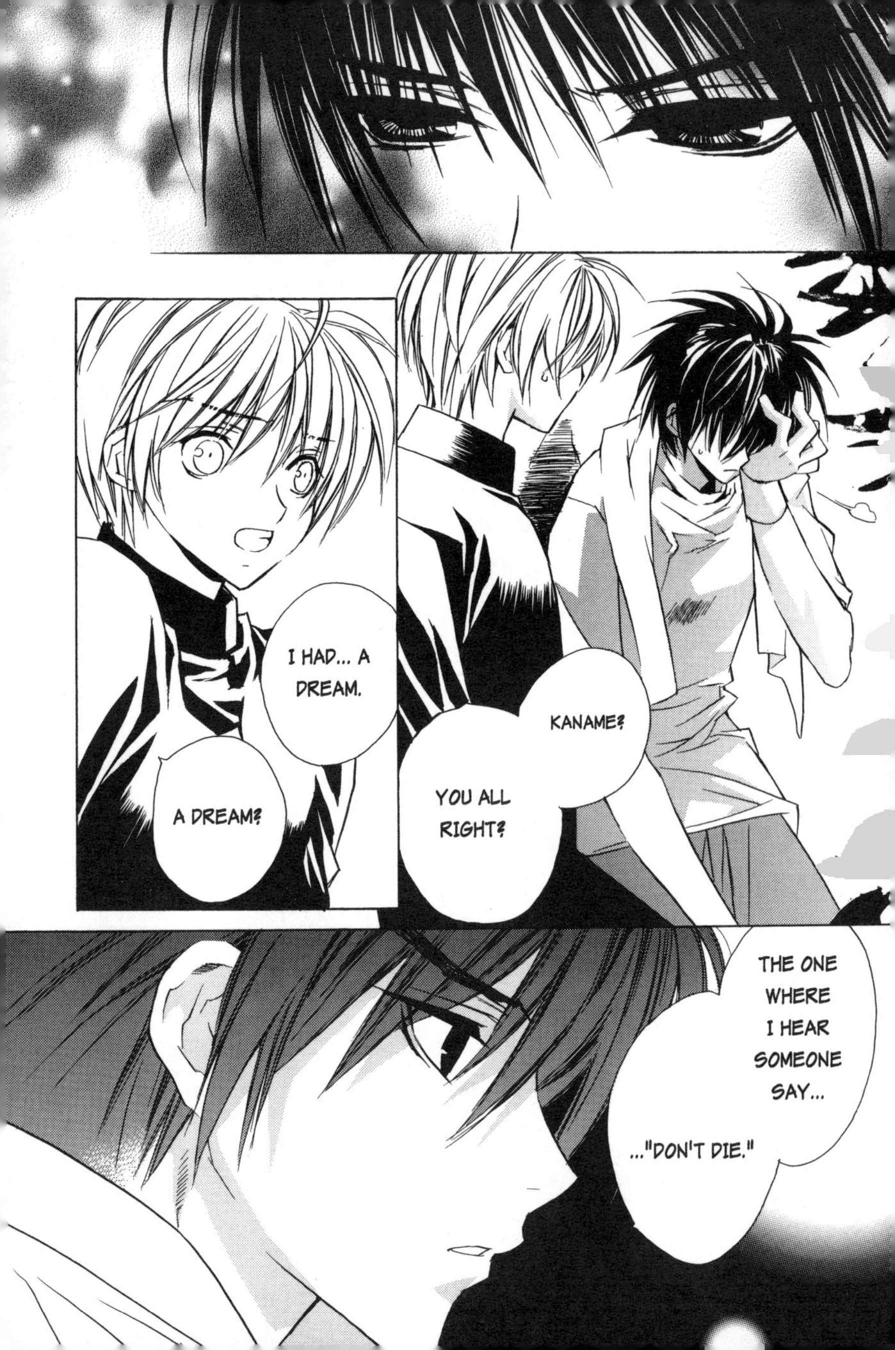
KANAME?
YOU ALL RIGHT?
I HAD... A DREAM.
A DREAM?
THE ONE WHERE I HEAR SOMEONE SAY...
..."DON'T DIE."

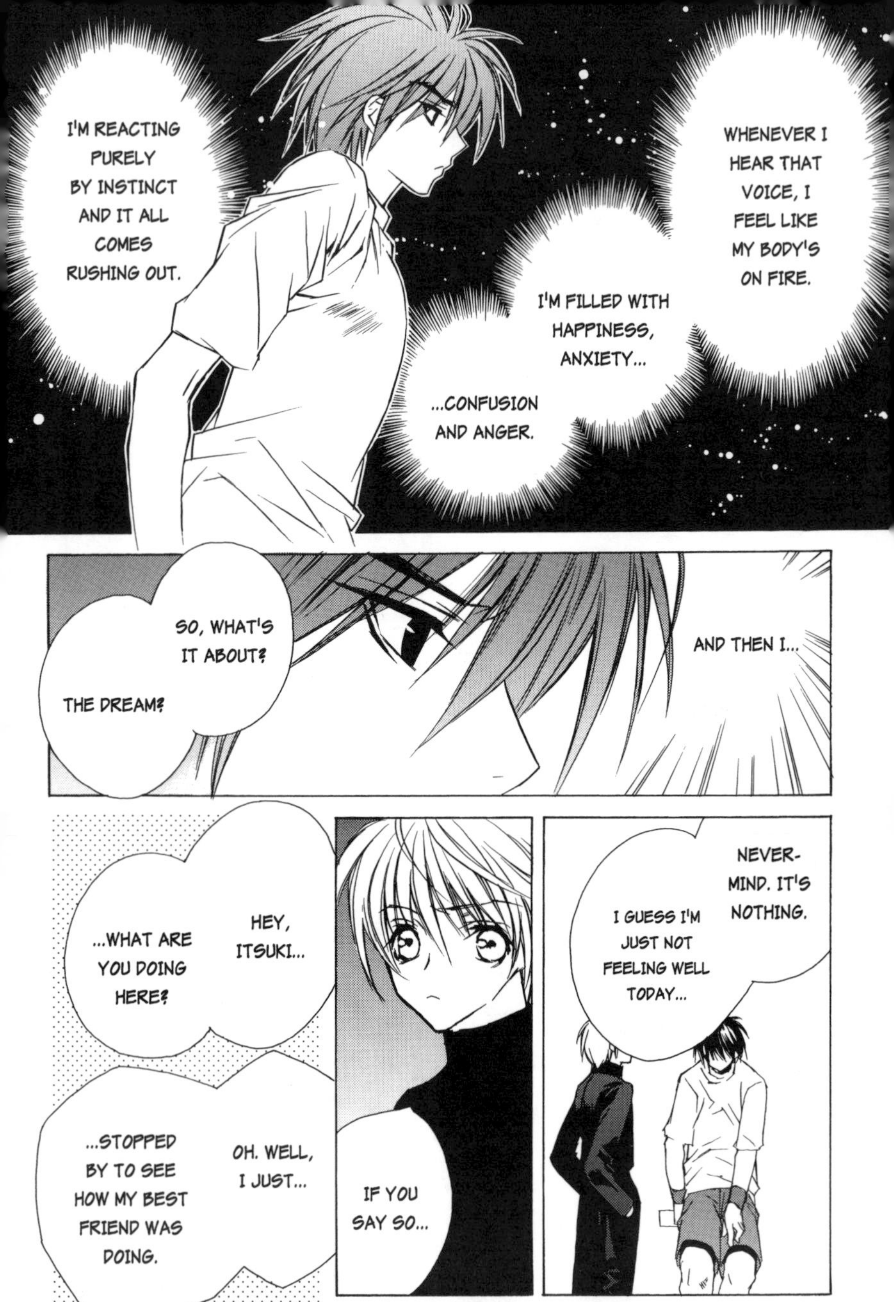
WHENEVER I HEAR THAT VOICE, I FEEL LIKE MY BODY'S ON FIRE.
I'M FILLED WITH HAPPINESS, ANXIETY...
...CONFUSION AND ANGER.
I'M REACTING PURELY BY INSTINCT AND IT ALL COMES RUSHING OUT.
AND THEN I...
SO, WHAT'S IT ABOUT?
THE DREAM?
NEVER-MIND. IT'S NOTHING.
I GUESS I'M JUST NOT FEELING WELL TODAY...
IF YOU SAY SO...
HEY, ITSUKI...
...WHAT ARE YOU DOING HERE?
OH. WELL, I JUST...
...STOPPED BY TO SEE HOW MY BEST FRIEND WAS DOING.

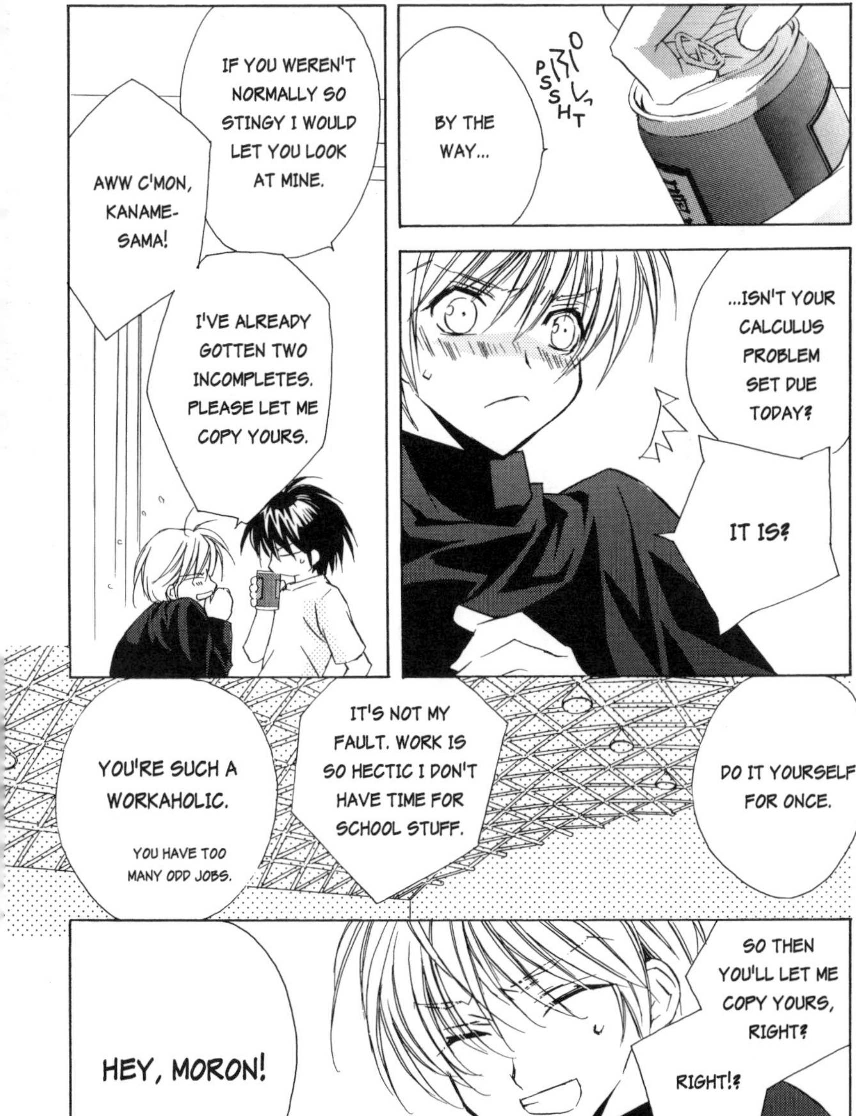
PSSHT
BY THE WAY...
...ISN'T YOUR CALCULUS PROBLEM SET DUE TODAY?
IT IS?
IF YOU WEREN'T NORMALLY SO STINGY I WOULD LET YOU LOOK AT MINE.
AWW C'MON, KANAME-SAMA!
I'VE ALREADY GOTTEN TWO INCOMPLETES. PLEASE LET ME COPY YOURS.
DO IT YOURSELF FOR ONCE.
IT'S NOT MY FAULT. WORK IS SO HECTIC I DON'T HAVE TIME FOR SCHOOL STUFF.
YOU'RE SUCH A WORKAHOLIC.
YOU HAVE TOO MANY ODD JOBS.
SO THEN YOU'LL LET ME COPY YOURS, RIGHT?
RIGHT!?
HEY, MORON!

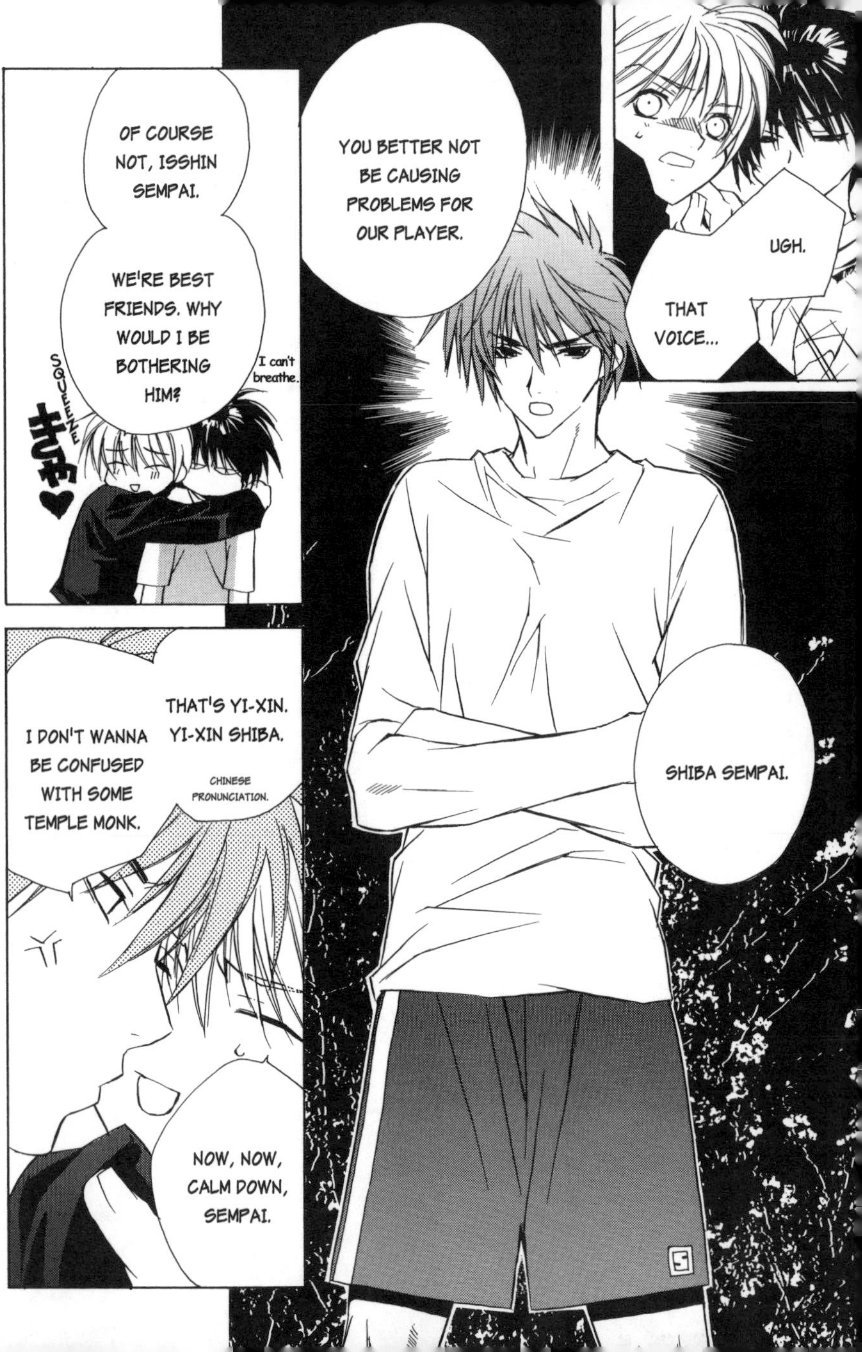
UGH.
THAT VOICE...
SHIBA SEMPAI.
YOU BETTER NOT BE CAUSING PROBLEMS FOR OUR PLAYER.
OF COURSE NOT, ISSHIN SEMPAI.
WE'RE BEST FRIENDS. WHY WOULD I BE BOTHERING HIM?
SQUEEZE
I can't breathe.
THAT'S YI-XIN. YI-XIN SHIBA.
CHINESE PRONUNCIATION.
I DON'T WANNA BE CONFUSED WITH SOME TEMPLE MONK.
NOW, NOW, CALM DOWN, SEMPAI.

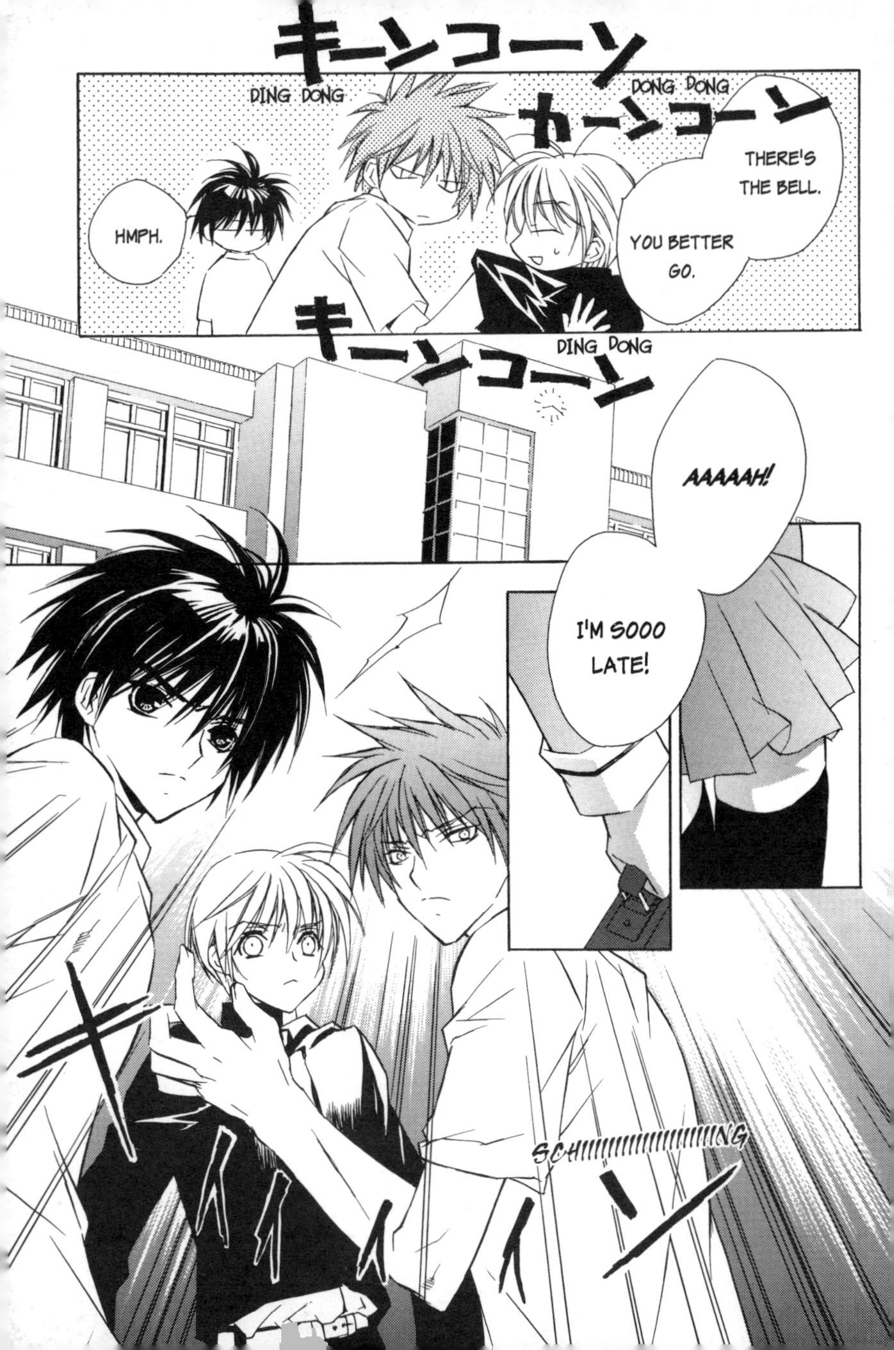
キーンコーン
DING DONG
カーンコーン
DONG DONG
THERE'S THE BELL.
YOU BETTER GO.
HMPH.
キーンコーン
DING DONG
AAAAAH!
I'M SOOO LATE!
SCHIIIIIIIIIIIIIIIIIIIIIING

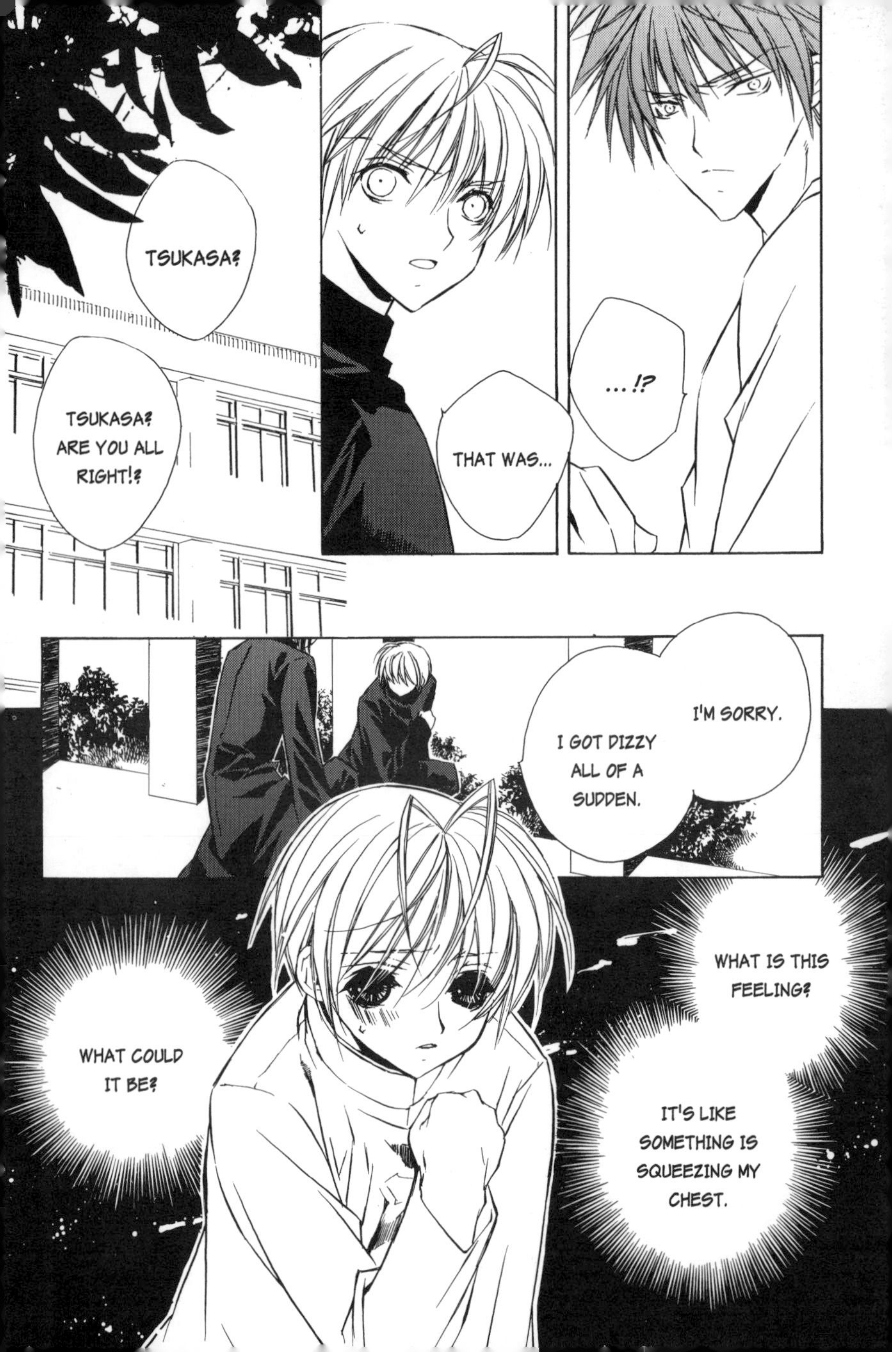
...!?
THAT WAS...
TSUKASA?
TSUKASA? ARE YOU ALL RIGHT!?
I'M SORRY.
I GOT DIZZY ALL OF A SUDDEN.
WHAT IS THIS FEELING?
IT'S LIKE SOMETHING IS SQUEEZING MY CHEST.
WHAT COULD IT BE?

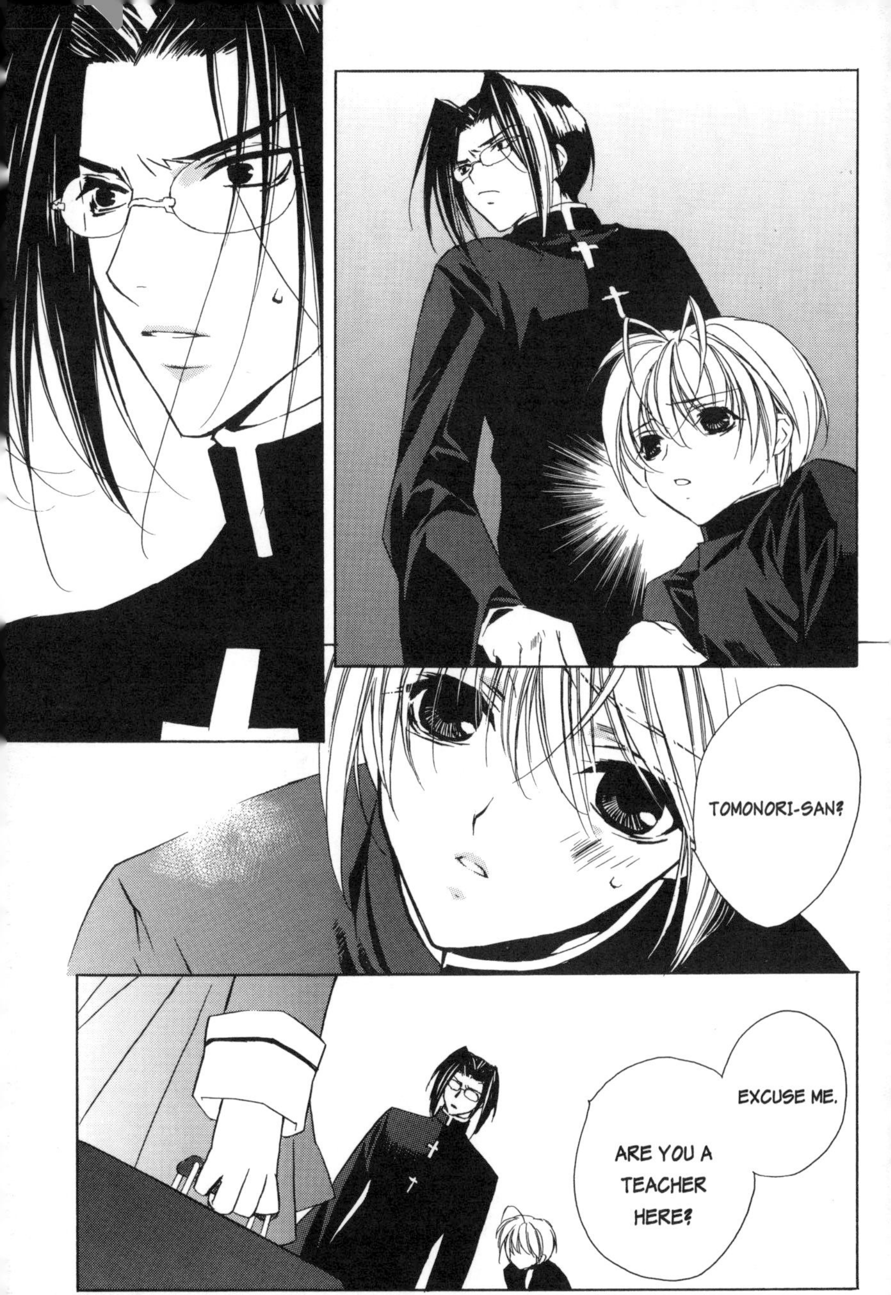
TOMONORI-SAN?
EXCUSE ME.
ARE YOU A TEACHER HERE?

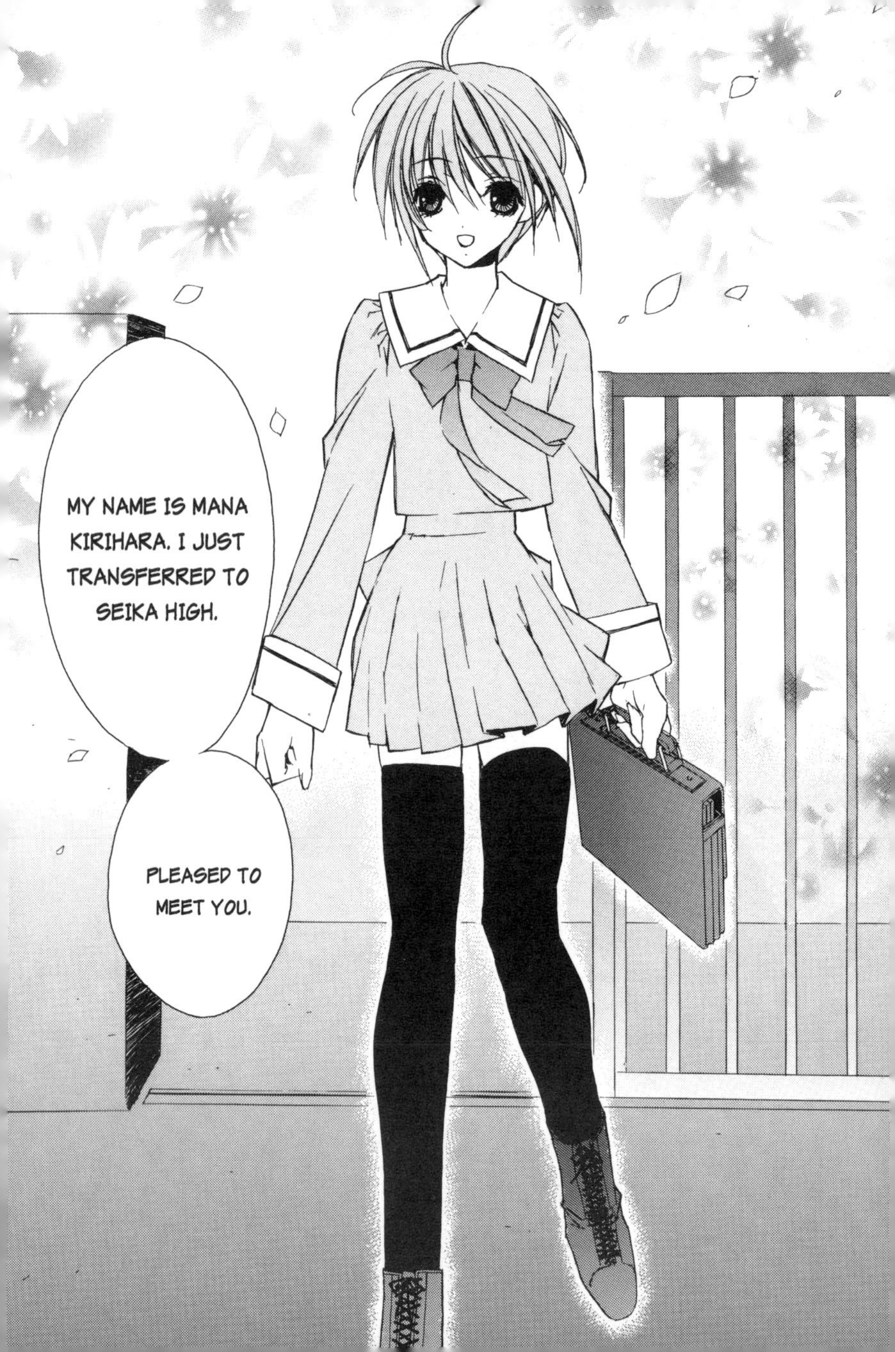
MY NAME IS MANA KIRIHARA. I JUST TRANSFERRED TO SEIKA HIGH.
PLEASED TO MEET YOU.

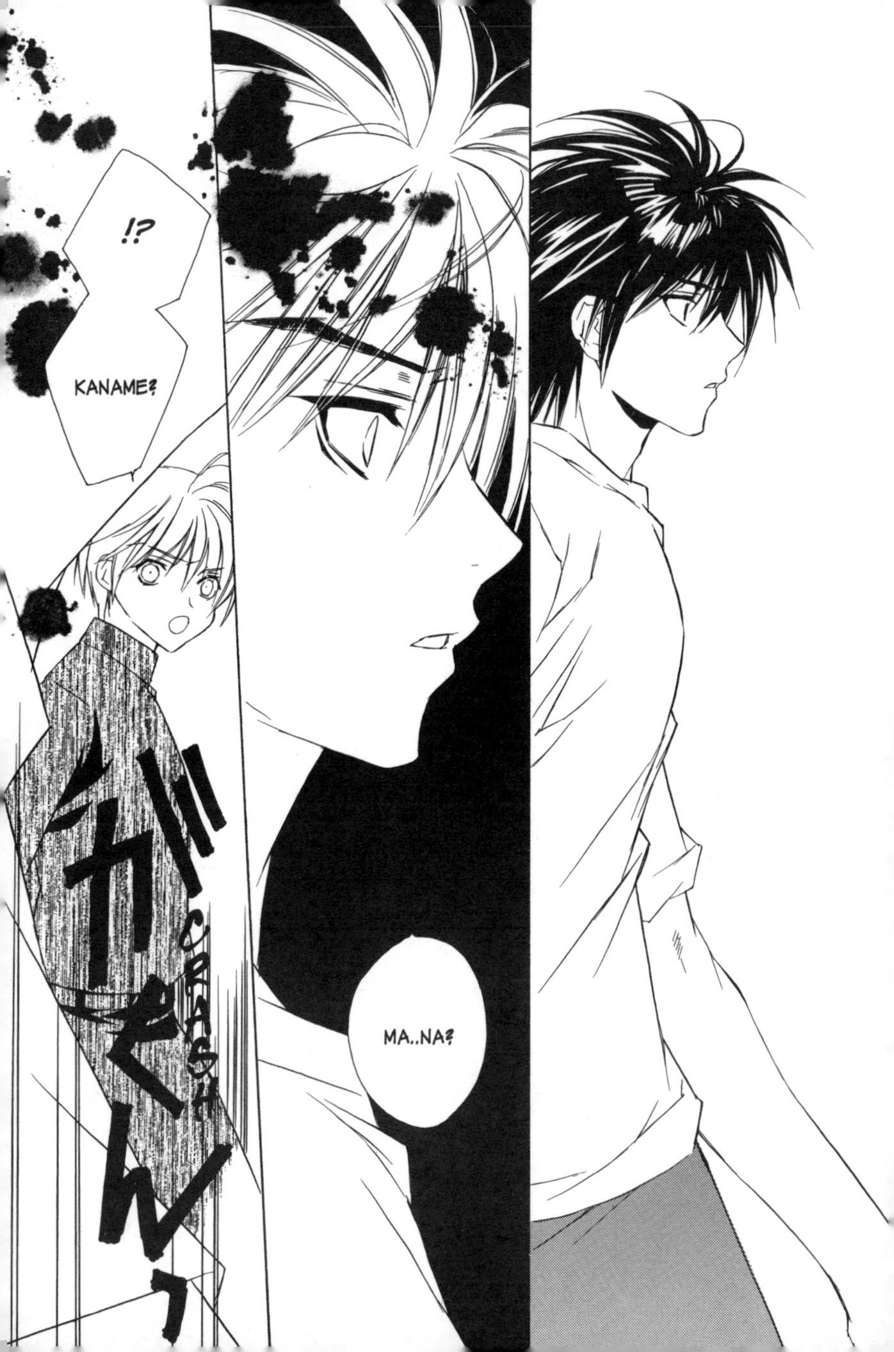
MA..NA?
!?
KANAME?
CRASH

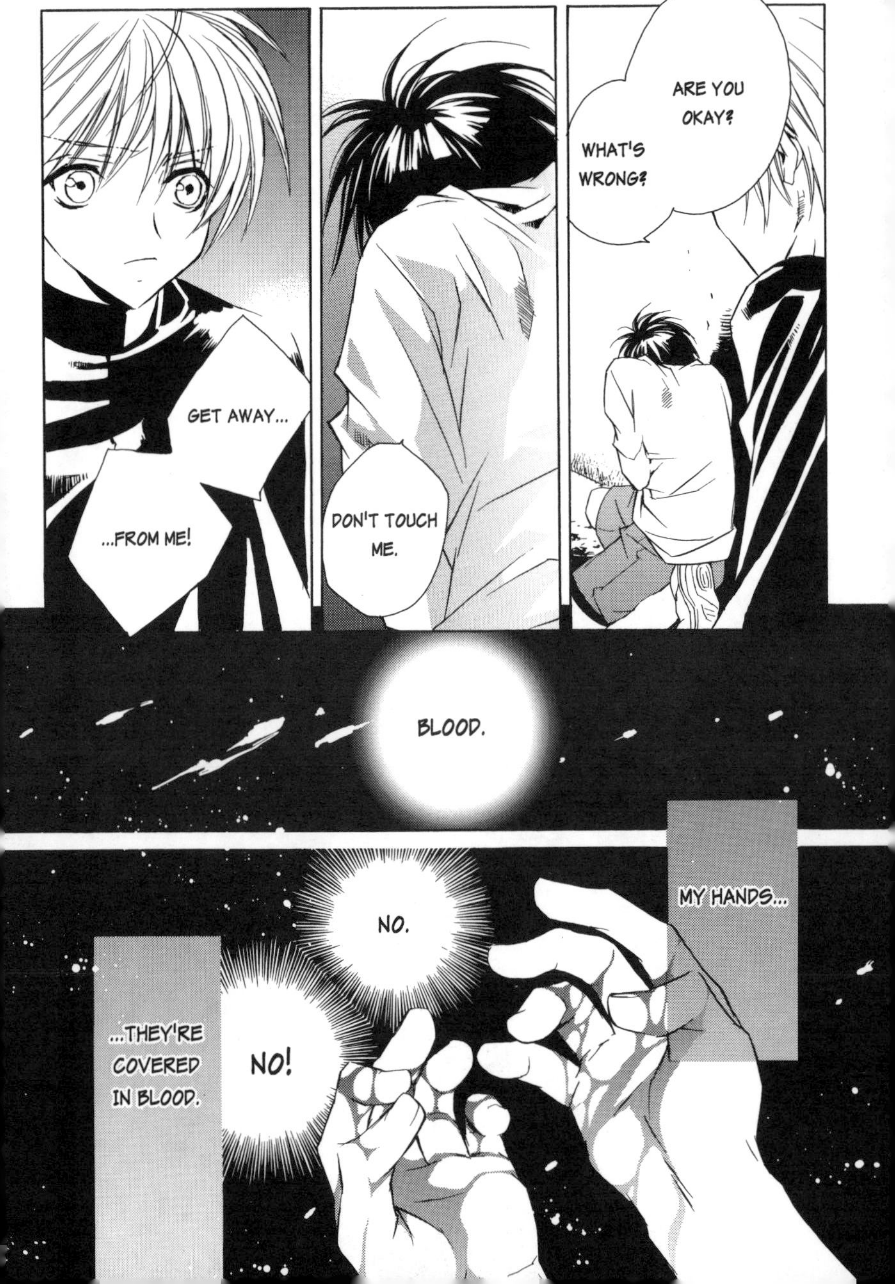
ARE YOU OKAY?
WHAT'S WRONG?
DON'T TOUCH ME.
GET AWAY...
...FROM ME!
BLOOD.
MY HANDS...
NO.
NO!
...THEY'RE COVERED IN BLOOD.

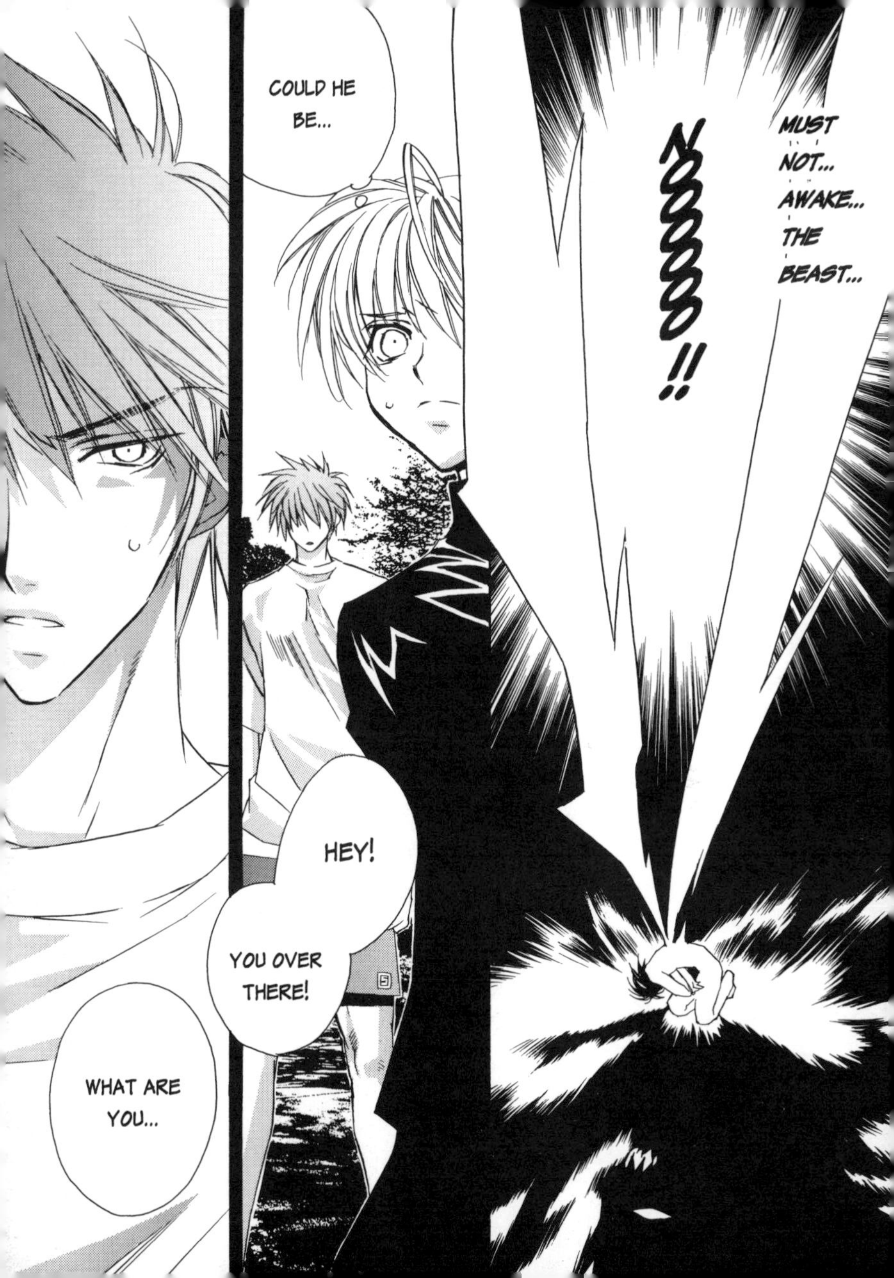
MUST NOT... AWAKE... THE BEAST...
NOOOOOOO!!
COULD HE BE...
HEY!
YOU OVER THERE!
WHAT ARE YOU...

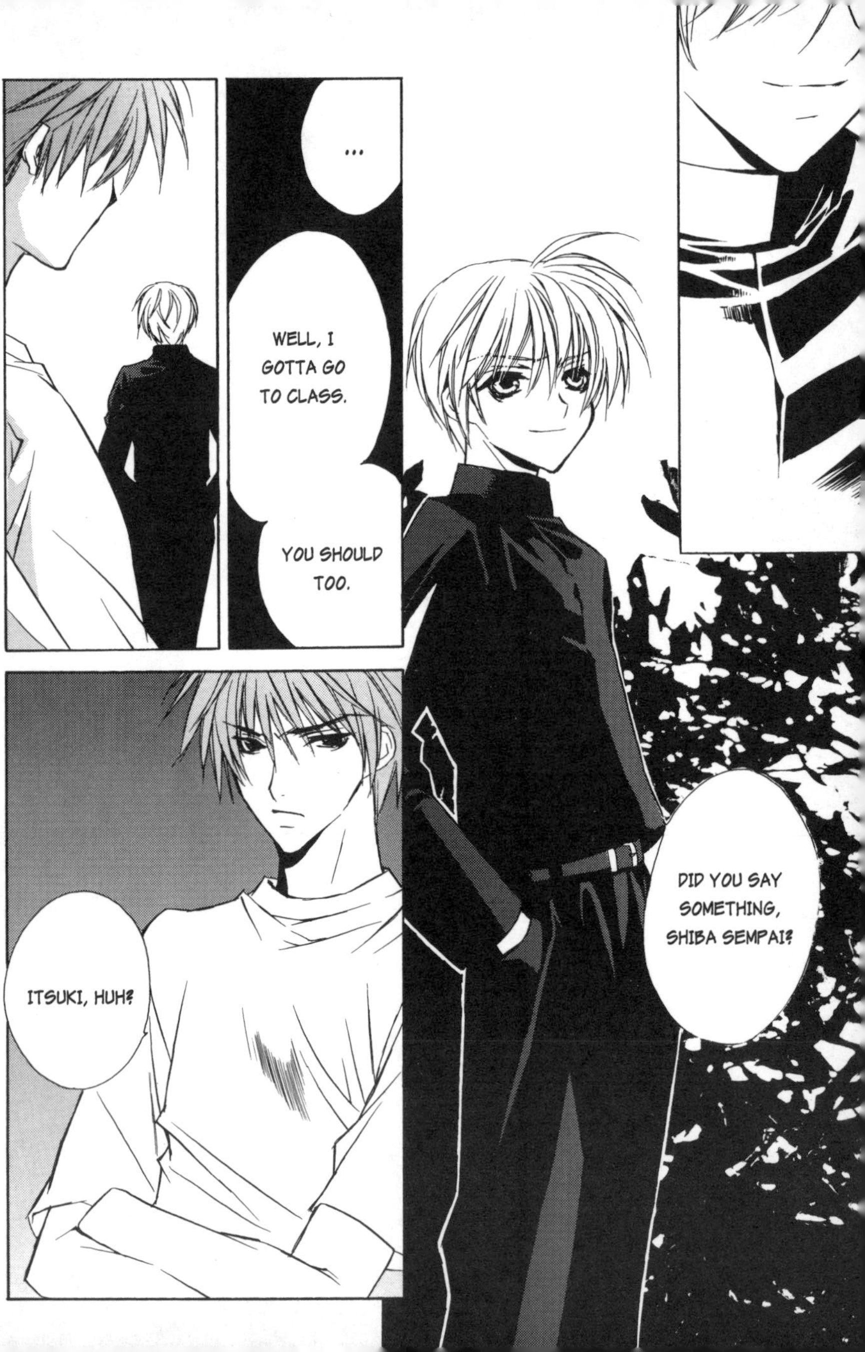
...
WELL, I GOTTA GO TO CLASS.
YOU SHOULD TOO.
DID YOU SAY SOMETHING, SHIBA SEMPAI?
ITSUKI, HUH?

PHEW.

THAT WAS CLOSE.

TRYING TO ACT LIKE A NORMAL STUDENT IS HARDER THAN IT LOOKS.

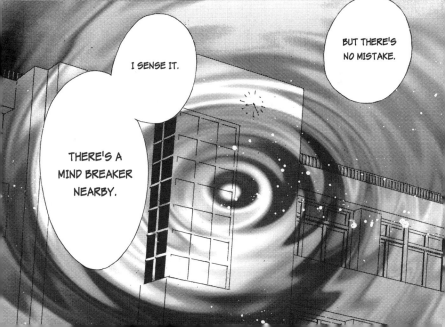

BUT THERE'S NO MISTAKE.

I SENSE IT.

THERE'S A MIND BREAKER NEARBY.

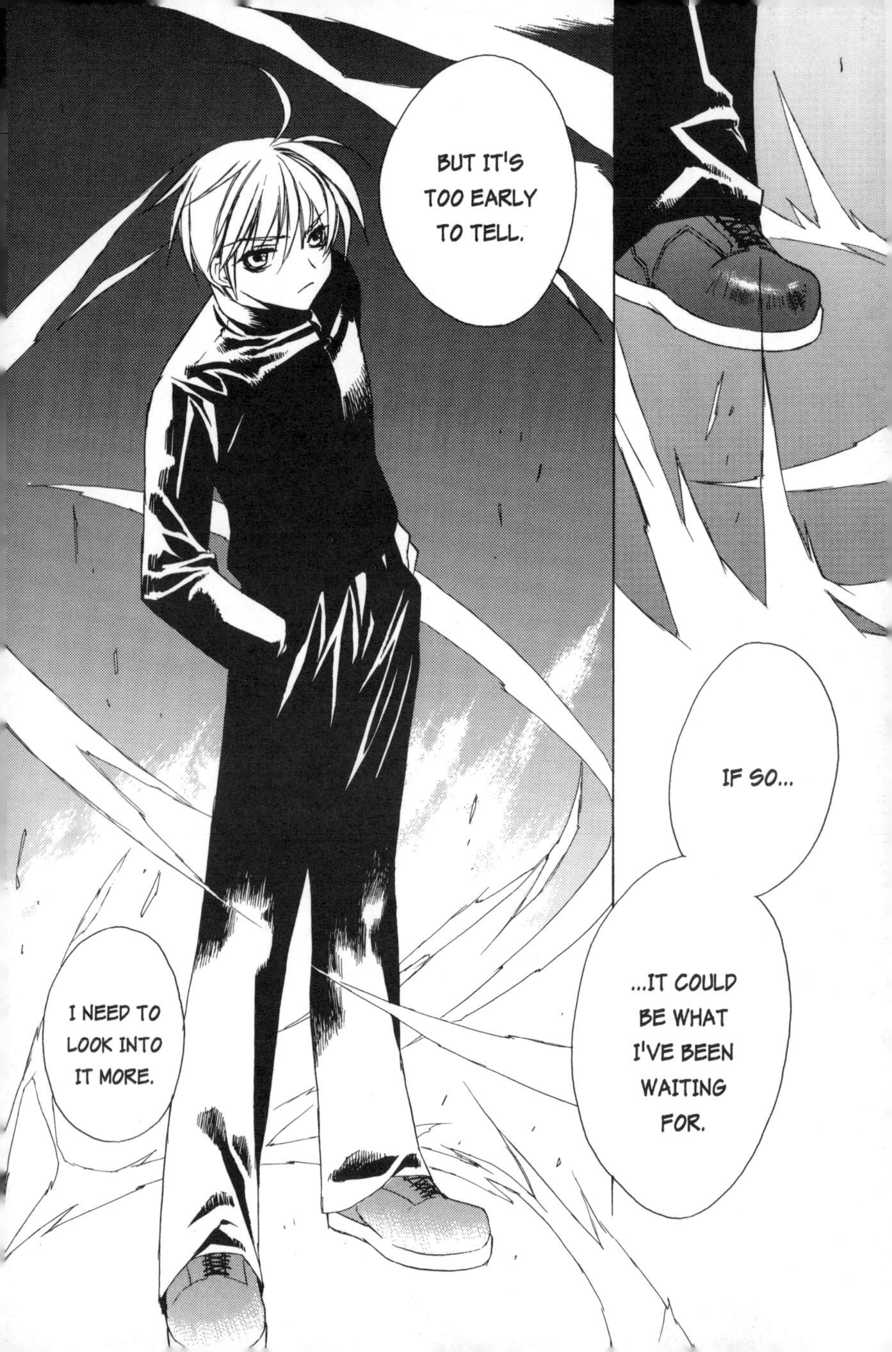
BUT IT'S TOO EARLY TO TELL.
IF SO...
...IT COULD BE WHAT I'VE BEEN WAITING FOR.
I NEED TO LOOK INTO IT MORE.

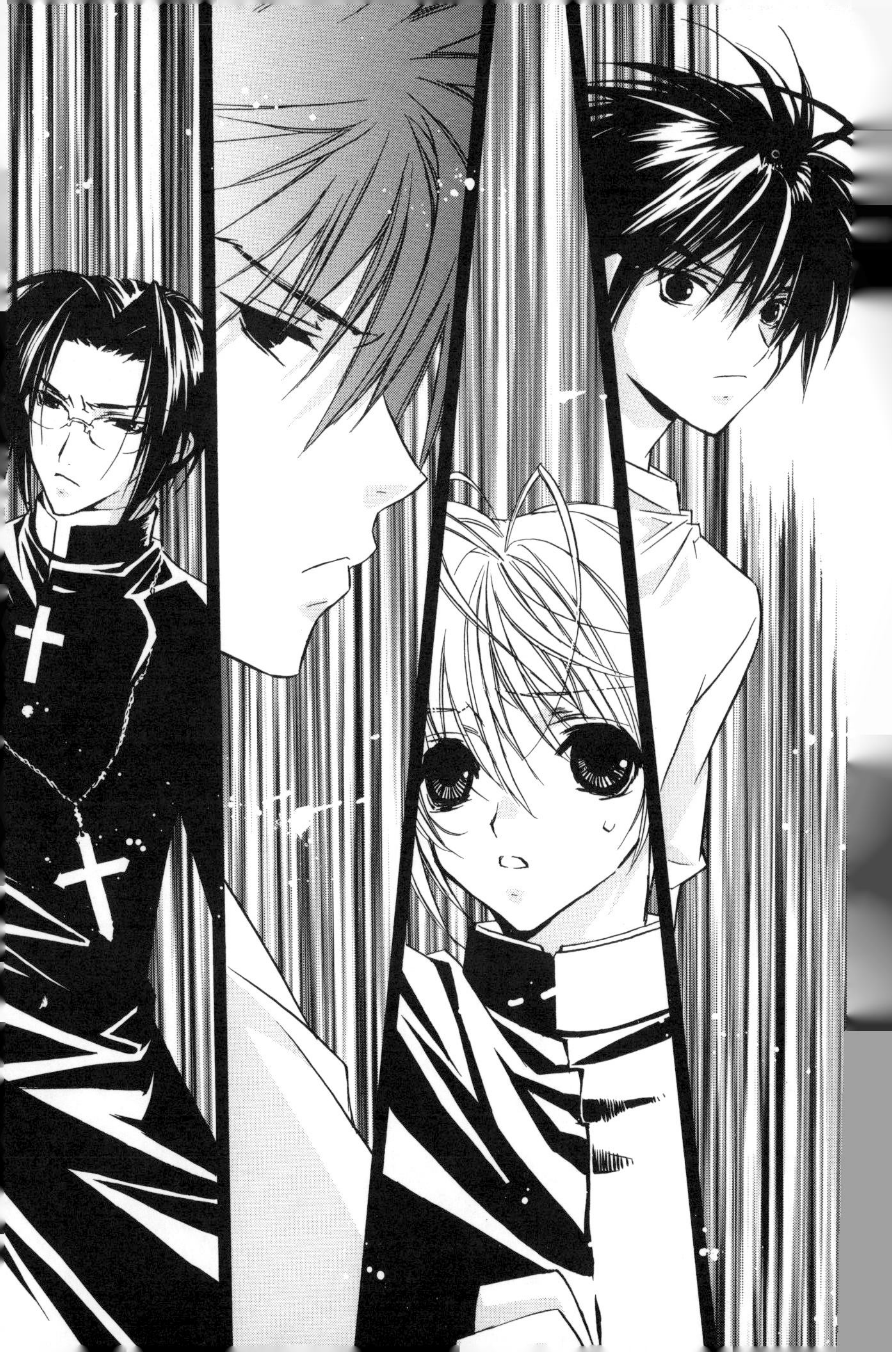

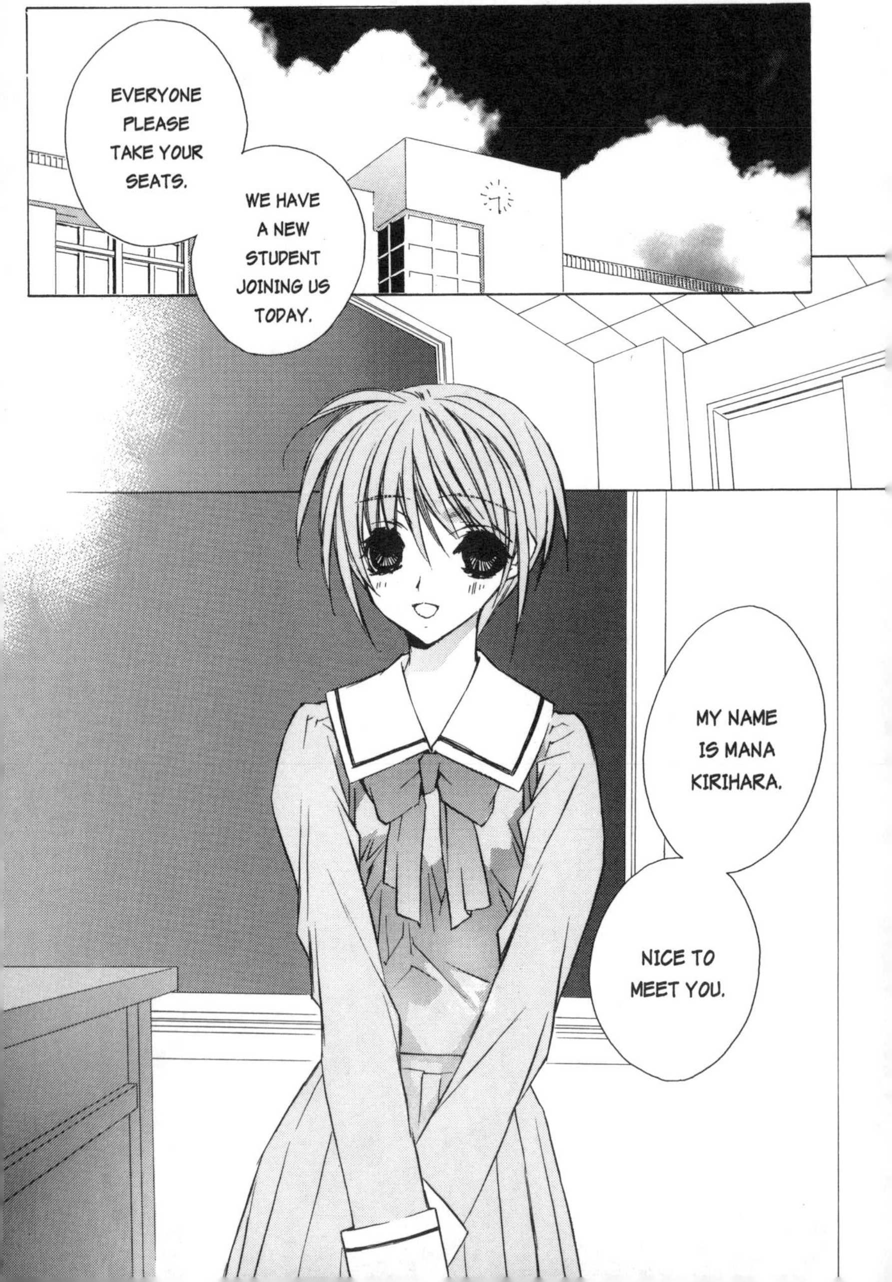
EVERYONE PLEASE TAKE YOUR SEATS.
WE HAVE A NEW STUDENT JOINING US TODAY.
MY NAME IS MANA KIRIHARA.
NICE TO MEET YOU.

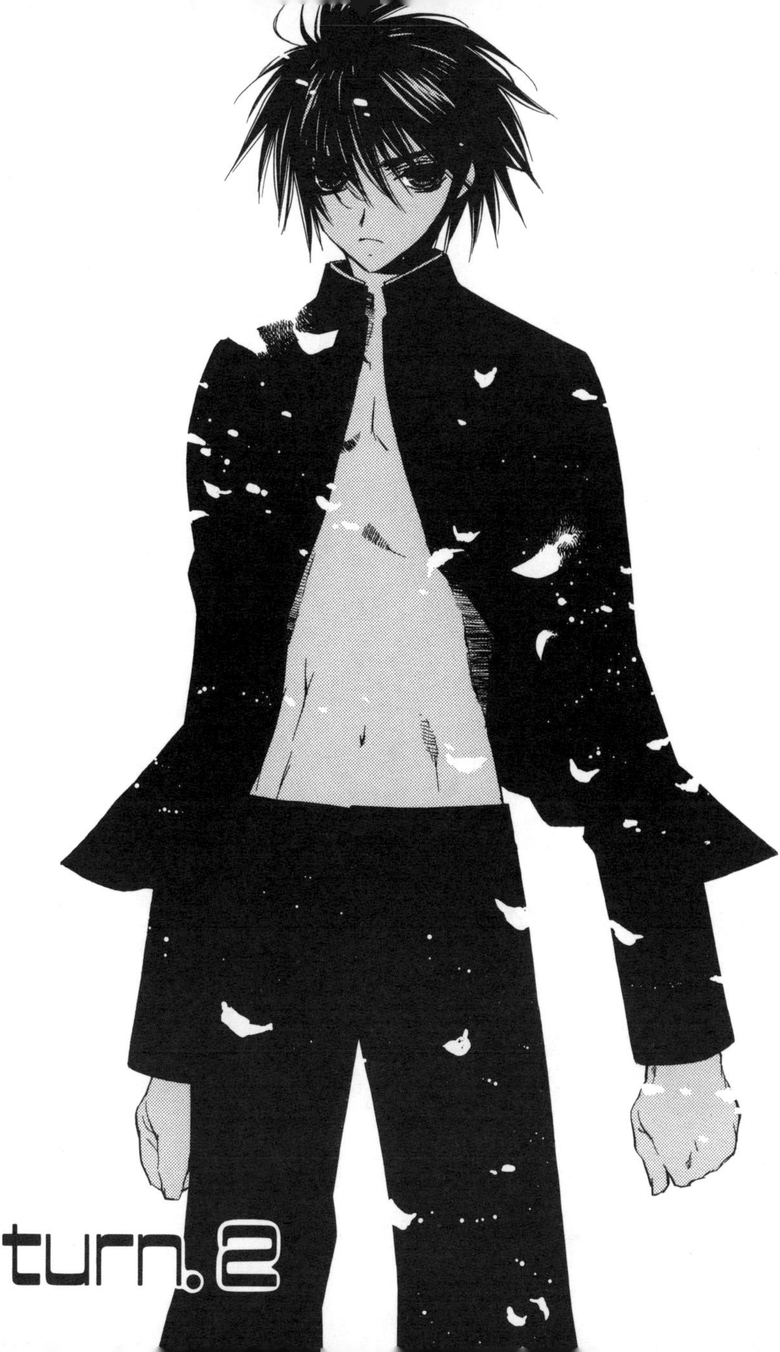
turn.2

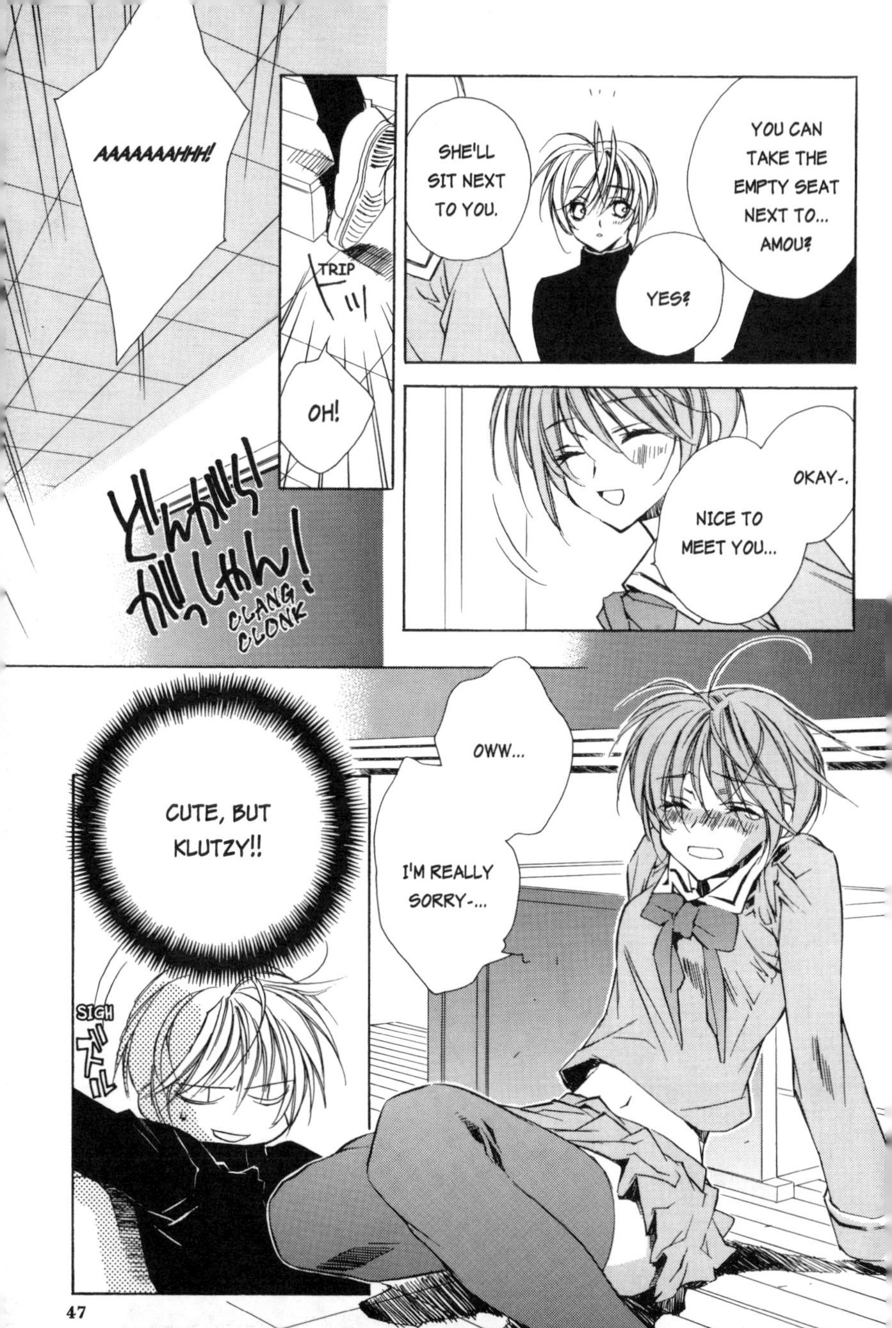
YOU CAN TAKE THE EMPTY SEAT NEXT TO... AMOU?
YES?
SHE'LL SIT NEXT TO YOU.
OKAY-.
NICE TO MEET YOU...
TRIP
OH!
AAAAAAAHHH!
CLANG CLONK
OWW...
I'M REALLY SORRY-...
CUTE, BUT KLUTZY!!
SIGH

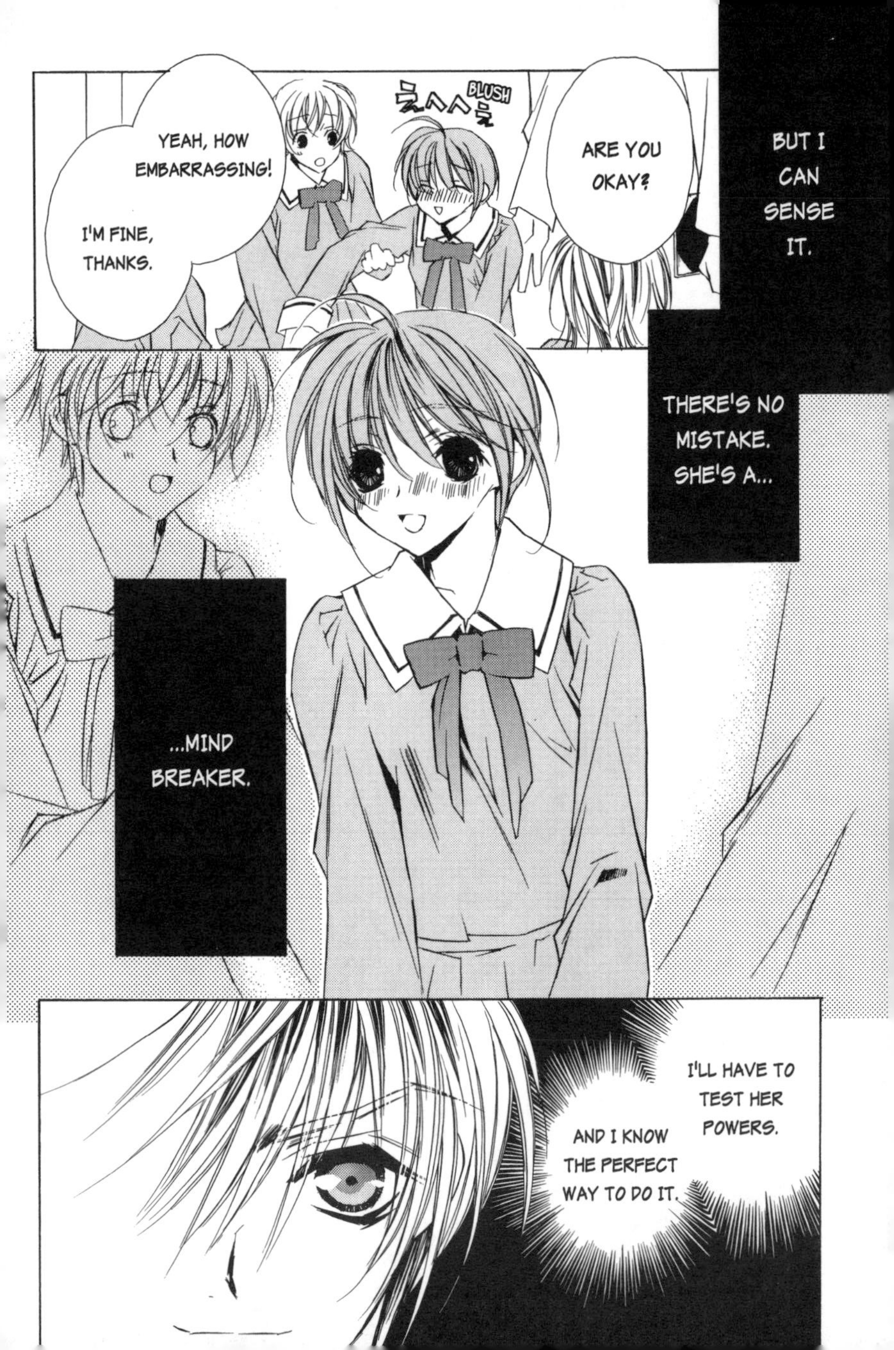
BUT I CAN SENSE IT.
ARE YOU OKAY?
BLUSH
えへへえ
YEAH, HOW EMBARRASSING!
I'M FINE, THANKS.
THERE'S NO MISTAKE. SHE'S A...
...MIND BREAKER.
I'LL HAVE TO TEST HER POWERS.
AND I KNOW THE PERFECT WAY TO DO IT.

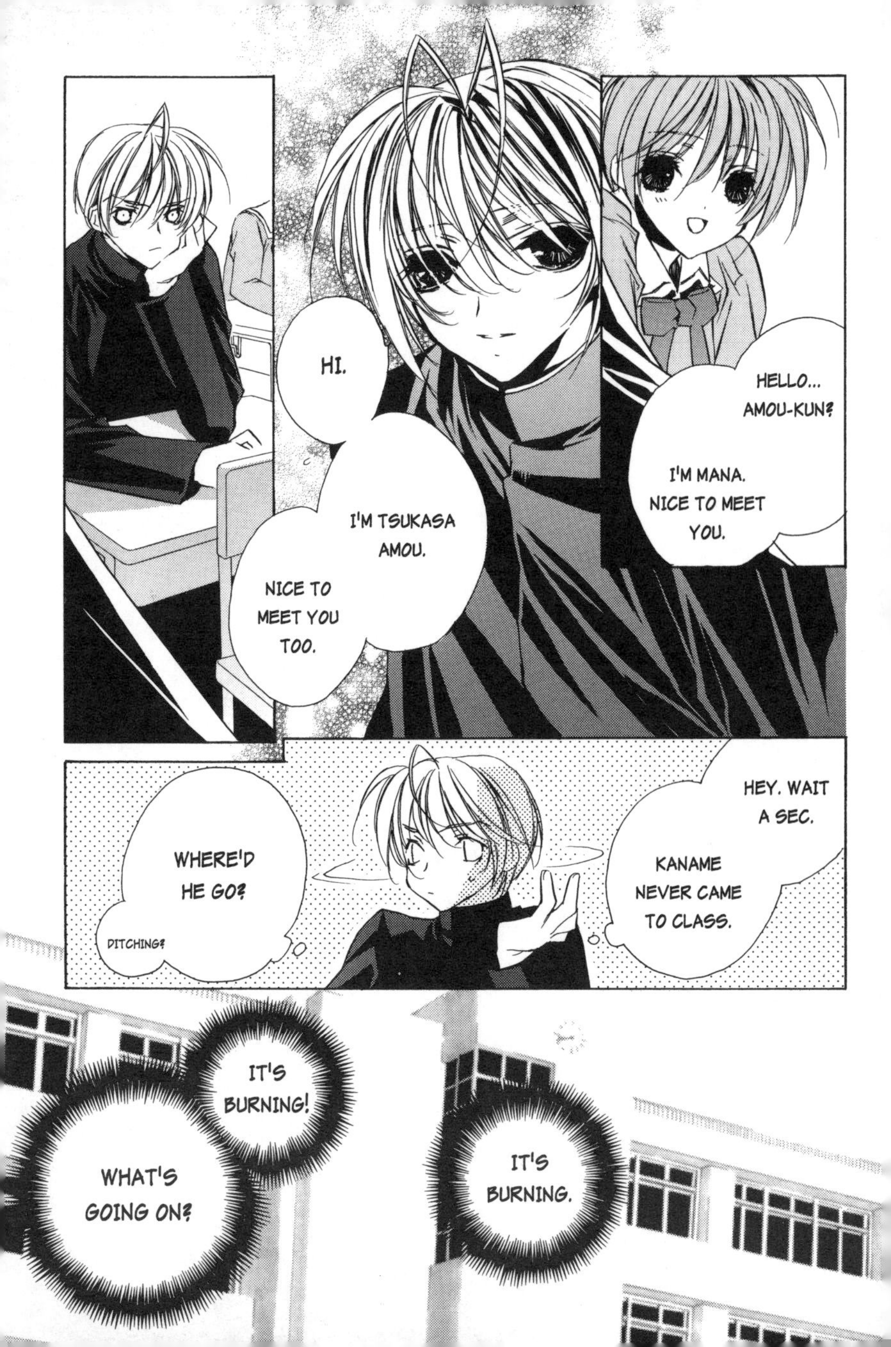
HELLO... AMOU-KUN?
I'M MANA. NICE TO MEET YOU.
HI.
I'M TSUKASA AMOU.
NICE TO MEET YOU TOO.
HEY. WAIT A SEC.
KANAME NEVER CAME TO CLASS.
WHERE'D HE GO?
DITCHING?
IT'S BURNING.
IT'S BURNING!
WHAT'S GOING ON?

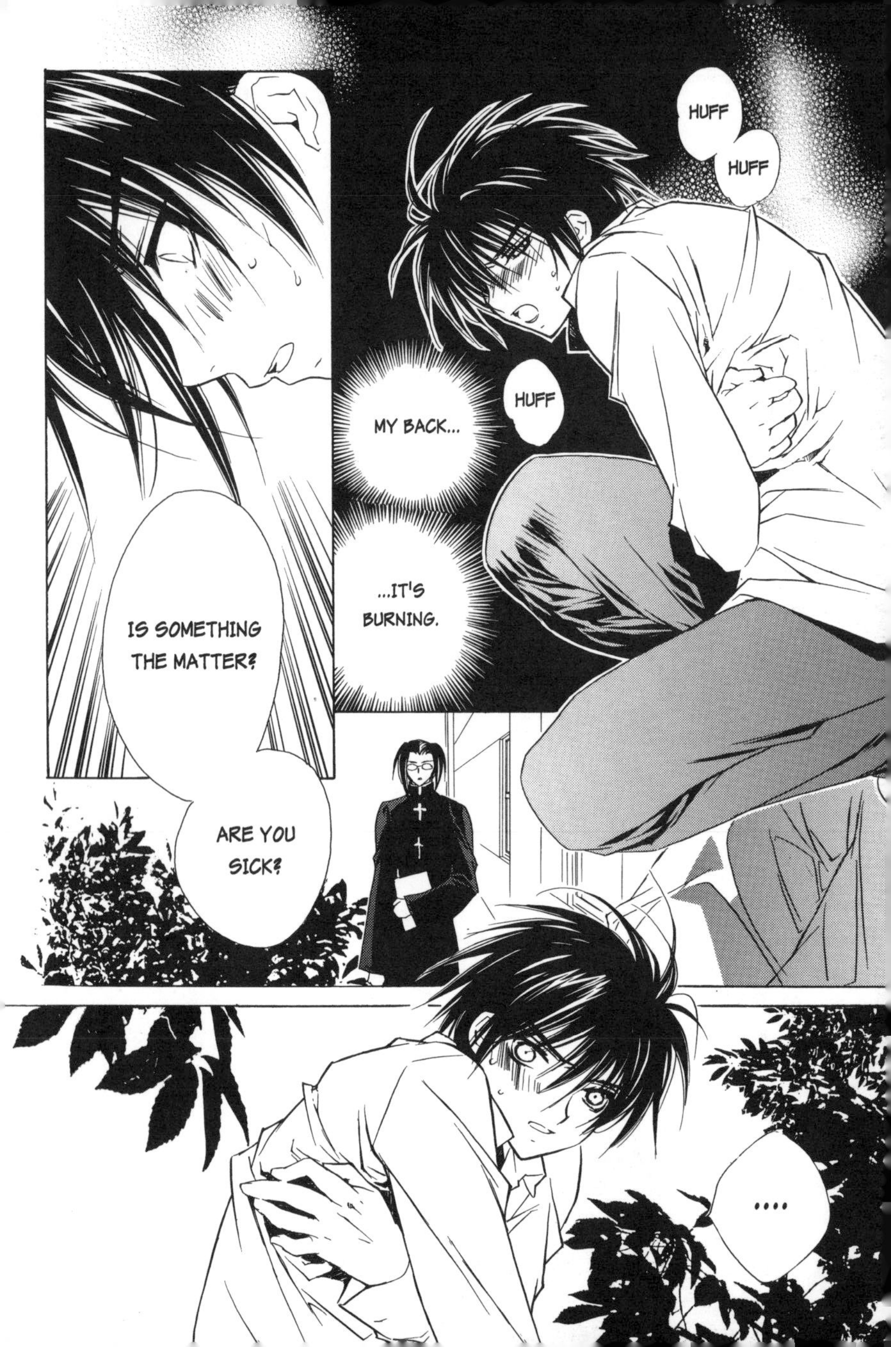
HUFF
HUFF
MY BACK...
HUFF
...IT'S BURNING.
IS SOMETHING THE MATTER?
ARE YOU SICK?
....

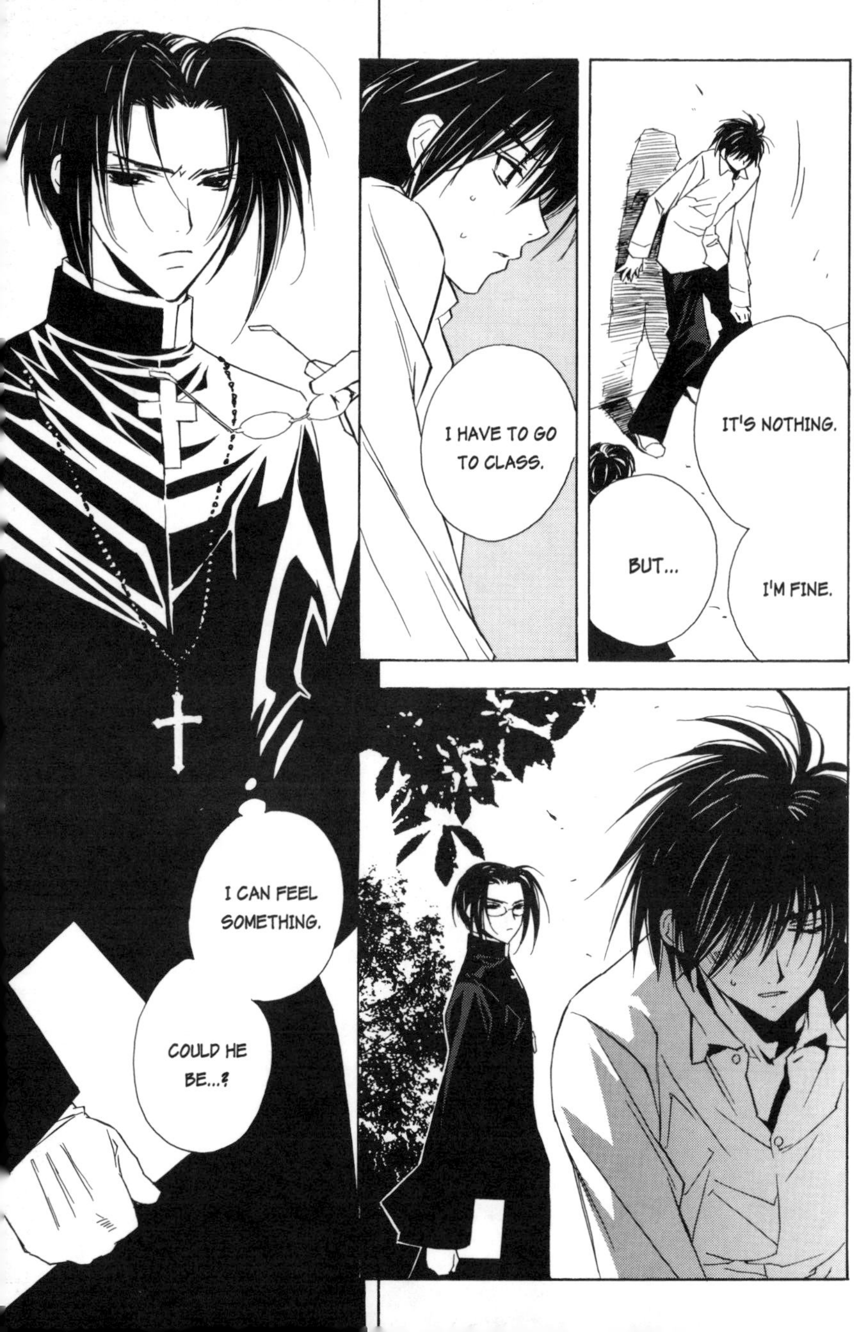
IT'S NOTHING.
BUT...
I'M FINE.
I HAVE TO GO TO CLASS.
I CAN FEEL SOMETHING.
COULD HE BE...?

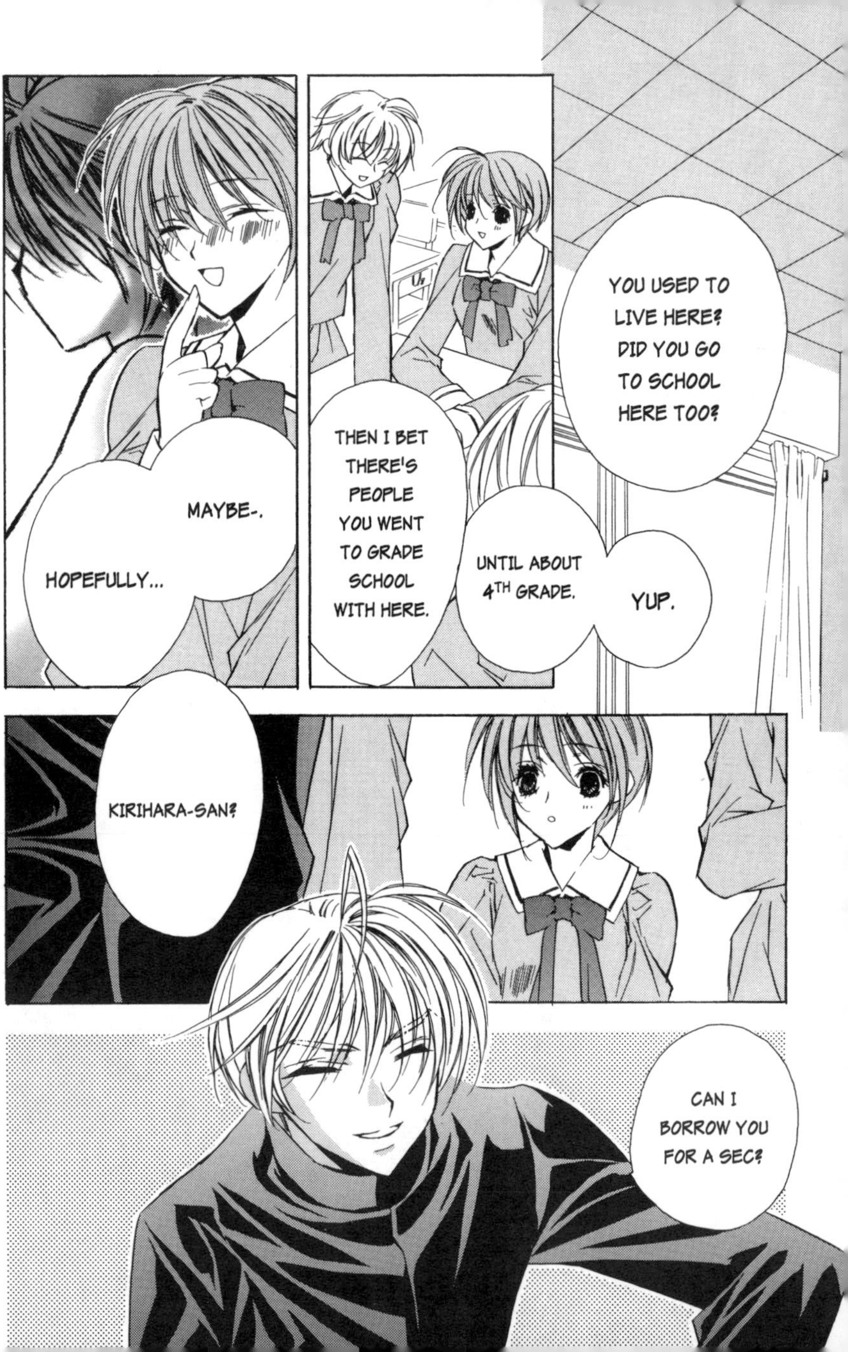
YOU USED TO LIVE HERE? DID YOU GO TO SCHOOL HERE TOO?
YUP.
UNTIL ABOUT 4TH GRADE.
THEN I BET THERE'S PEOPLE YOU WENT TO GRADE SCHOOL WITH HERE.
MAYBE-.
HOPEFULLY...
KIRIHARA-SAN?
CAN I BORROW YOU FOR A SEC?

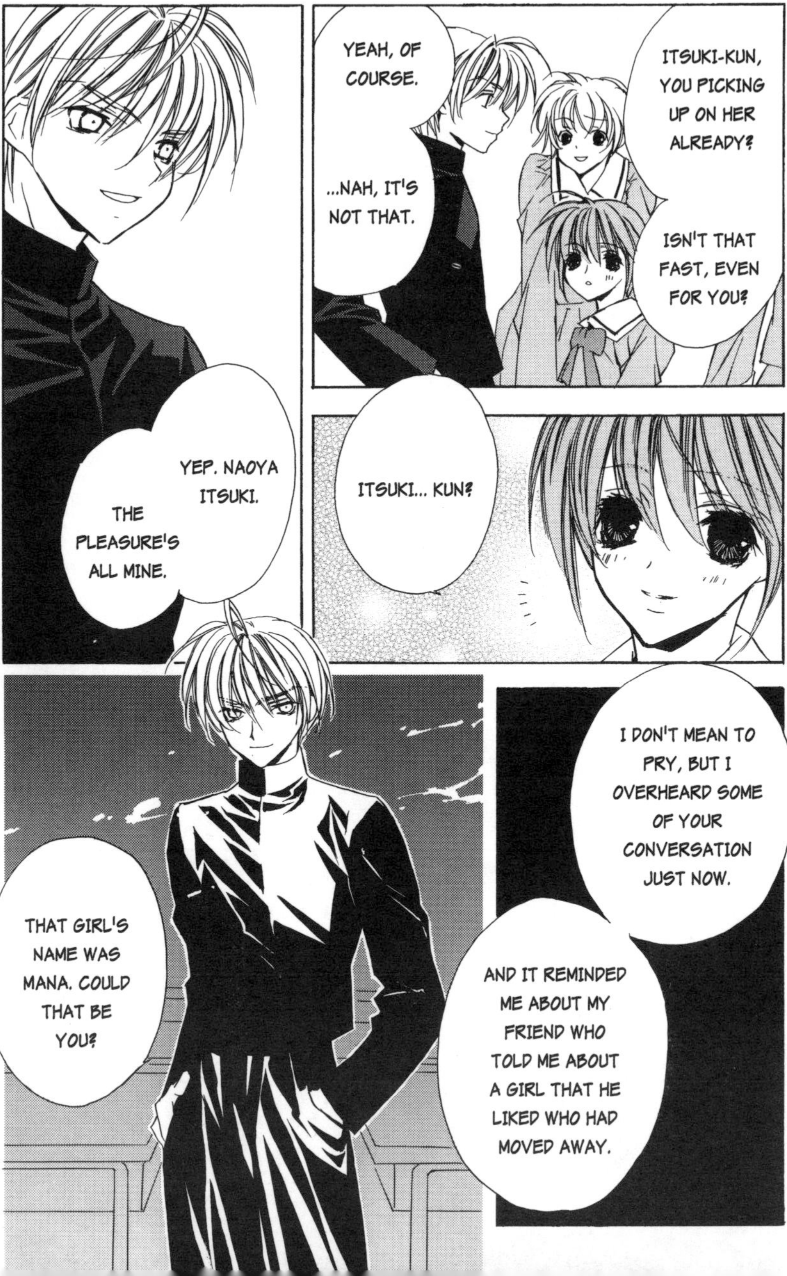
ITSUKI-KUN, YOU PICKING UP ON HER ALREADY?
ISN'T THAT FAST, EVEN FOR YOU?
YEAH, OF COURSE.
...NAH, IT'S NOT THAT.
ITSUKI... KUN?
YEP. NAOYA ITSUKI.
THE PLEASURE'S ALL MINE.
I DON'T MEAN TO PRY, BUT I OVERHEARD SOME OF YOUR CONVERSATION JUST NOW.
AND IT REMINDED ME ABOUT MY FRIEND WHO TOLD ME ABOUT A GIRL THAT HE LIKED WHO HAD MOVED AWAY.
THAT GIRL'S NAME WAS MANA. COULD THAT BE YOU?

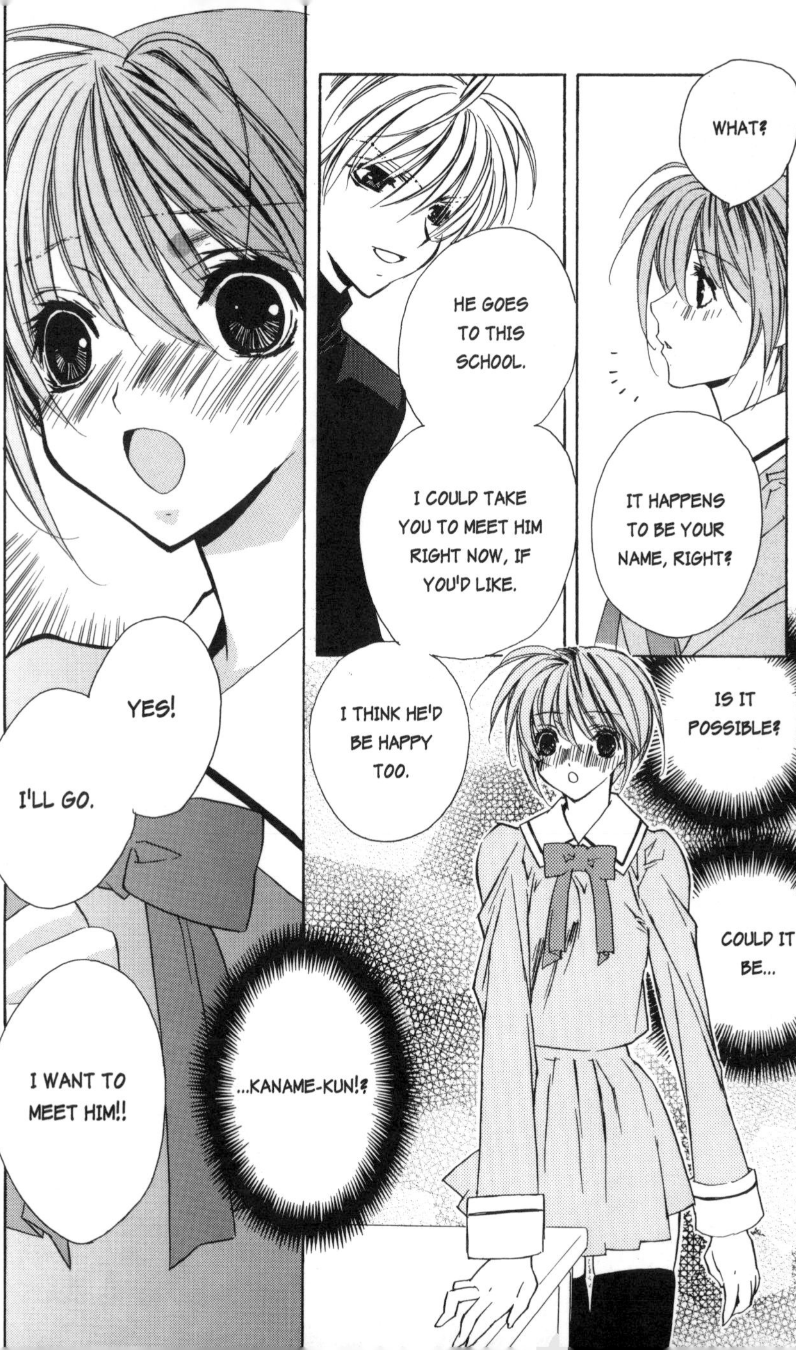
WHAT?
IT HAPPENS TO BE YOUR NAME, RIGHT?
HE GOES TO THIS SCHOOL.
I COULD TAKE YOU TO MEET HIM RIGHT NOW, IF YOU'D LIKE.
I THINK HE'D BE HAPPY TOO.
IS IT POSSIBLE?
COULD IT BE...
...KANAME-KUN!?
YES!
I'LL GO.
I WANT TO MEET HIM!!

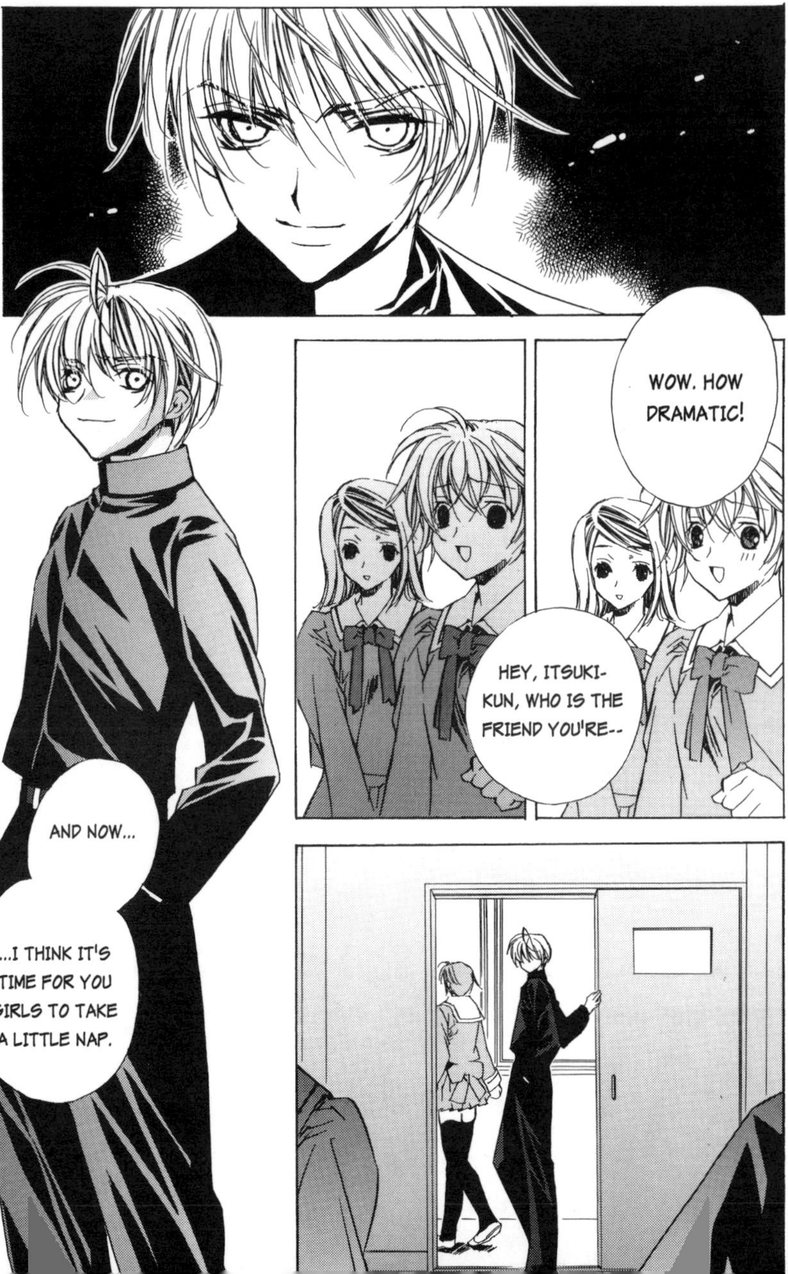
WOW. HOW DRAMATIC!
HEY, ITSUKI-KUN, WHO IS THE FRIEND YOU'RE--
AND NOW...
...I THINK IT'S TIME FOR YOU GIRLS TO TAKE A LITTLE NAP.

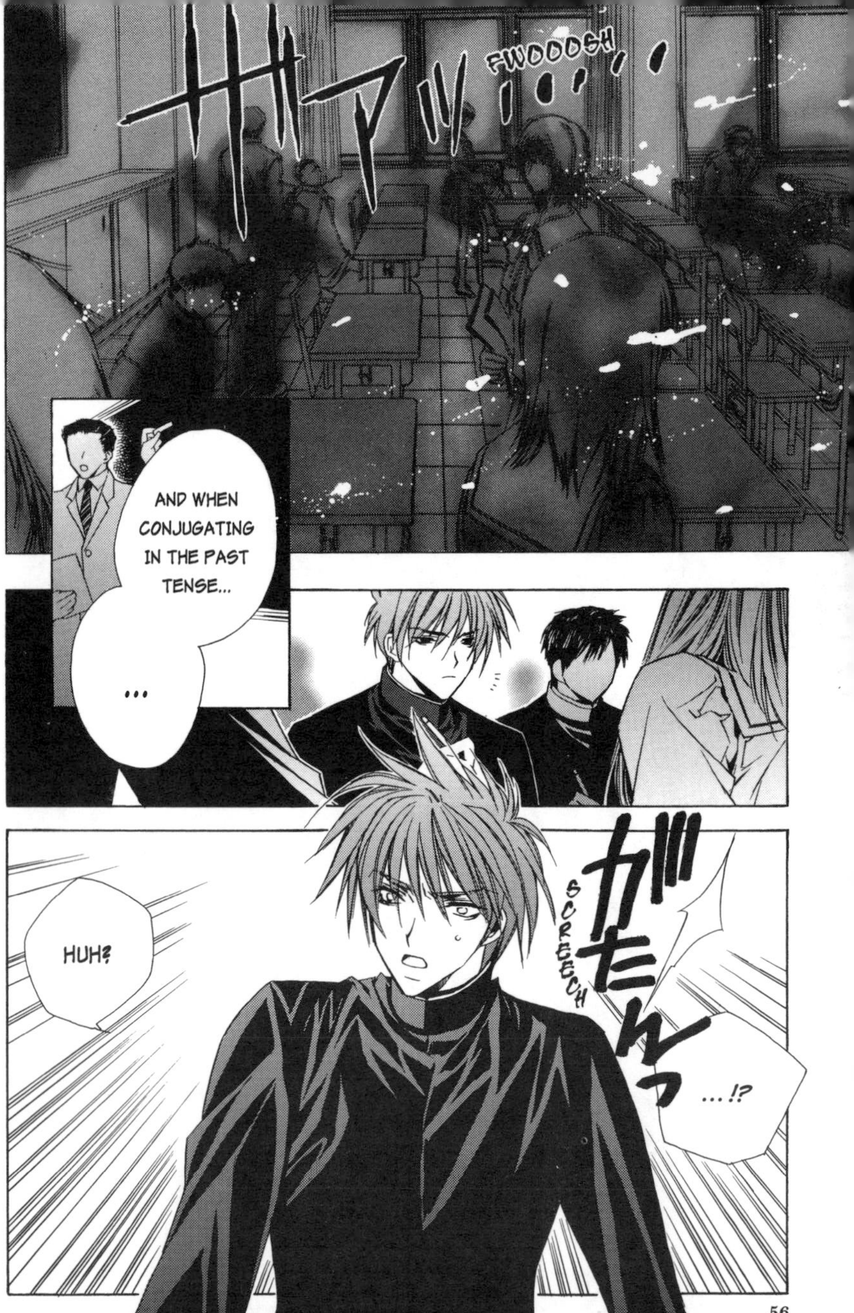
FWOOOSH
AND WHEN CONJUGATING IN THE PAST TENSE...
...
SCREECH
...!?
HUH?

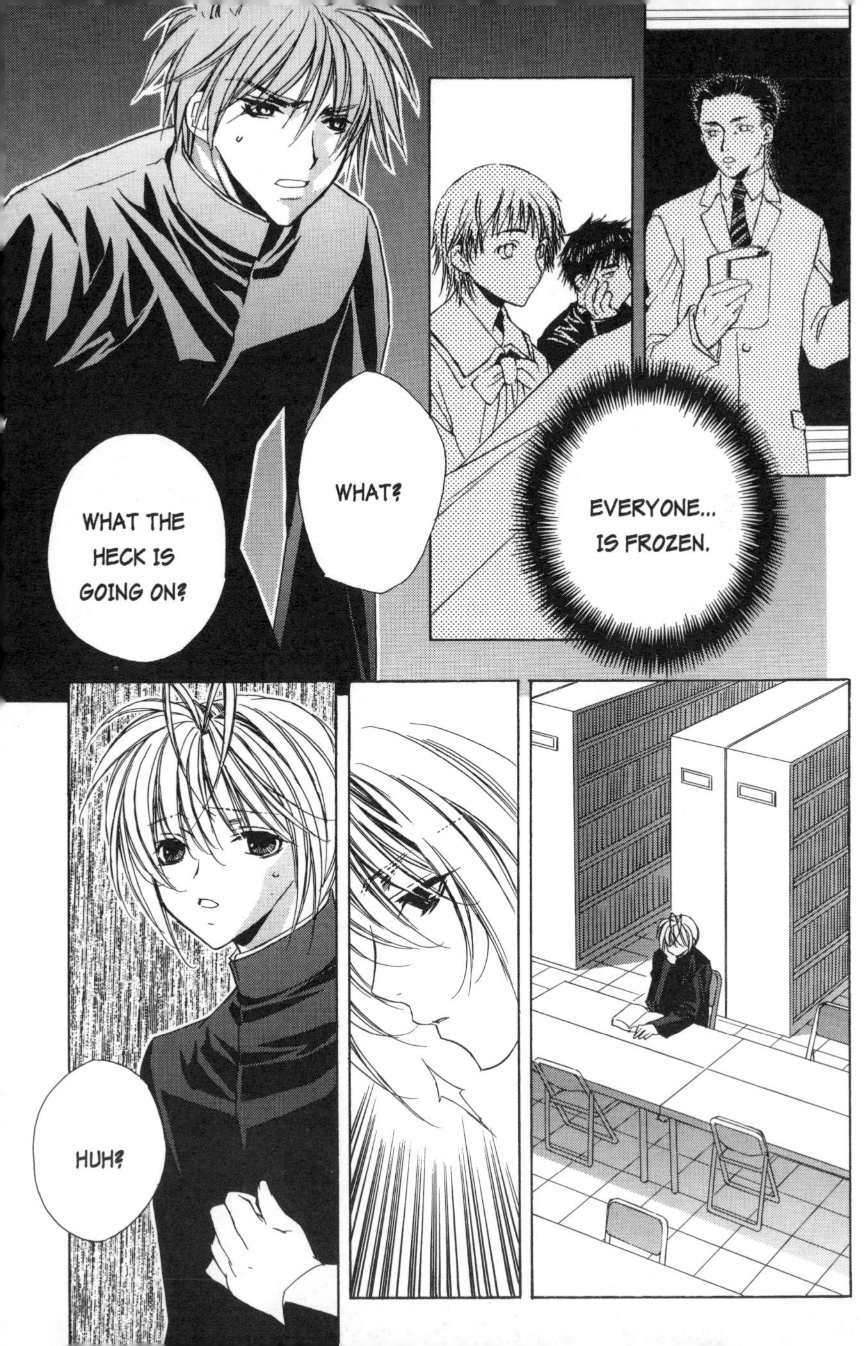
EVERYONE...
IS FROZEN.
WHAT?
WHAT THE HECK IS GOING ON?
HUH?

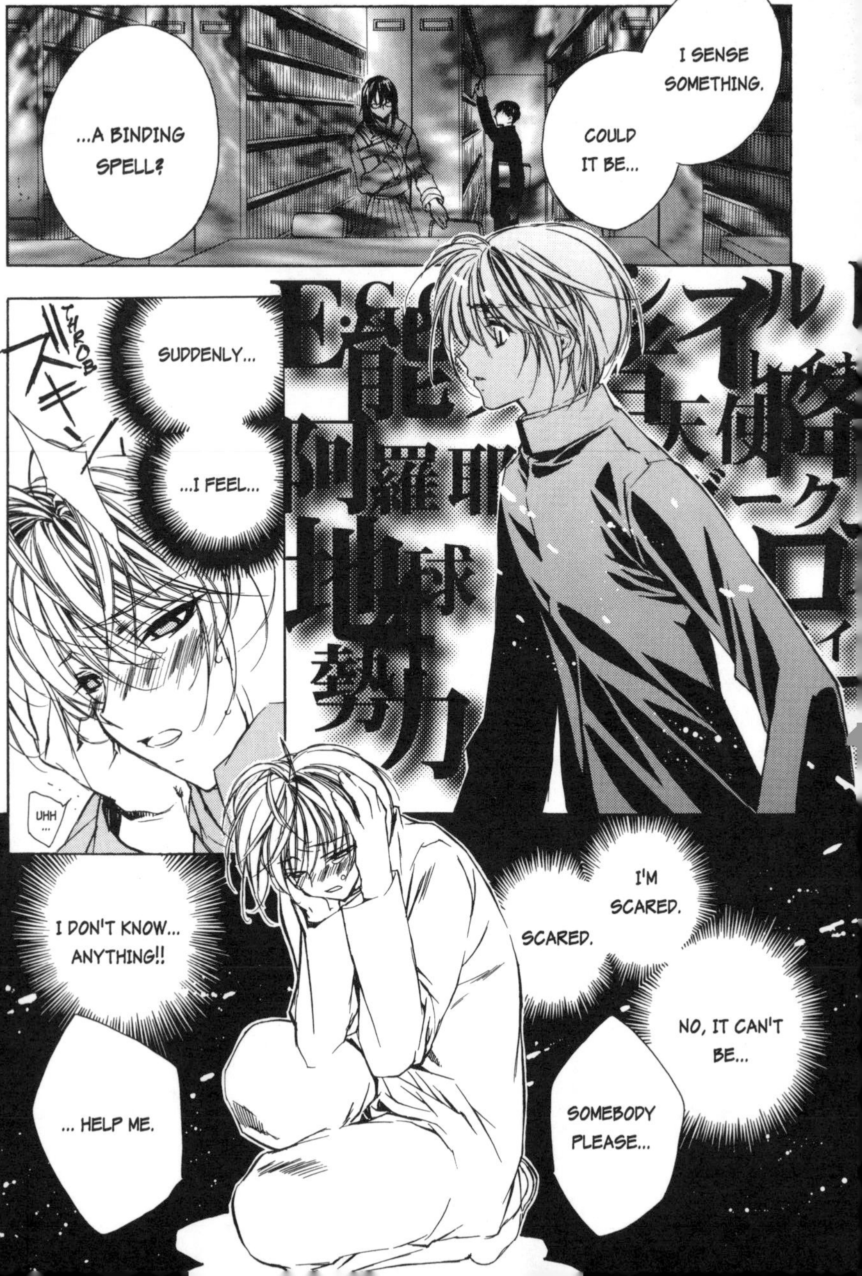
I SENSE SOMETHING.
COULD IT BE...
...A BINDING SPELL?
THROB
SUDDENLY...
...I FEEL...
UHH ...
I'M SCARED.
SCARED.
I DON'T KNOW... ANYTHING!!
NO, IT CAN'T BE...
SOMEBODY PLEASE...
... HELP ME.

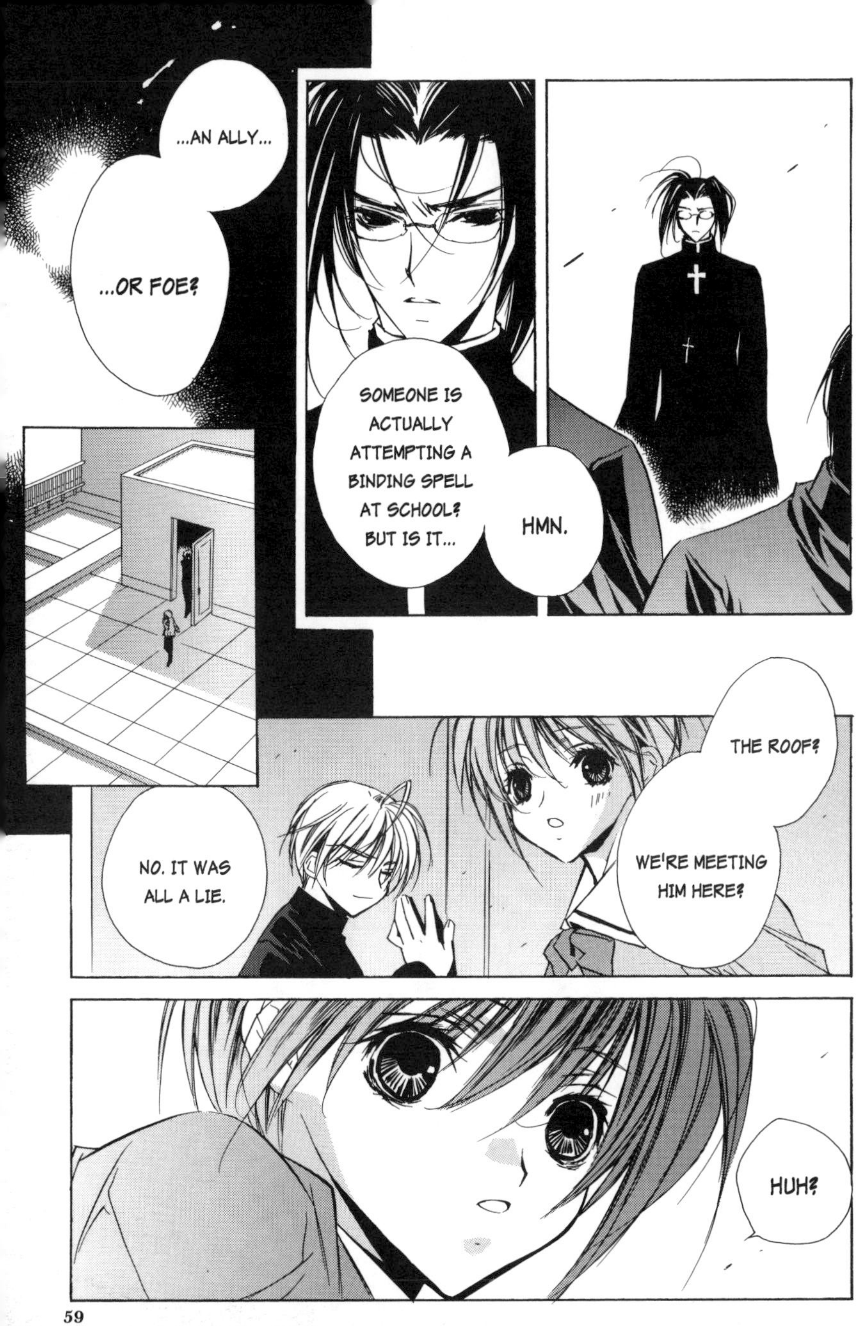
HMN.
SOMEONE IS ACTUALLY ATTEMPTING A BINDING SPELL AT SCHOOL? BUT IS IT...
...AN ALLY...
...OR FOE?
THE ROOF?
WE'RE MEETING HIM HERE?
NO. IT WAS ALL A LIE.
HUH?

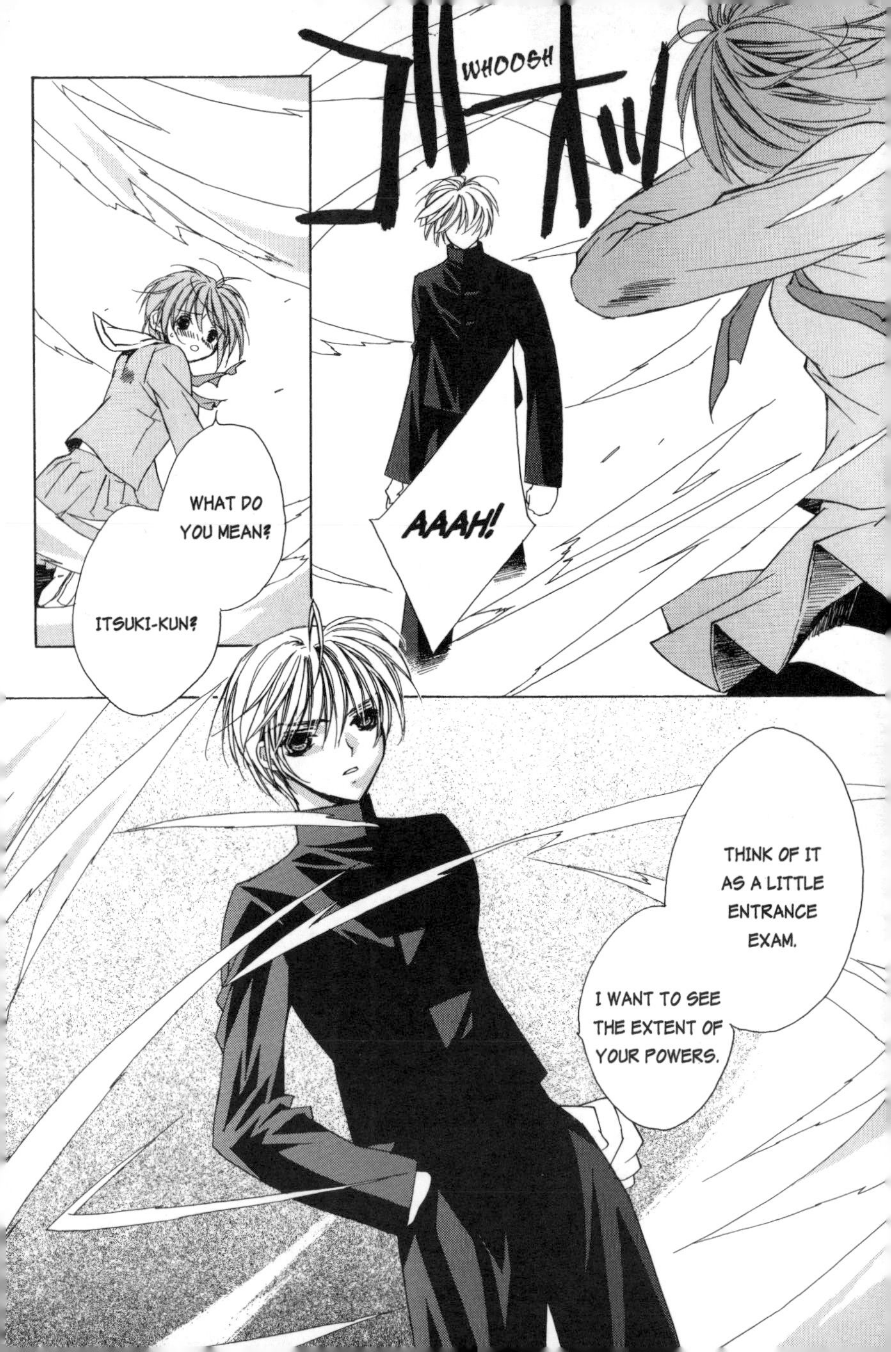
WHOOSH
AAAH!
WHAT DO YOU MEAN?
ITSUKI-KUN?
THINK OF IT AS A LITTLE ENTRANCE EXAM.
I WANT TO SEE THE EXTENT OF YOUR POWERS.

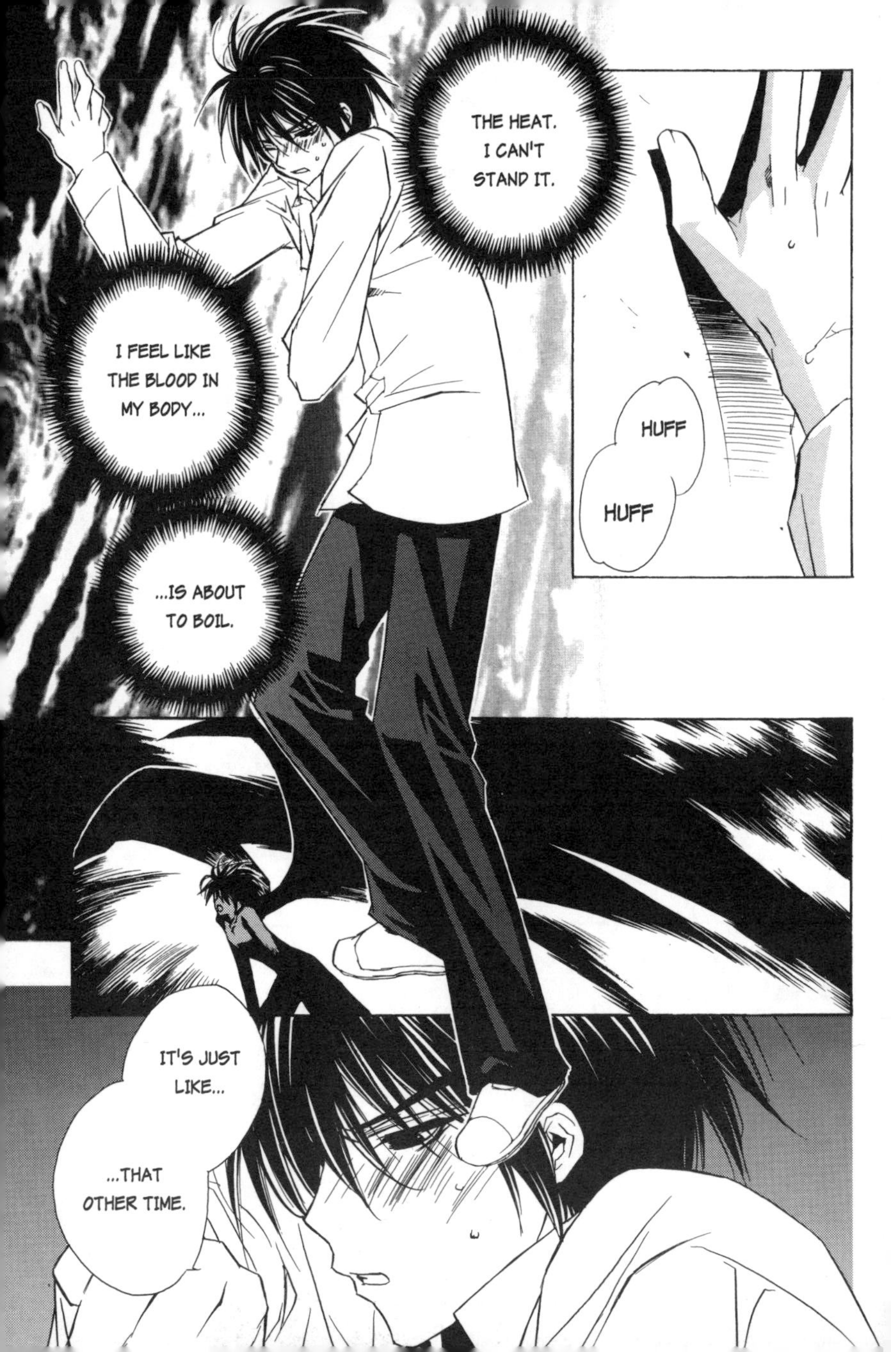
HUFF
HUFF
THE HEAT. I CAN'T STAND IT.
I FEEL LIKE THE BLOOD IN MY BODY...
...IS ABOUT TO BOIL.
IT'S JUST LIKE...
...THAT OTHER TIME.

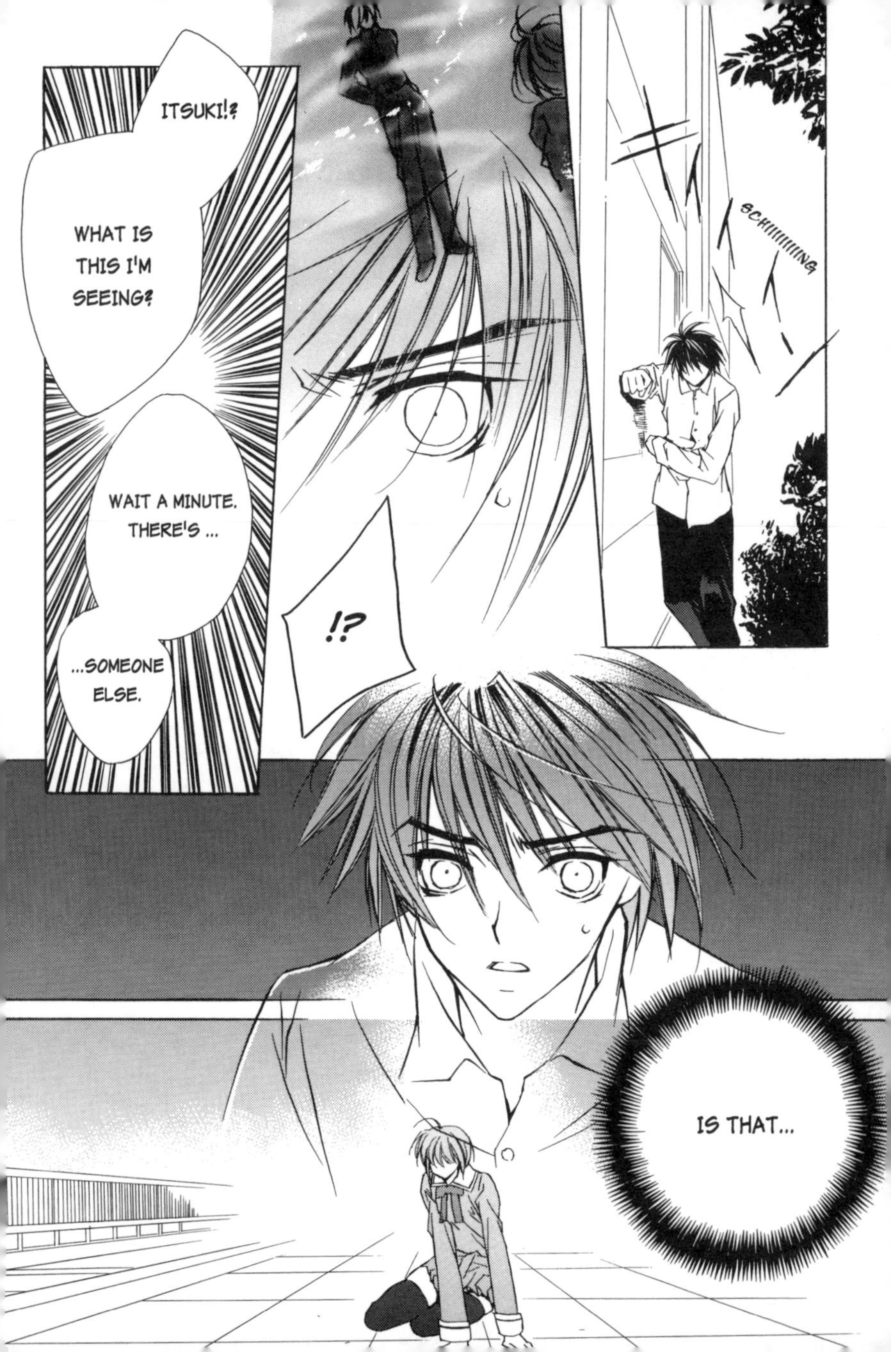
SCHIIIIIIING
!?
ITSUKI!?
WHAT IS THIS I'M SEEING?
WAIT A MINUTE. THERE'S ...
...SOMEONE ELSE.
IS THAT...

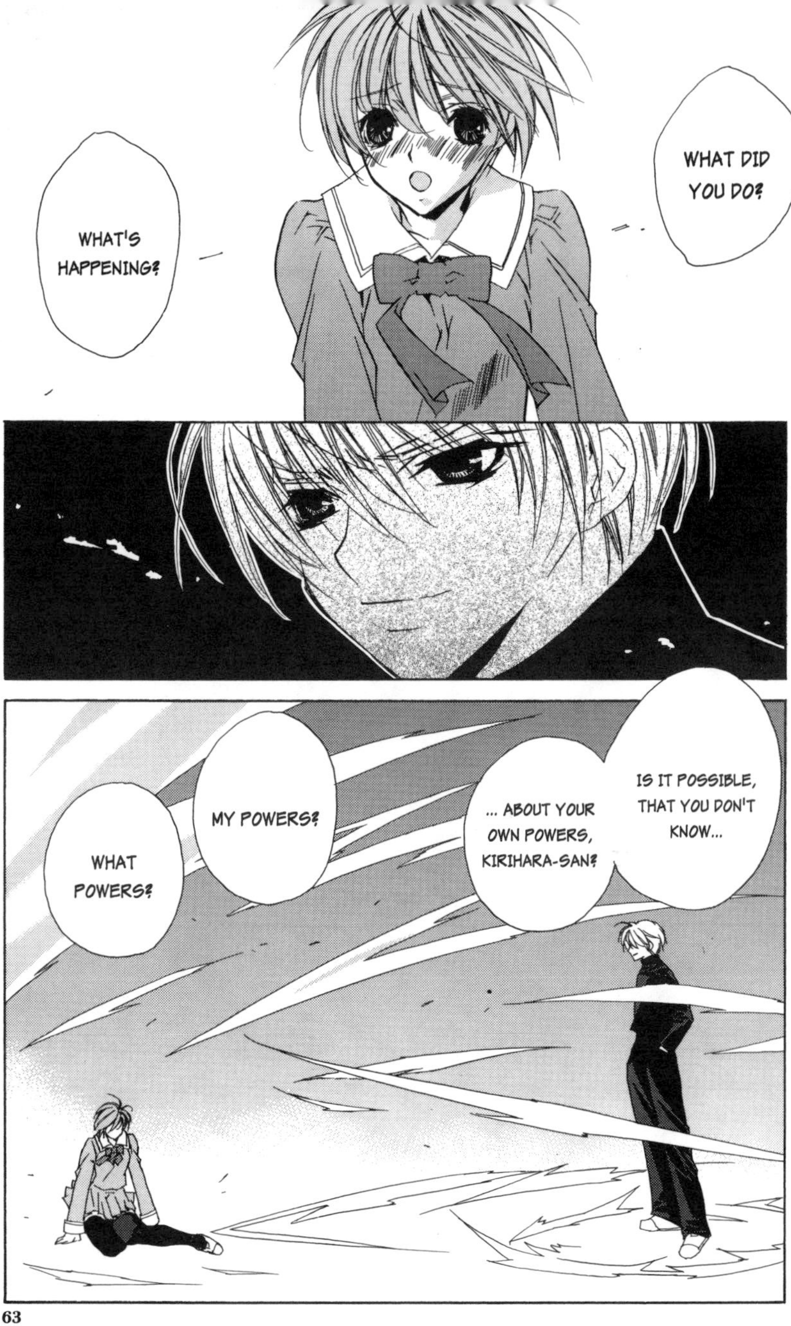
WHAT DID YOU DO?
WHAT'S HAPPENING?
IS IT POSSIBLE, THAT YOU DON'T KNOW...
... ABOUT YOUR OWN POWERS, KIRIHARA-SAN?
MY POWERS?
WHAT POWERS?

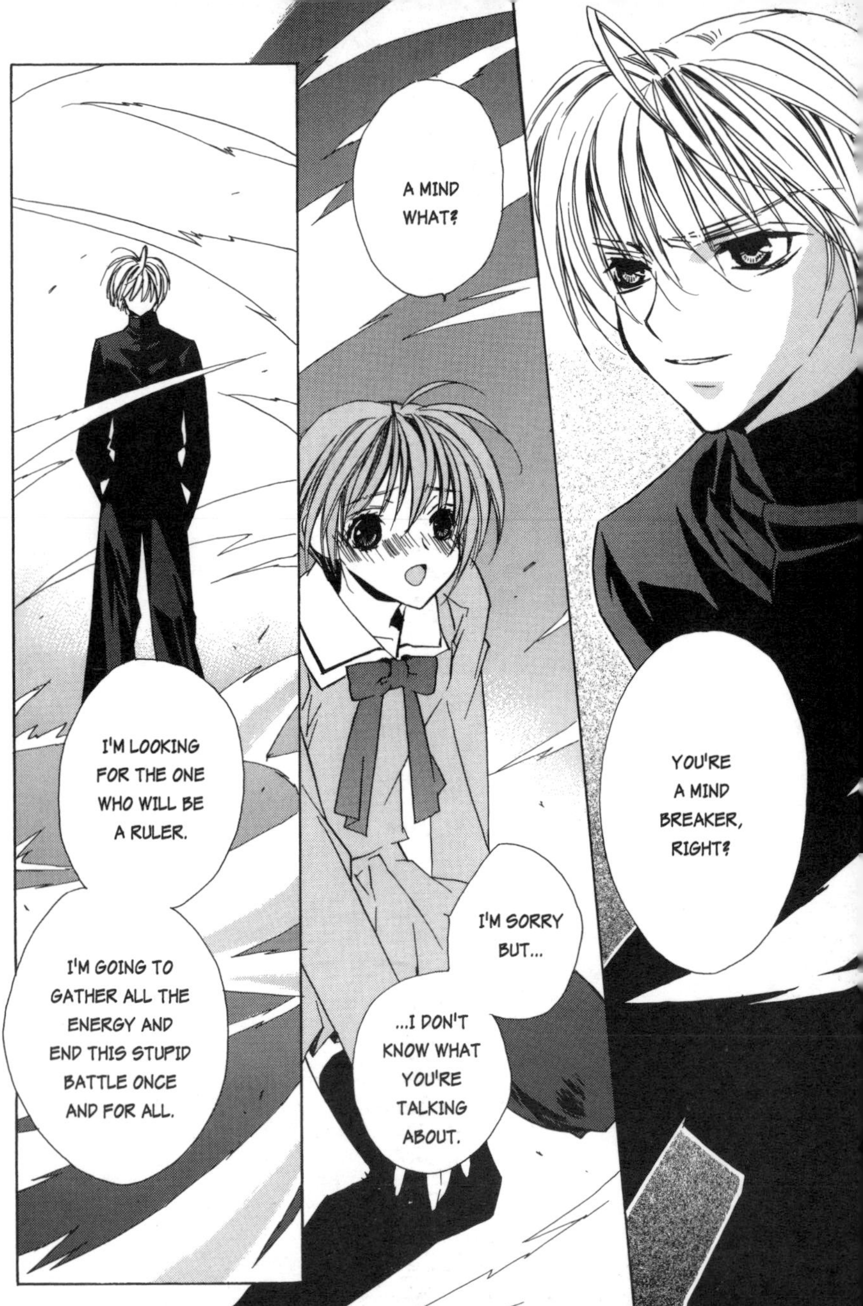
YOU'RE A MIND BREAKER, RIGHT?
A MIND WHAT?
I'M SORRY BUT...
...I DON'T KNOW WHAT YOU'RE TALKING ABOUT.
I'M LOOKING FOR THE ONE WHO WILL BE A RULER.
I'M GOING TO GATHER ALL THE ENERGY AND END THIS STUPID BATTLE ONCE AND FOR ALL.

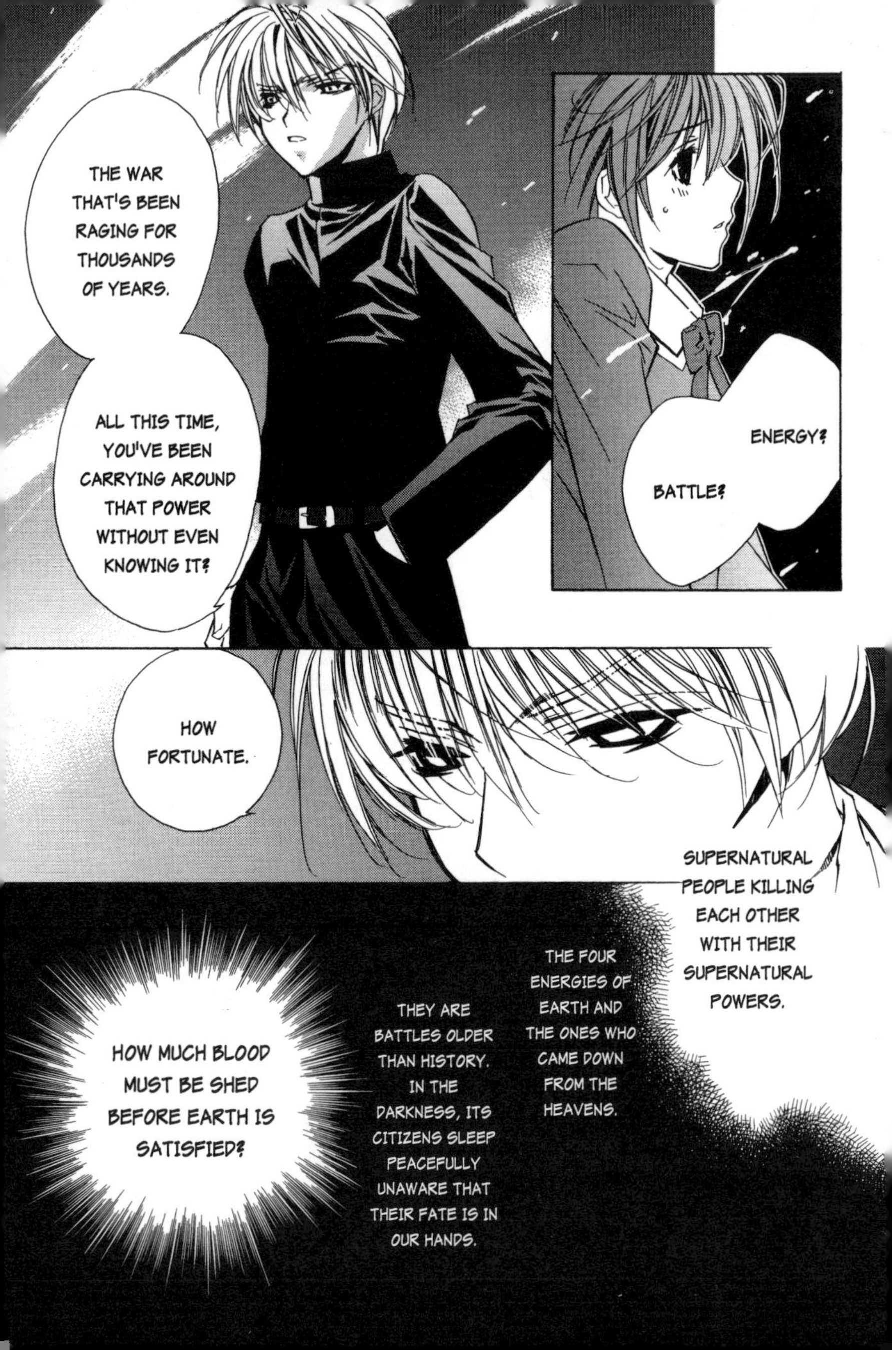
ENERGY?
BATTLE?
THE WAR THAT'S BEEN RAGING FOR THOUSANDS OF YEARS.
ALL THIS TIME, YOU'VE BEEN CARRYING AROUND THAT POWER WITHOUT EVEN KNOWING IT?
HOW FORTUNATE.
SUPERNATURAL PEOPLE KILLING EACH OTHER WITH THEIR SUPERNATURAL POWERS.
THE FOUR ENERGIES OF EARTH AND THE ONES WHO CAME DOWN FROM THE HEAVENS.
THEY ARE BATTLES OLDER THAN HISTORY. IN THE DARKNESS, ITS CITIZENS SLEEP PEACEFULLY UNAWARE THAT THEIR FATE IS IN OUR HANDS.
HOW MUCH BLOOD MUST BE SHED BEFORE EARTH IS SATISFIED?

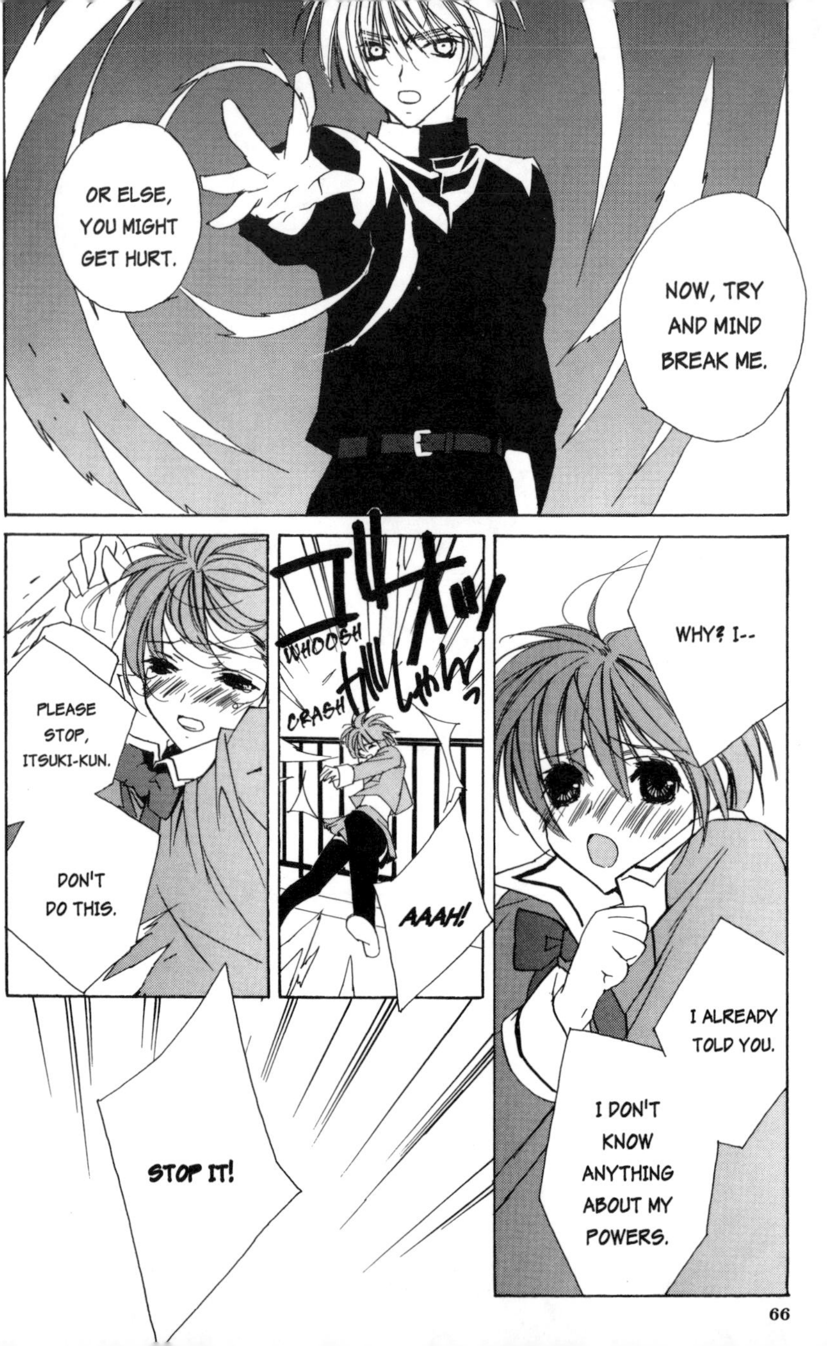
NOW, TRY AND MIND BREAK ME.
OR ELSE, YOU MIGHT GET HURT.
WHY? I--
I ALREADY TOLD YOU.
I DON'T KNOW ANYTHING ABOUT MY POWERS.
WHOOSH
CRASH
AAAH!
PLEASE STOP, ITSUKI-KUN.
DON'T DO THIS.
STOP IT!

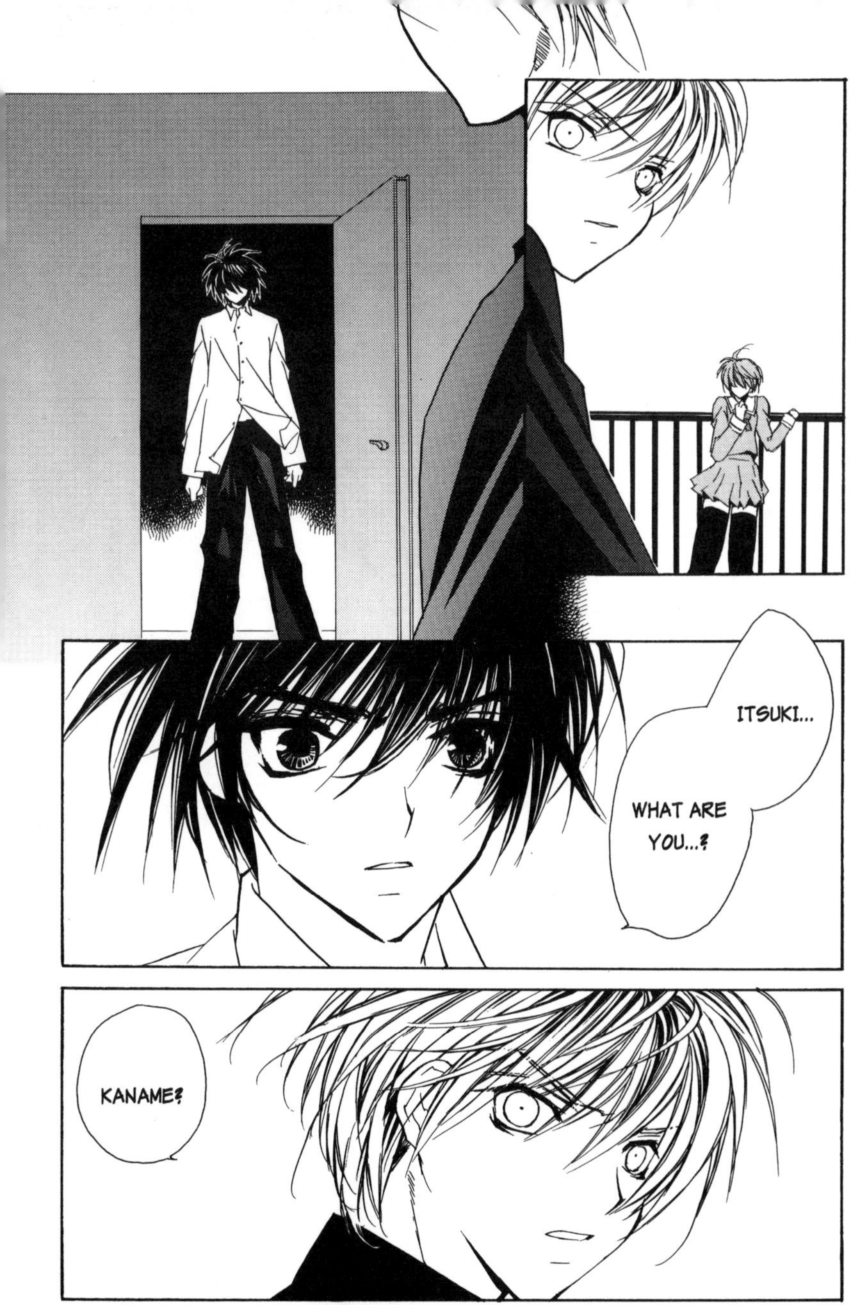
ITSUKI...
WHAT ARE YOU...?
KANAME?

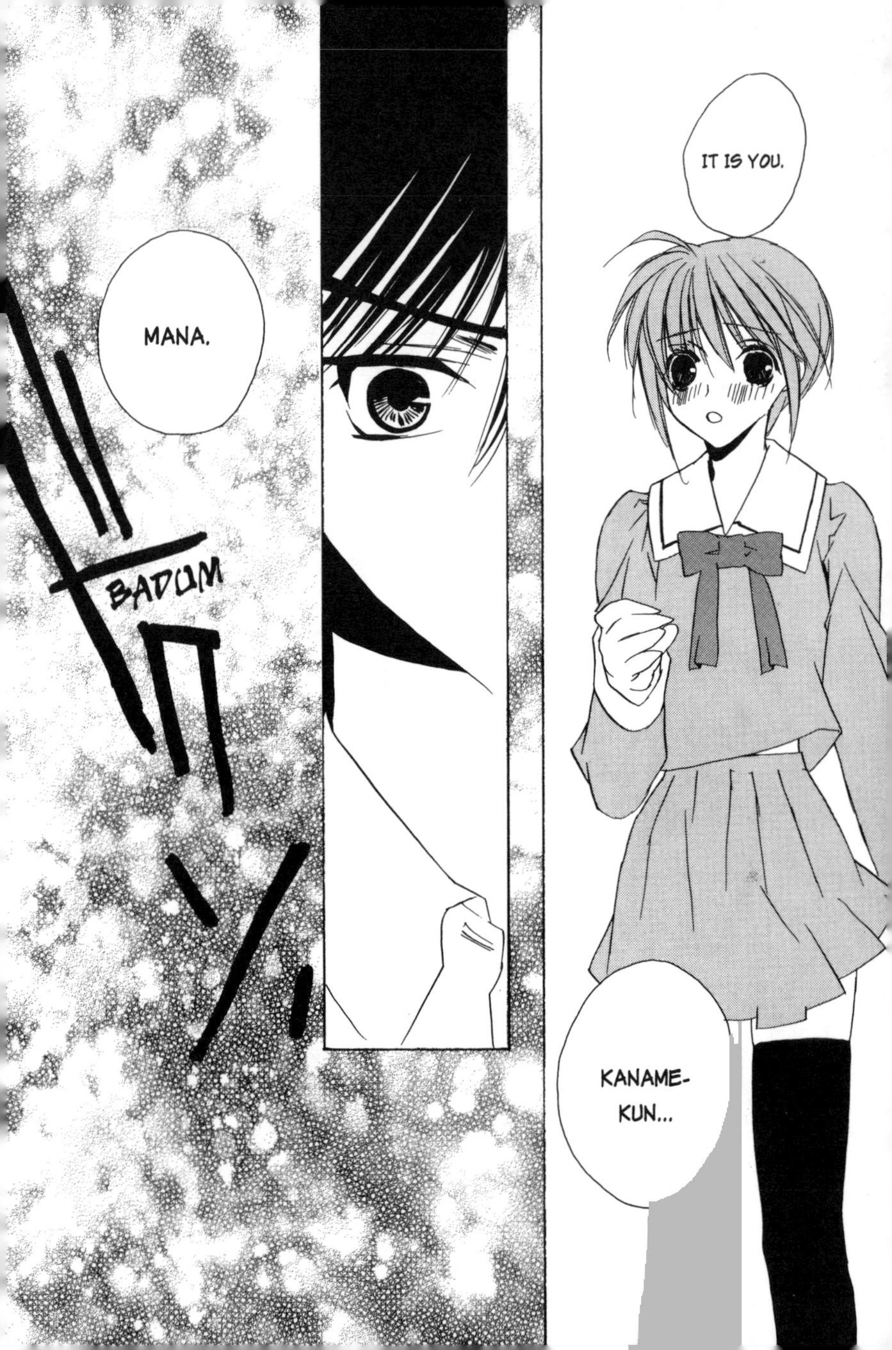
IT IS YOU.
KANAME-KUN...
MANA.
BADUM

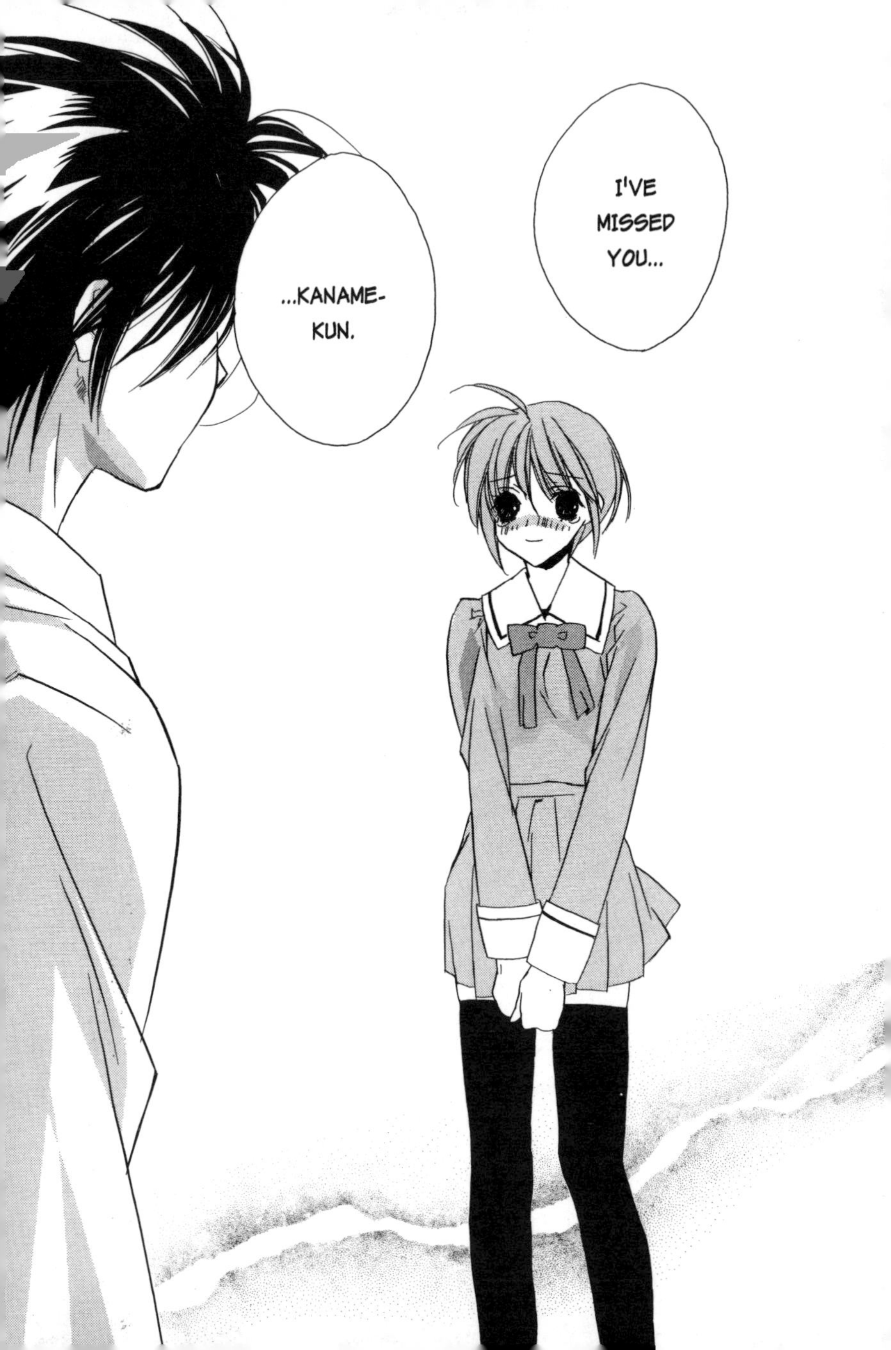
I'VE MISSED YOU...
...KANAME-KUN.

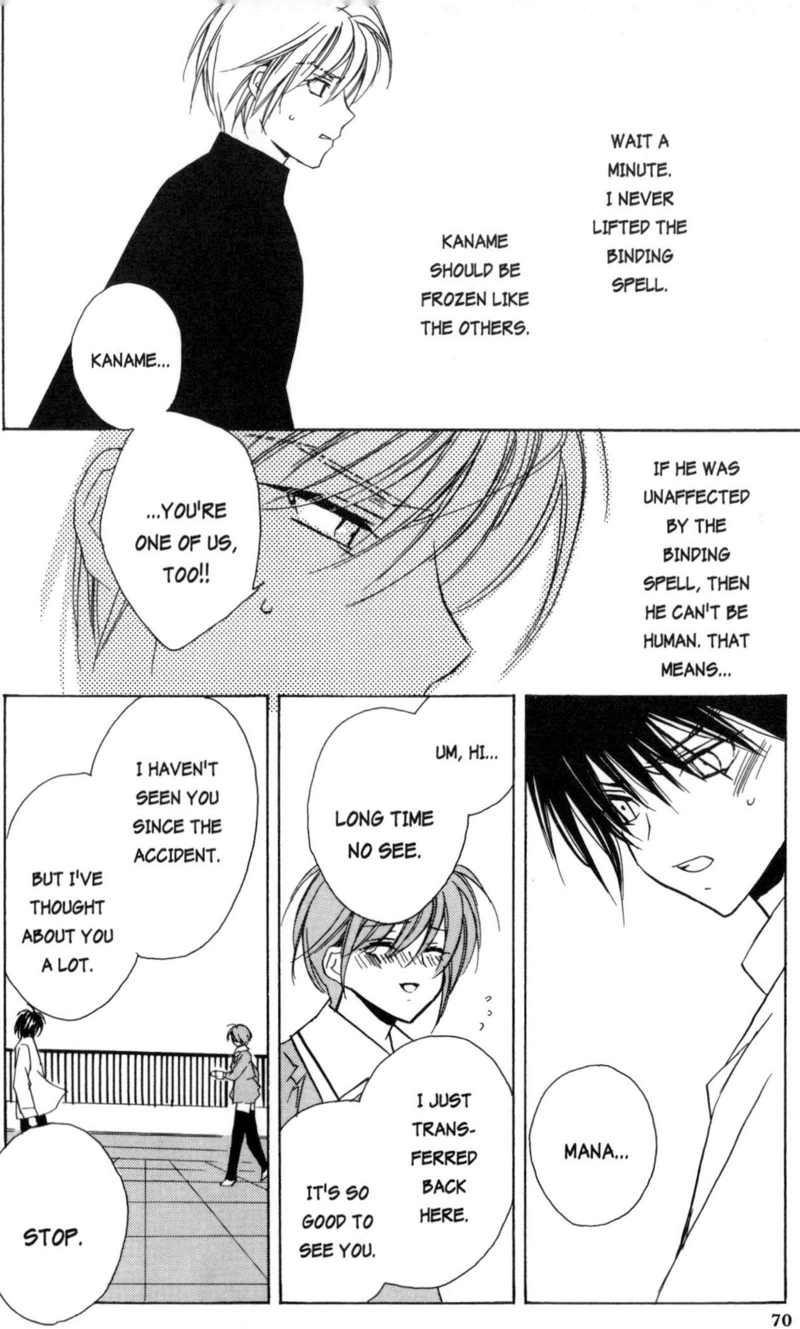
WAIT A MINUTE. I NEVER LIFTED THE BINDING SPELL.
KANAME SHOULD BE FROZEN LIKE THE OTHERS.
KANAME...
IF HE WAS UNAFFECTED BY THE BINDING SPELL, THEN HE CAN'T BE HUMAN. THAT MEANS...
...YOU'RE ONE OF US, TOO!!
MANA...
UM, HI...
LONG TIME NO SEE.
I JUST TRANS-FERRED BACK HERE.
IT'S SO GOOD TO SEE YOU.
I HAVEN'T SEEN YOU SINCE THE ACCIDENT.
BUT I'VE THOUGHT ABOUT YOU A LOT.
STOP.

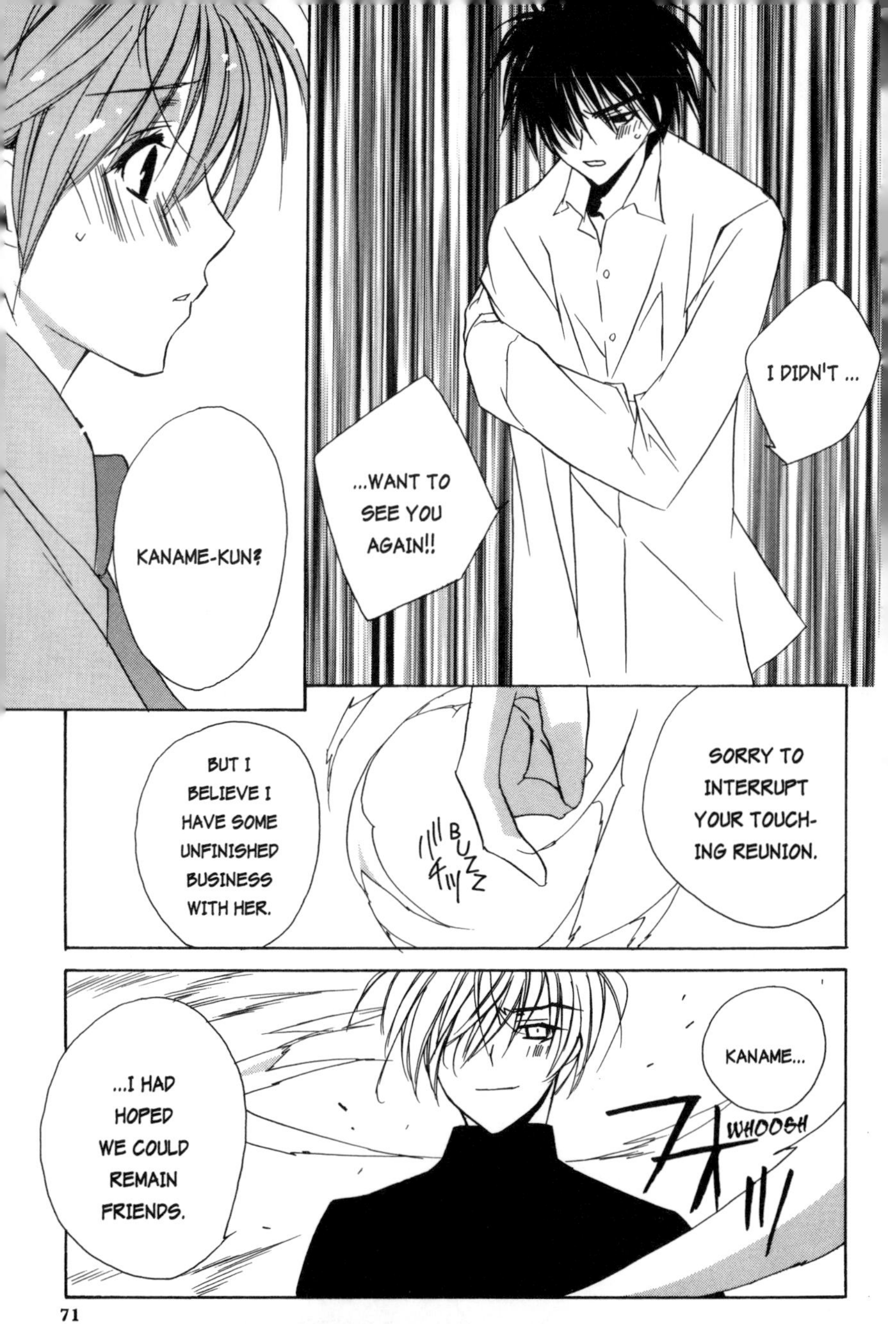
I DIDN'T ...
...WANT TO SEE YOU AGAIN!!
KANAME-KUN?
SORRY TO INTERRUPT YOUR TOUCH-ING REUNION.
BUZZ
BUT I BELIEVE I HAVE SOME UNFINISHED BUSINESS WITH HER.
KANAME...
WHOOSH
...I HAD HOPED WE COULD REMAIN FRIENDS.

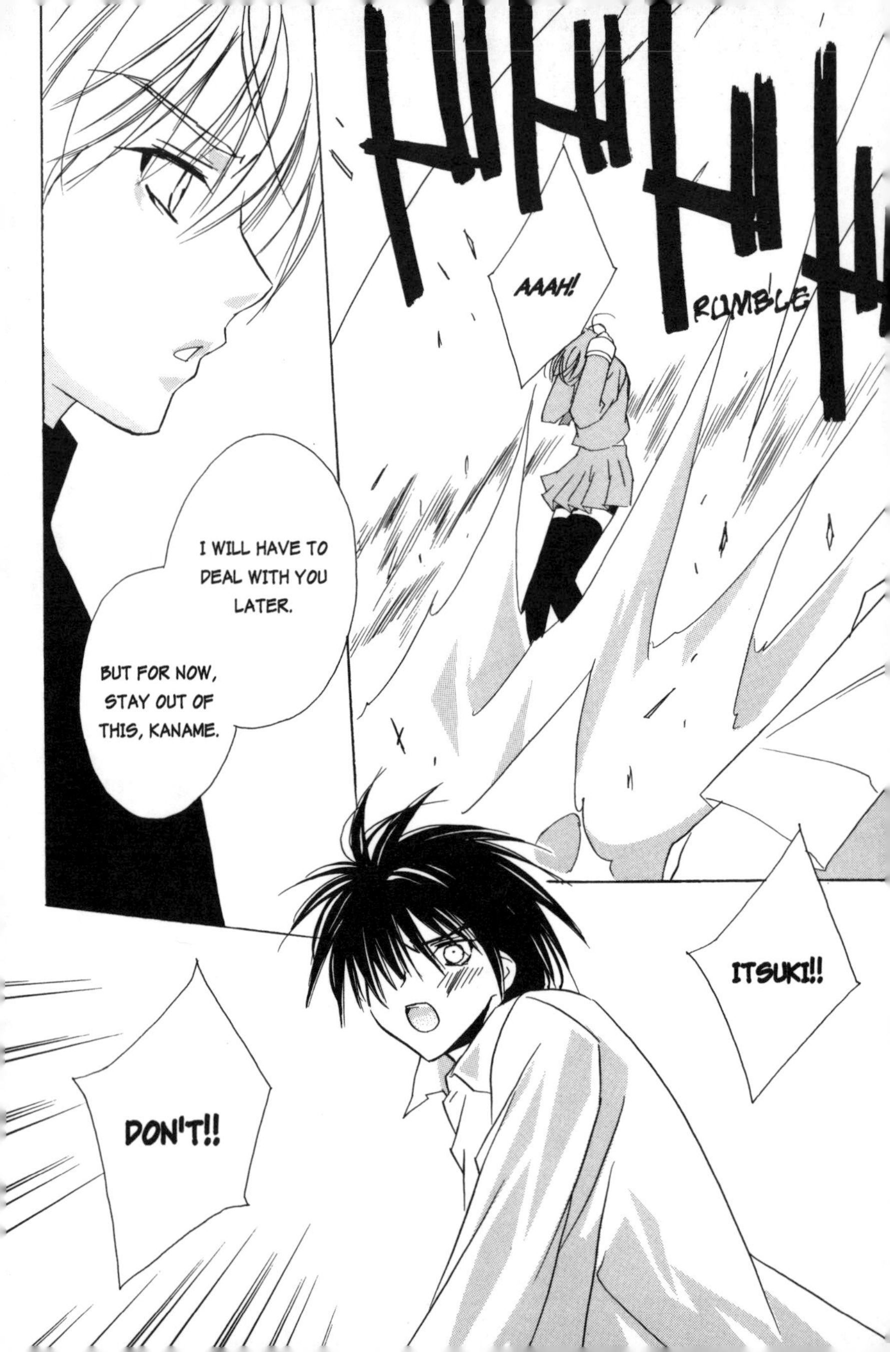
AAAH!
RUMBLE
I WILL HAVE TO DEAL WITH YOU LATER.
BUT FOR NOW, STAY OUT OF THIS, KANAME.
ITSUKI!!
DON'T!!

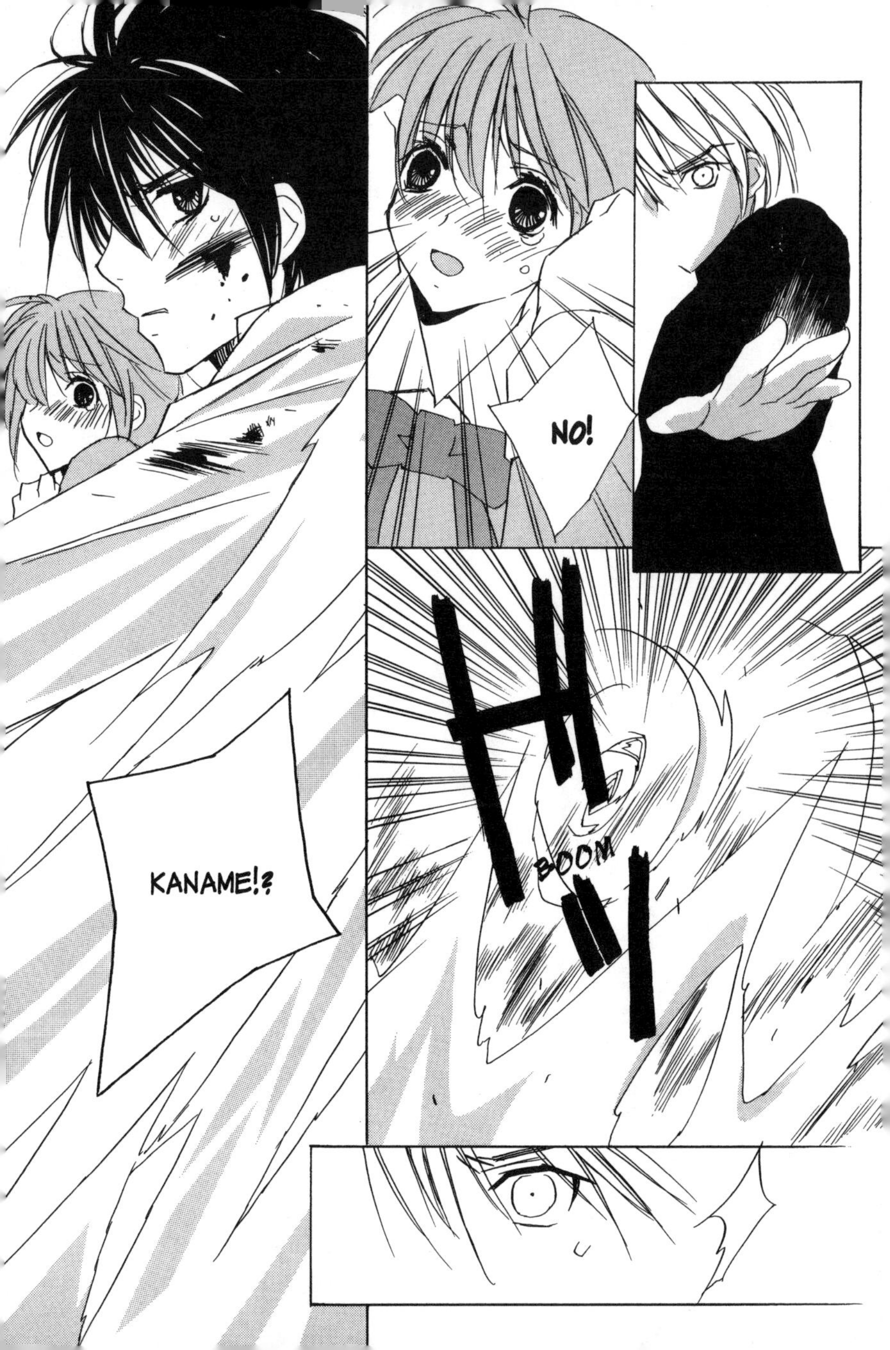
NO!
BOOM
KANAME!?

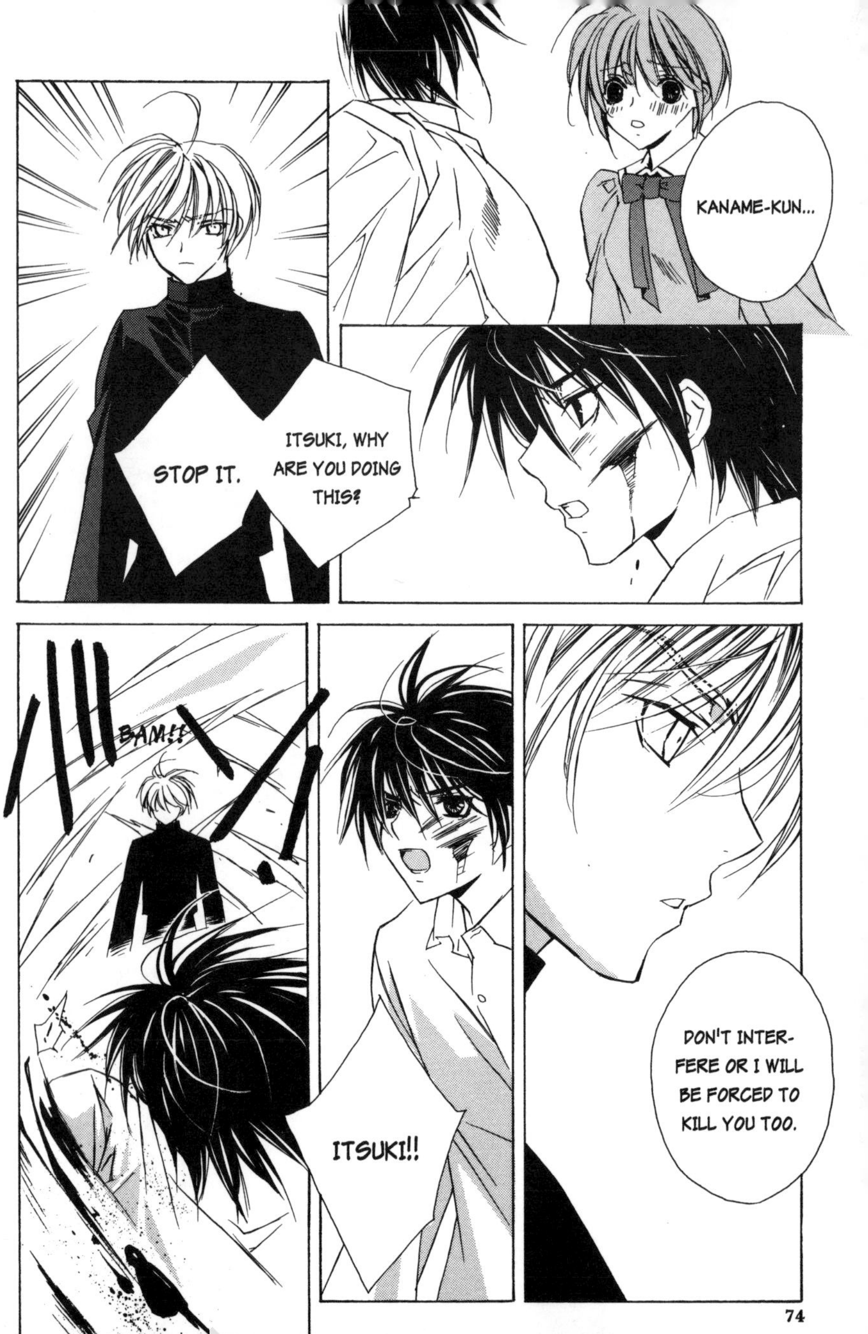
KANAME-KUN...
ITSUKI, WHY ARE YOU DOING THIS?
STOP IT.
DON'T INTER-FERE OR I WILL BE FORCED TO KILL YOU TOO.
ITSUKI!!
BAM!!

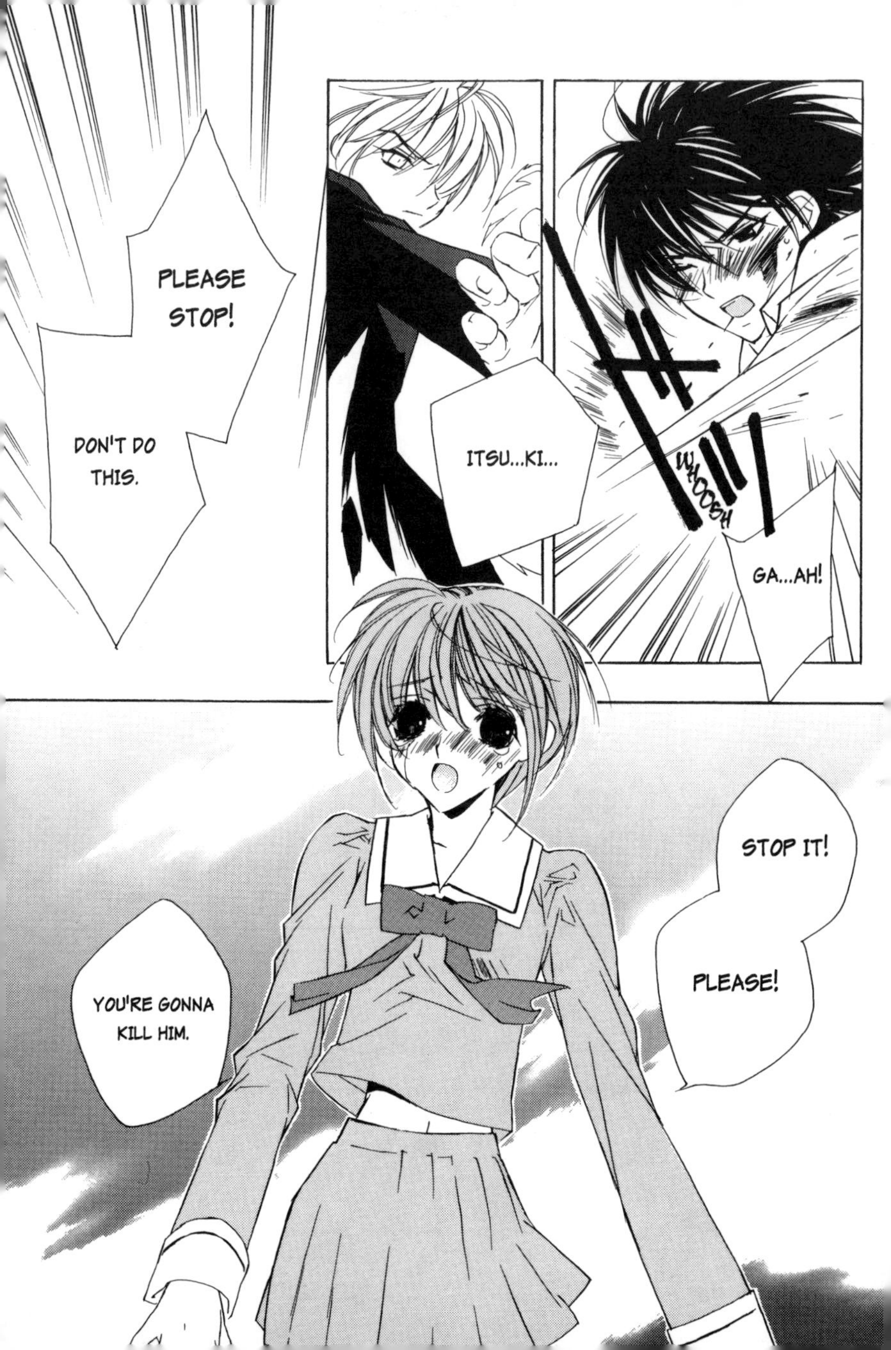
WHOOSH
GA...AH!
ITSU...KI...
PLEASE STOP!
DON'T DO THIS.
STOP IT!
PLEASE!
YOU'RE GONNA KILL HIM.

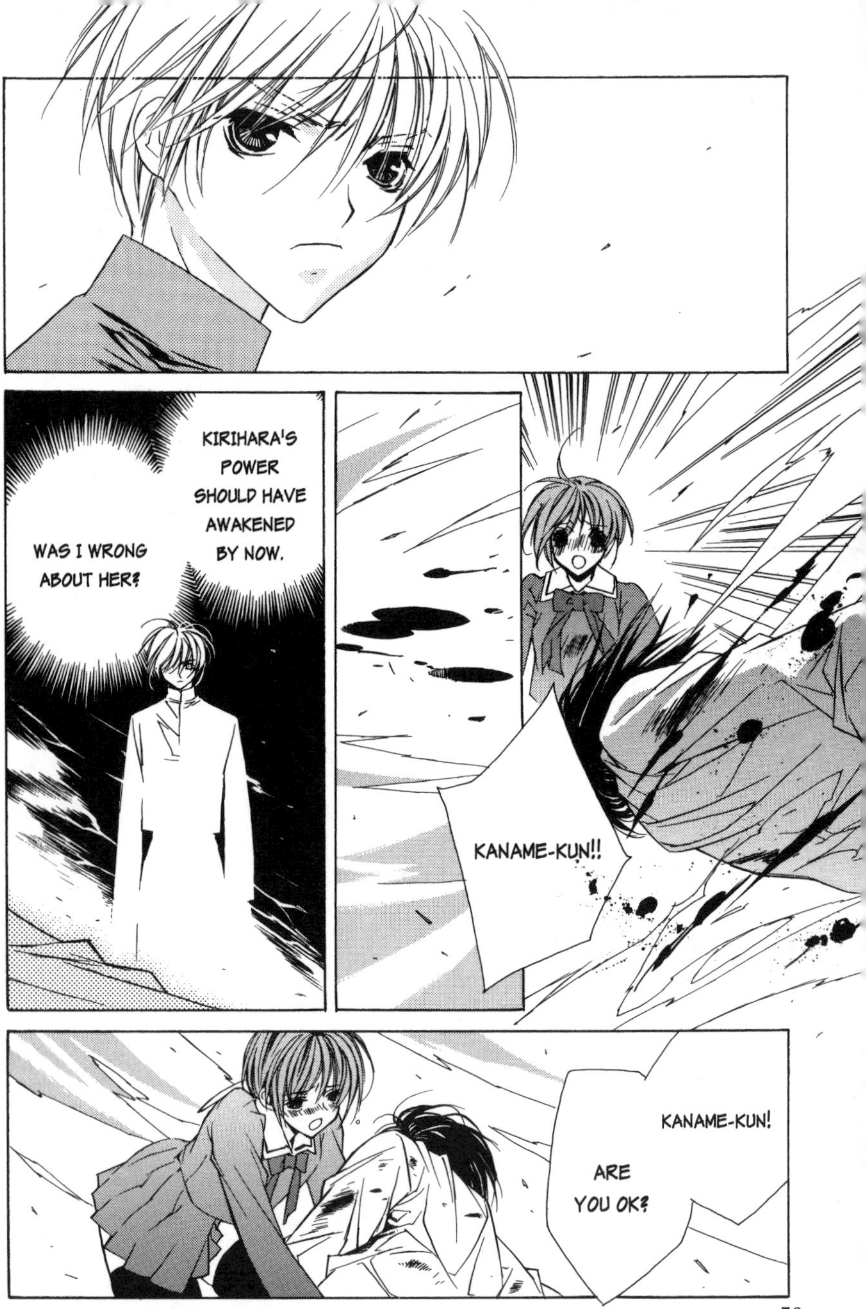
KANAME-KUN!!
KIRIHARA'S POWER SHOULD HAVE AWAKENED BY NOW.
WAS I WRONG ABOUT HER?
KANAME-KUN!
ARE YOU OK?

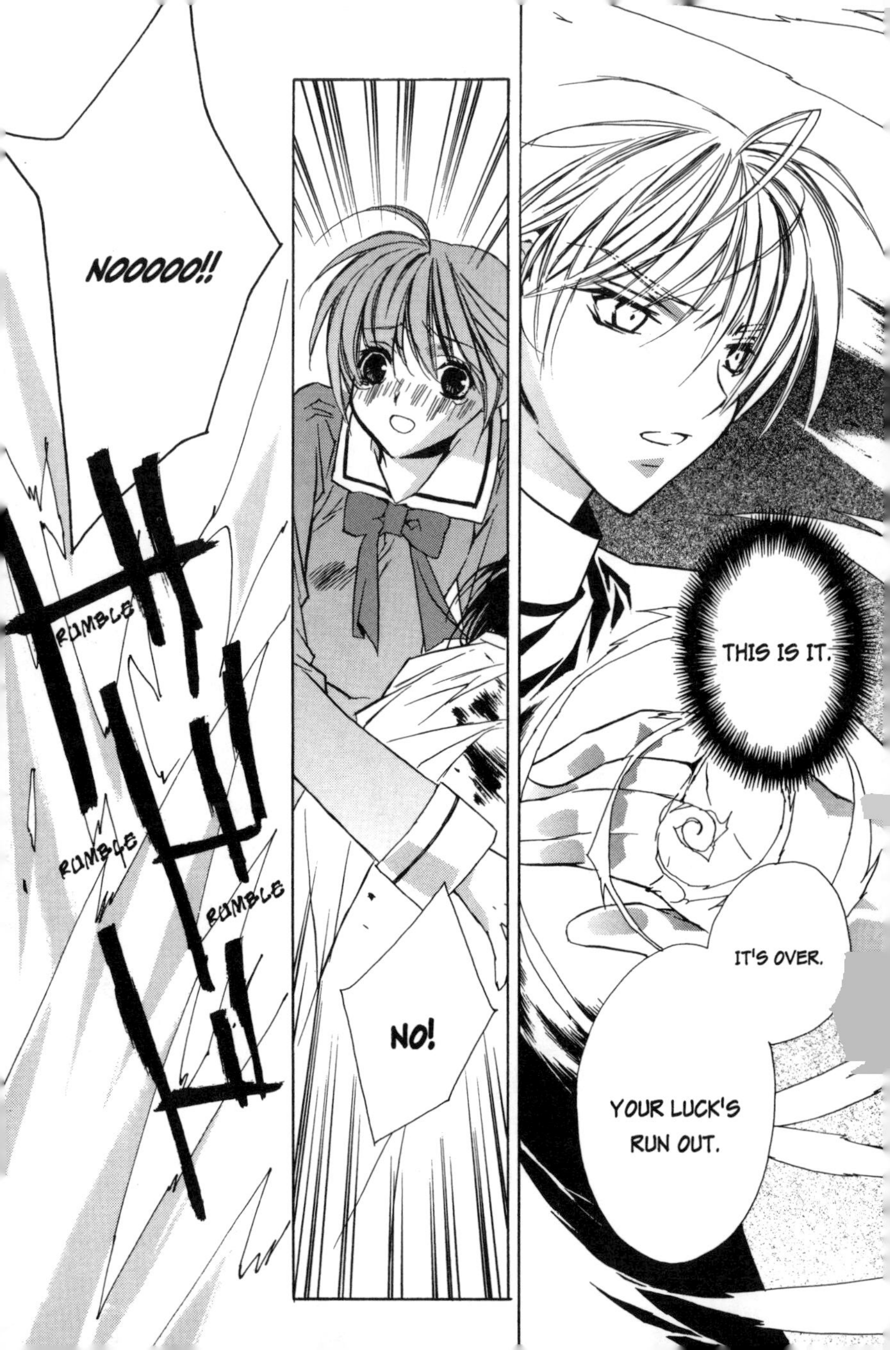
THIS IS IT.
IT'S OVER.
YOUR LUCK'S RUN OUT.
NO!
NOOOOO!!
RUMBLE
RUMBLE
RUMBLE

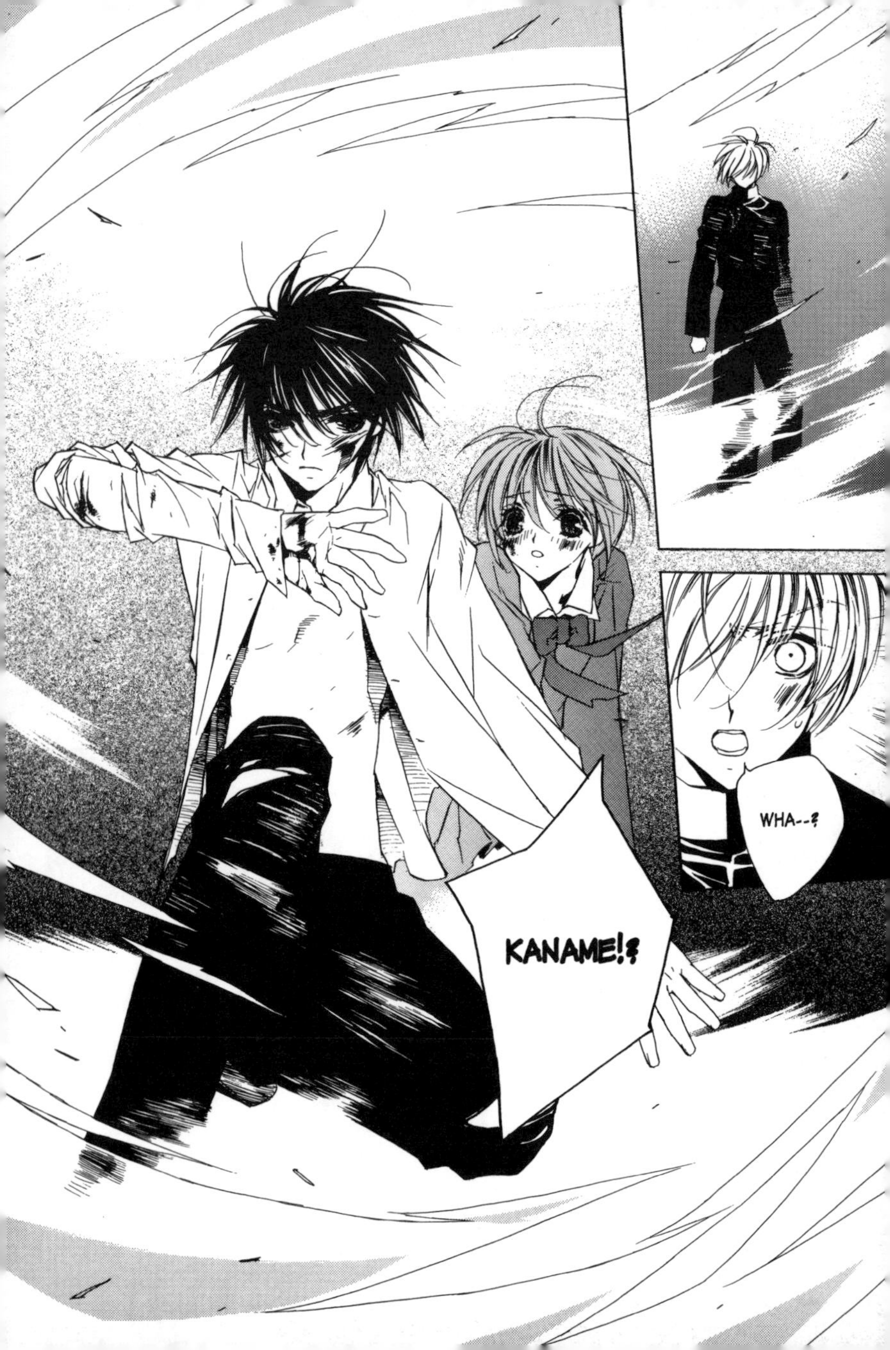
WHA--?
KANAME!?

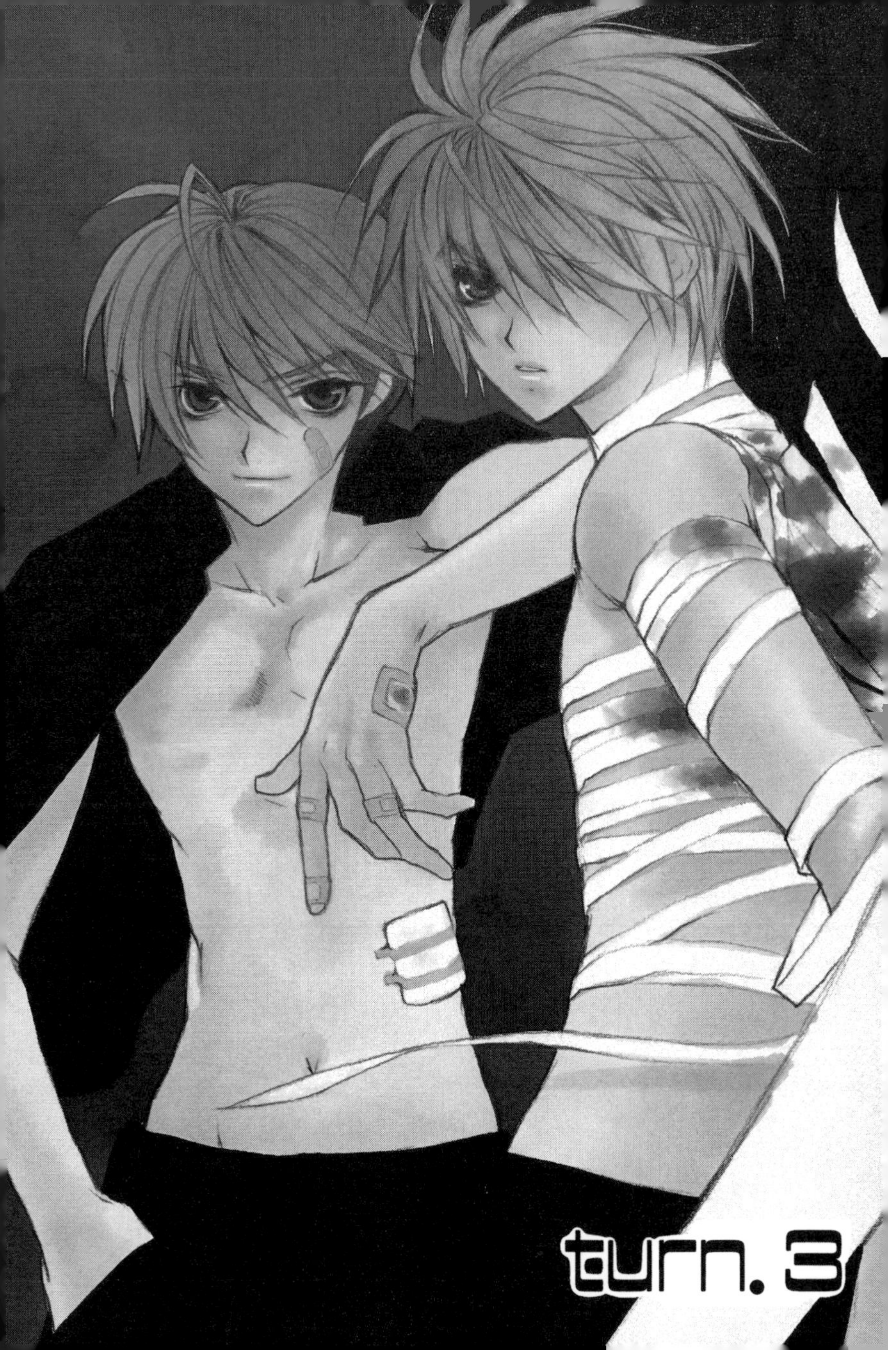
turn. 3

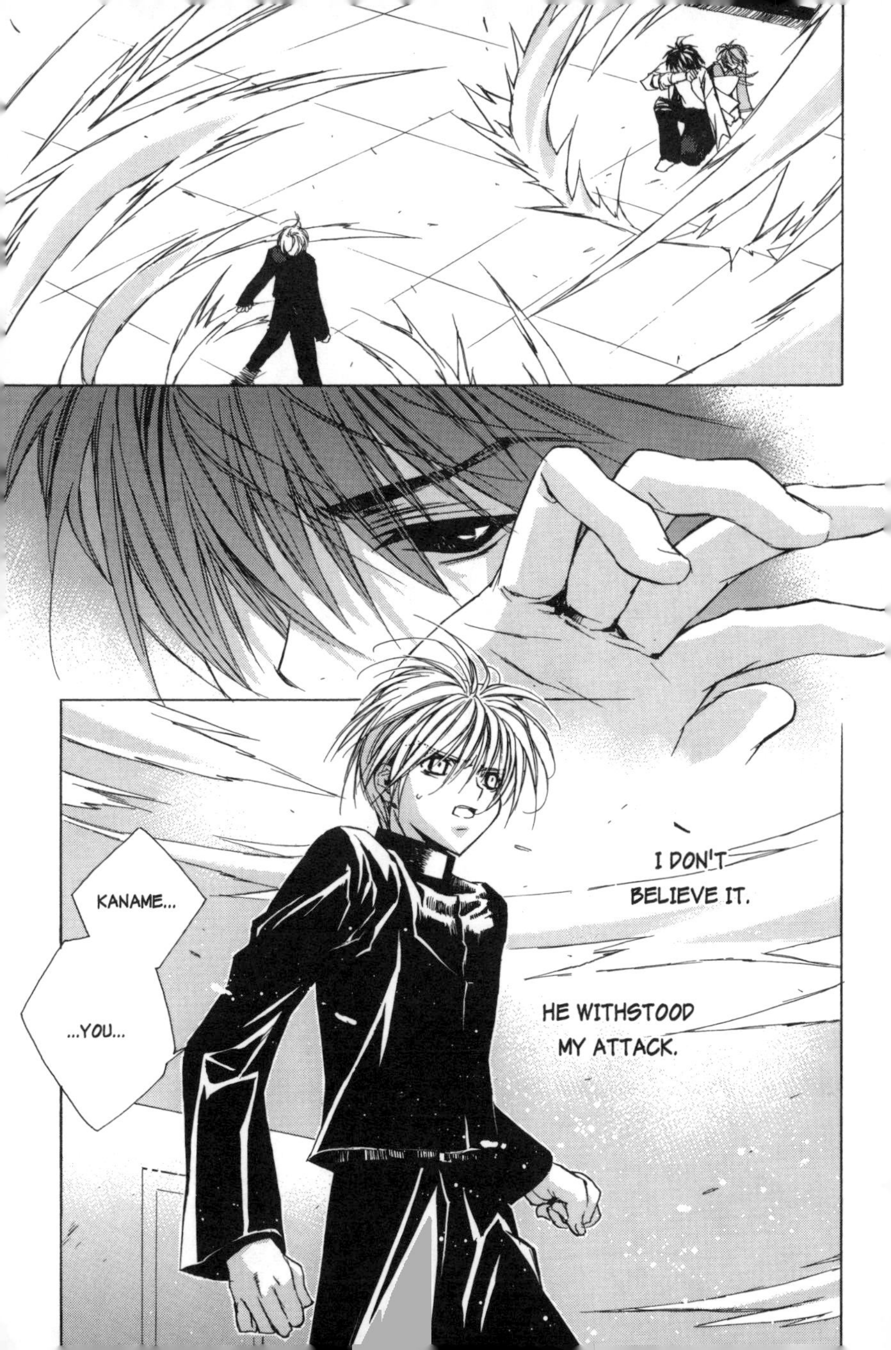
I DON'T BELIEVE IT.
HE WITHSTOOD MY ATTACK.
KANAME...
...YOU...

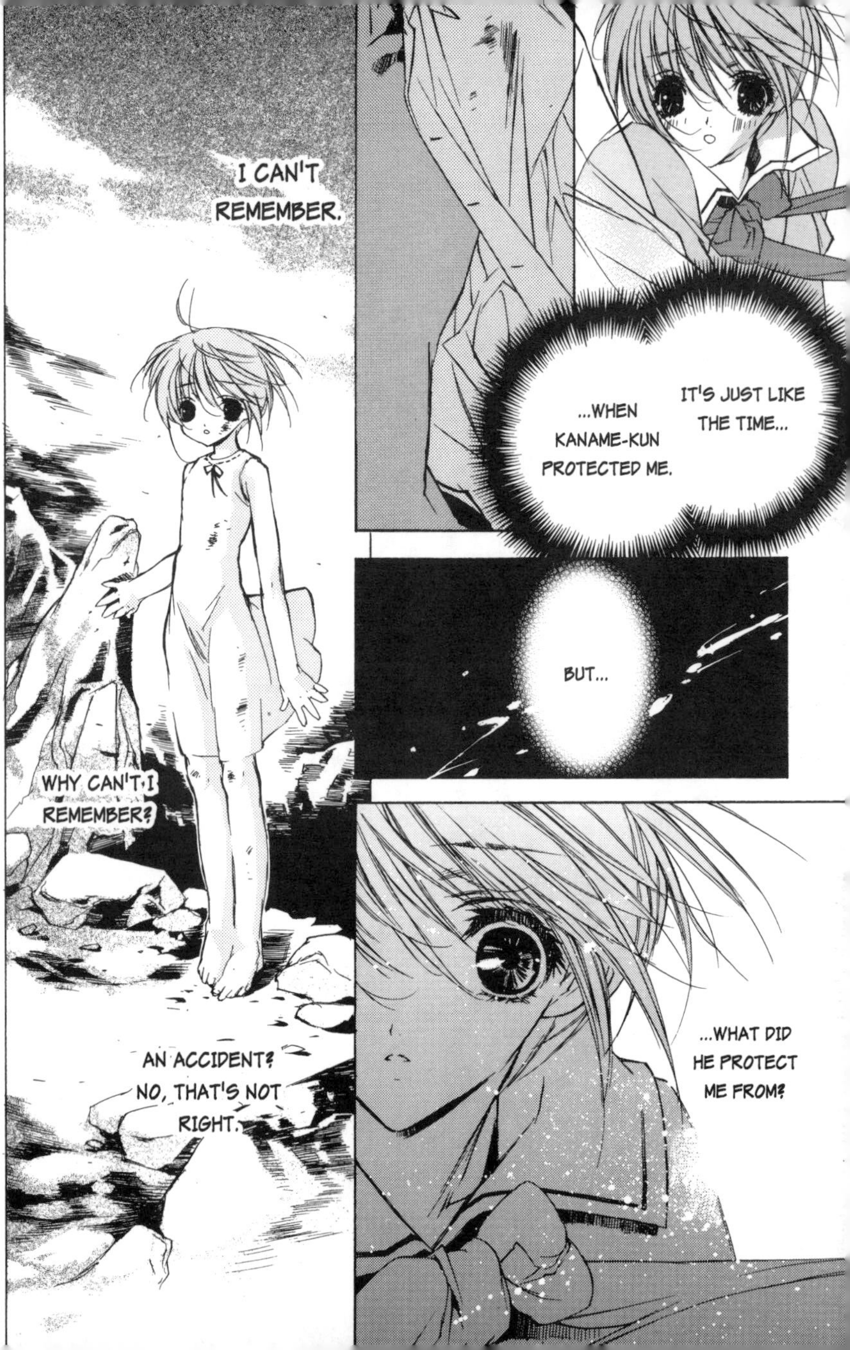
IT'S JUST LIKE THE TIME...
...WHEN KANAME-KUN PROTECTED ME.
BUT...
...WHAT DID HE PROTECT ME FROM?
I CAN'T REMEMBER.
WHY CAN'T I REMEMBER?
AN ACCIDENT? NO, THAT'S NOT RIGHT.

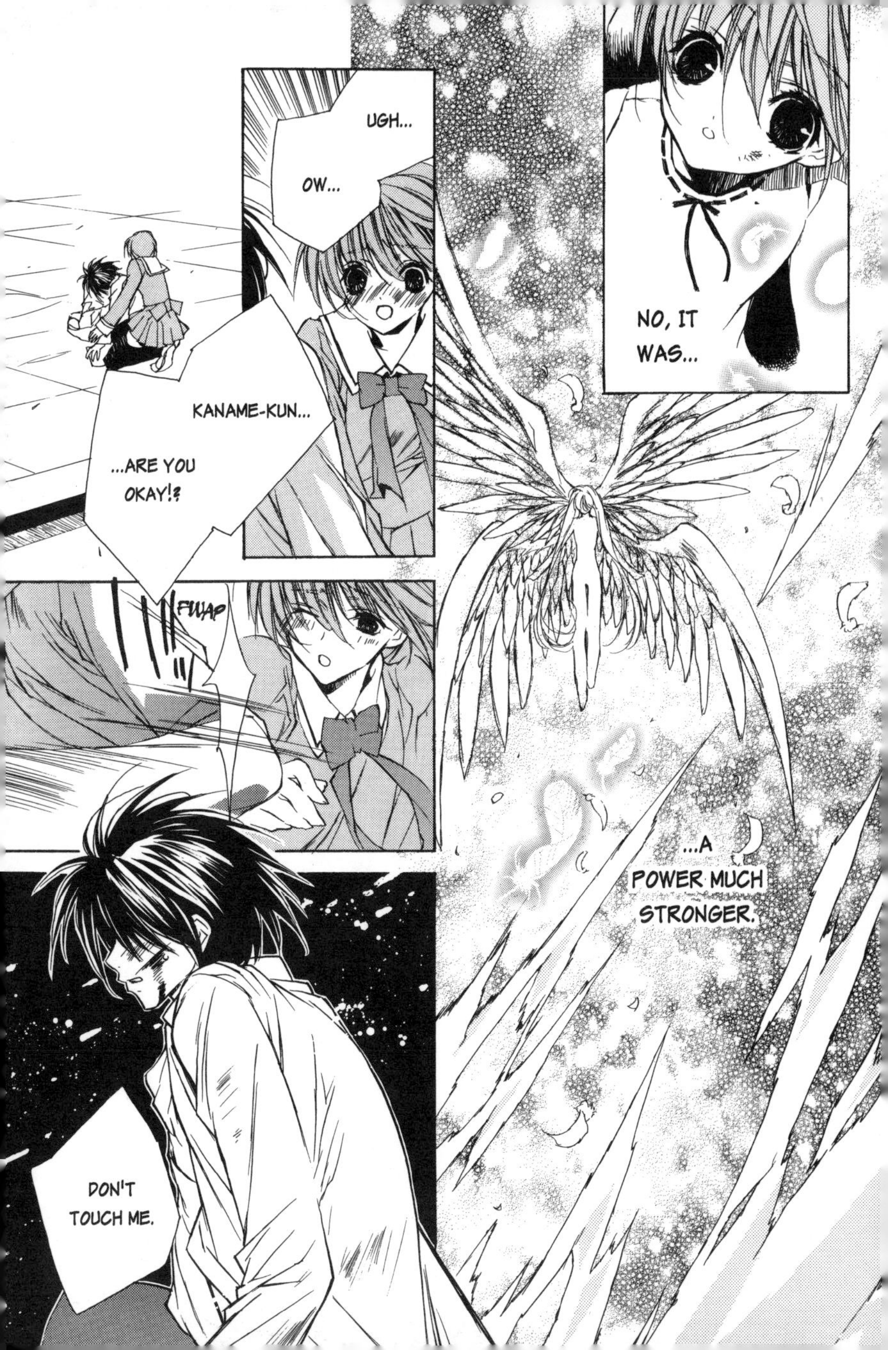
NO, IT WAS...
...A POWER MUCH STRONGER.
UGH...
OW...
KANAME-KUN...
...ARE YOU OKAY!?
FWAP
DON'T TOUCH ME.

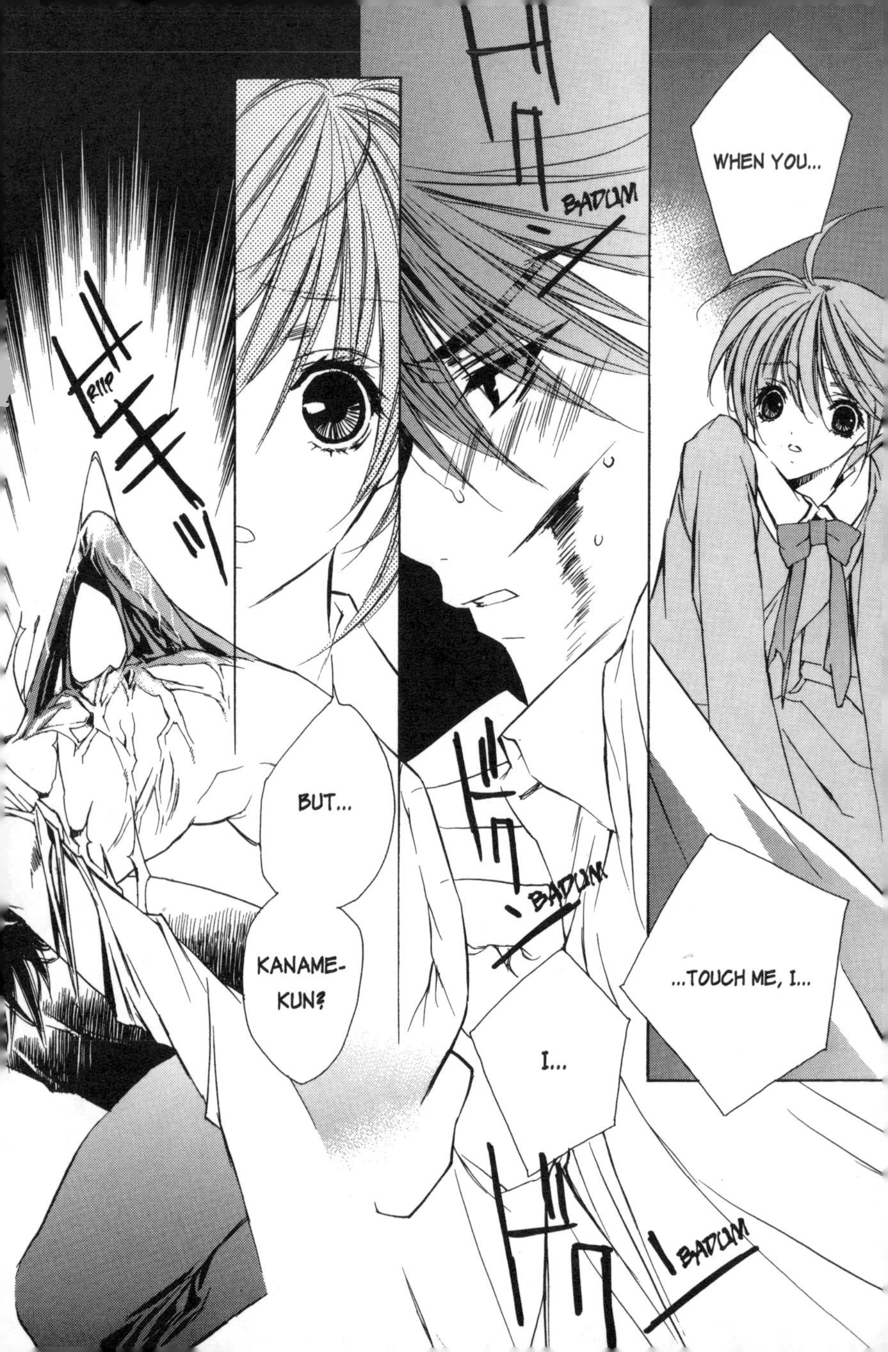

WHEN YOU...
...TOUCH ME, I...
BADUM
BADUM
I...
BADUM
BUT...
KANAME-KUN?
RIIP

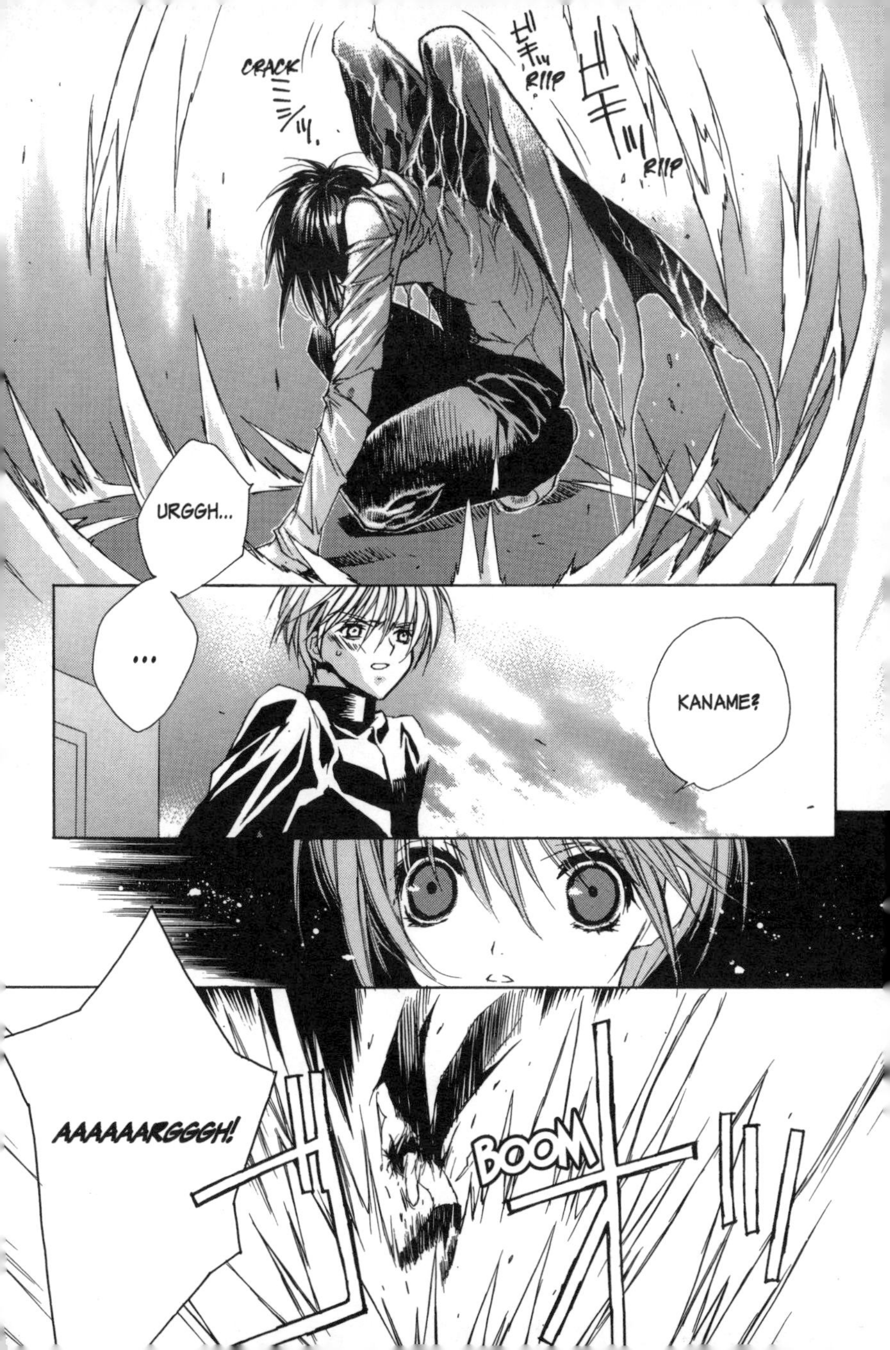
RIIP
RIIP
CRACK
URGGH...
KANAME?
...
BOOM
AAAAAARGGGH!

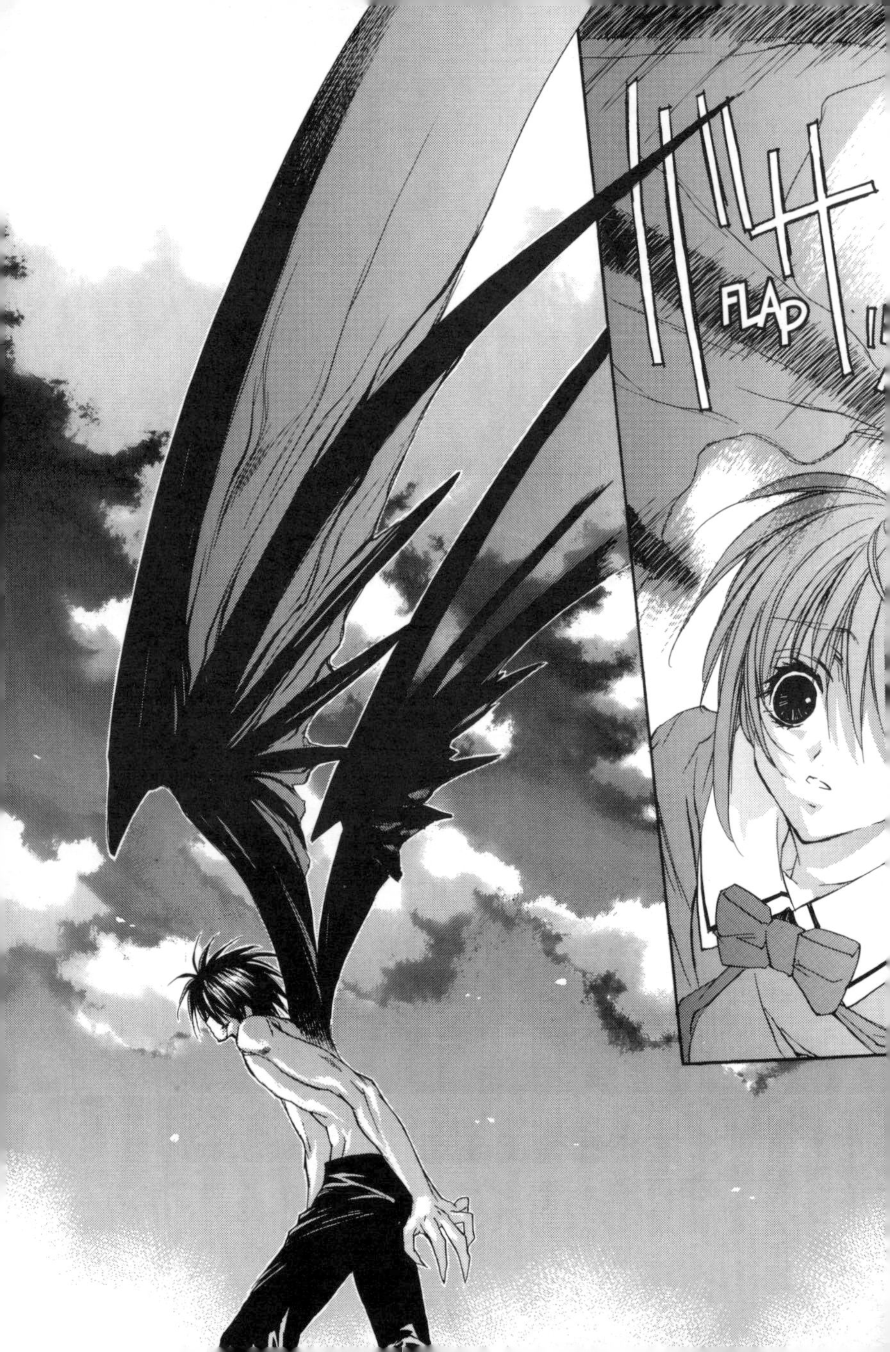
FLAP

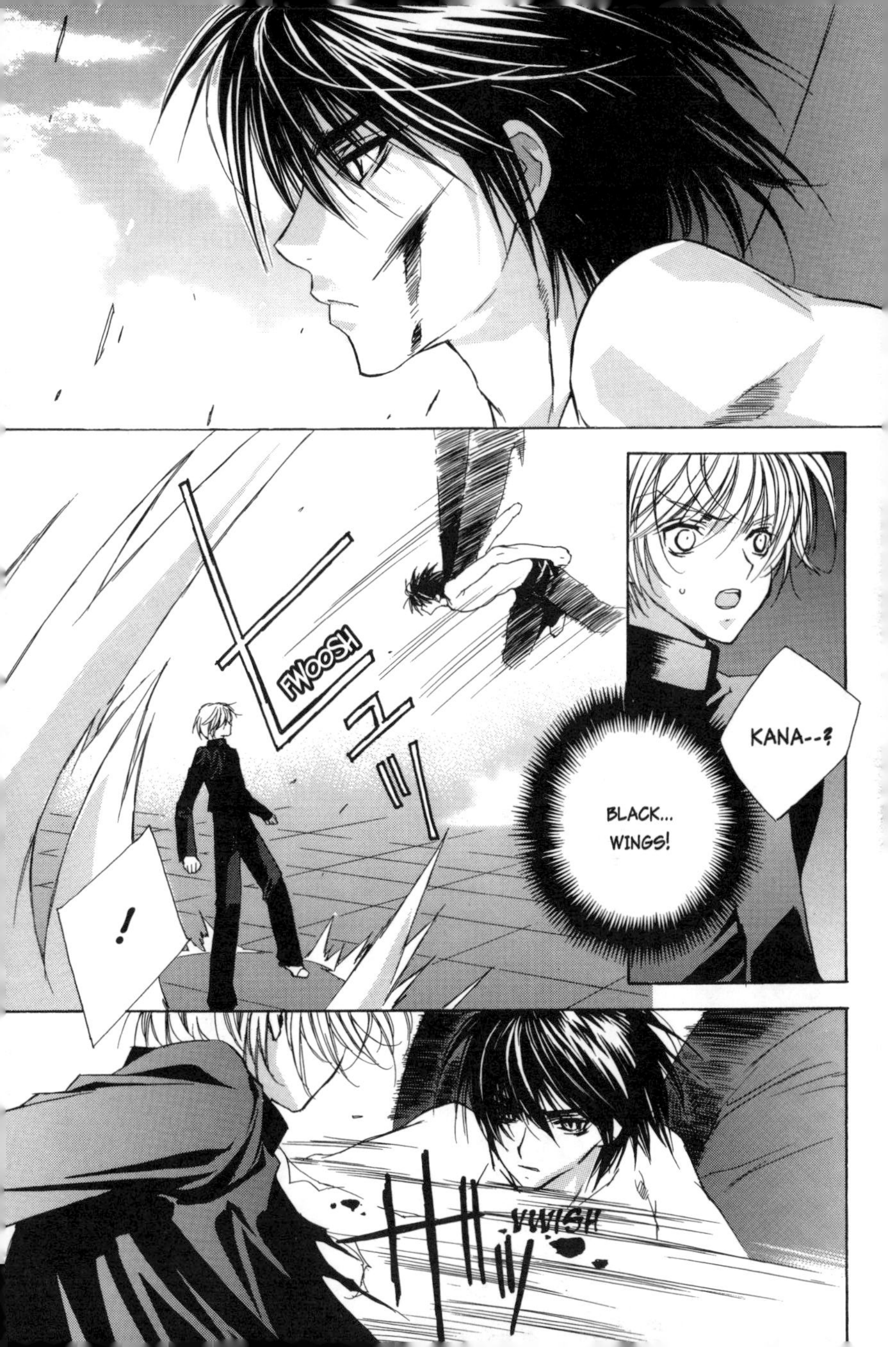

KANA--?
BLACK... WINGS!
FWOOSH
!
VWISH

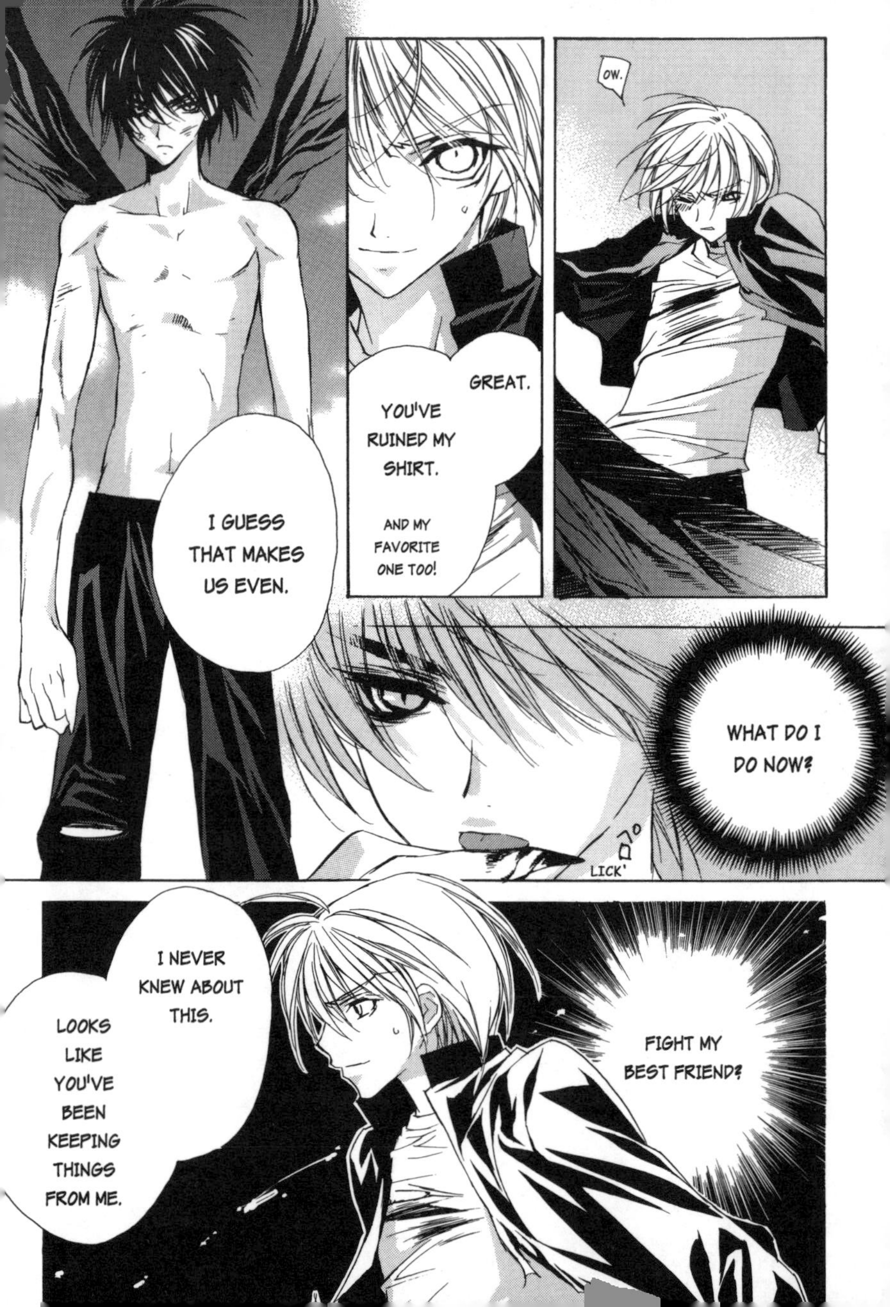
OW.
GREAT.
YOU'VE RUINED MY SHIRT.
AND MY FAVORITE ONE TOO!
WHAT DO I DO NOW?
LICK
I GUESS THAT MAKES US EVEN.
I NEVER KNEW ABOUT THIS.
LOOKS LIKE YOU'VE BEEN KEEPING THINGS FROM ME.
FIGHT MY BEST FRIEND?

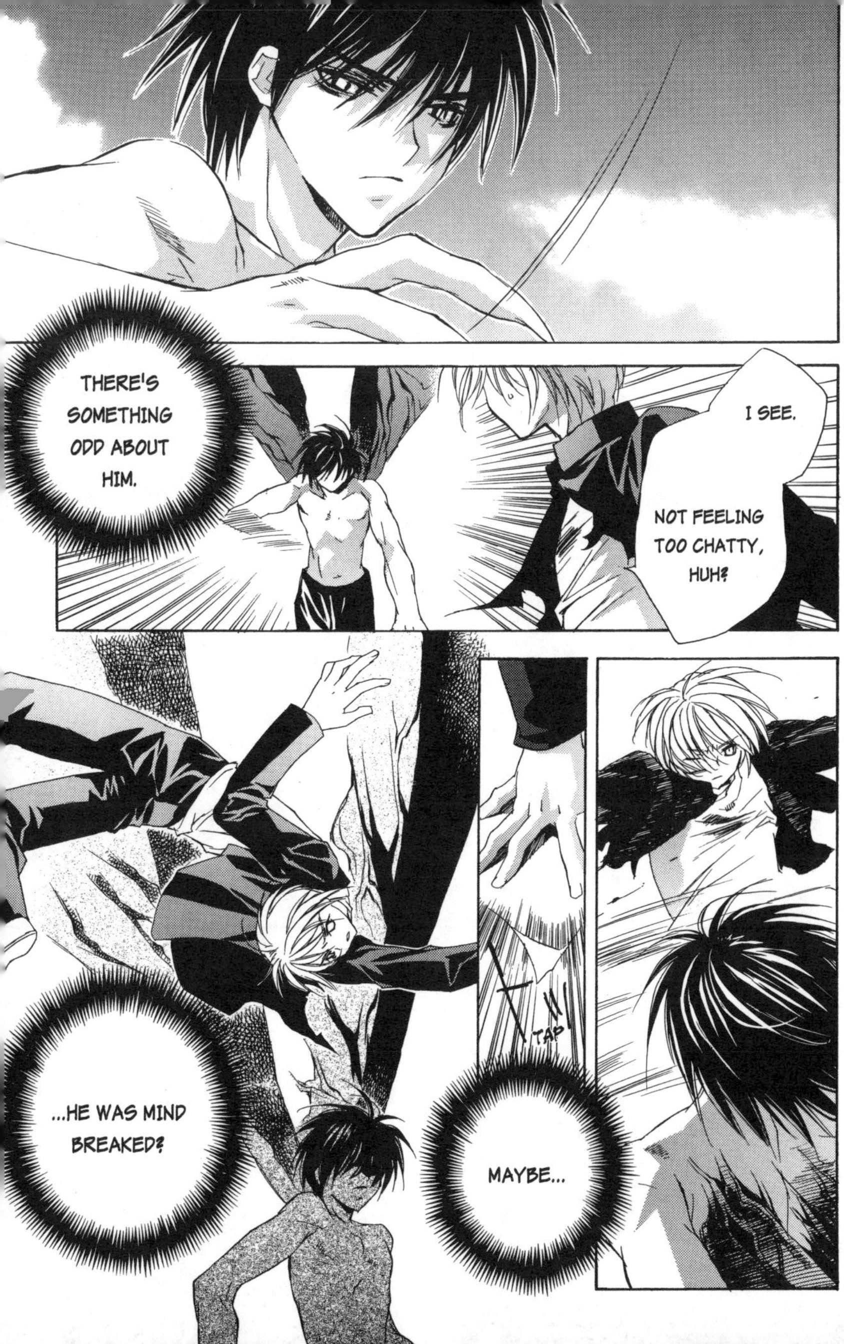
I SEE.
NOT FEELING TOO CHATTY, HUH?
THERE'S SOMETHING ODD ABOUT HIM.
TAP
...HE WAS MIND BREAKED?
MAYBE...

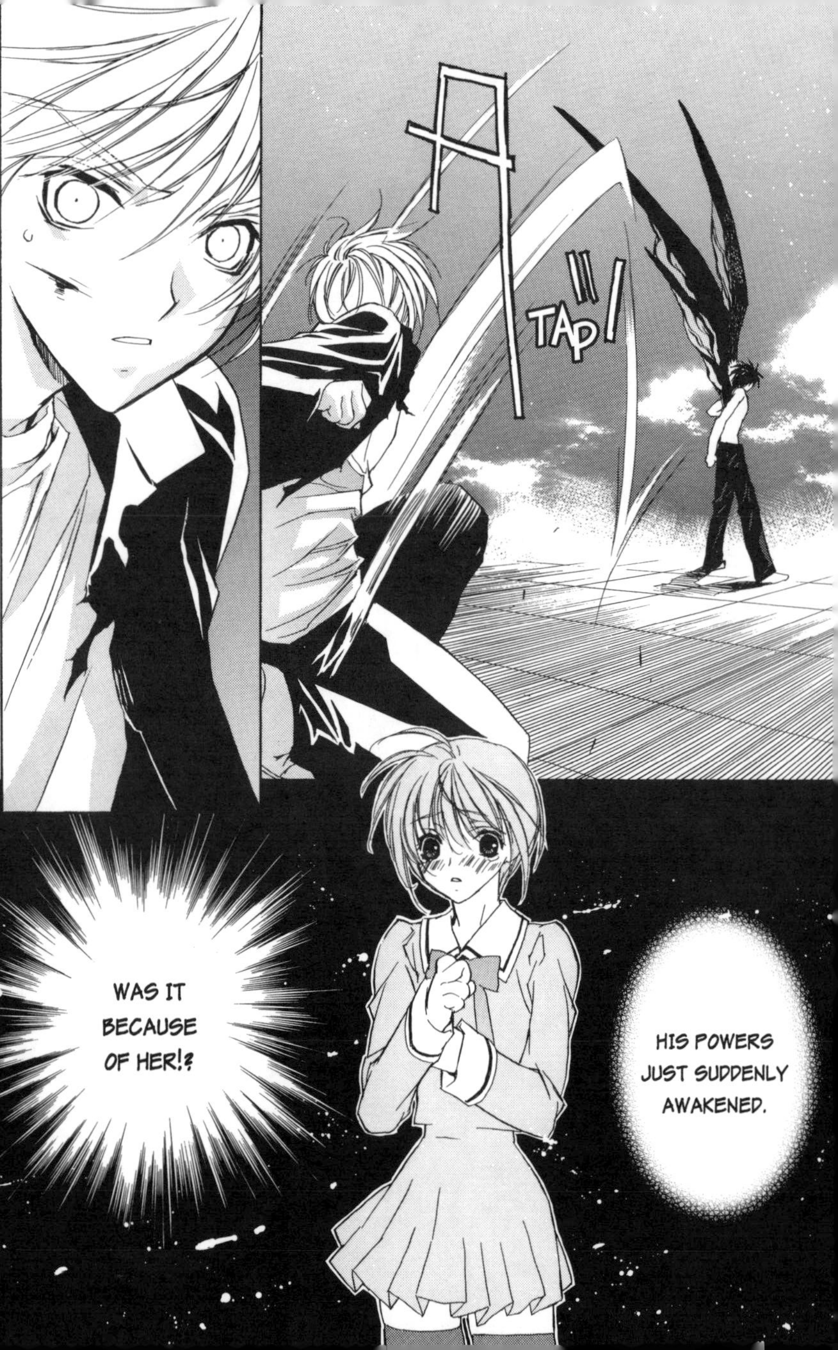
TAP
HIS POWERS JUST SUDDENLY AWAKENED.
WAS IT BECAUSE OF HER!?

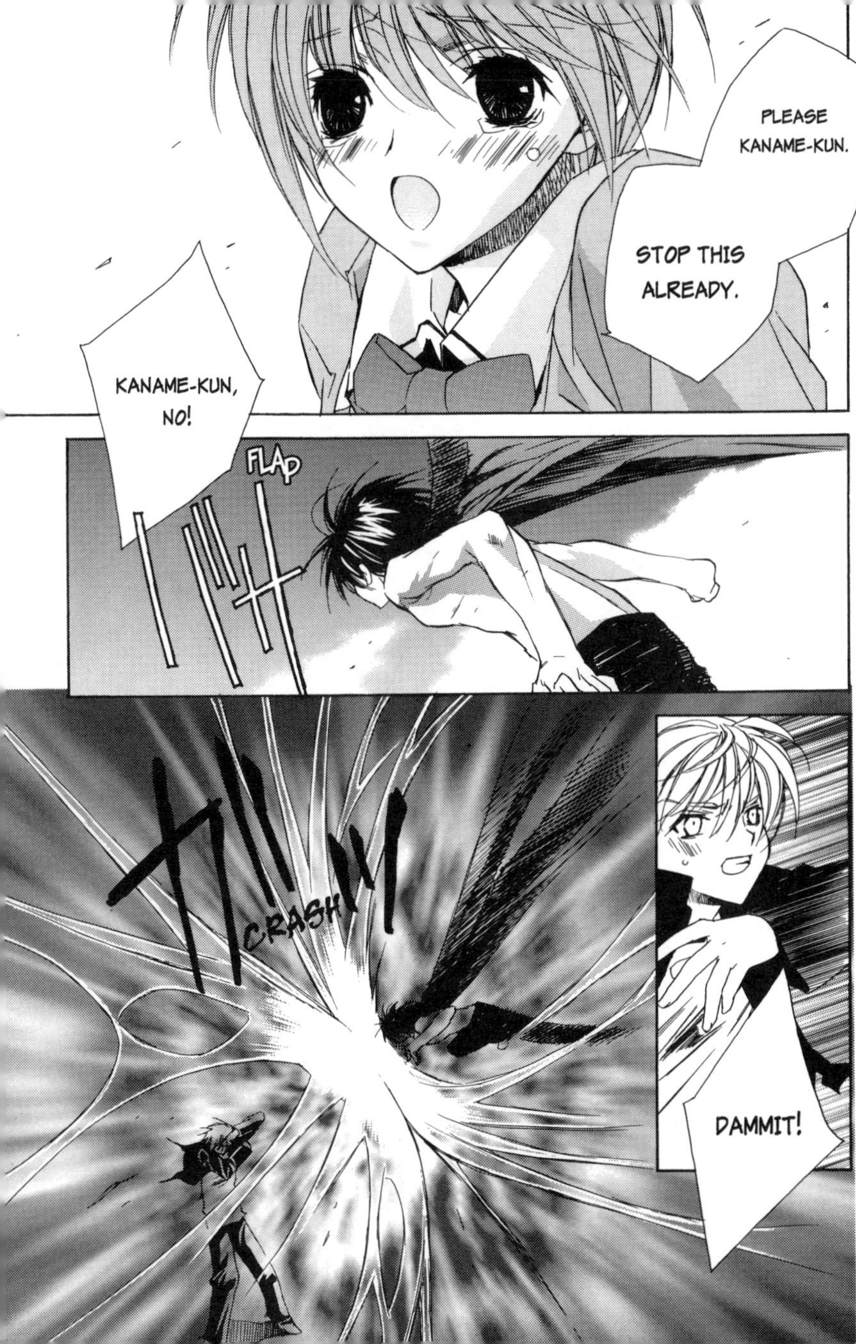
PLEASE KANAME-KUN.
STOP THIS ALREADY.
KANAME-KUN, NO!
FLAP
DAMMIT!
CRASH

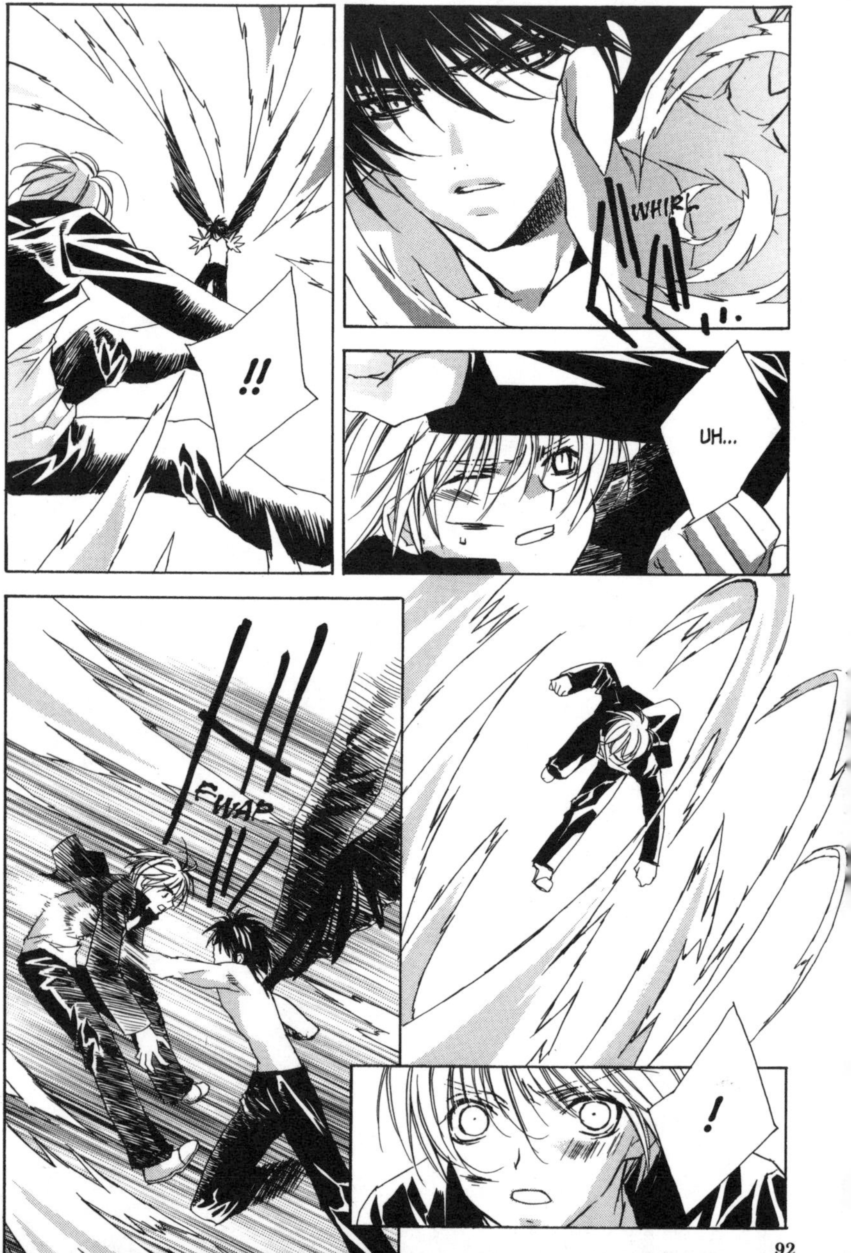
WHIRL
UH...
!!
!
FWAP

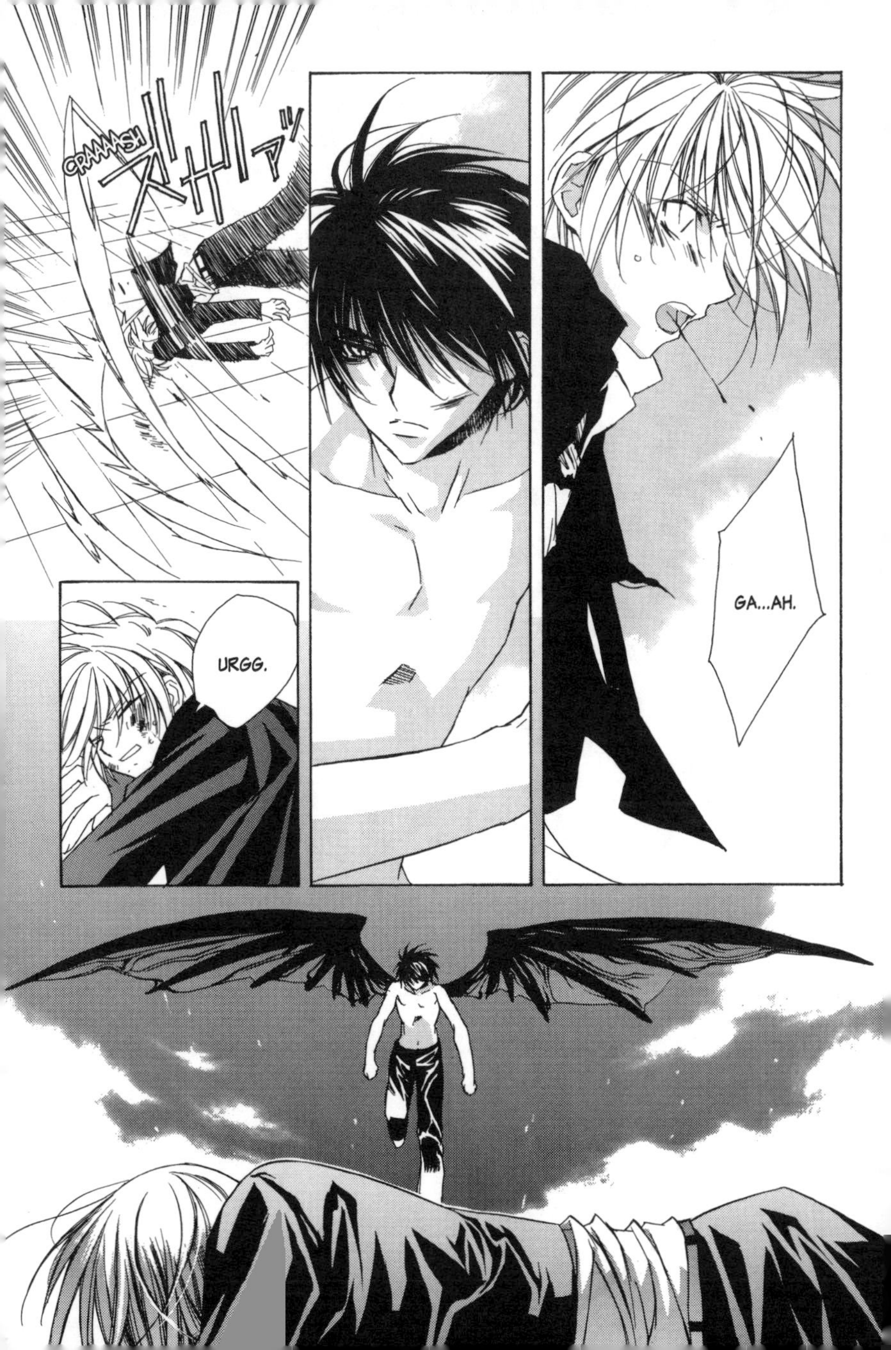
GA...AH.
CRAAAASH
URGG.

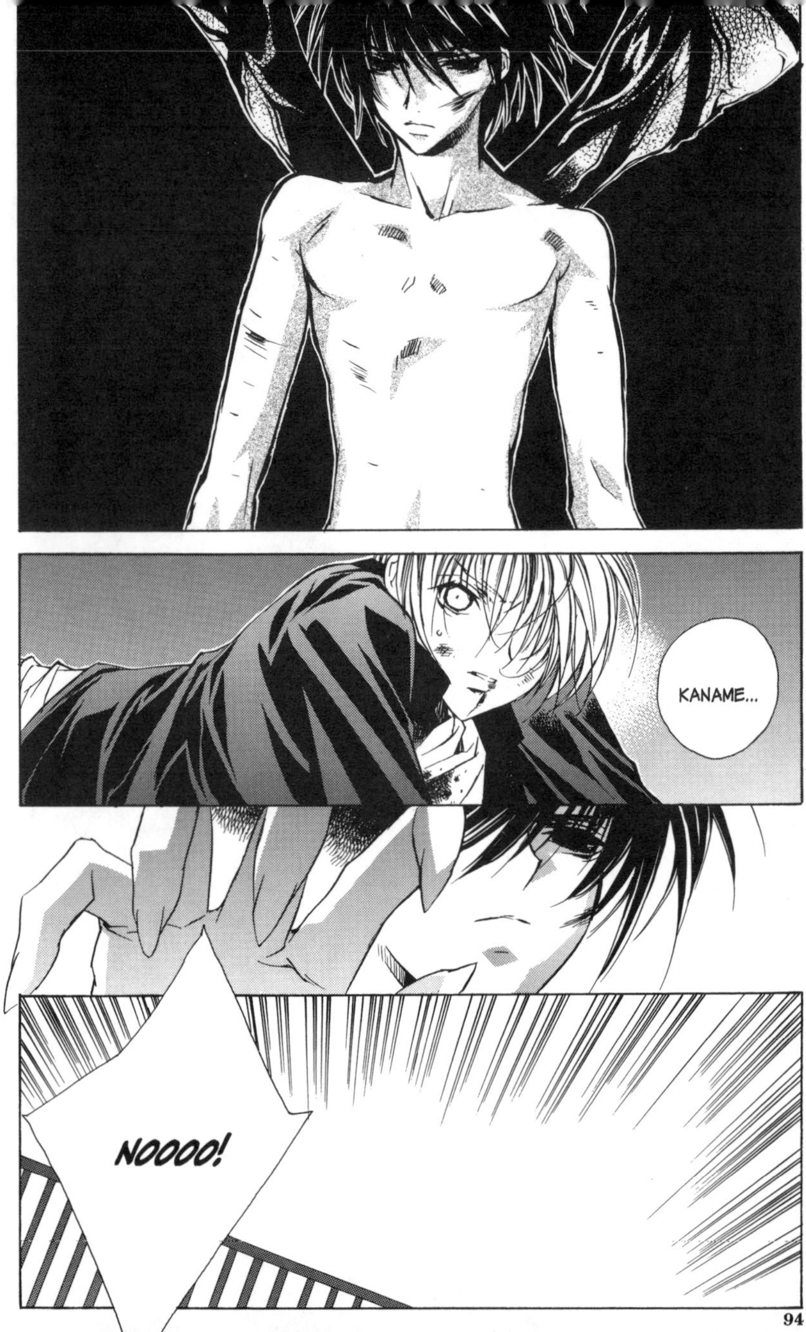
KANAME...
NOOOO!

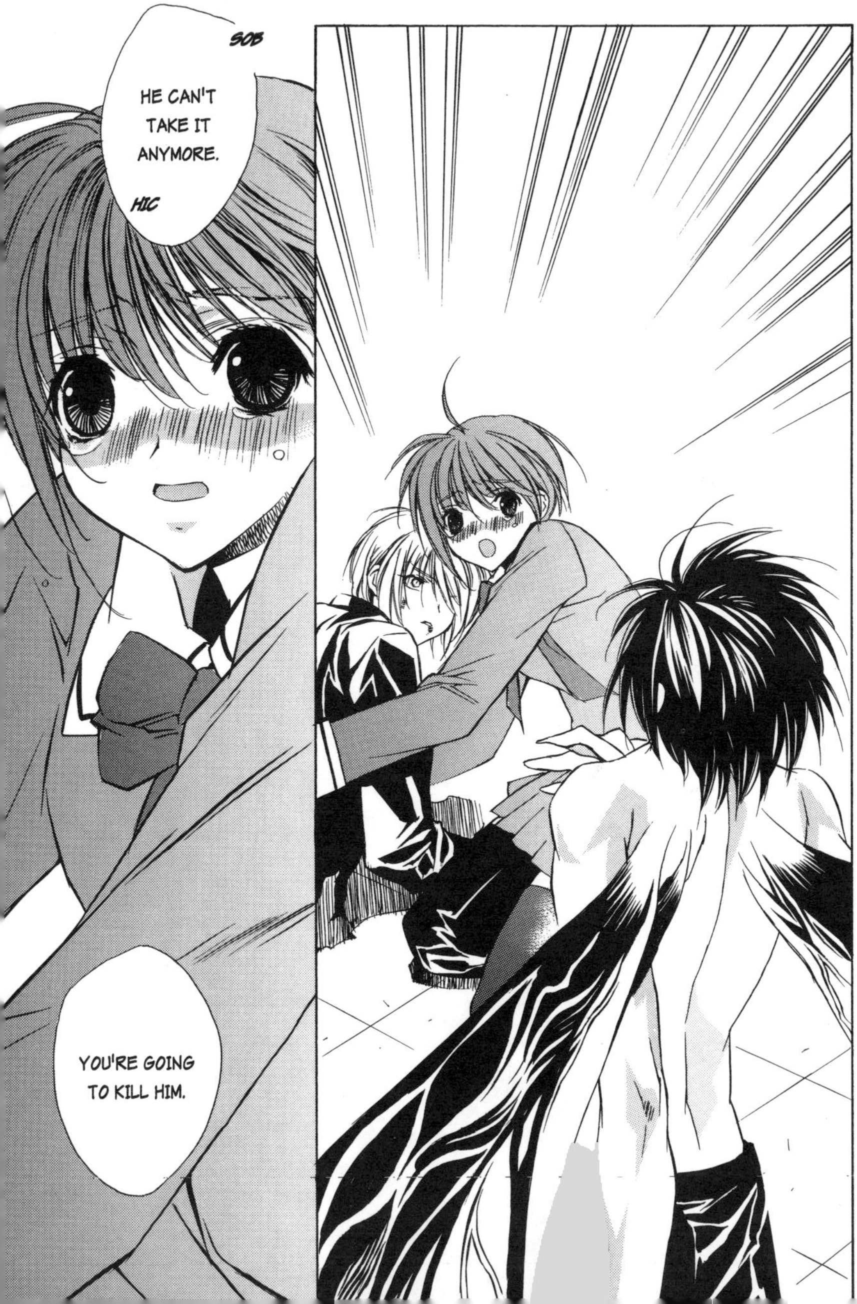
SOB
HE CAN'T TAKE IT ANYMORE.
HIC
YOU'RE GOING TO KILL HIM.

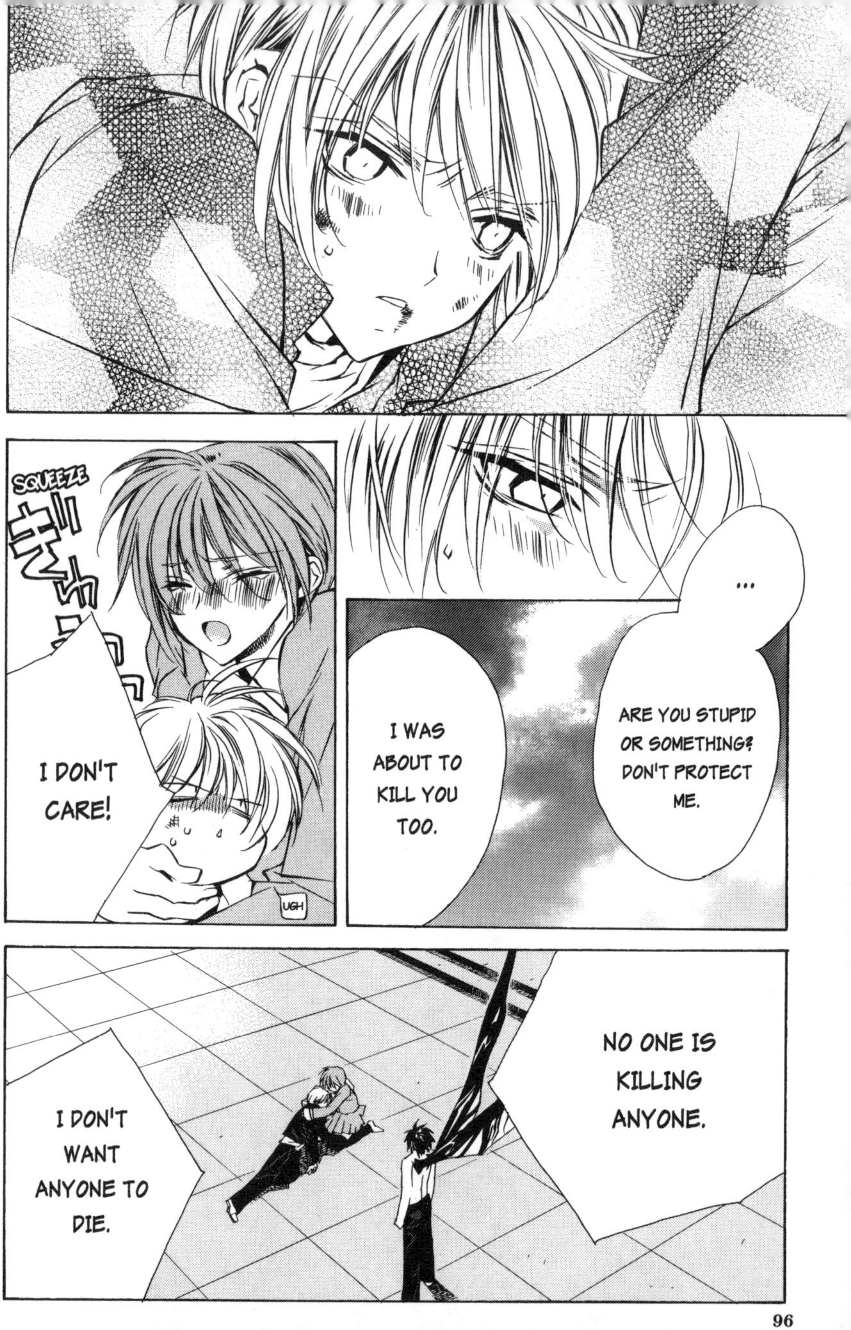
...
ARE YOU STUPID OR SOMETHING? DON'T PROTECT ME.
I WAS ABOUT TO KILL YOU TOO.
SQUEEZE
I DON'T CARE!
UGH
NO ONE IS KILLING ANYONE.
I DON'T WANT ANYONE TO DIE.

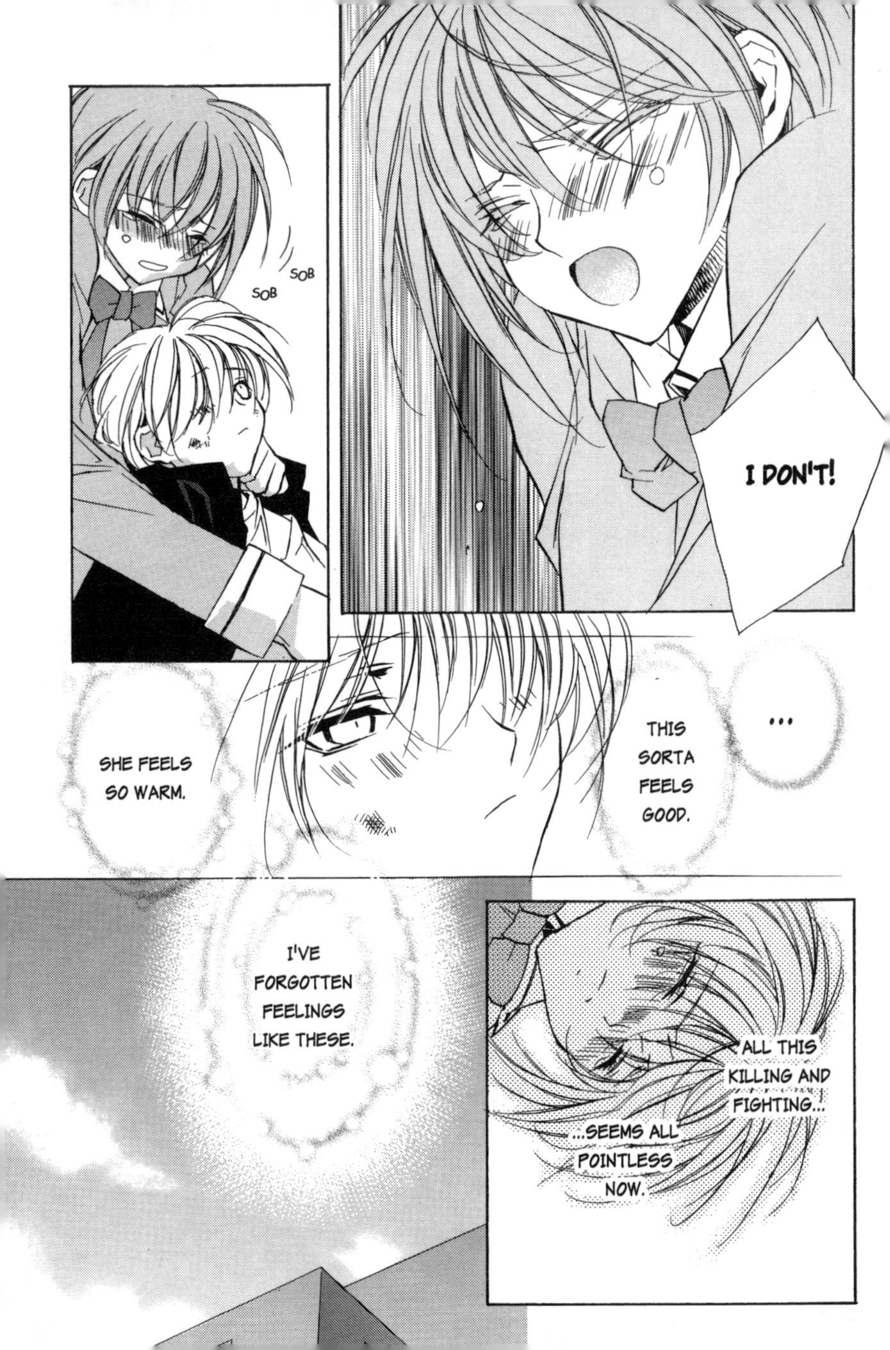
I DON'T!
SOB
SOB
...
THIS SORTA FEELS GOOD.
SHE FEELS SO WARM.
ALL THIS KILLING AND FIGHTING...
...SEEMS ALL POINTLESS NOW.
I'VE FORGOTTEN FEELINGS LIKE THESE.

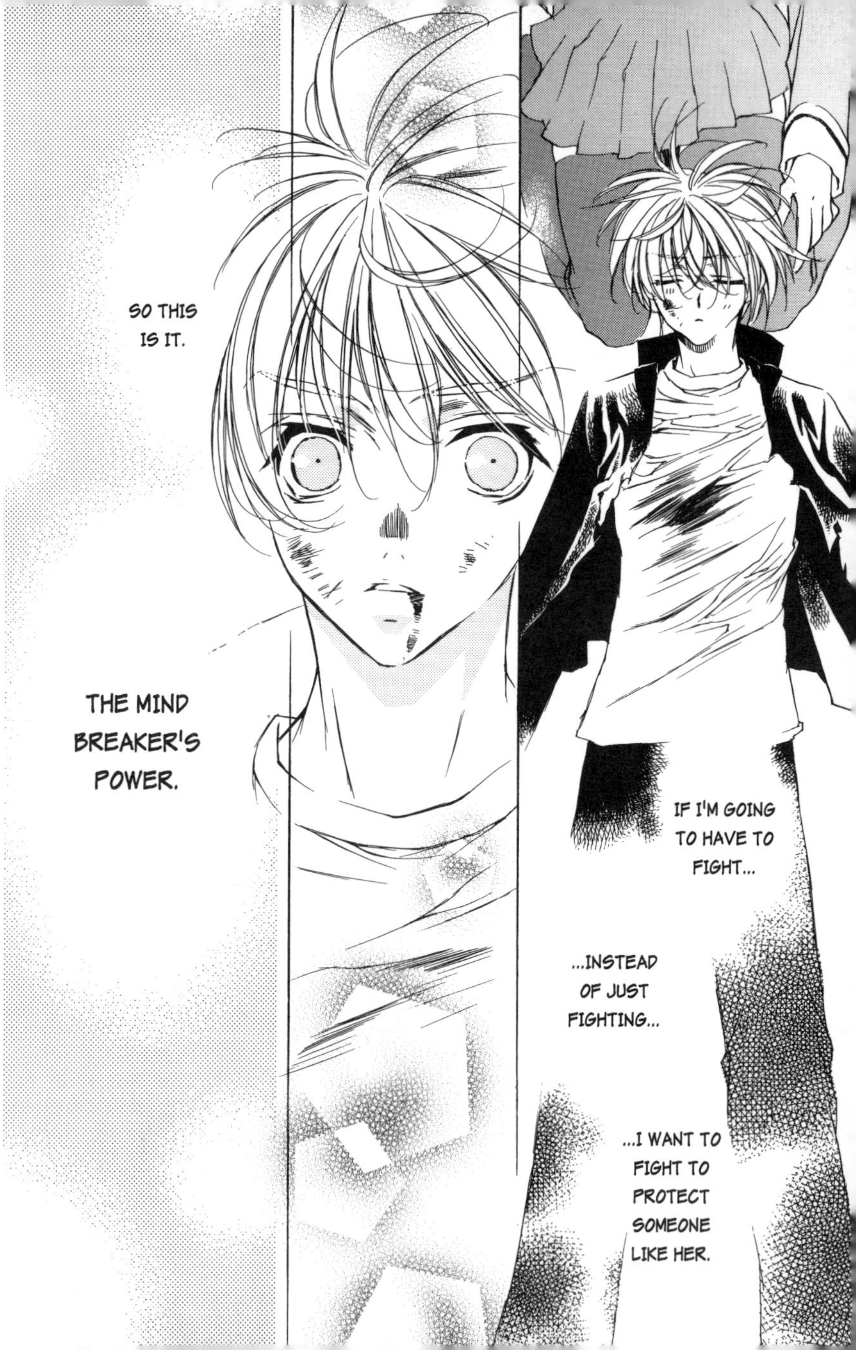
IF I'M GOING TO HAVE TO FIGHT...
...INSTEAD OF JUST FIGHTING...
...I WANT TO FIGHT TO PROTECT SOMEONE LIKE HER.
SO THIS IS IT.
THE MIND BREAKER'S POWER.

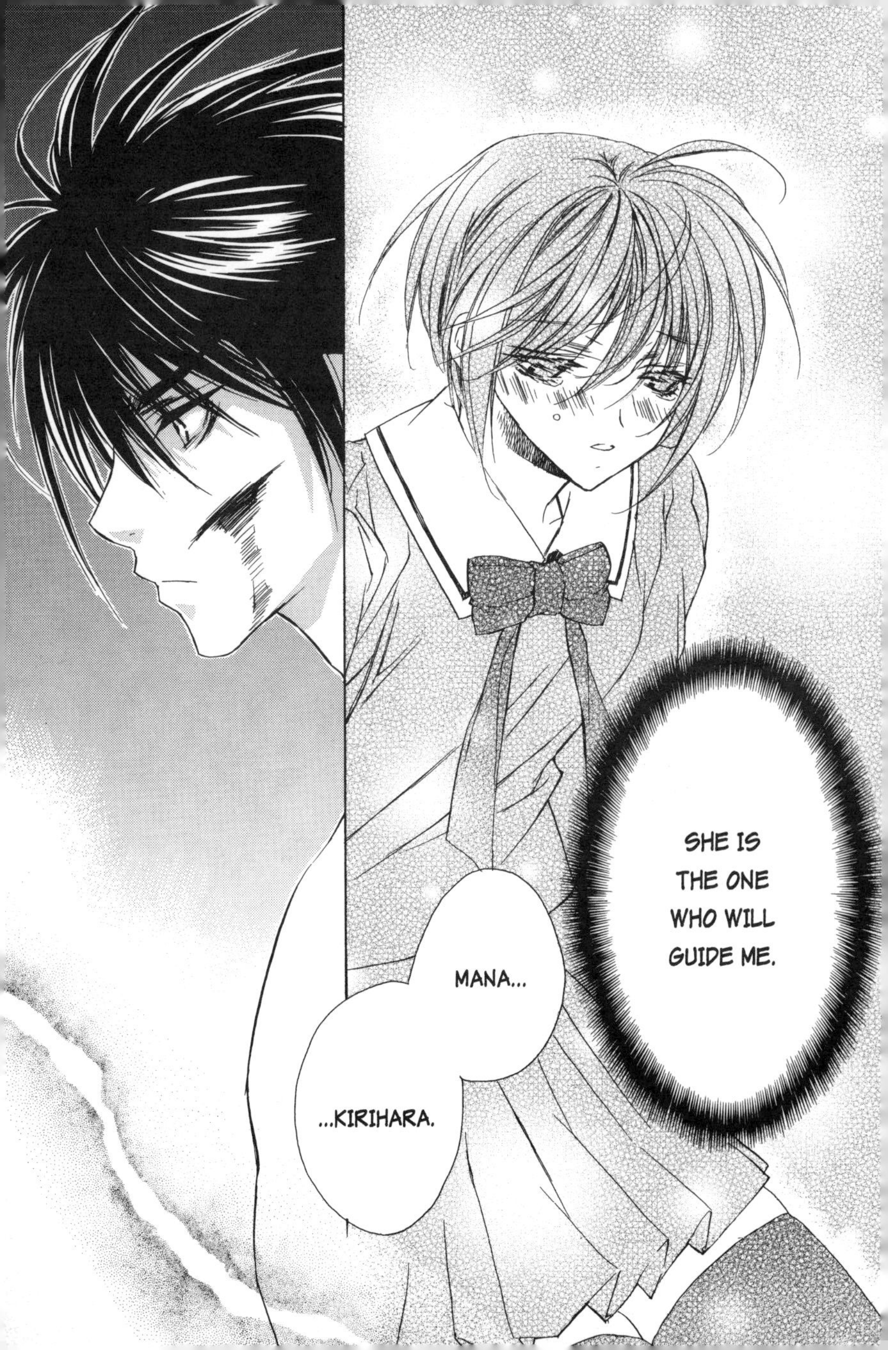
SHE IS THE ONE WHO WILL GUIDE ME.
MANA...
...KIRIHARA.

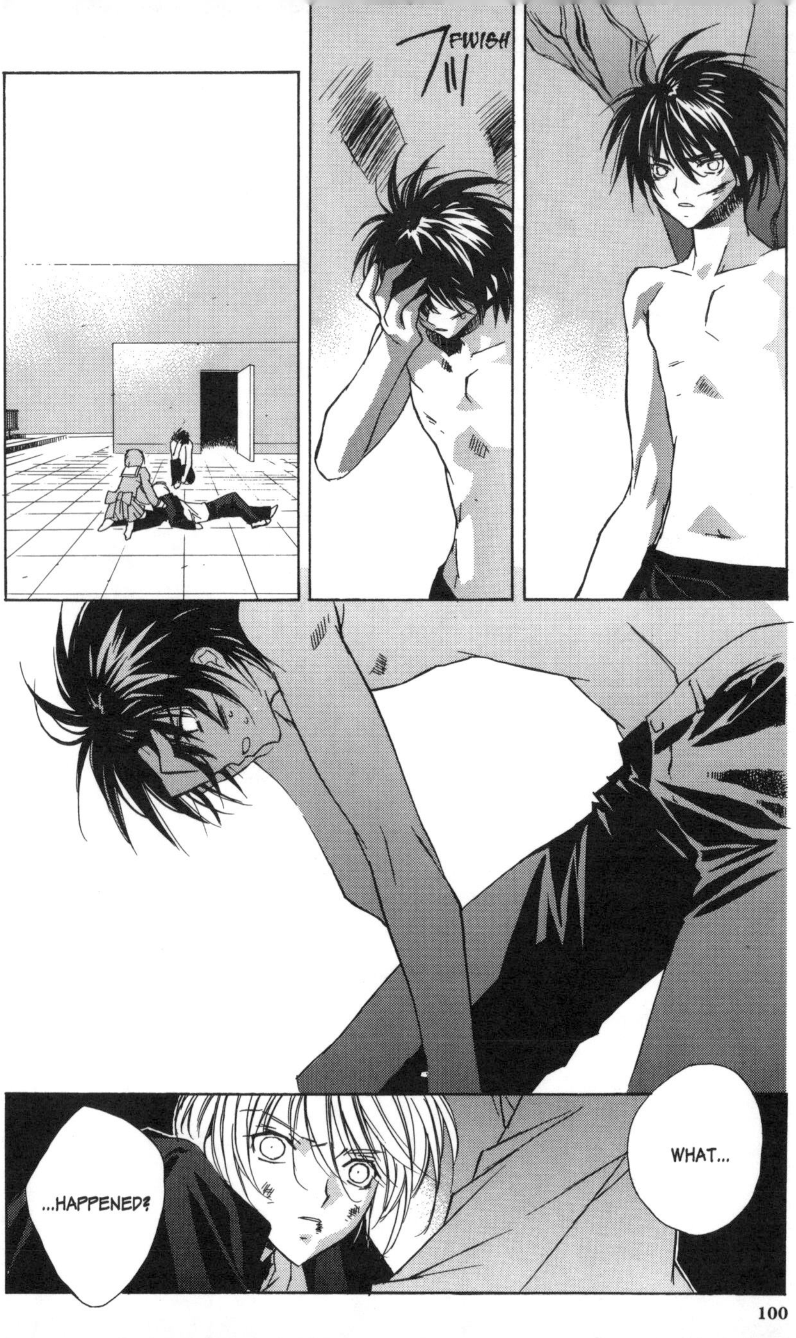
FWISH
WHAT...
...HAPPENED?

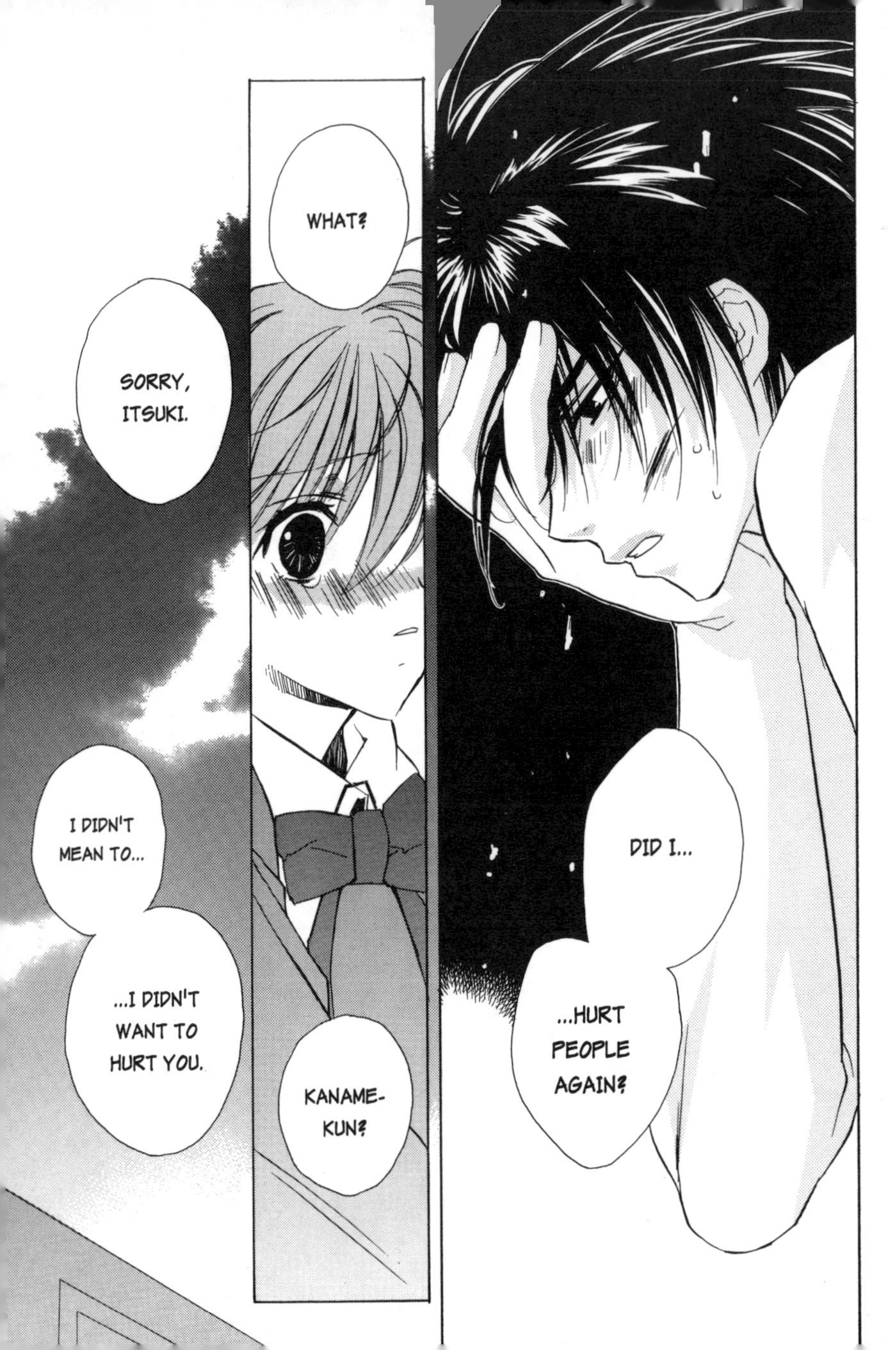
DID I...
...HURT PEOPLE AGAIN?
WHAT?
KANAME-KUN?
SORRY, ITSUKI.
I DIDN'T MEAN TO...
...I DIDN'T WANT TO HURT YOU.

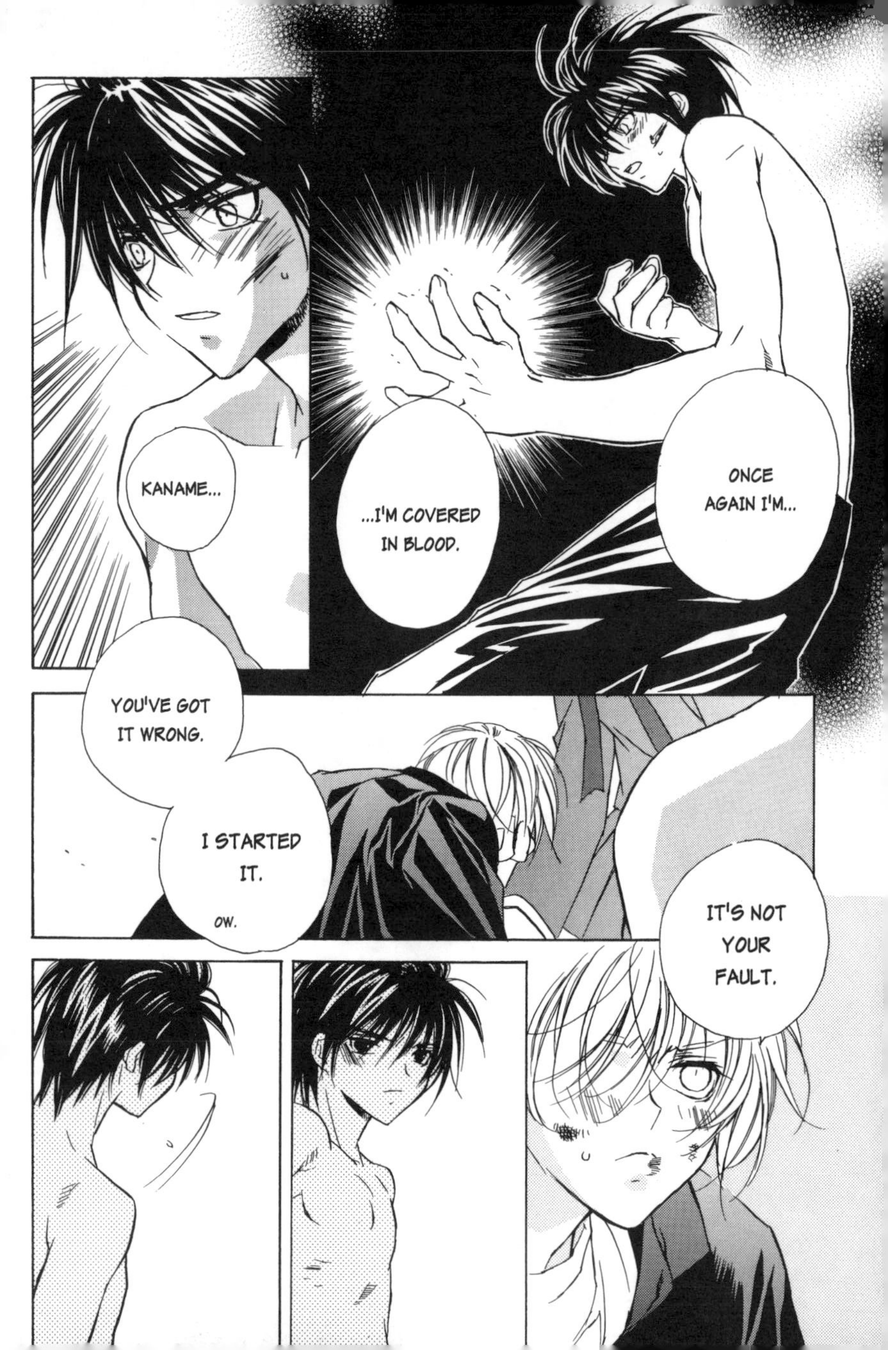
ONCE AGAIN I'M...
...I'M COVERED IN BLOOD.
KANAME...
YOU'VE GOT IT WRONG.
I STARTED IT.
OW.
IT'S NOT YOUR FAULT.

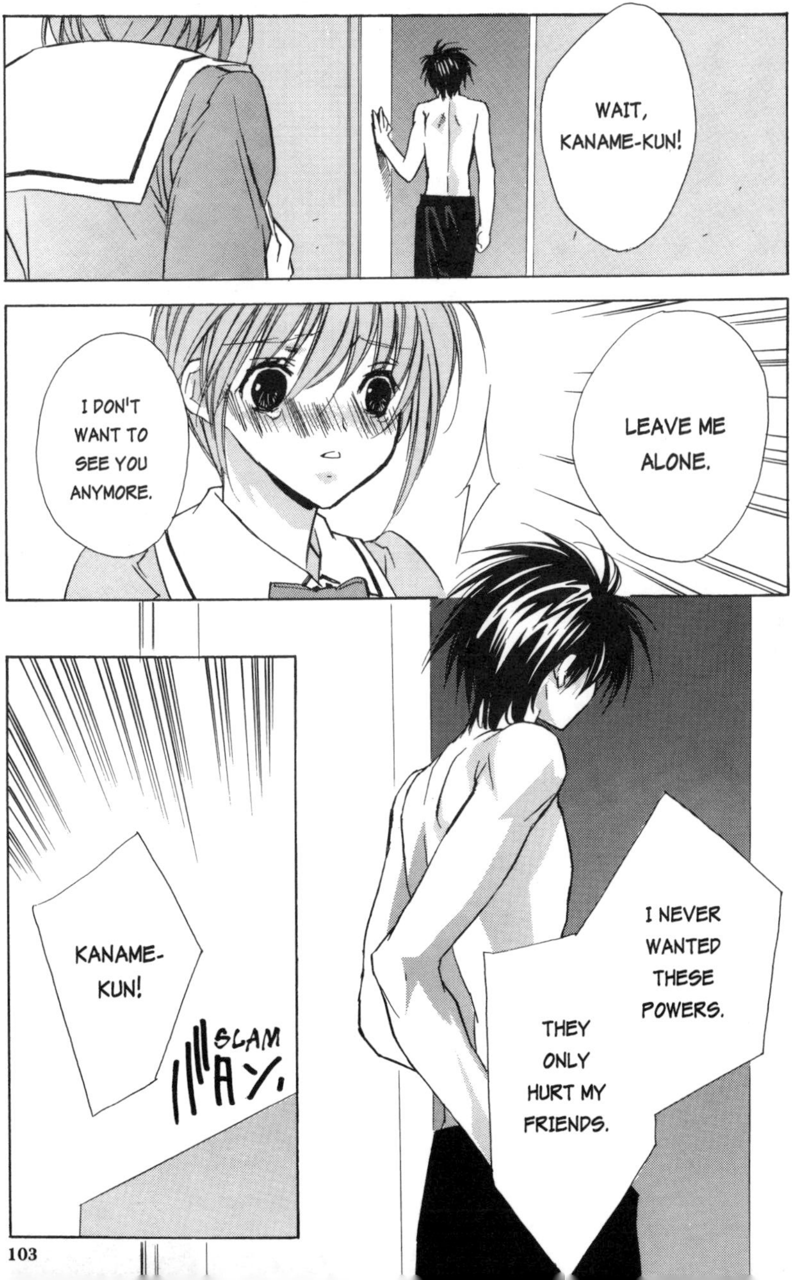
WAIT, KANAME-KUN!
LEAVE ME ALONE.
I DON'T WANT TO SEE YOU ANYMORE.
I NEVER WANTED THESE POWERS.
THEY ONLY HURT MY FRIENDS.
KANAME-KUN!
SLAM

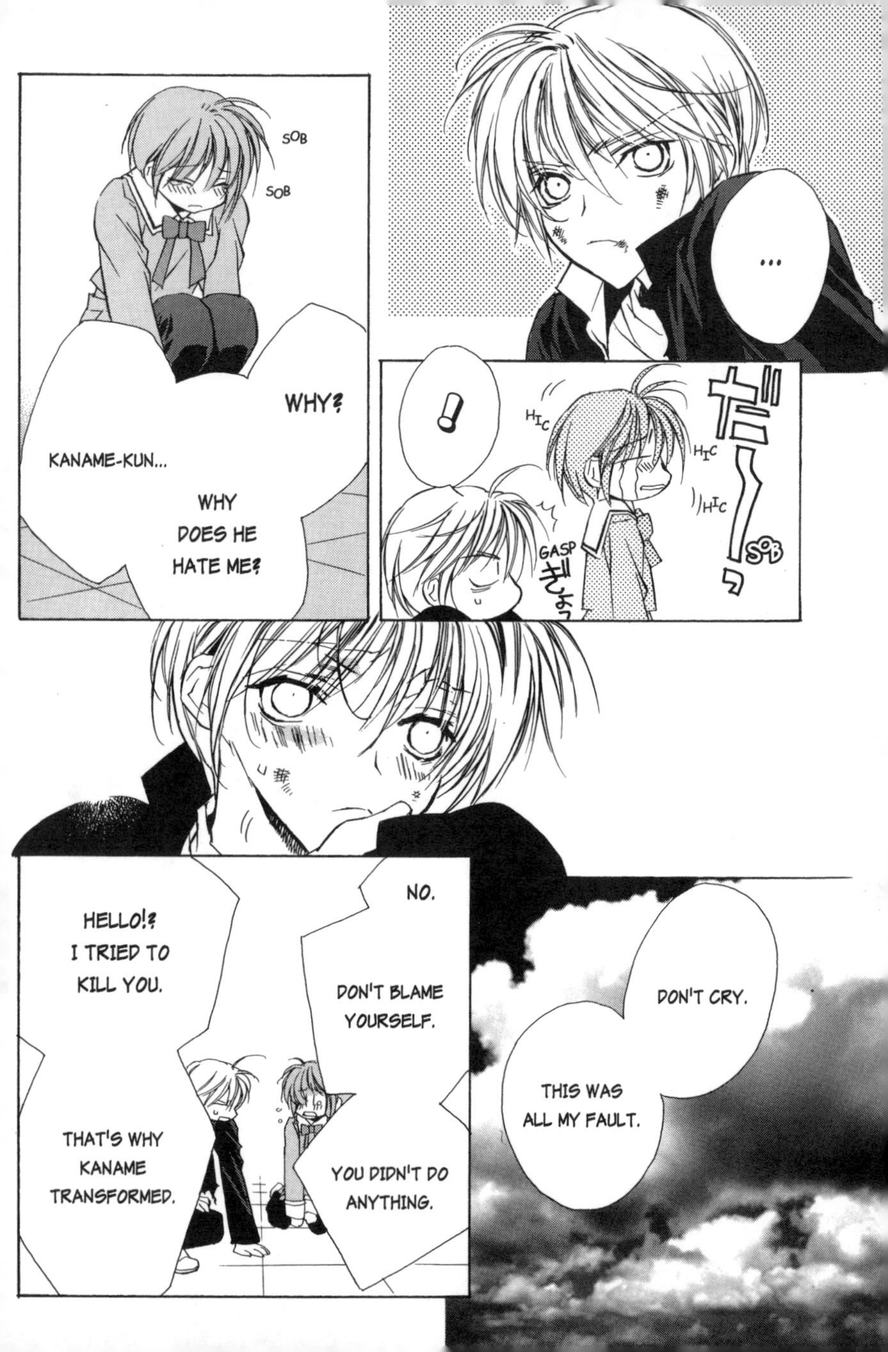
...
!
HIC
HIC
HIC
だ〜っ
SOB
GASP
ぎょっ
SOB
SOB
WHY?
KANAME-KUN...
WHY DOES HE HATE ME?
DON'T CRY.
THIS WAS ALL MY FAULT.
NO.
DON'T BLAME YOURSELF.
YOU DIDN'T DO ANYTHING.
HELLO!? I TRIED TO KILL YOU.
THAT'S WHY KANAME TRANSFORMED.

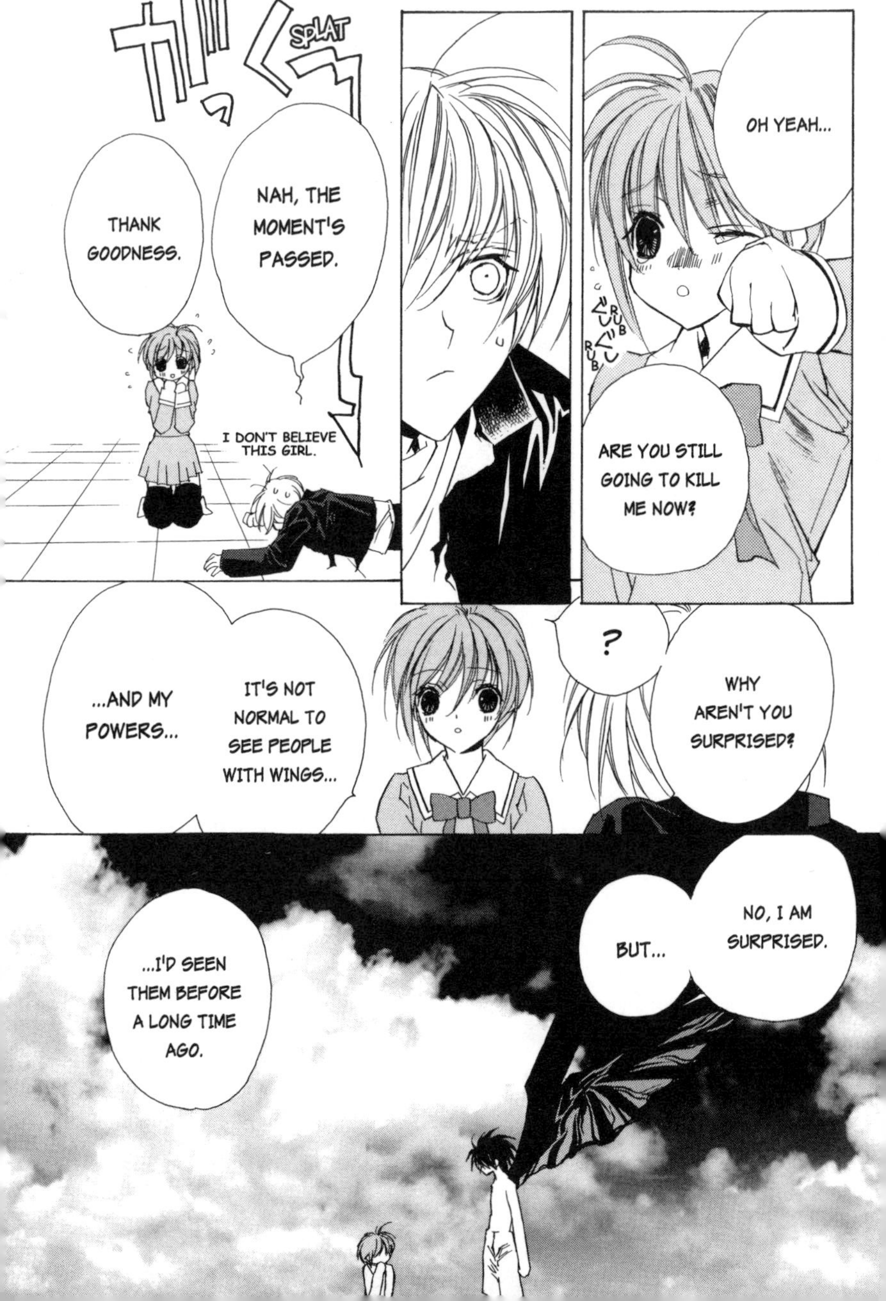
OH YEAH...
RUB RUB
ARE YOU STILL GOING TO KILL ME NOW?
SPLAT
NAH, THE MOMENT'S PASSED.
THANK GOODNESS.
I DON'T BELIEVE THIS GIRL.
?
WHY AREN'T YOU SURPRISED?
IT'S NOT NORMAL TO SEE PEOPLE WITH WINGS...
...AND MY POWERS...
NO, I AM SURPRISED.
BUT...
...I'D SEEN THEM BEFORE A LONG TIME AGO.

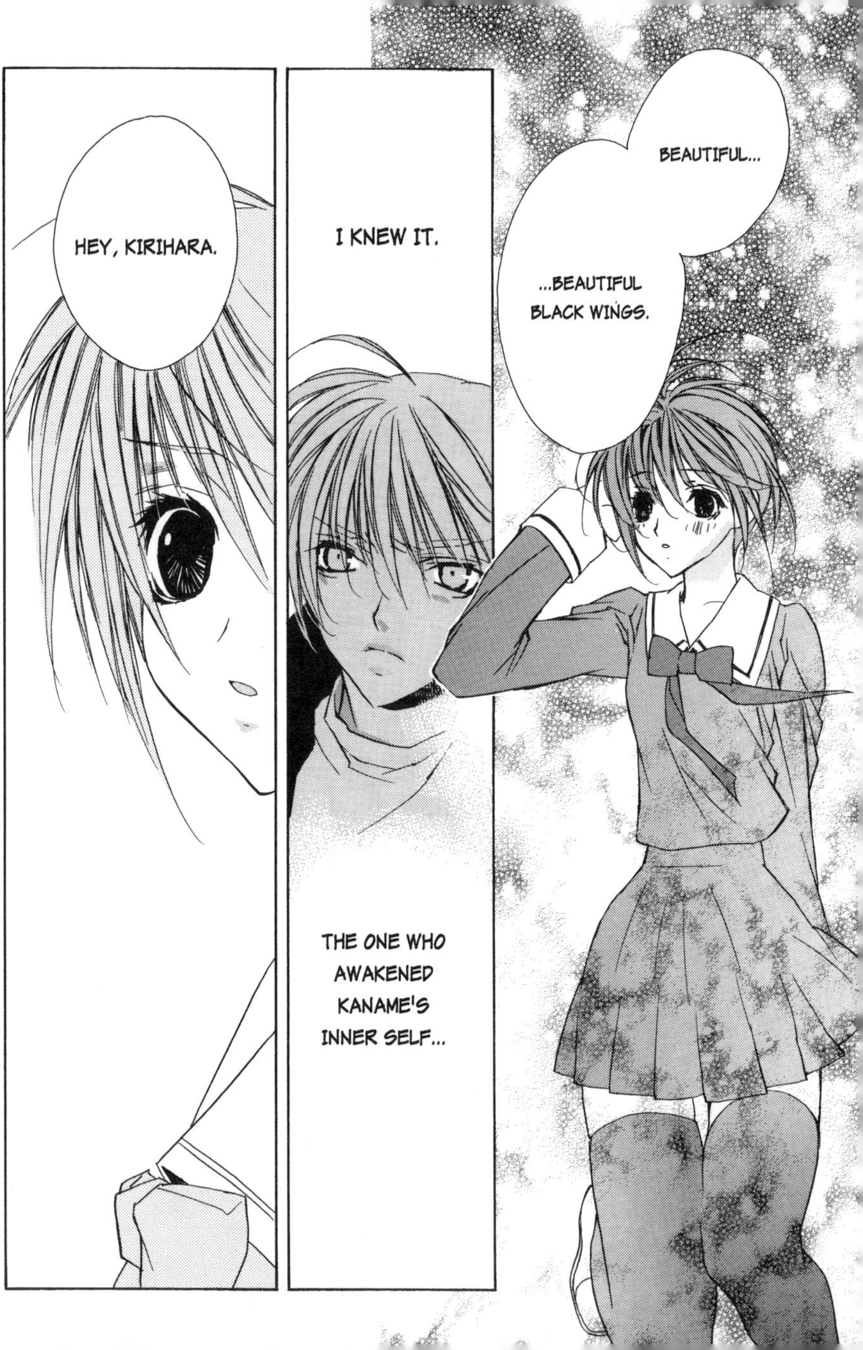
BEAUTIFUL...
...BEAUTIFUL BLACK WINGS.
I KNEW IT.
THE ONE WHO AWAKENED KANAME'S INNER SELF...
HEY, KIRIHARA.

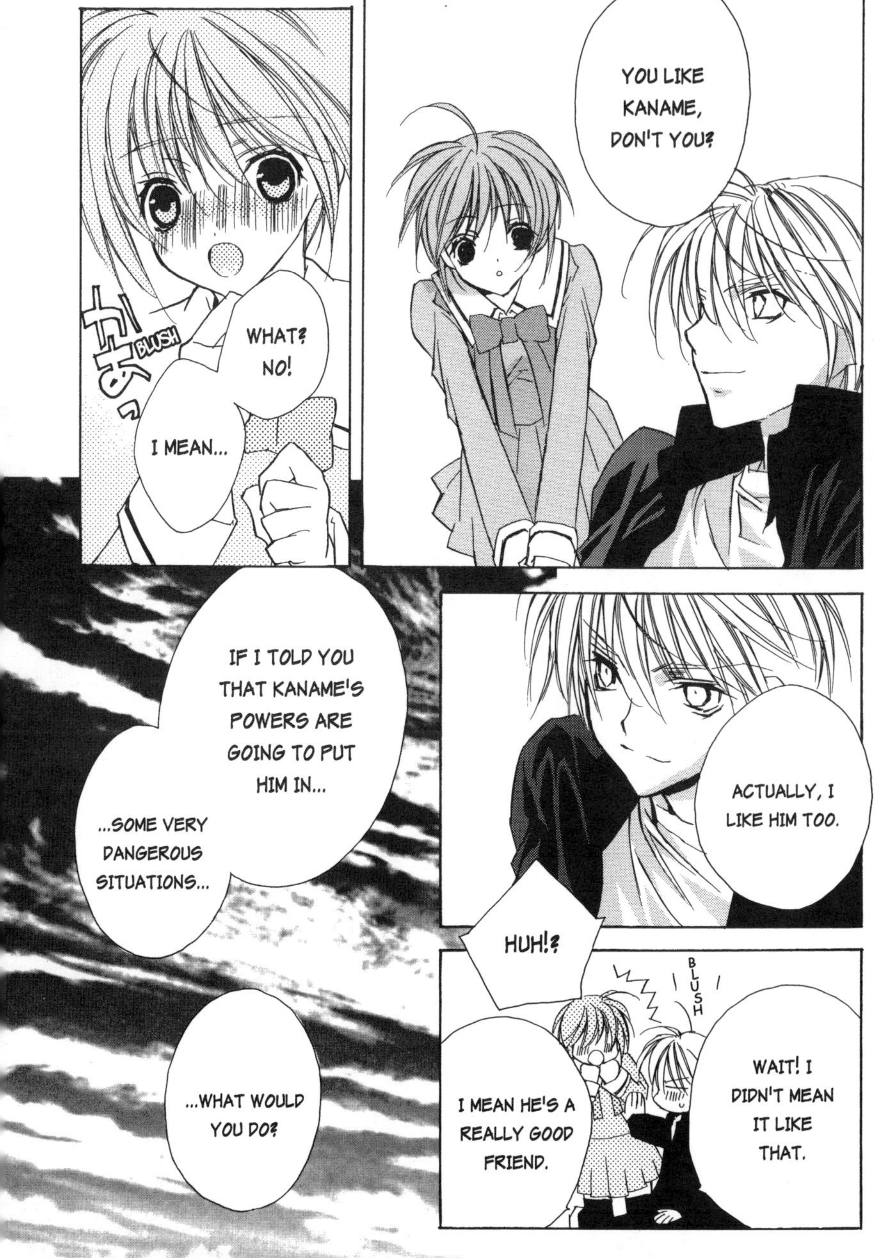
YOU LIKE KANAME, DON'T YOU?
WHAT? NO!
BLUSH
I MEAN...
ACTUALLY, I LIKE HIM TOO.
HUH!?
BLUSH
WAIT! I DIDN'T MEAN IT LIKE THAT.
I MEAN HE'S A REALLY GOOD FRIEND.
IF I TOLD YOU THAT KANAME'S POWERS ARE GOING TO PUT HIM IN...
...SOME VERY DANGEROUS SITUATIONS...
...WHAT WOULD YOU DO?

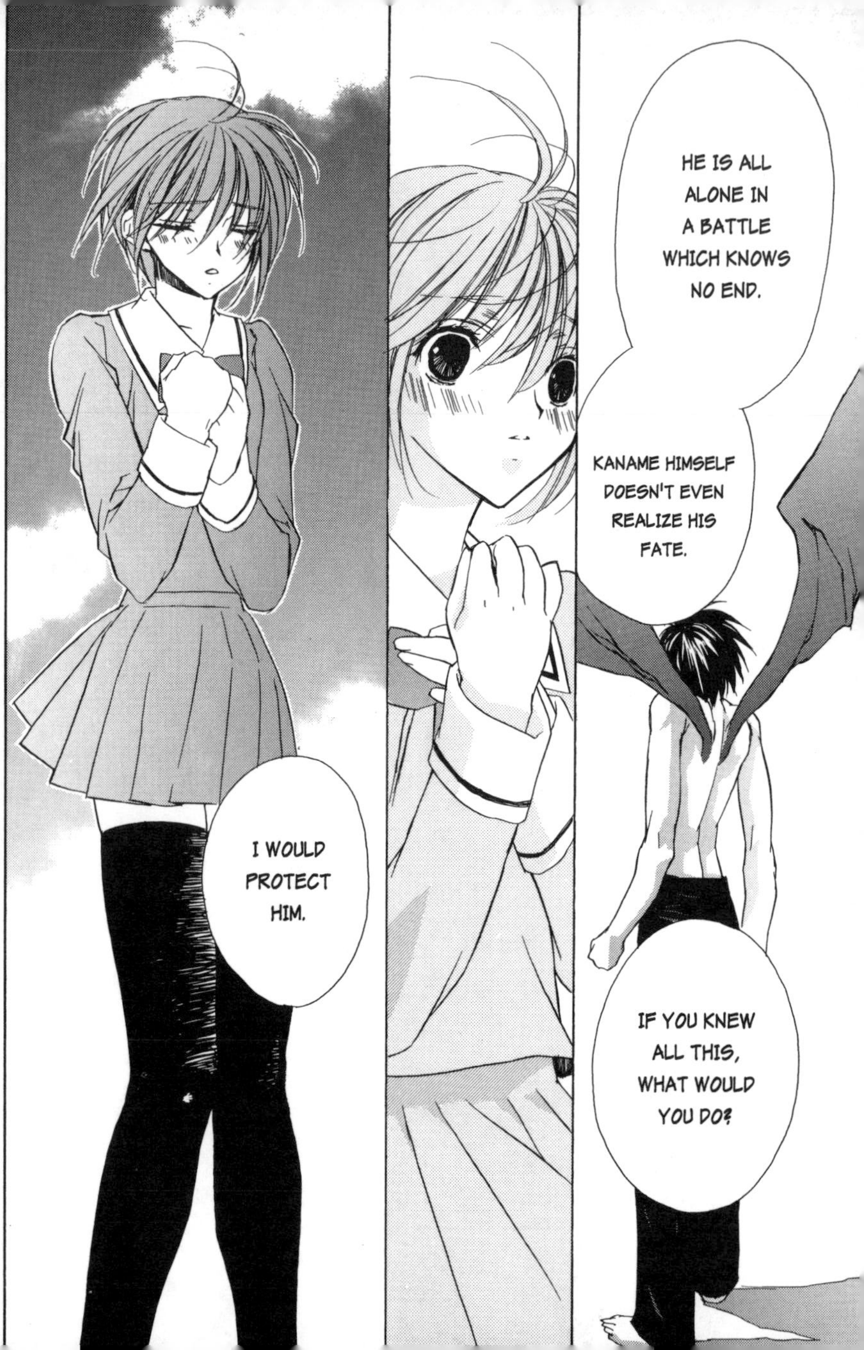
HE IS ALL ALONE IN A BATTLE WHICH KNOWS NO END.
KANAME HIMSELF DOESN'T EVEN REALIZE HIS FATE.
IF YOU KNEW ALL THIS, WHAT WOULD YOU DO?
I WOULD PROTECT HIM.

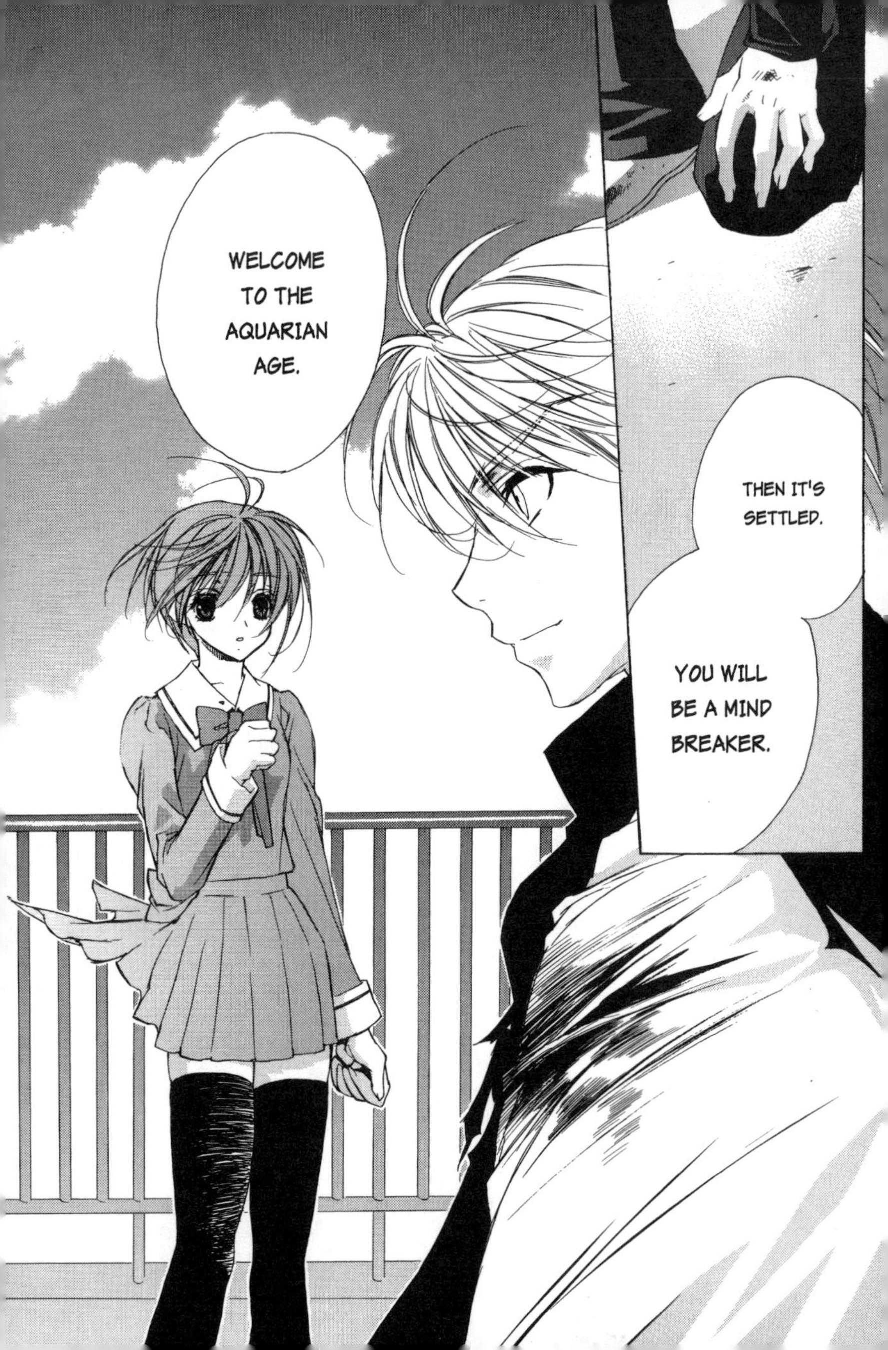
THEN IT'S SETTLED.
YOU WILL BE A MIND BREAKER.
WELCOME TO THE AQUARIAN AGE.

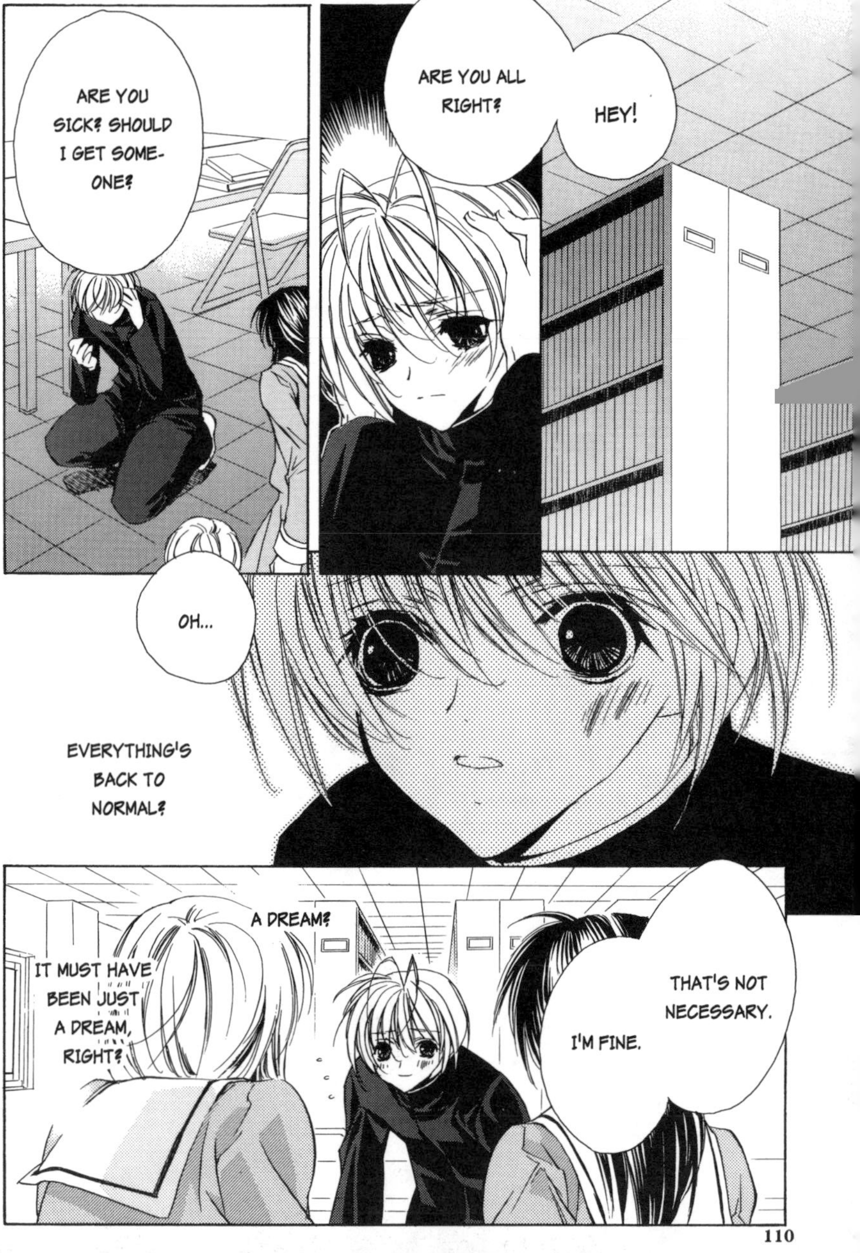
HEY!
ARE YOU ALL RIGHT?
ARE YOU SICK? SHOULD I GET SOME-ONE?
OH...
EVERYTHING'S BACK TO NORMAL?
THAT'S NOT NECESSARY.
I'M FINE.
A DREAM?
IT MUST HAVE BEEN JUST A DREAM, RIGHT?

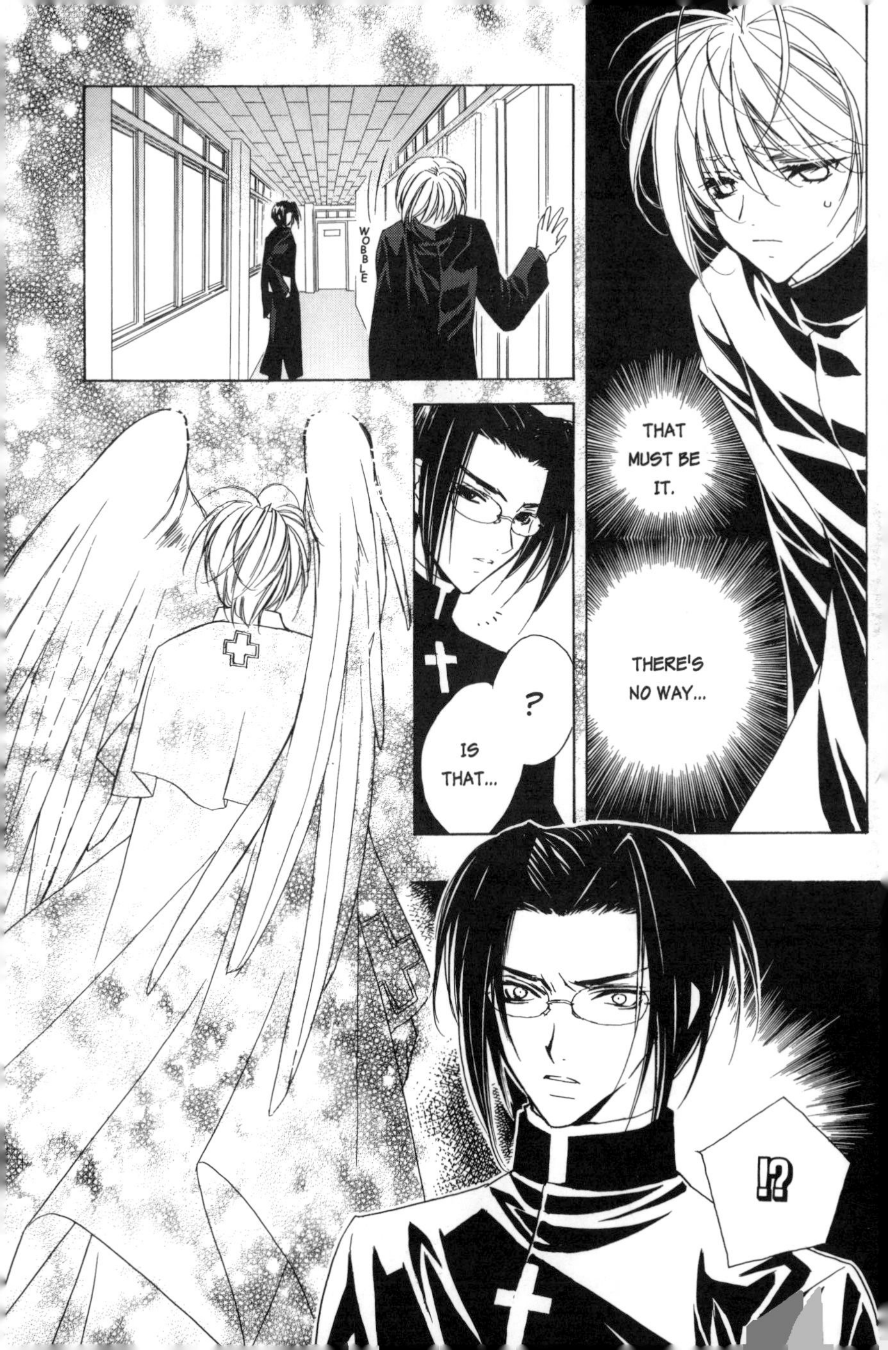
THAT MUST BE IT.
THERE'S NO WAY...
WOBBLE
?
IS THAT...
!?

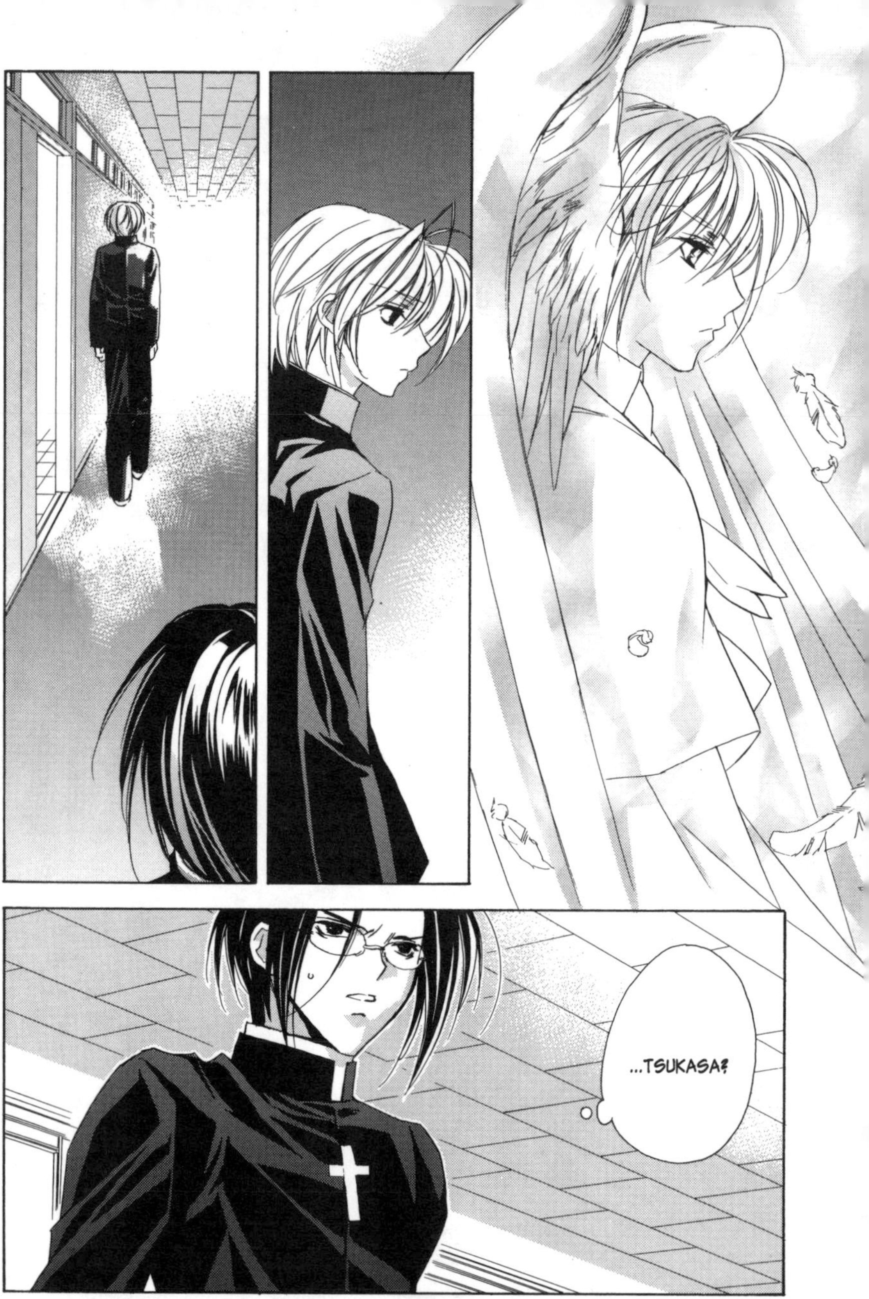
...TSUKASA?

turn.4

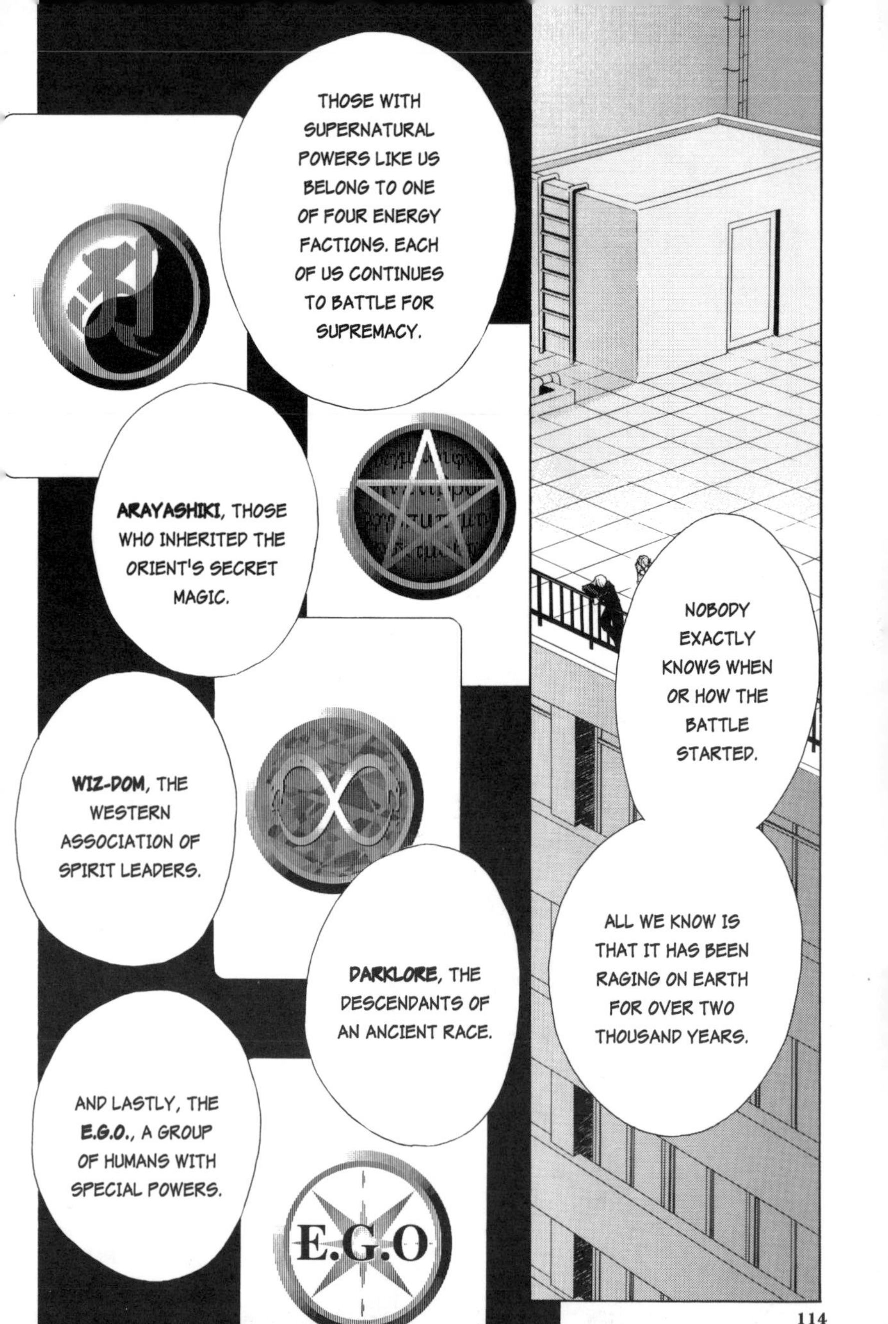
NOBODY EXACTLY KNOWS WHEN OR HOW THE BATTLE STARTED.
ALL WE KNOW IS THAT IT HAS BEEN RAGING ON EARTH FOR OVER TWO THOUSAND YEARS.
THOSE WITH SUPERNATURAL POWERS LIKE US BELONG TO ONE OF FOUR ENERGY FACTIONS. EACH OF US CONTINUES TO BATTLE FOR SUPREMACY.
ARAYASHIKI, THOSE WHO INHERITED THE ORIENT'S SECRET MAGIC.
WIZ-DOM, THE WESTERN ASSOCIATION OF SPIRIT LEADERS.
DARKLORE, THE DESCENDANTS OF AN ANCIENT RACE.
AND LASTLY, THE E.G.O., A GROUP OF HUMANS WITH SPECIAL POWERS.
E.G.O

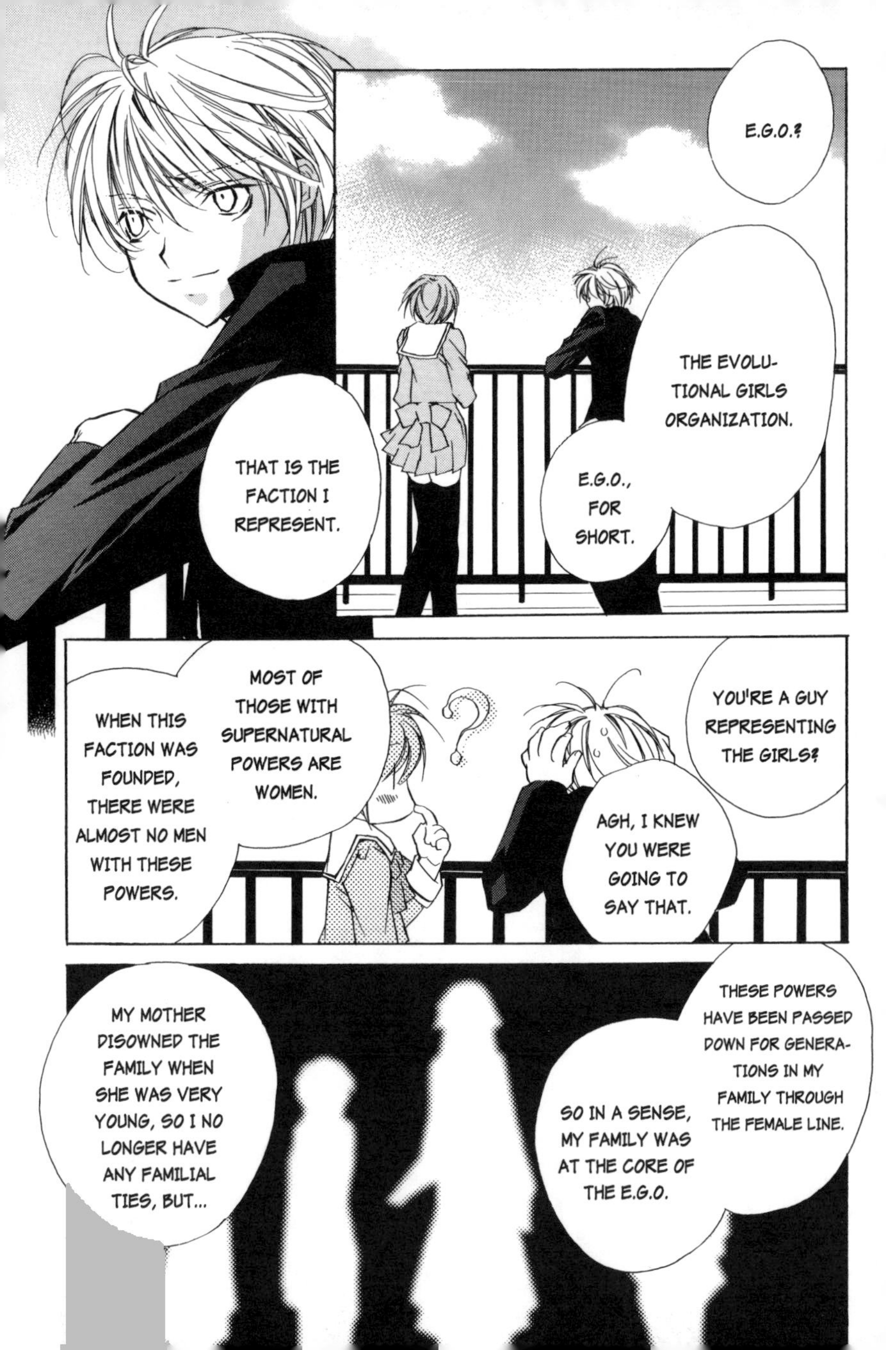
E.G.O.?
THE EVOLUTIONAL GIRLS ORGANIZATION.
E.G.O., FOR SHORT.
THAT IS THE FACTION I REPRESENT.
YOU'RE A GUY REPRESENTING THE GIRLS?
AGH, I KNEW YOU WERE GOING TO SAY THAT.
MOST OF THOSE WITH SUPERNATURAL POWERS ARE WOMEN.
WHEN THIS FACTION WAS FOUNDED, THERE WERE ALMOST NO MEN WITH THESE POWERS.
THESE POWERS HAVE BEEN PASSED DOWN FOR GENERATIONS IN MY FAMILY THROUGH THE FEMALE LINE.
SO IN A SENSE, MY FAMILY WAS AT THE CORE OF THE E.G.O.
MY MOTHER DISOWNED THE FAMILY WHEN SHE WAS VERY YOUNG, SO I NO LONGER HAVE ANY FAMILIAL TIES, BUT...

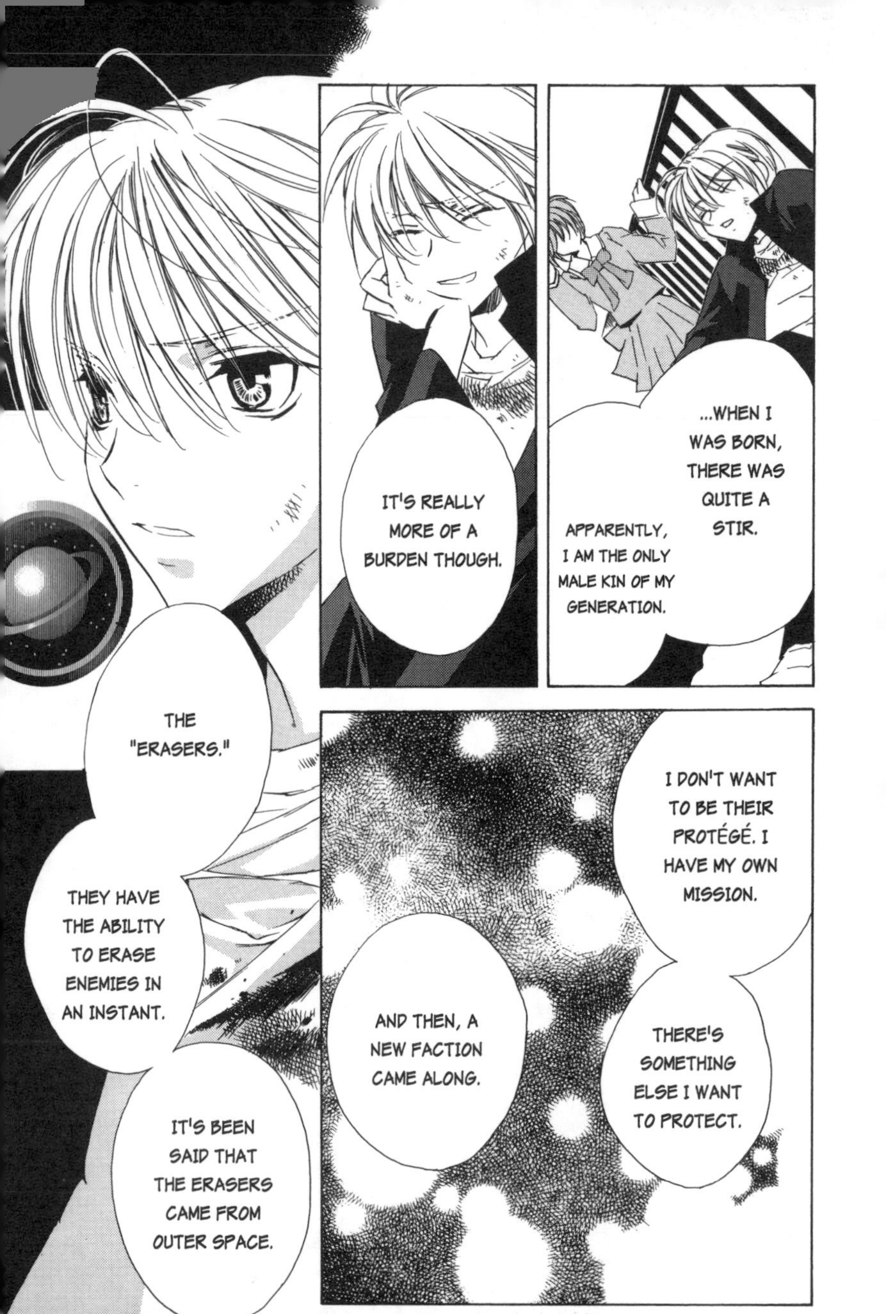
...WHEN I WAS BORN, THERE WAS QUITE A STIR.
APPARENTLY, I AM THE ONLY MALE KIN OF MY GENERATION.
IT'S REALLY MORE OF A BURDEN THOUGH.
I DON'T WANT TO BE THEIR PROTÉGÉ. I HAVE MY OWN MISSION.
THERE'S SOMETHING ELSE I WANT TO PROTECT.
AND THEN, A NEW FACTION CAME ALONG.
THE "ERASERS."
THEY HAVE THE ABILITY TO ERASE ENEMIES IN AN INSTANT.
IT'S BEEN SAID THAT THE ERASERS CAME FROM OUTER SPACE.

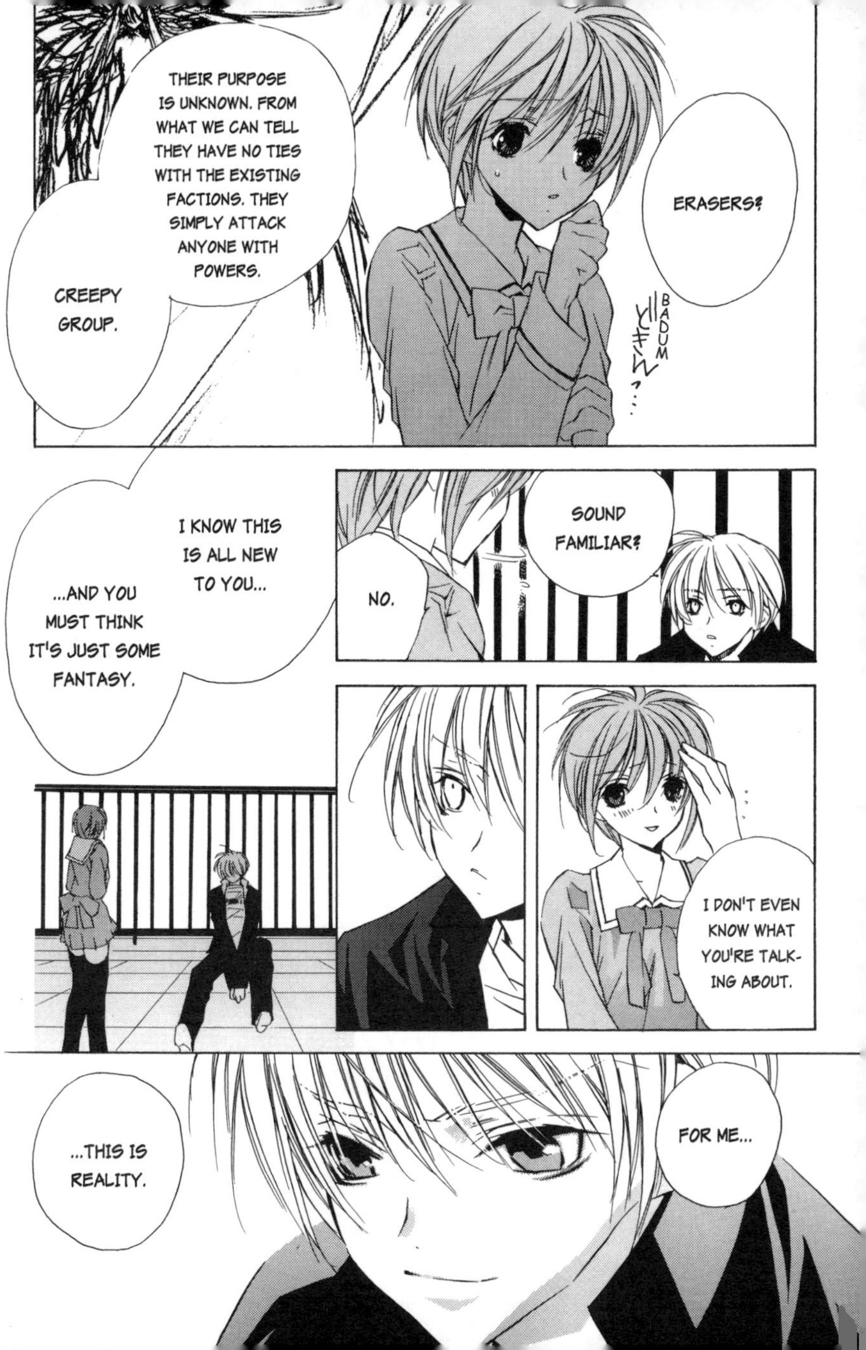
ERASERS?
THEIR PURPOSE IS UNKNOWN. FROM WHAT WE CAN TELL THEY HAVE NO TIES WITH THE EXISTING FACTIONS. THEY SIMPLY ATTACK ANYONE WITH POWERS.
CREEPY GROUP.
BADUM
SOUND FAMILIAR?
NO.
I DON'T EVEN KNOW WHAT YOU'RE TALK-ING ABOUT.
I KNOW THIS IS ALL NEW TO YOU...
...AND YOU MUST THINK IT'S JUST SOME FANTASY.
FOR ME...
...THIS IS REALITY.

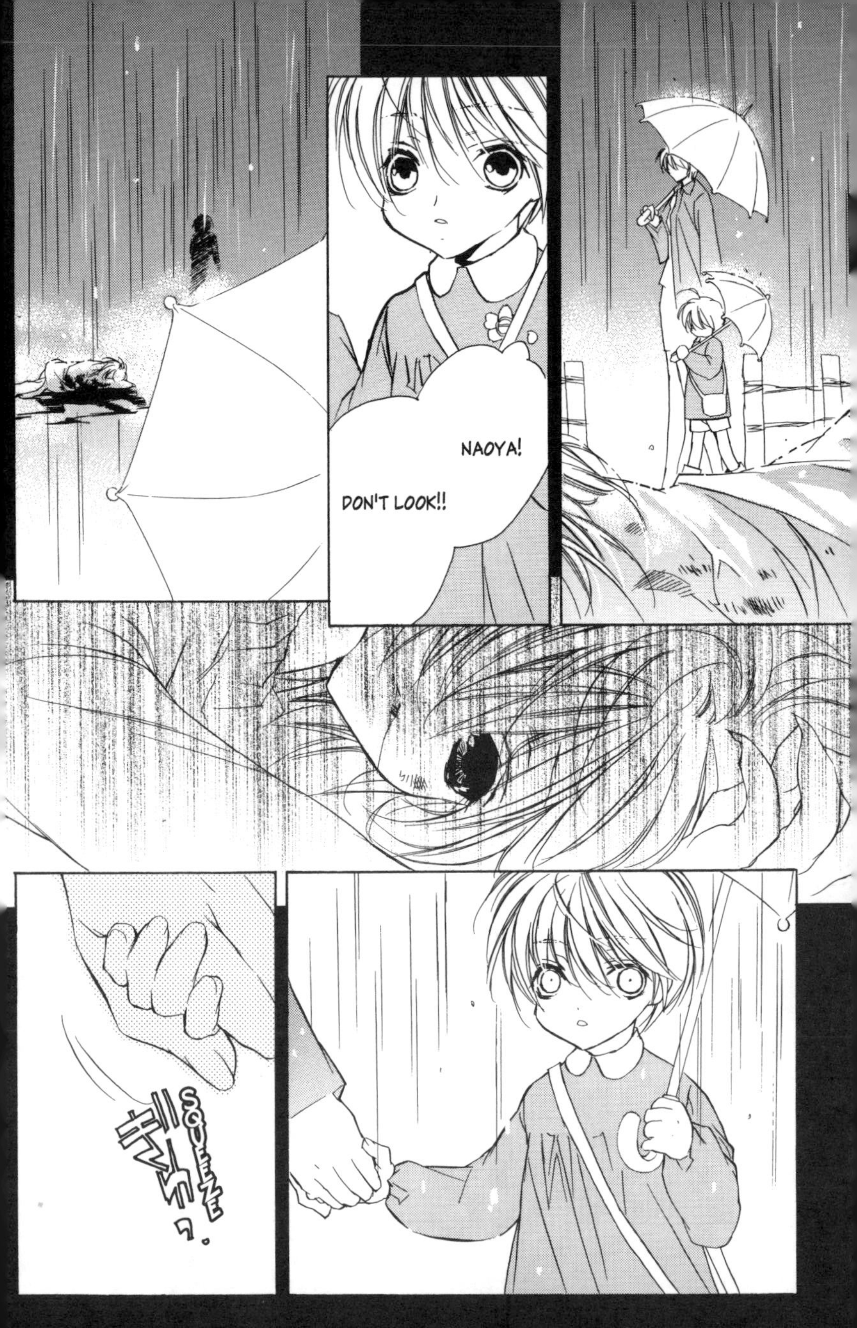
NAOYA!
DON'T LOOK!!
SQUEEZE

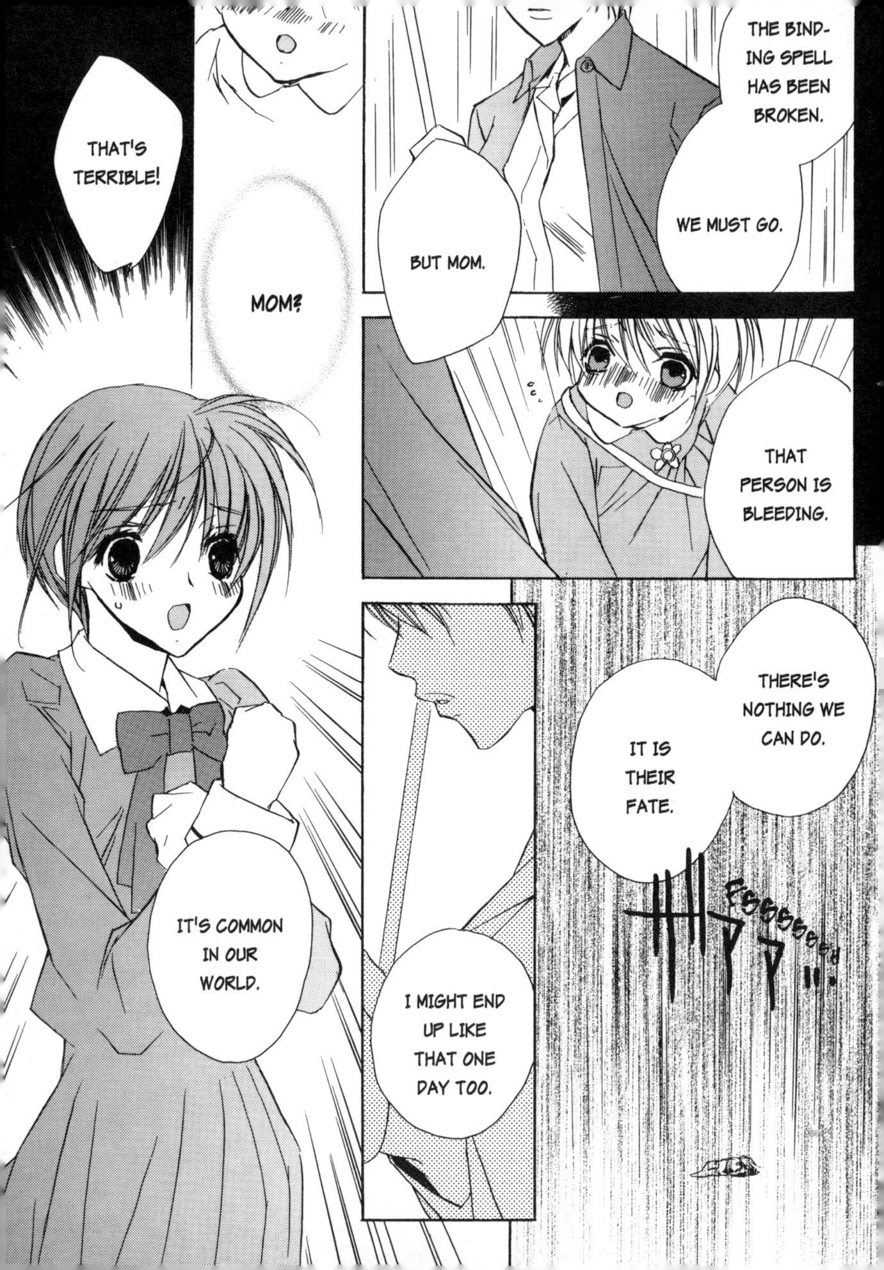
THE BINDING-ING SPELL HAS BEEN BROKEN.
WE MUST GO.
BUT MOM.
THAT PERSON IS BLEEDING.
THERE'S NOTHING WE CAN DO.
IT IS THEIR FATE.
FSSSSSSH!!
I MIGHT END UP LIKE THAT ONE DAY TOO.
MOM?
THAT'S TERRIBLE!
IT'S COMMON IN OUR WORLD.

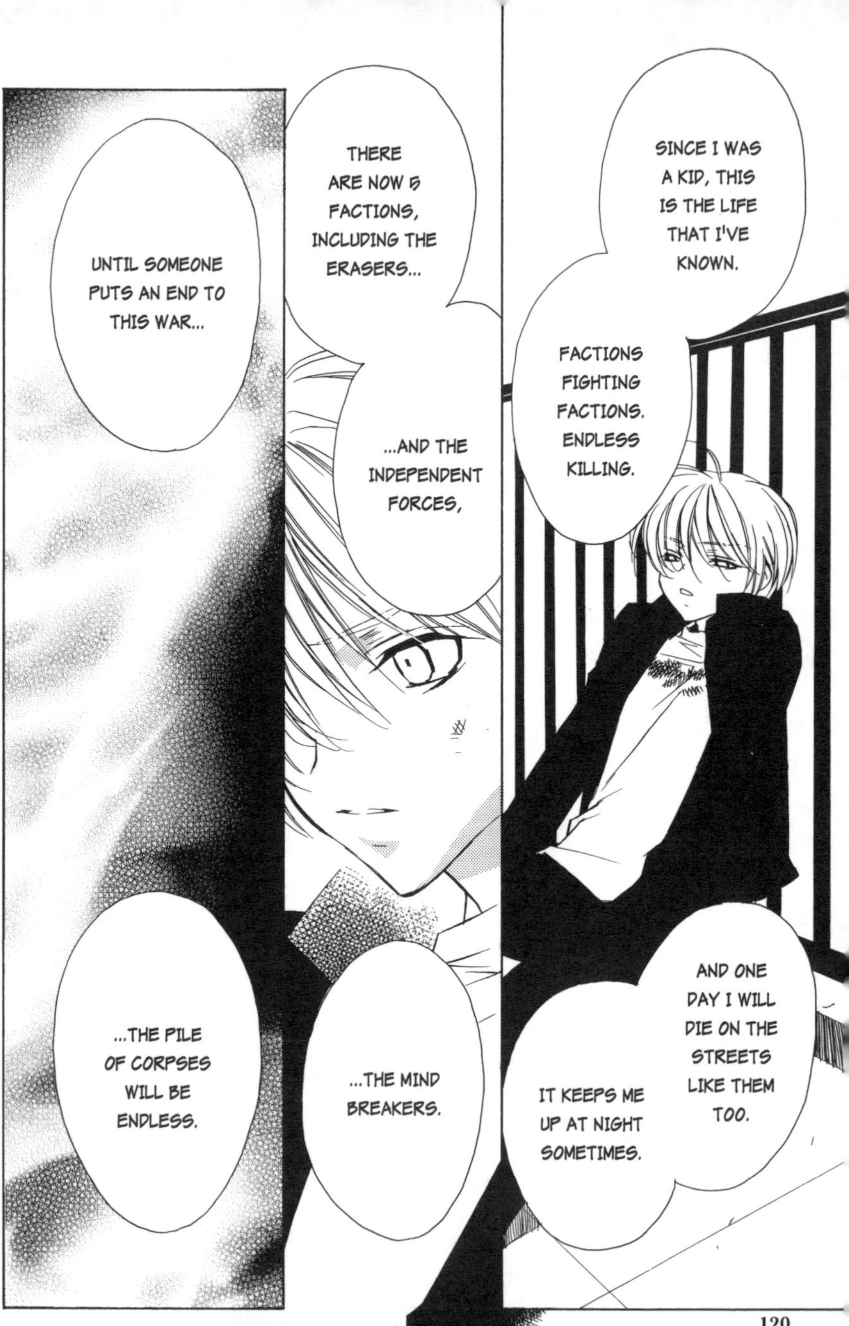
SINCE I WAS A KID, THIS IS THE LIFE THAT I'VE KNOWN.
FACTIONS FIGHTING FACTIONS. ENDLESS KILLING.
AND ONE DAY I WILL DIE ON THE STREETS LIKE THEM TOO.
IT KEEPS ME UP AT NIGHT SOMETIMES.
THERE ARE NOW 5 FACTIONS, INCLUDING THE ERASERS...
...AND THE INDEPENDENT FORCES,
...THE MIND BREAKERS.
UNTIL SOMEONE PUTS AN END TO THIS WAR...
...THE PILE OF CORPSES WILL BE ENDLESS.

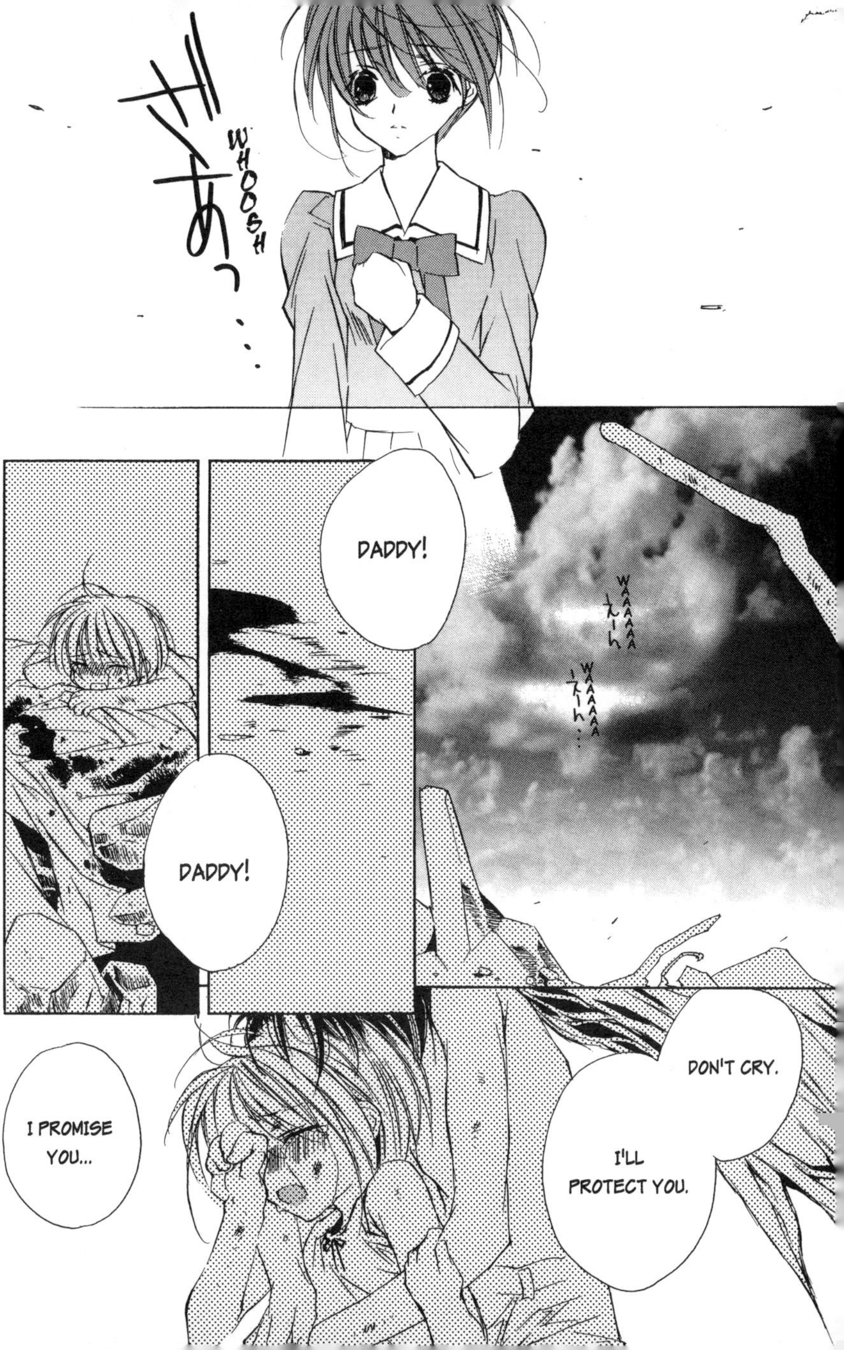

WHOOSH
WAAAAAA
WAAAAAA...
DADDY!
DADDY!
DON'T CRY.
I'LL PROTECT YOU.
I PROMISE YOU...

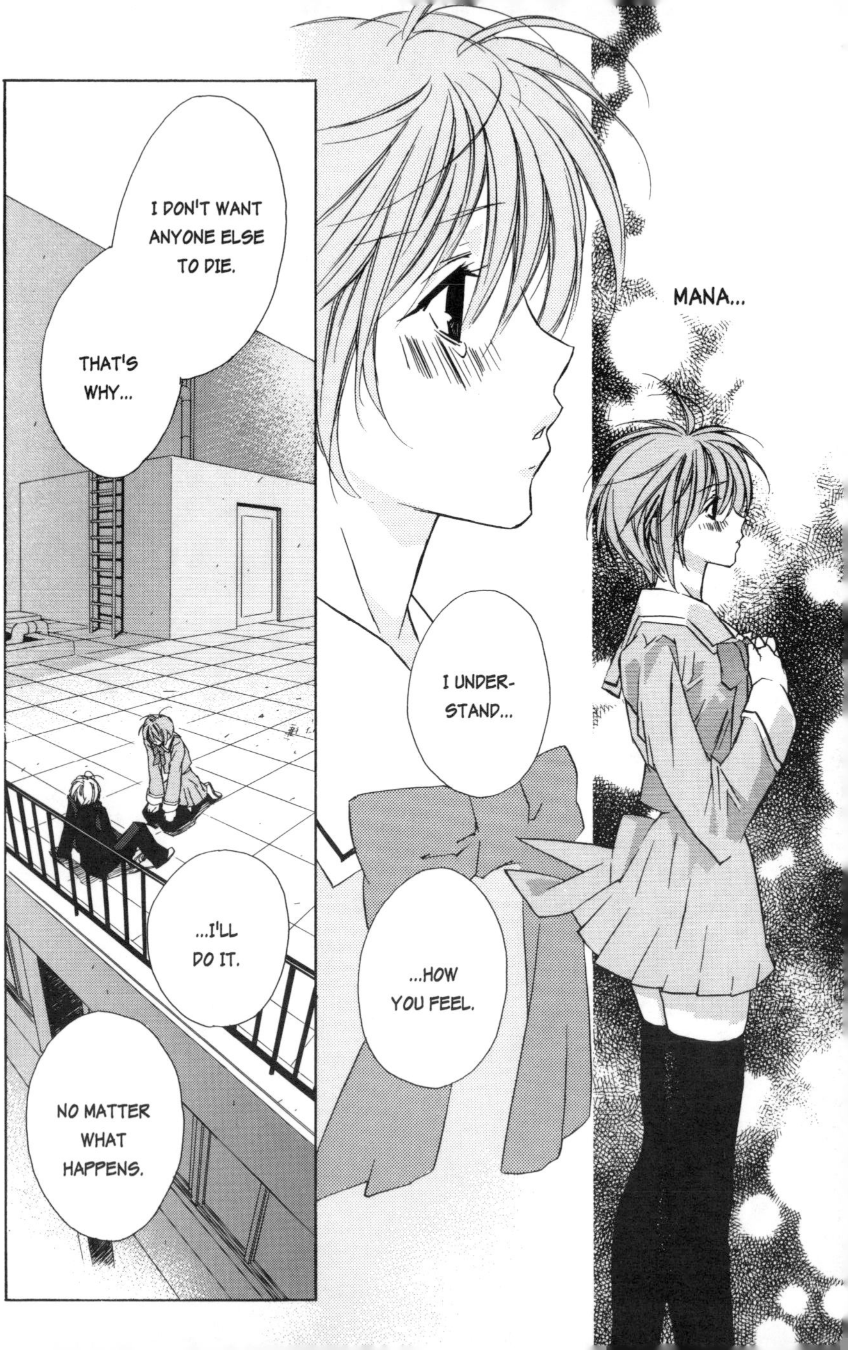
MANA...
I UNDER-STAND...
...HOW YOU FEEL.
I DON'T WANT ANYONE ELSE TO DIE.
THAT'S WHY...
...I'LL DO IT.
NO MATTER WHAT HAPPENS.

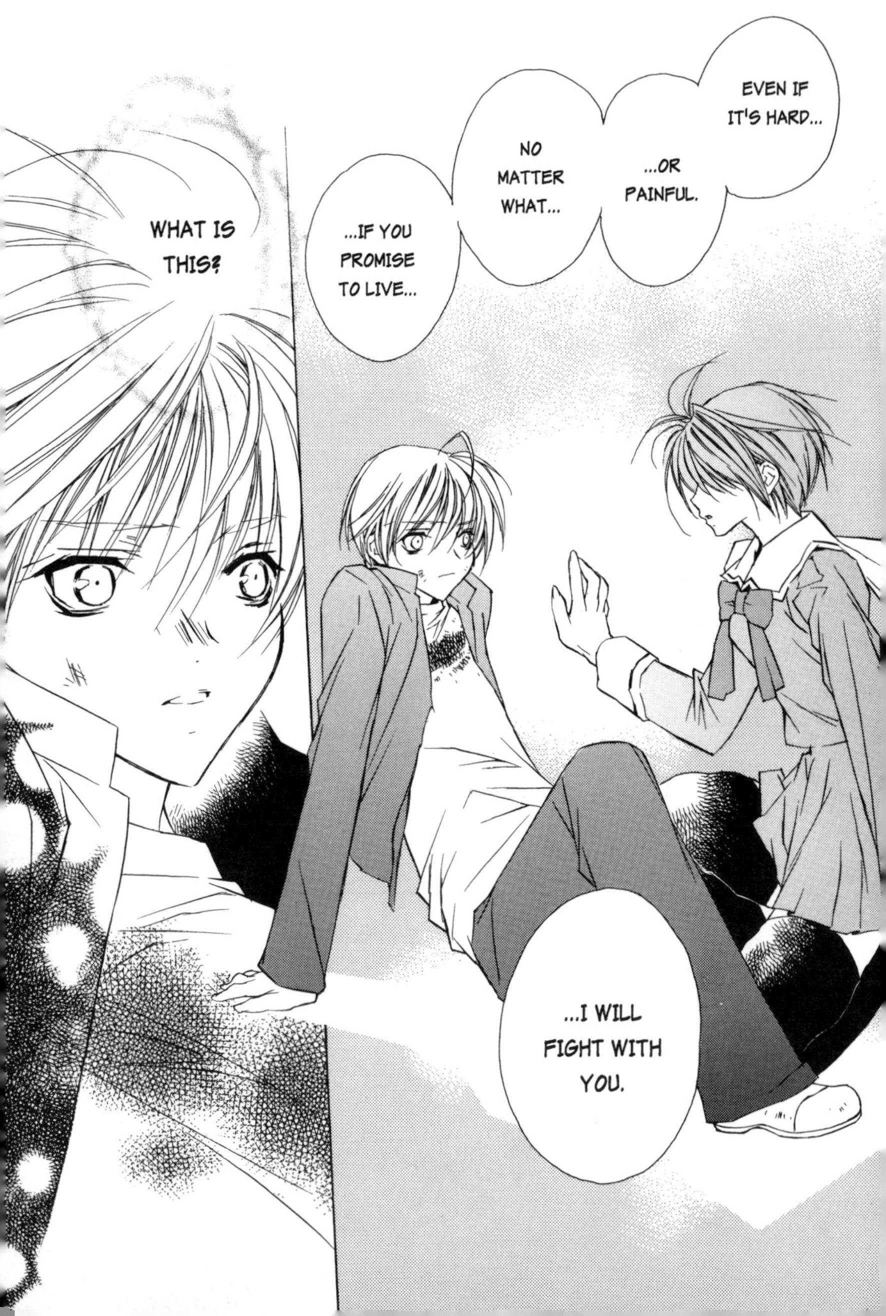
EVEN IF IT'S HARD...
...OR PAINFUL.
NO MATTER WHAT...
...IF YOU PROMISE TO LIVE...
...I WILL FIGHT WITH YOU.
WHAT IS THIS?

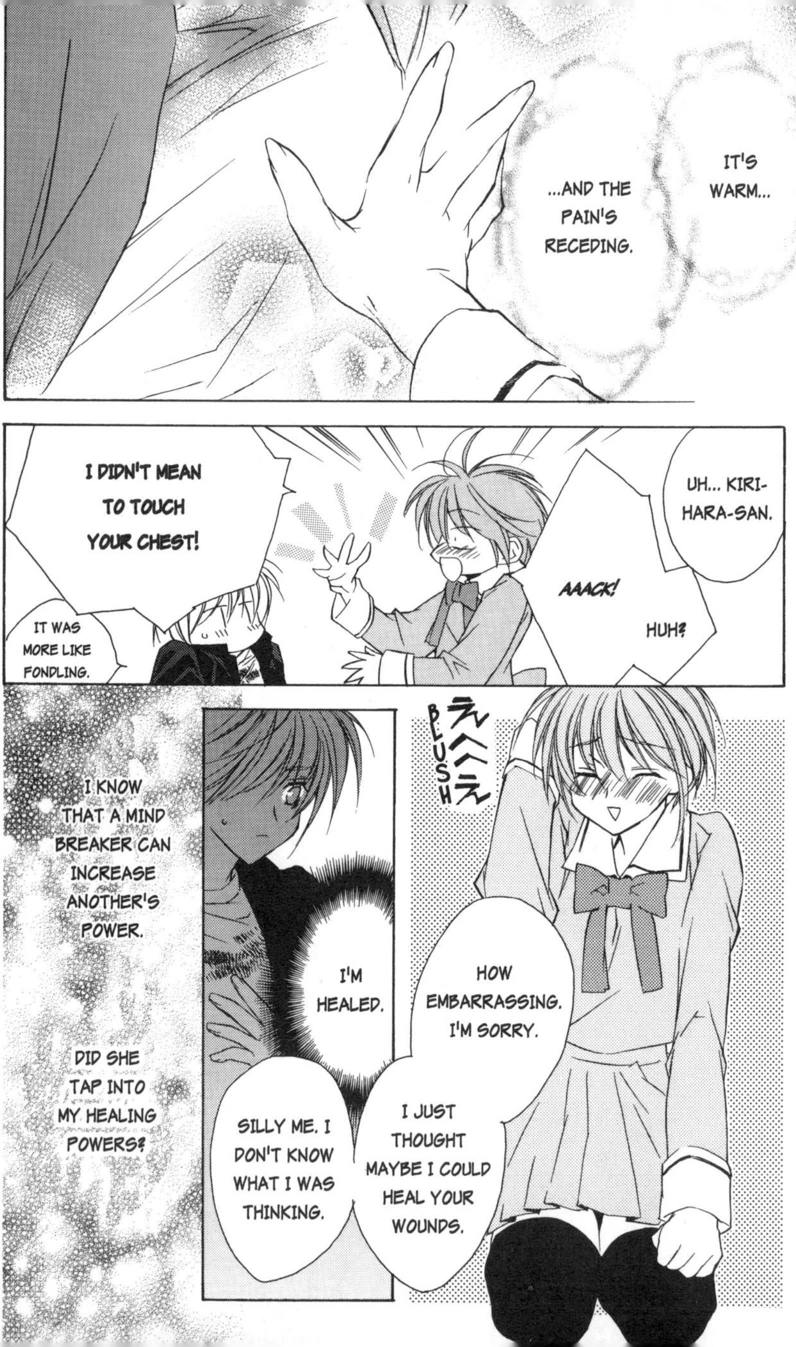
IT'S WARM...
...AND THE PAIN'S RECEDING.
UH... KIRI-HARA-SAN.
HUH?
AAACK!
I DIDN'T MEAN TO TOUCH YOUR CHEST!
IT WAS MORE LIKE FONDLING.
BLUSH
HOW EMBARRASSING. I'M SORRY.
I JUST THOUGHT MAYBE I COULD HEAL YOUR WOUNDS.
SILLY ME. I DON'T KNOW WHAT I WAS THINKING.
I'M HEALED.
I KNOW THAT A MIND BREAKER CAN INCREASE ANOTHER'S POWER.
DID SHE TAP INTO MY HEALING POWERS?

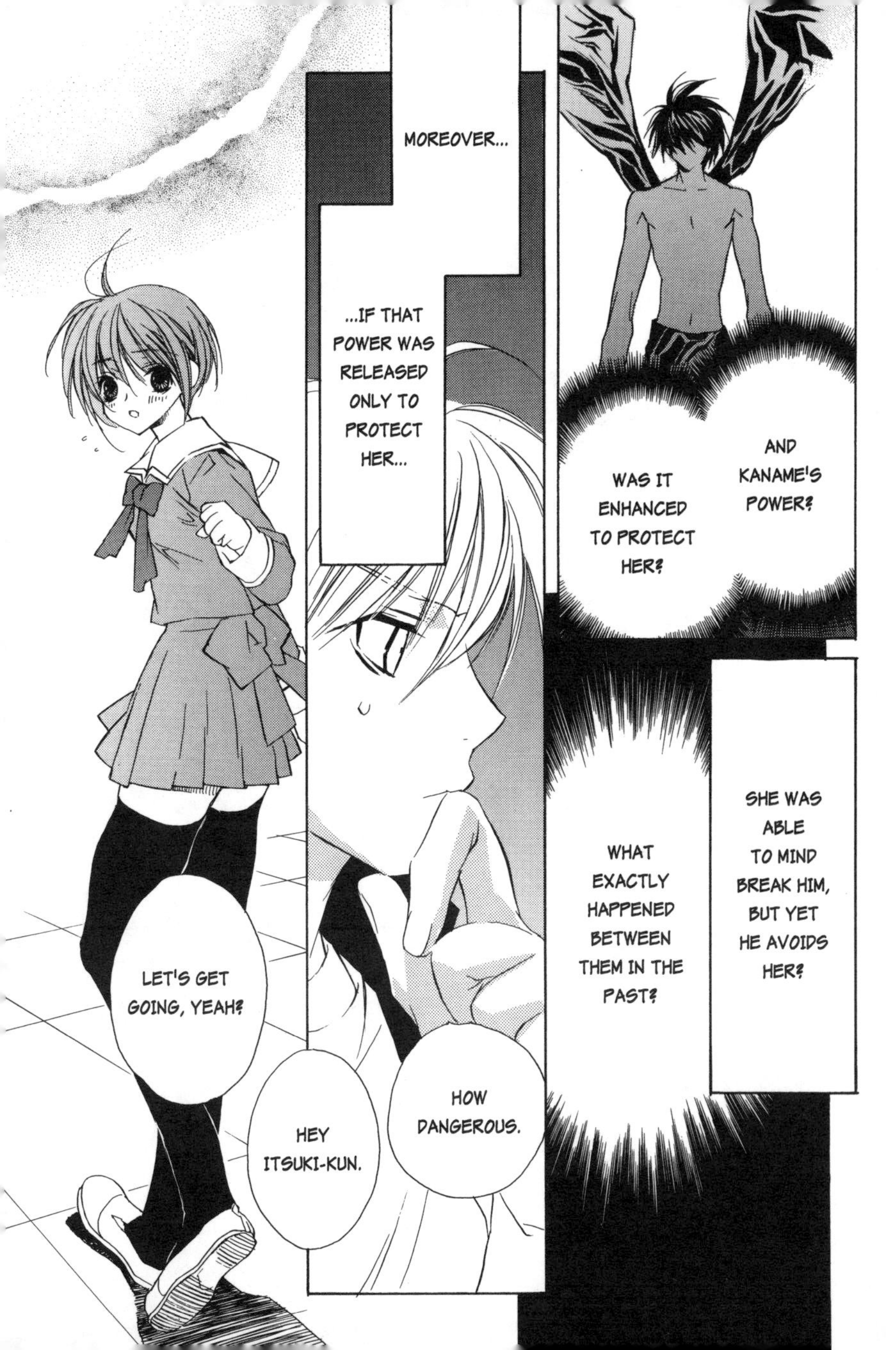
AND KANAME'S POWER?
WAS IT ENHANCED TO PROTECT HER?
SHE WAS ABLE TO MIND BREAK HIM, BUT YET HE AVOIDS HER?
WHAT EXACTLY HAPPENED BETWEEN THEM IN THE PAST?
MOREOVER...
...IF THAT POWER WAS RELEASED ONLY TO PROTECT HER...
HOW DANGEROUS.
HEY ITSUKI-KUN.
LET'S GET GOING, YEAH?

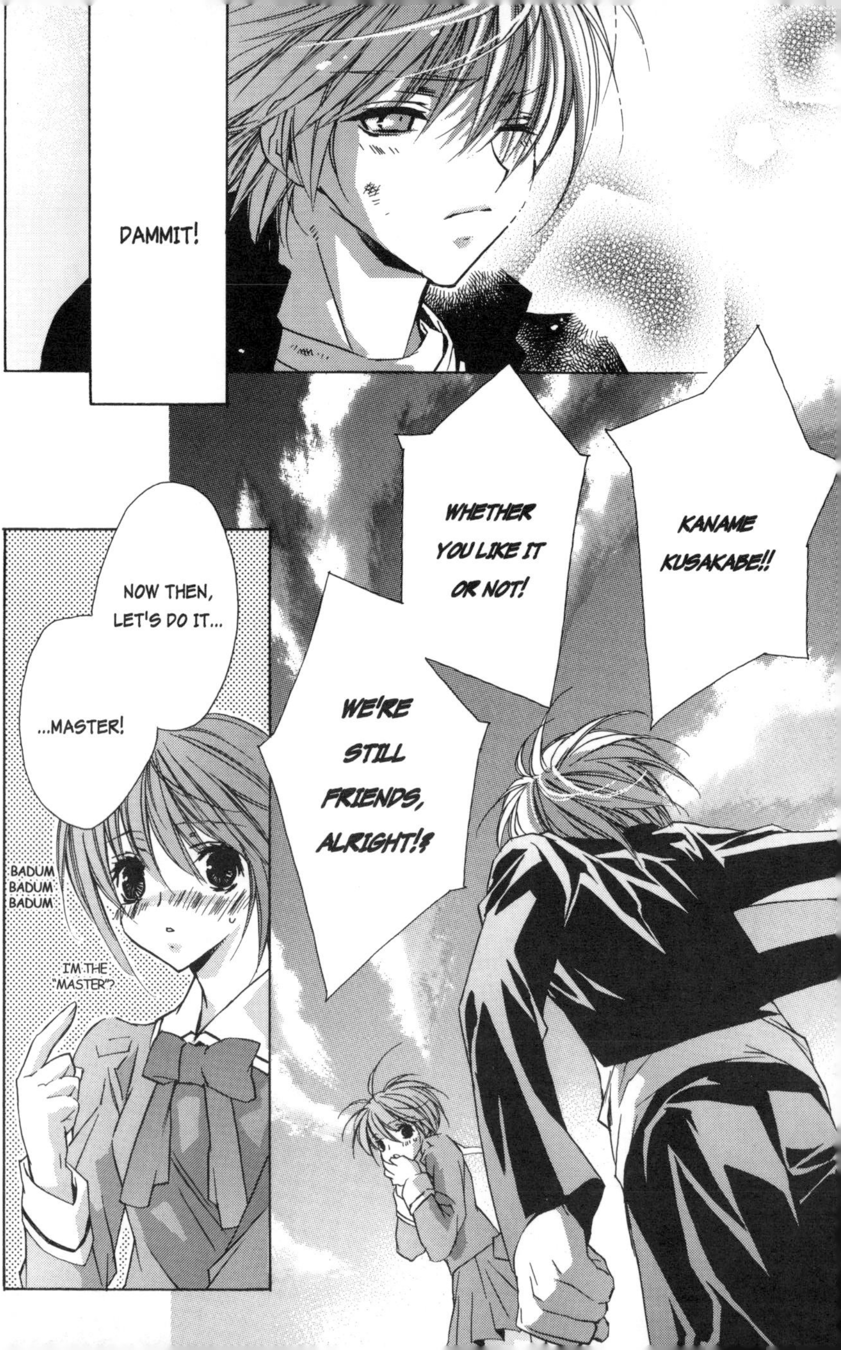
DAMMIT!
KANAME KUSAKABE!!
WHETHER YOU LIKE IT OR NOT!
WE'RE STILL FRIENDS, ALRIGHT!?
NOW THEN, LET'S DO IT...
...MASTER!
BADUM BADUM BADUM
I'M THE "MASTER"?

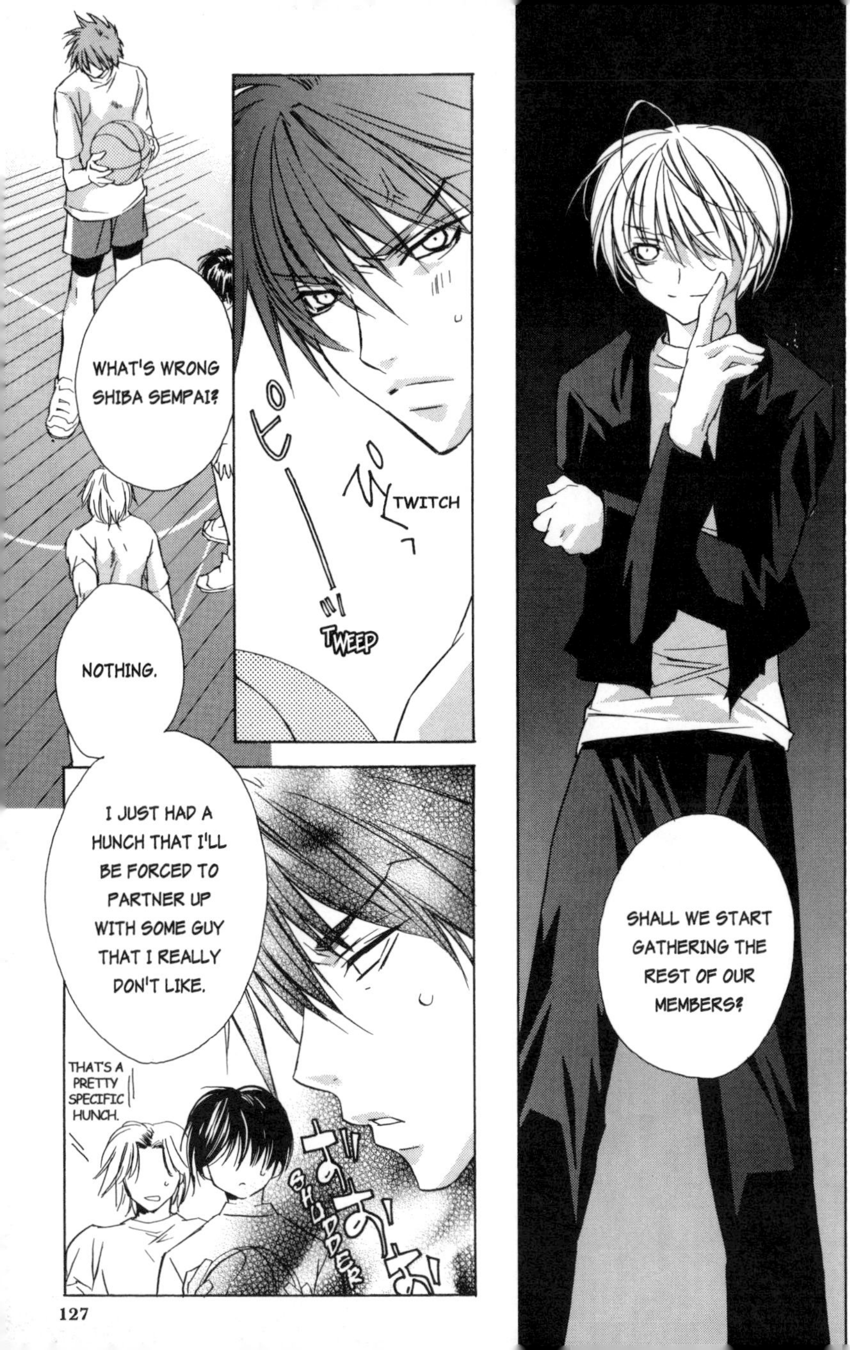
SHALL WE START GATHERING THE REST OF OUR MEMBERS?
TWITCH
TWEEP
WHAT'S WRONG SHIBA SEMPAI?
NOTHING.
I JUST HAD A HUNCH THAT I'LL BE FORCED TO PARTNER UP WITH SOME GUY THAT I REALLY DON'T LIKE.
THAT'S A PRETTY SPECIFIC HUNCH.
SHUDDER

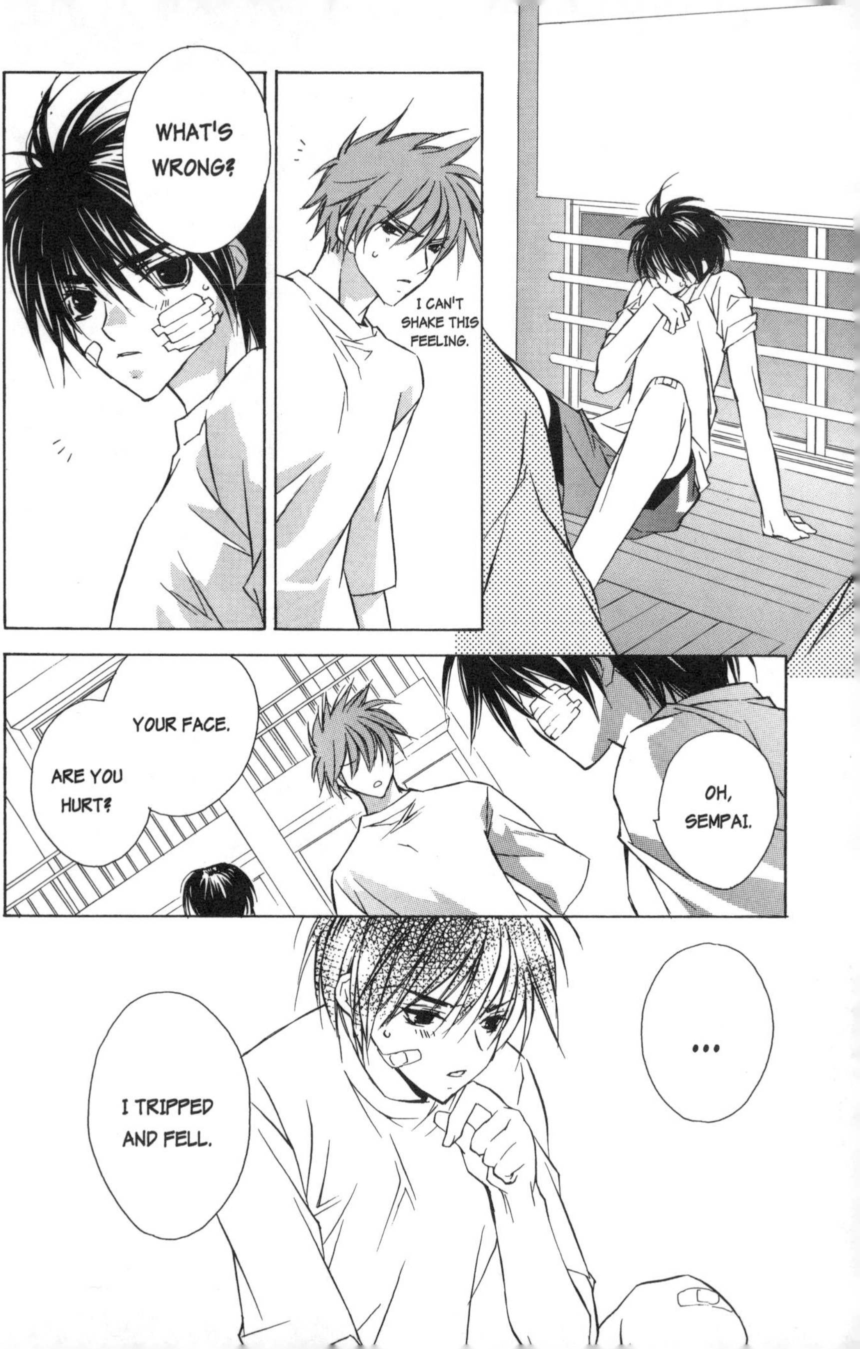
I CAN'T SHAKE THIS FEELING.
WHAT'S WRONG?
OH, SEMPAI.
YOUR FACE.
ARE YOU HURT?
...
I TRIPPED AND FELL.

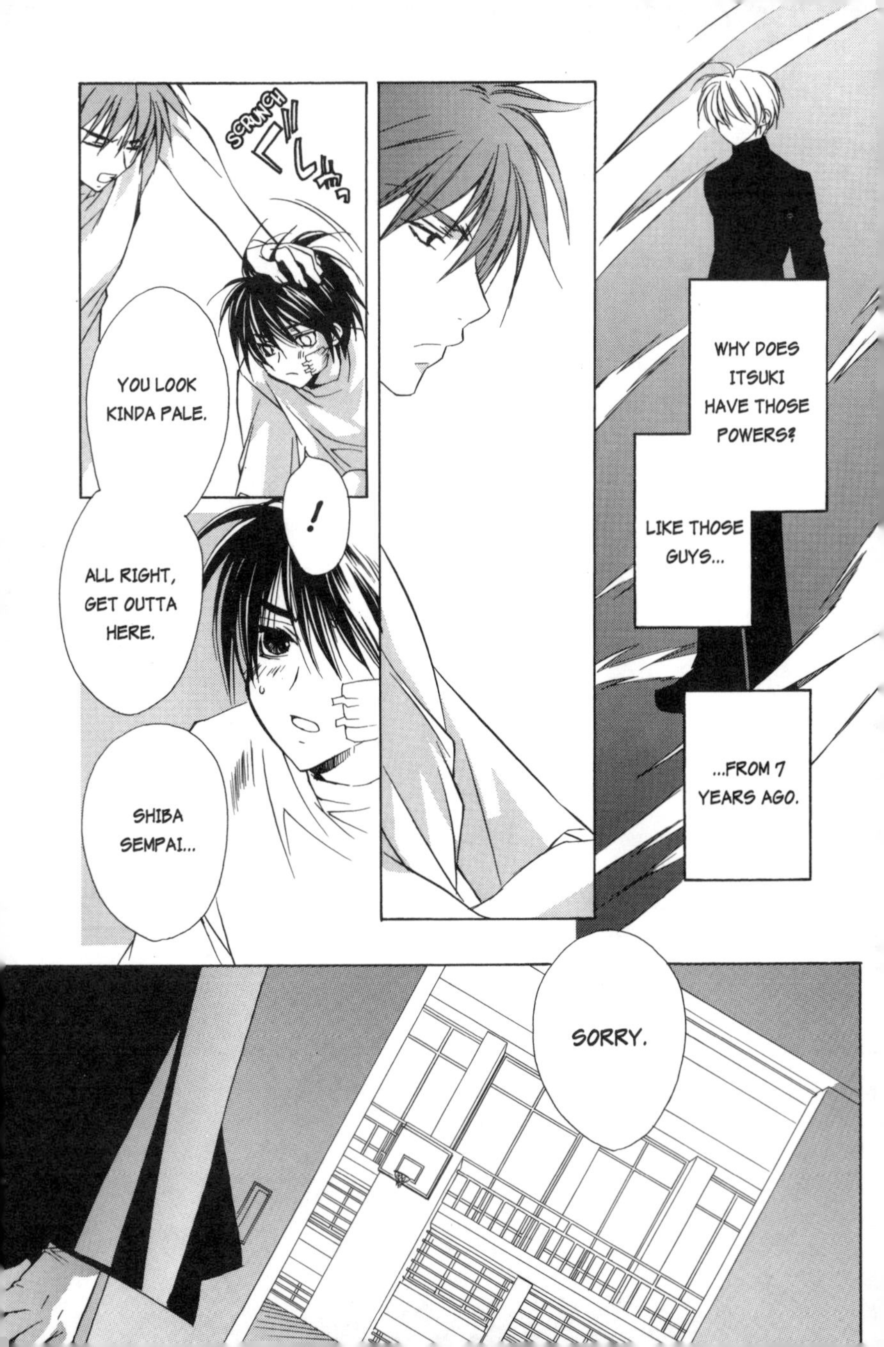
WHY DOES ITSUKI HAVE THOSE POWERS?
LIKE THOSE GUYS...
...FROM 7 YEARS AGO.
SCRUNCH
YOU LOOK KINDA PALE.
!
ALL RIGHT, GET OUTTA HERE.
SHIBA SEMPAI...
SORRY.

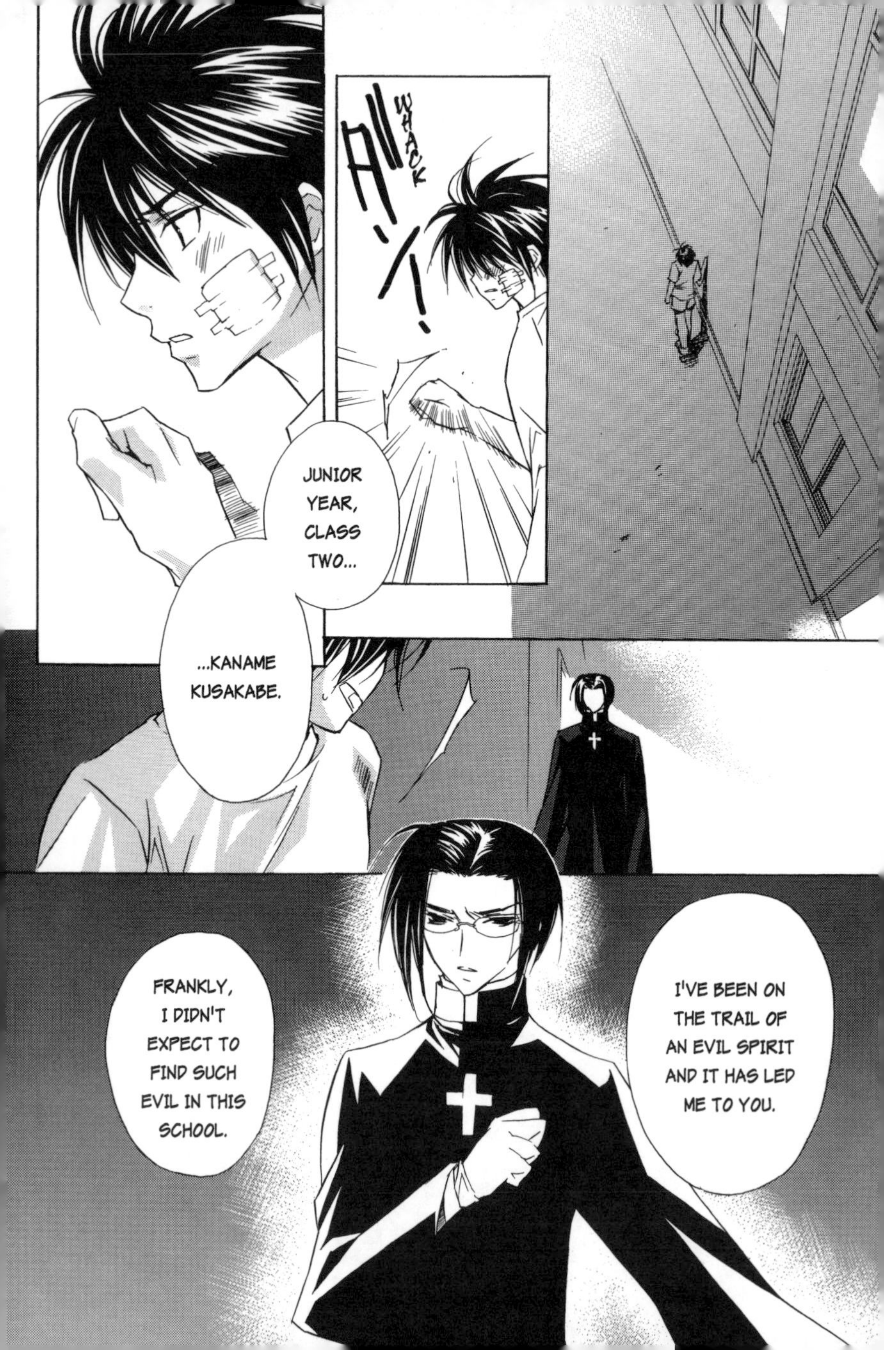
WHACK
JUNIOR YEAR, CLASS TWO...
...KANAME KUSAKABE.
I'VE BEEN ON THE TRAIL OF AN EVIL SPIRIT AND IT HAS LED ME TO YOU.
FRANKLY, I DIDN'T EXPECT TO FIND SUCH EVIL IN THIS SCHOOL.

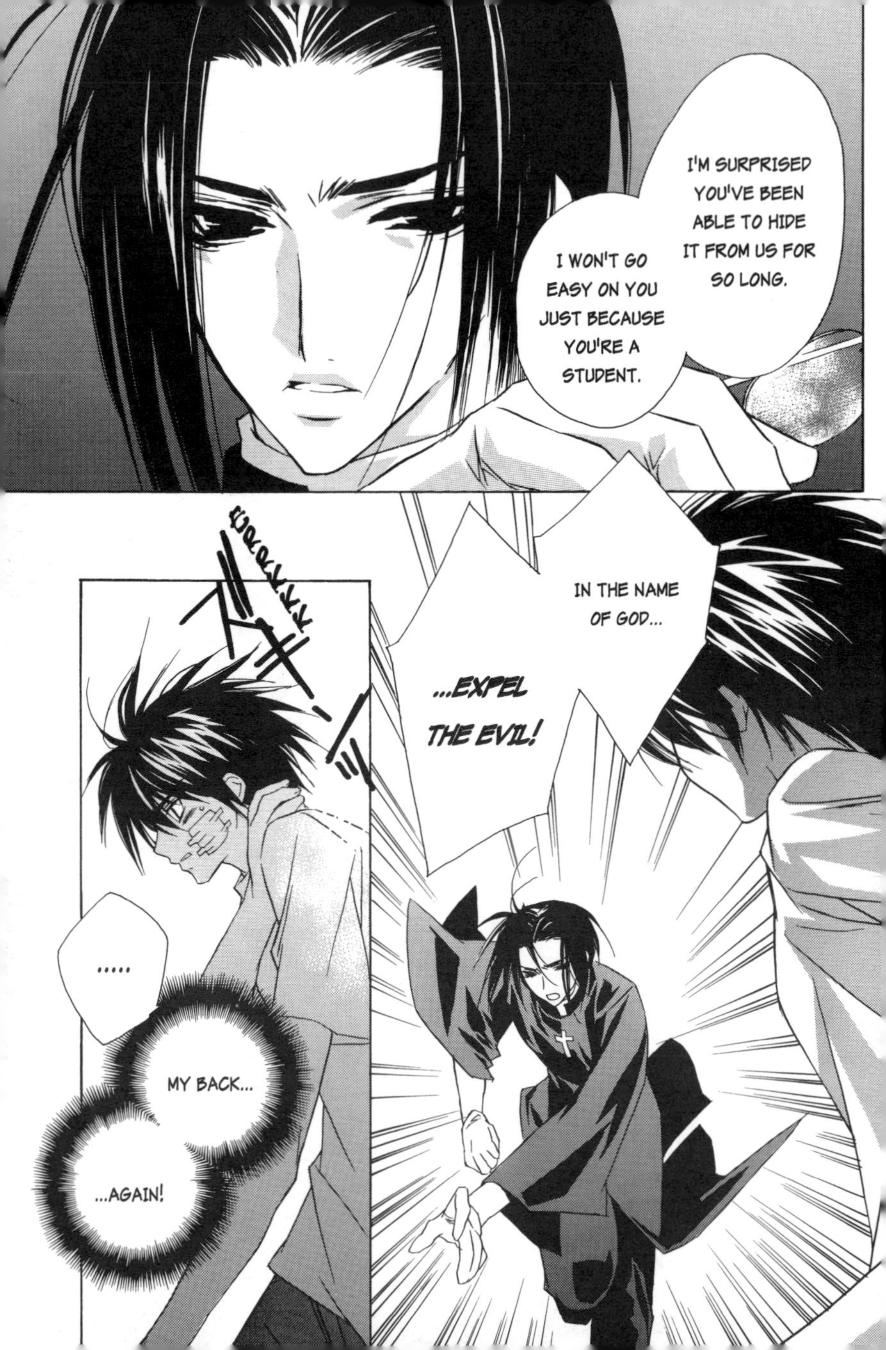

I'M SURPRISED YOU'VE BEEN ABLE TO HIDE IT FROM US FOR SO LONG.
I WON'T GO EASY ON YOU JUST BECAUSE YOU'RE A STUDENT.
IN THE NAME OF GOD...
...EXPEL THE EVIL!
GRRRKKKK
.....
MY BACK...
...AGAIN!

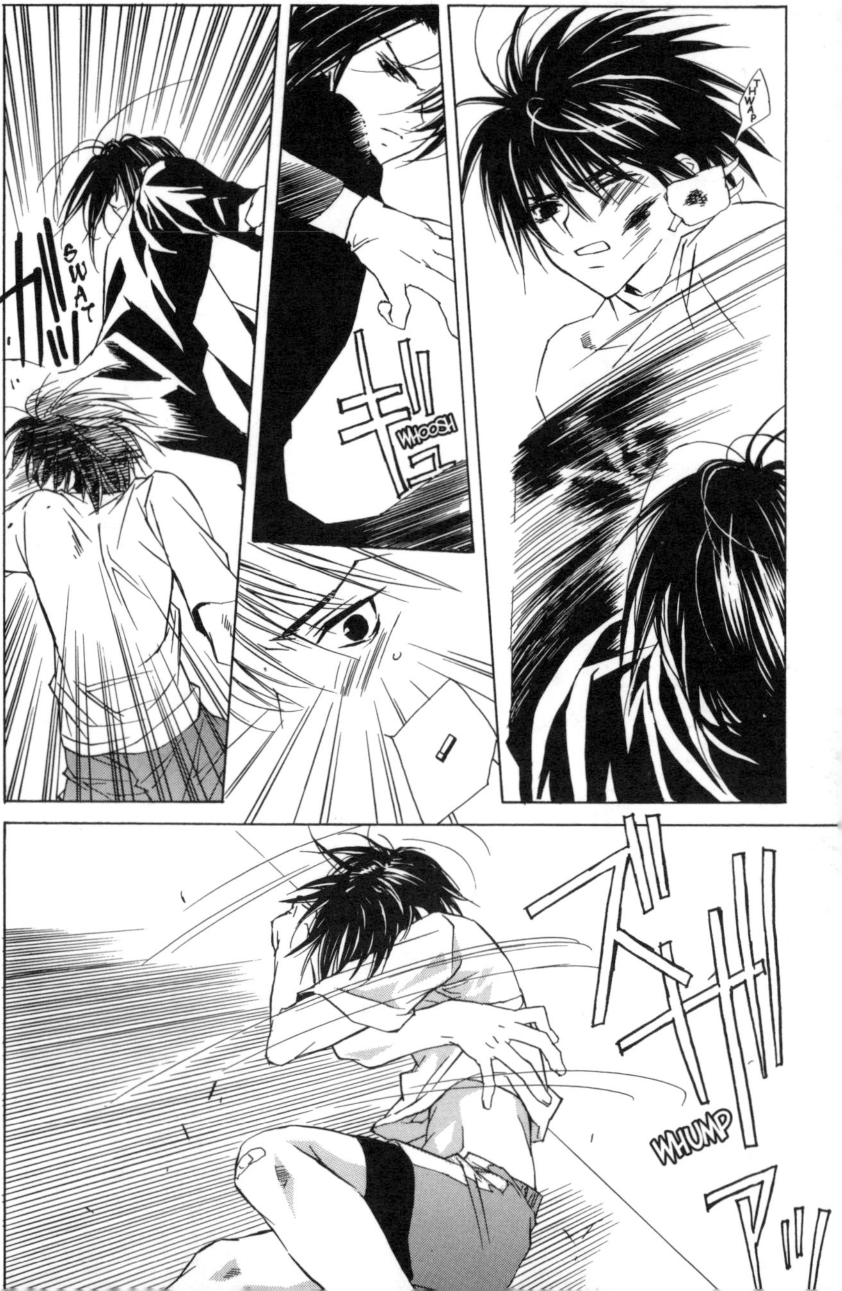
THWAP
WHOOSH
SWAT
WHUMP

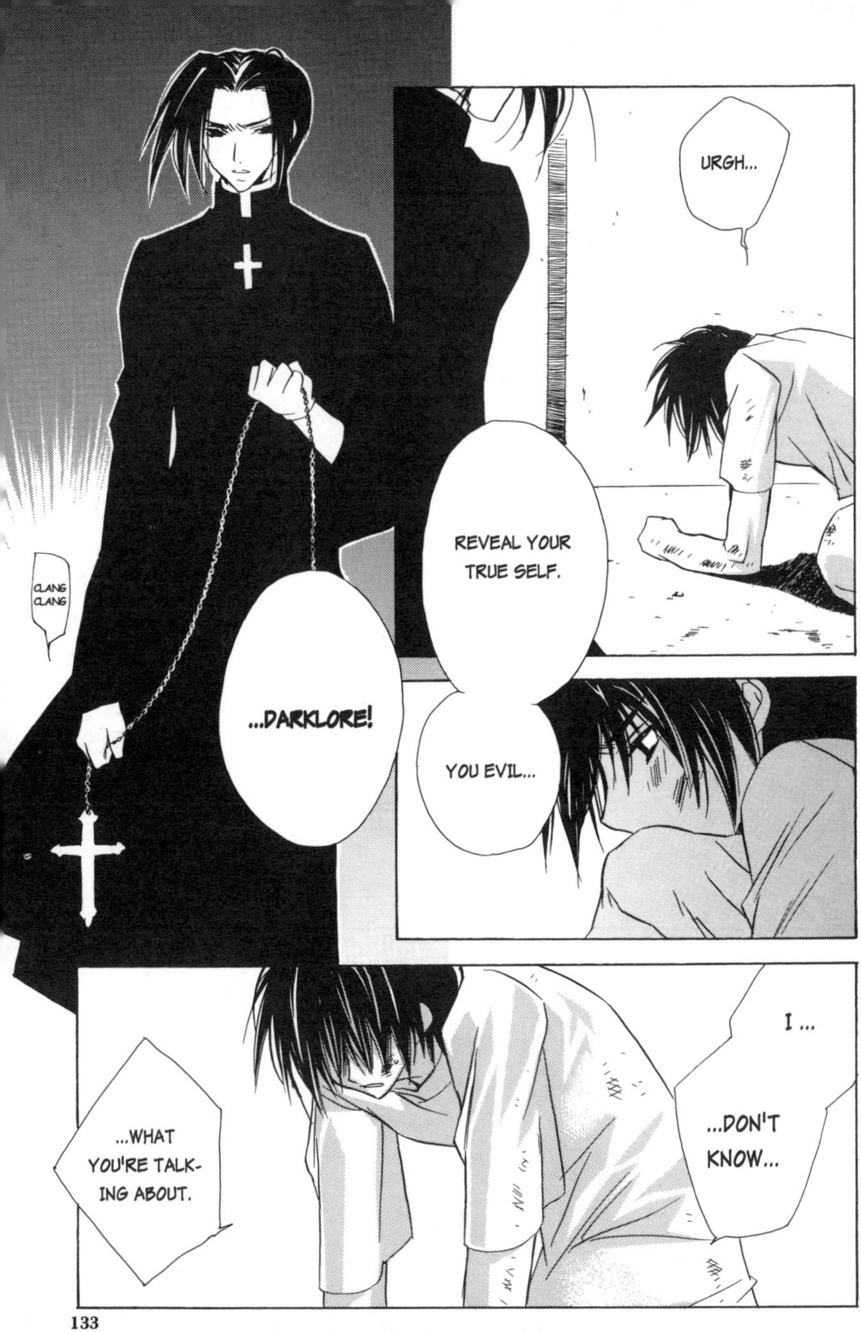
URGH...
REVEAL YOUR TRUE SELF.
YOU EVIL...
...DARKLORE!
CLANG CLANG
I ...
...DON'T KNOW...
...WHAT YOU'RE TALK-ING ABOUT.

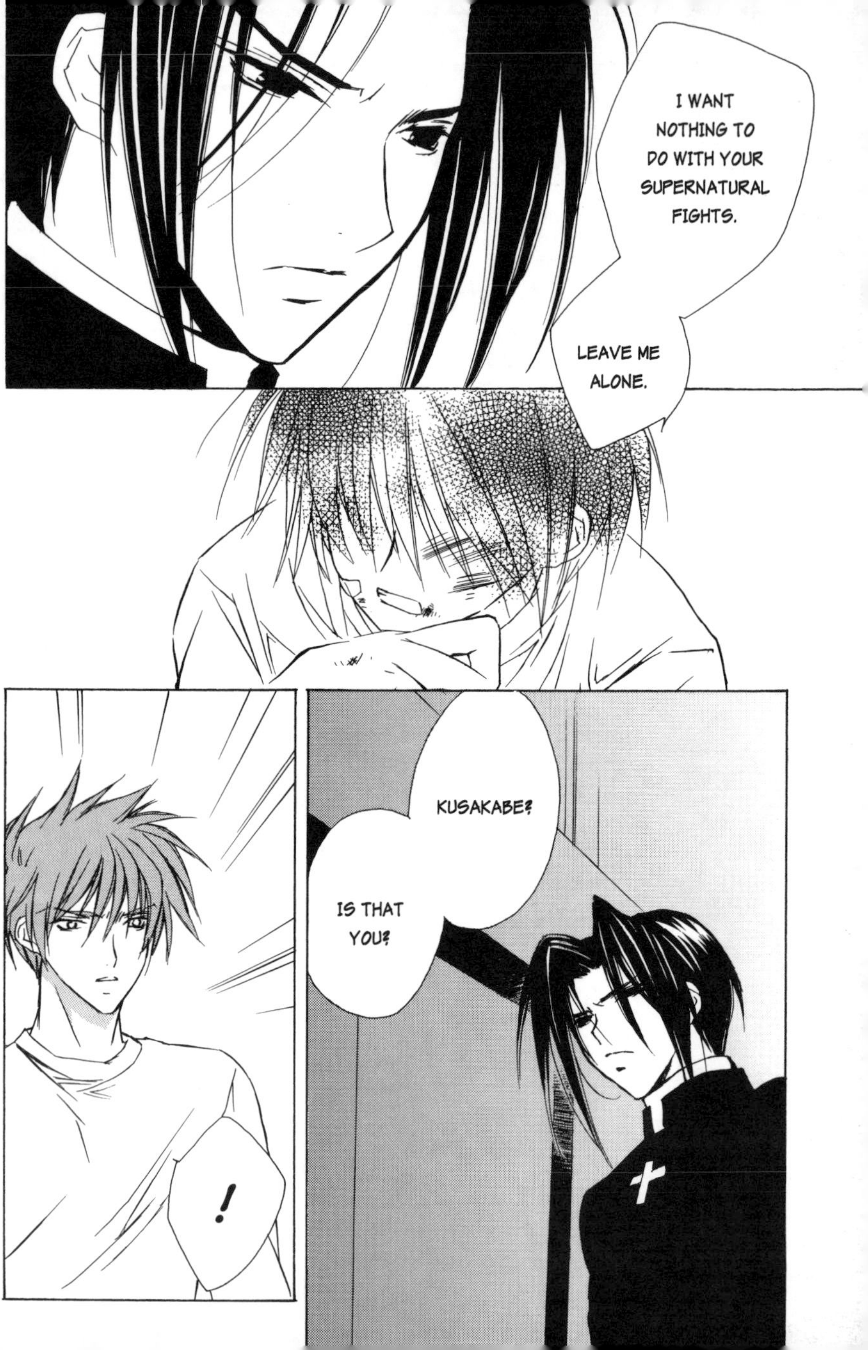
I WANT NOTHING TO DO WITH YOUR SUPERNATURAL FIGHTS.
LEAVE ME ALONE.
KUSAKABE?
IS THAT YOU?
!

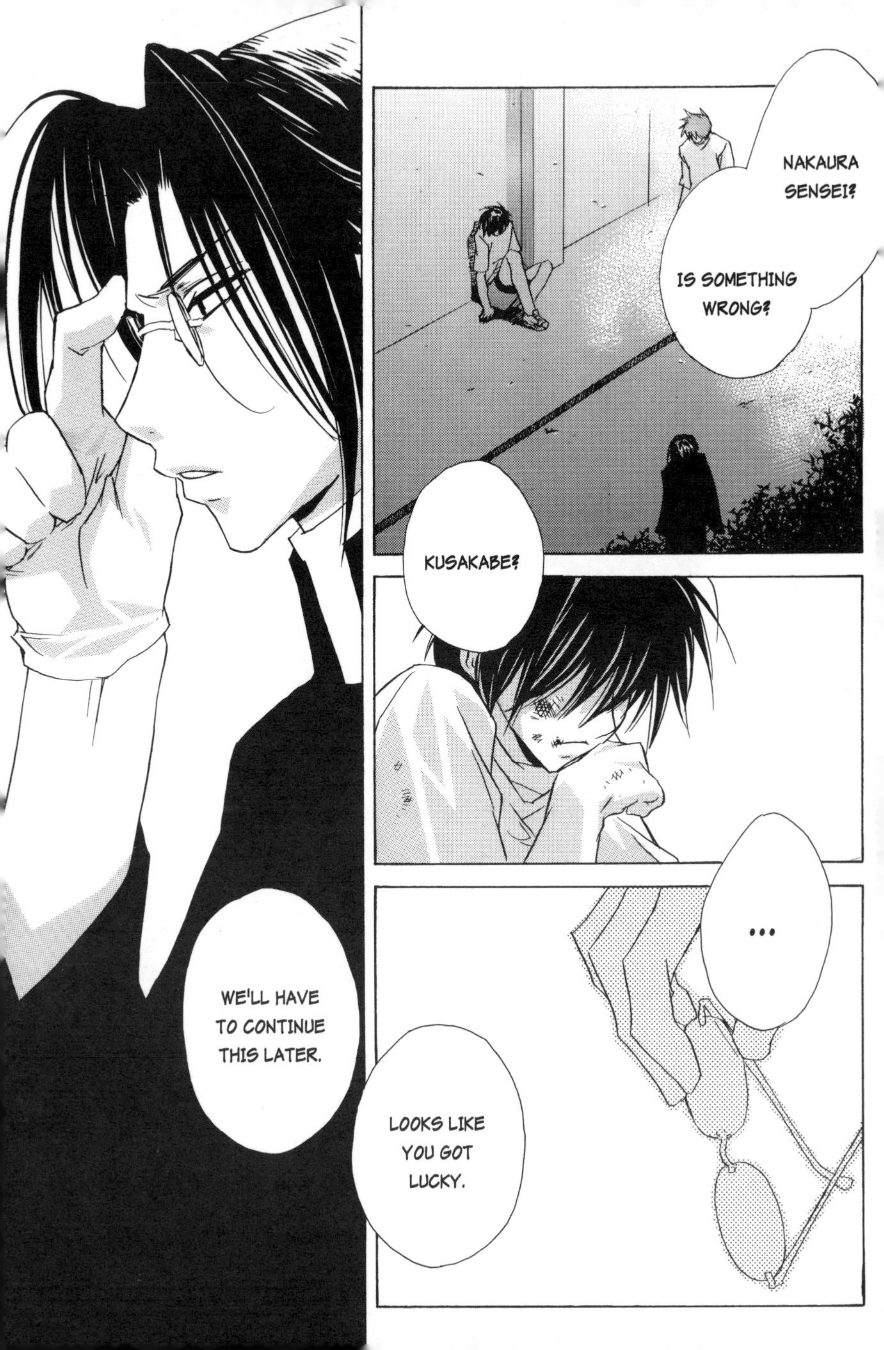
NAKAURA SENSEI?
IS SOMETHING WRONG?
KUSAKABE?
...
WE'LL HAVE TO CONTINUE THIS LATER.
LOOKS LIKE YOU GOT LUCKY.

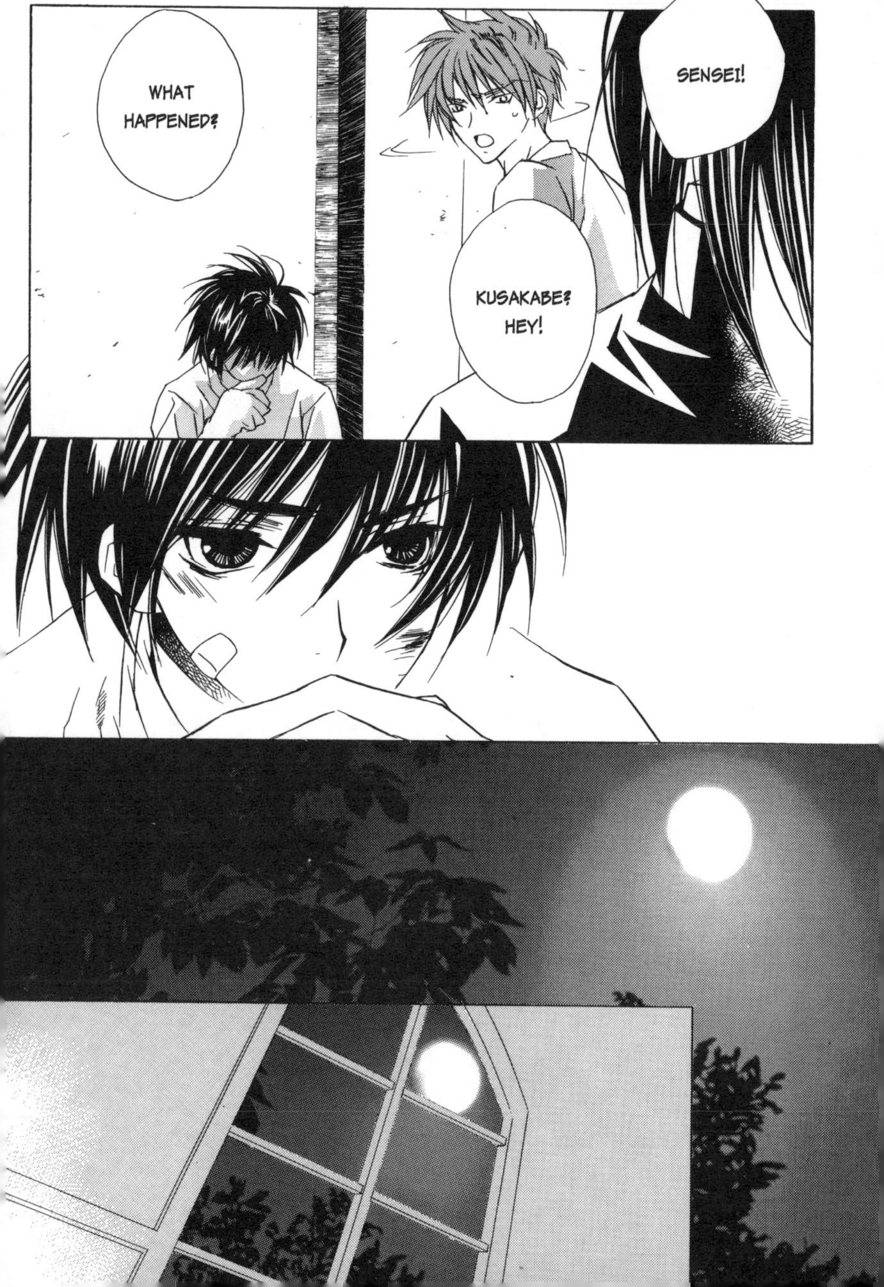
SENSEI!
KUSAKABE? HEY!
WHAT HAPPENED?

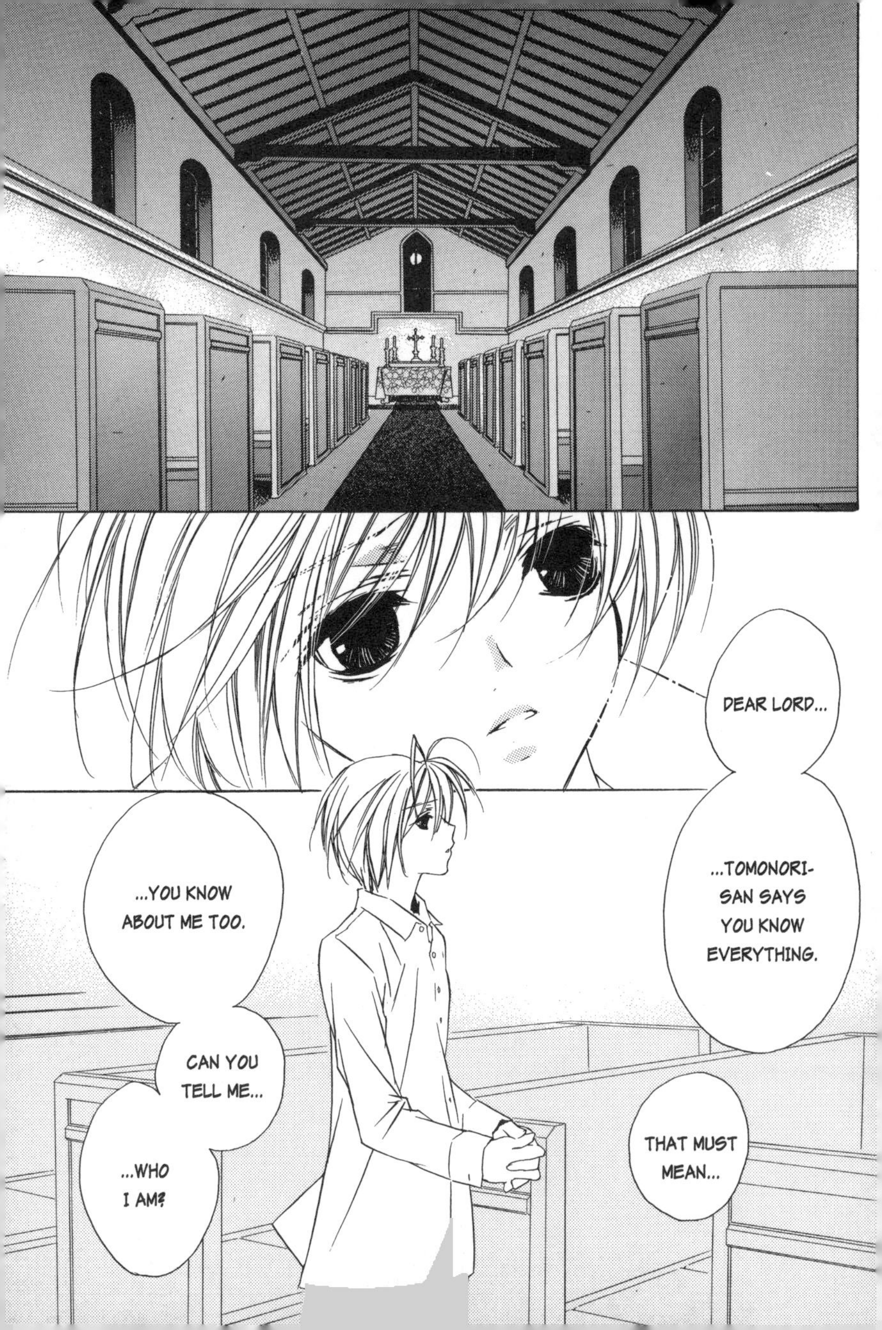
DEAR LORD...
...TOMONORI-SAN SAYS YOU KNOW EVERYTHING.
THAT MUST MEAN...
...YOU KNOW ABOUT ME TOO.
CAN YOU TELL ME...
...WHO I AM?

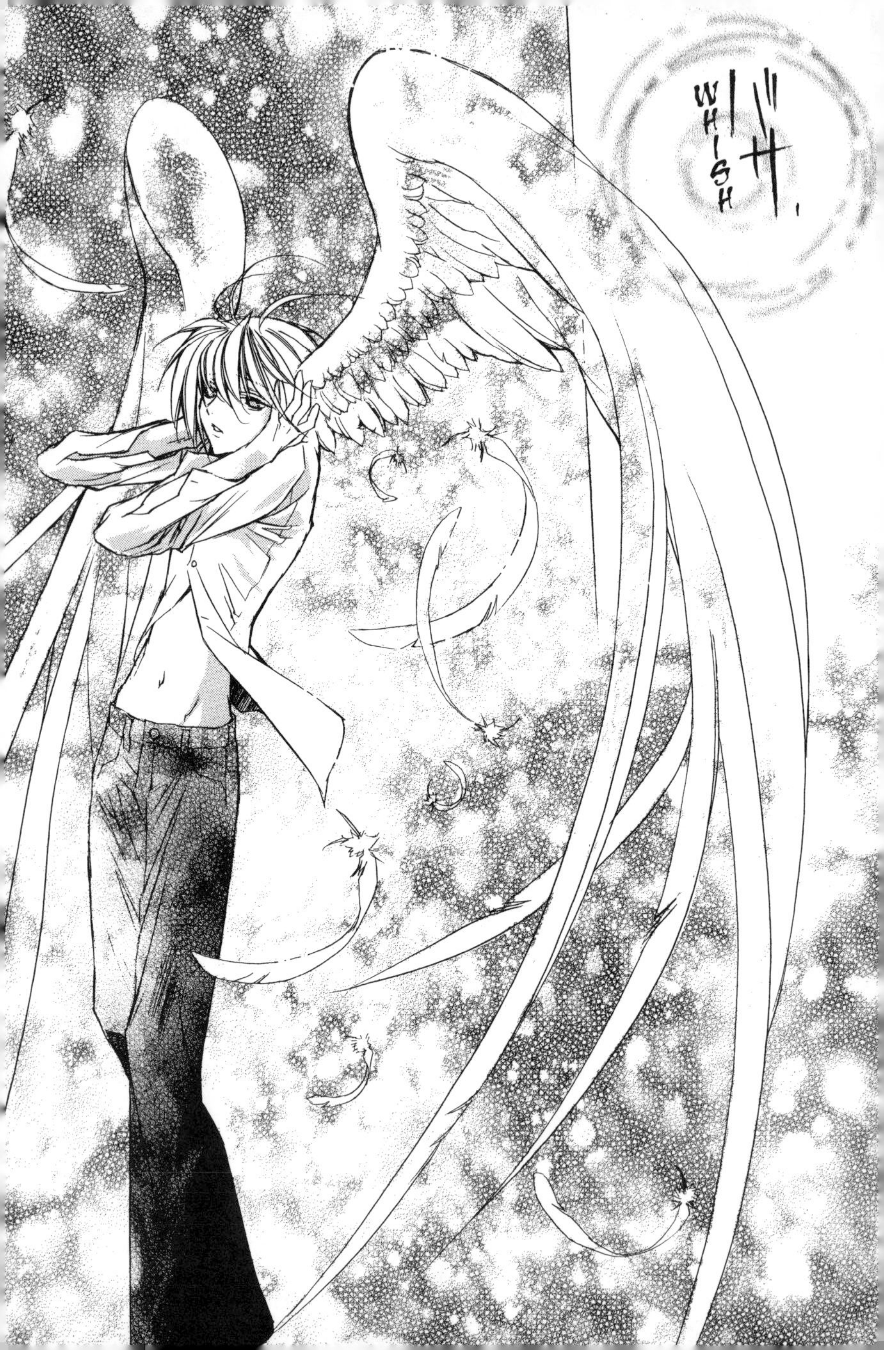
バサ
WHISH

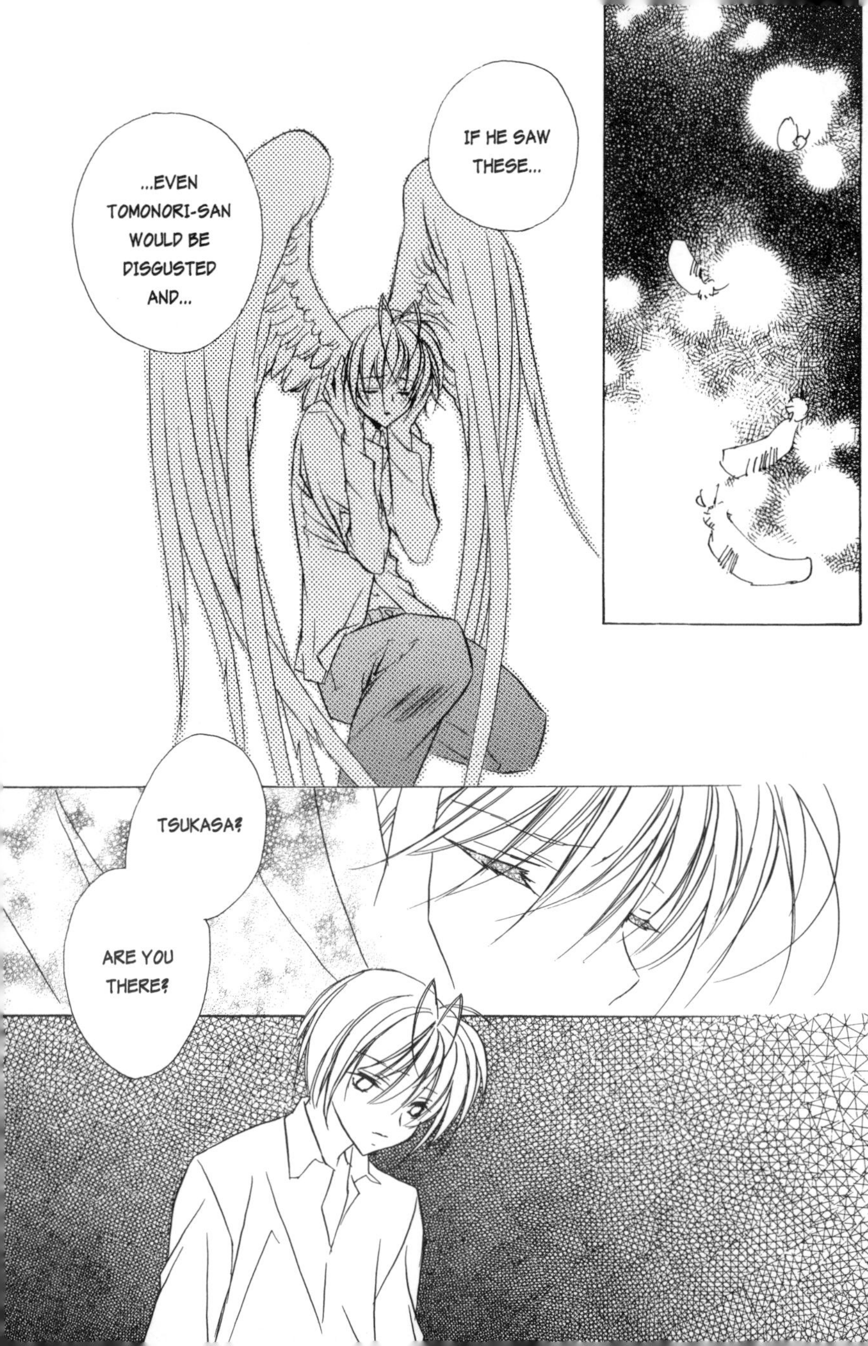
IF HE SAW THESE...
...EVEN TOMONORI-SAN WOULD BE DISGUSTED AND...
TSUKASA?
ARE YOU THERE?

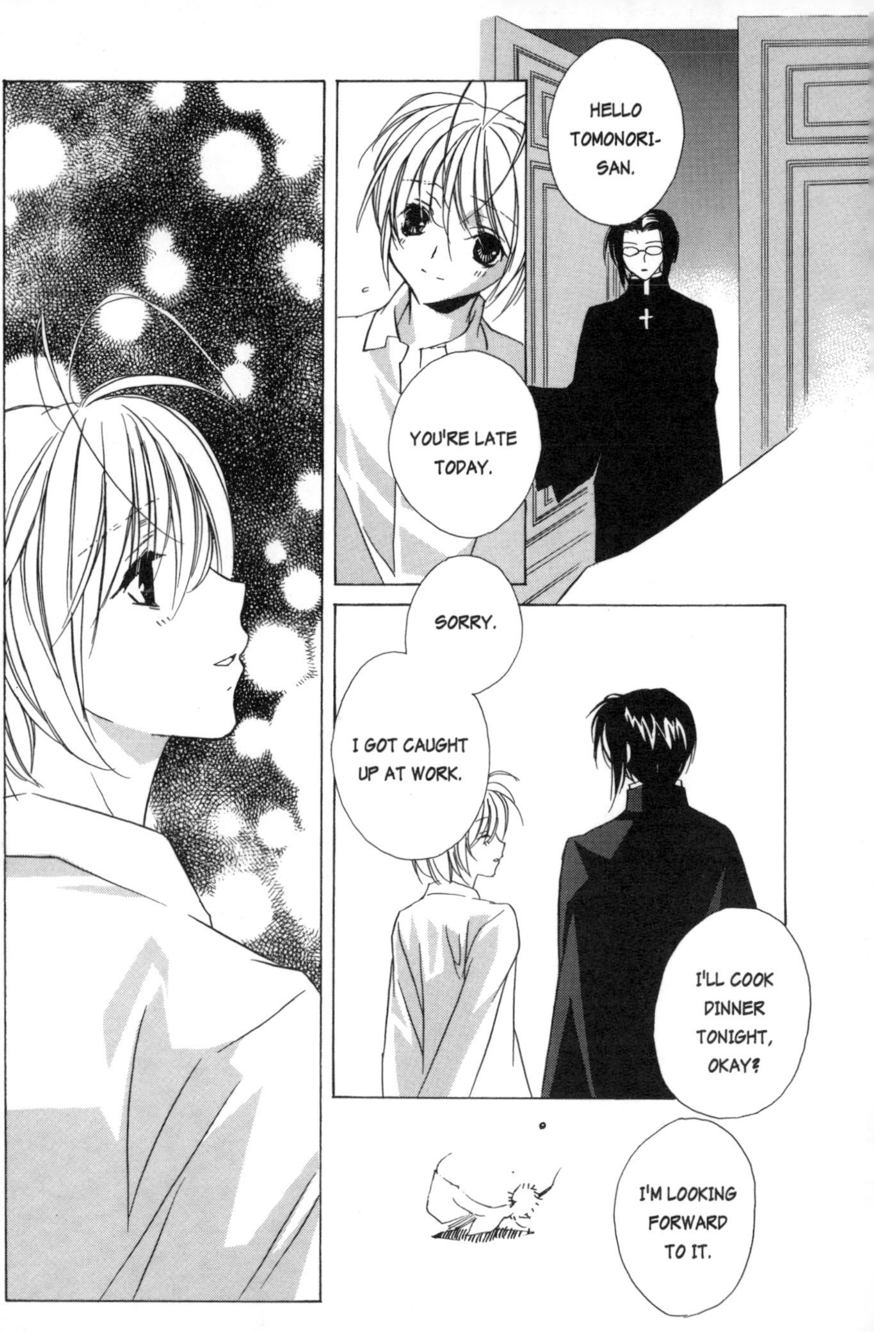
HELLO TOMONORI-SAN.
YOU'RE LATE TODAY.
SORRY.
I GOT CAUGHT UP AT WORK.
I'LL COOK DINNER TONIGHT, OKAY?
I'M LOOKING FORWARD TO IT.

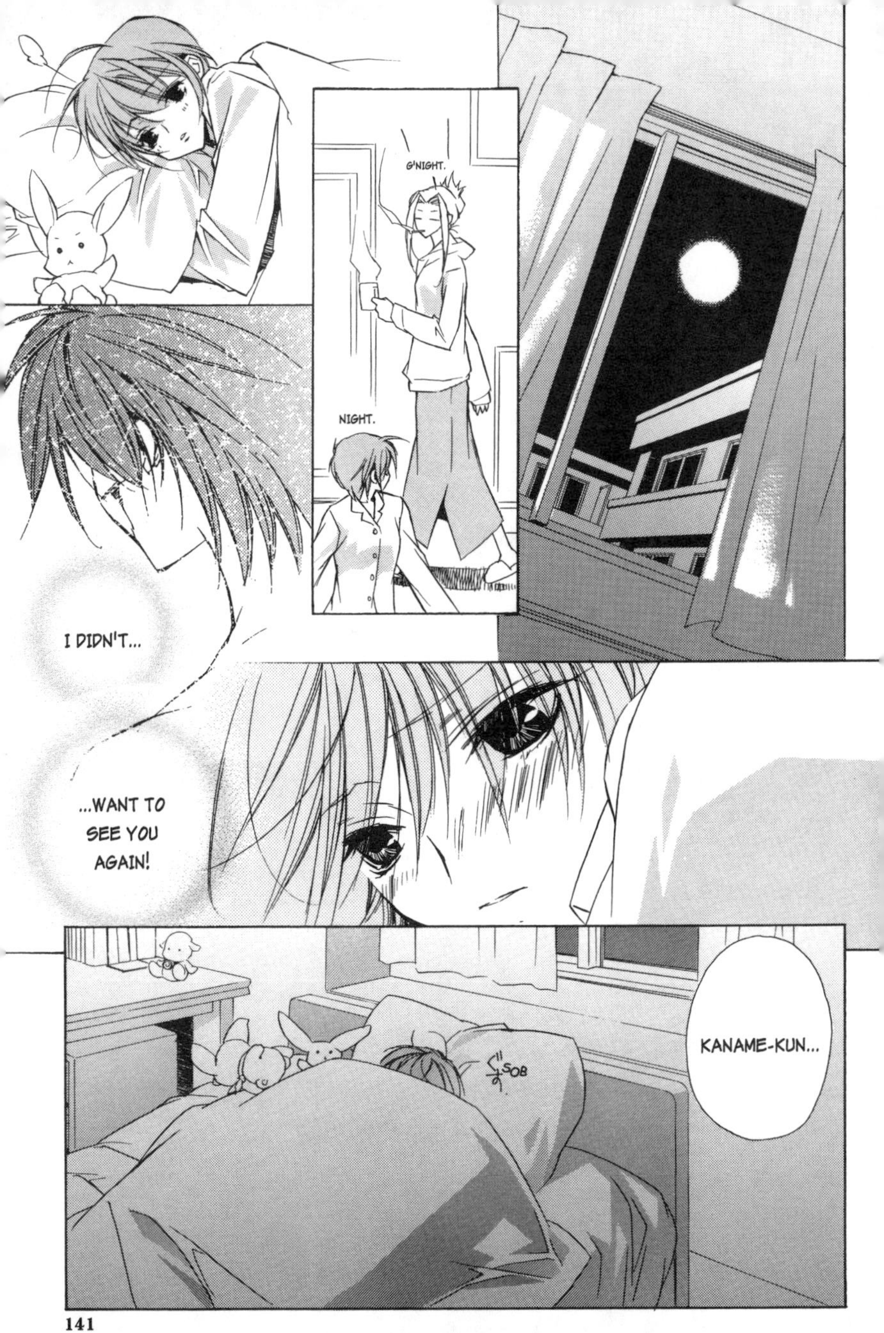
G'NIGHT.
NIGHT.
I DIDN'T...
...WANT TO SEE YOU AGAIN!
SOB
KANAME-KUN...

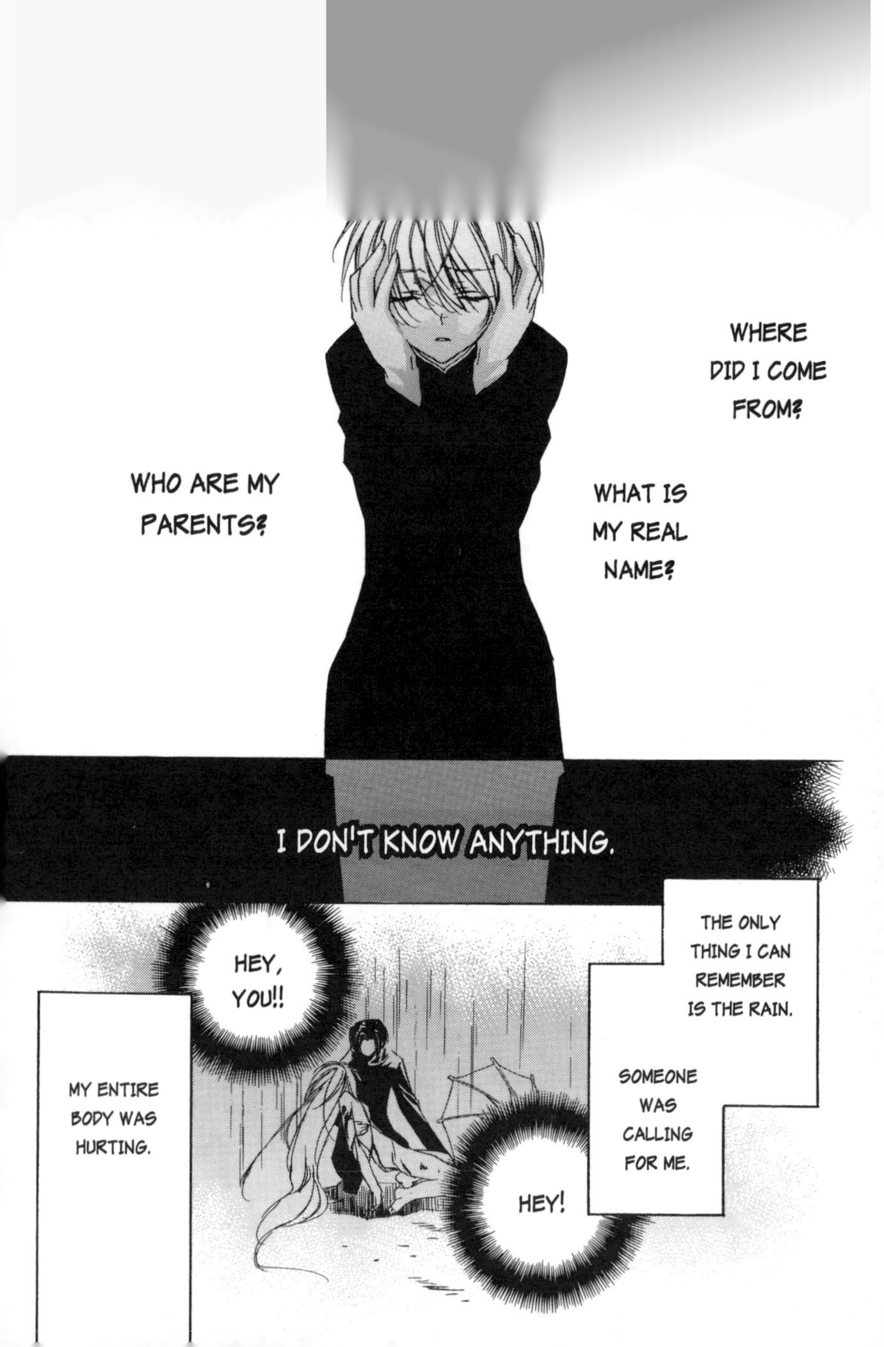
WHERE DID I COME FROM?
WHAT IS MY REAL NAME?
WHO ARE MY PARENTS?
I DON'T KNOW ANYTHING.
THE ONLY THING I CAN REMEMBER IS THE RAIN.
SOMEONE WAS CALLING FOR ME.
HEY, YOU!!
HEY!
MY ENTIRE BODY WAS HURTING.

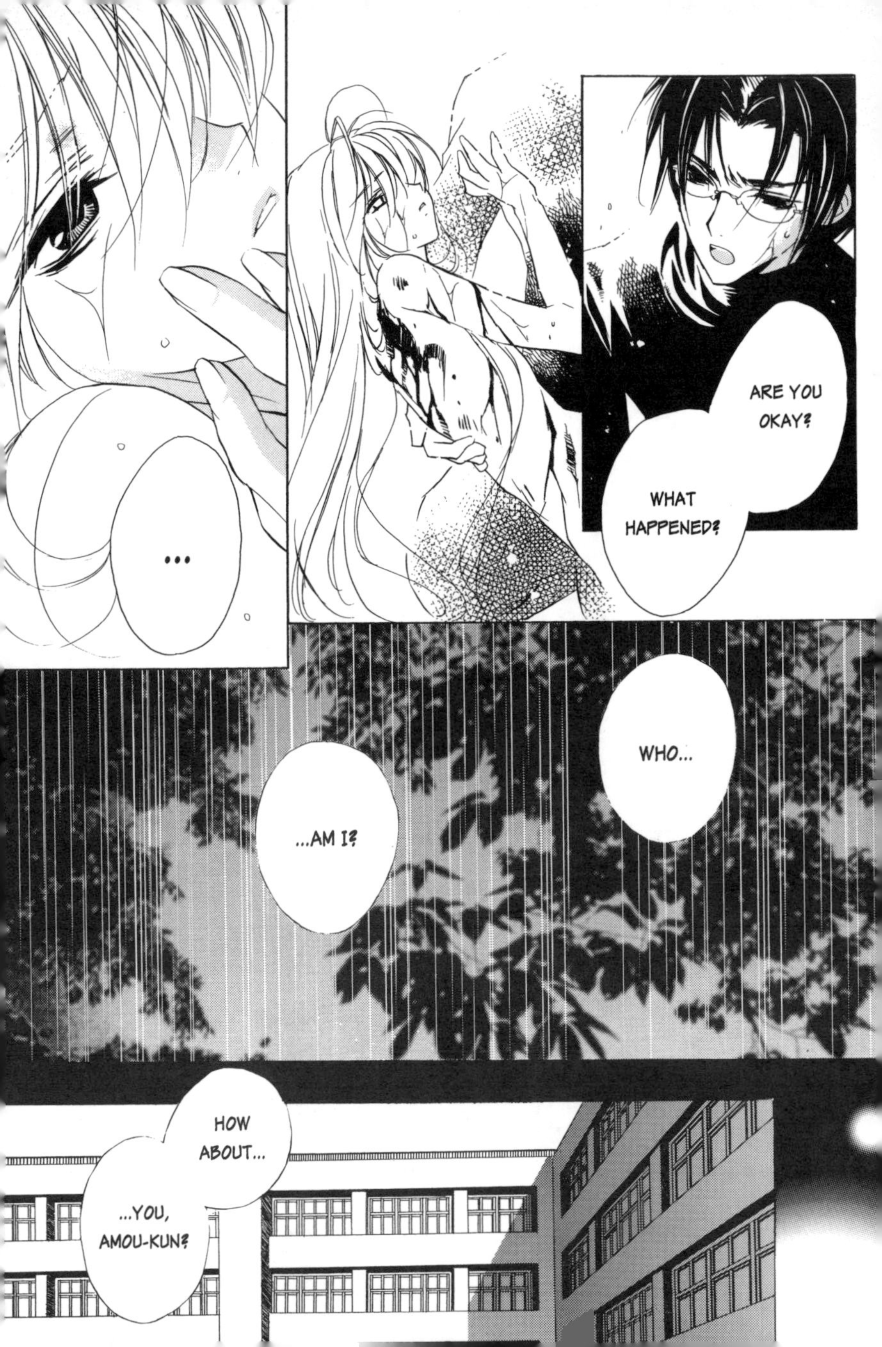
ARE YOU OKAY?
WHAT HAPPENED?
...
WHO...
...AM I?
HOW ABOUT...
...YOU, AMOU-KUN?

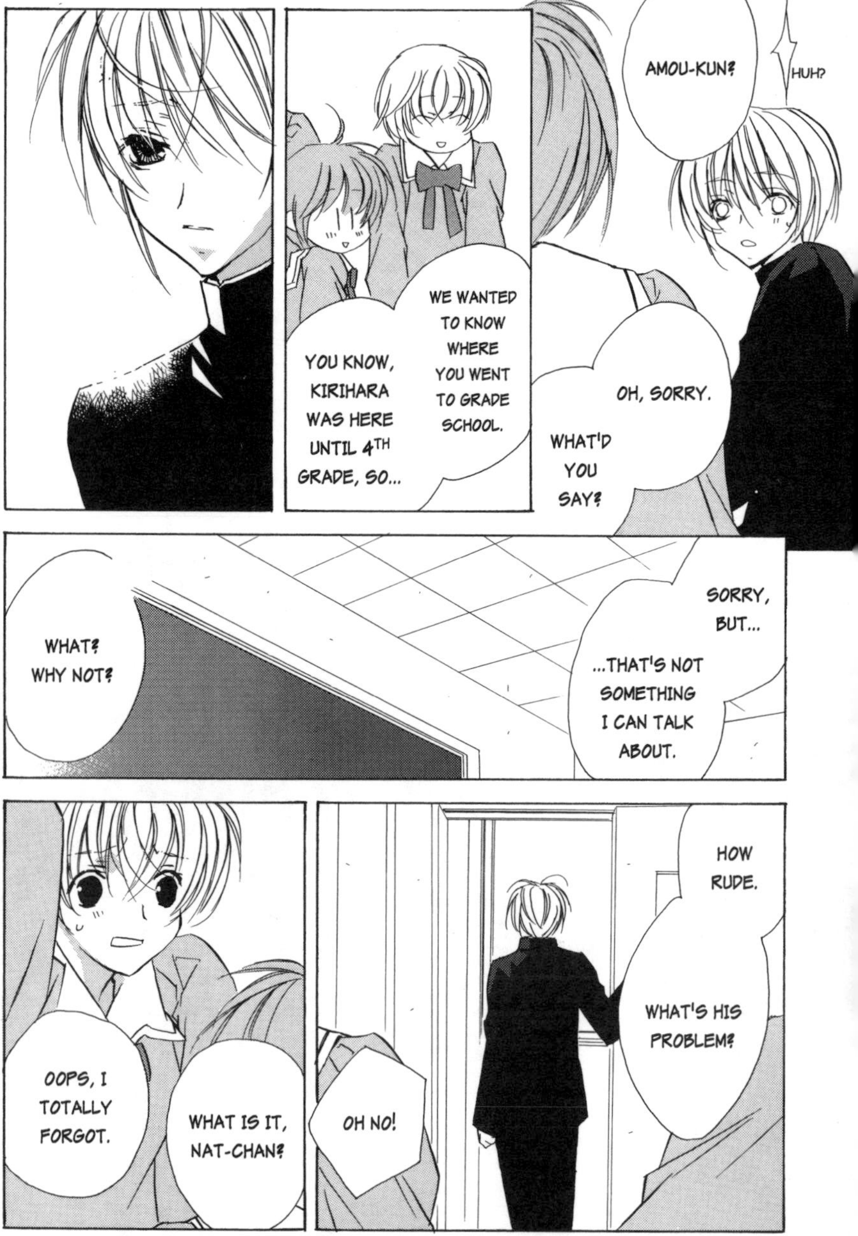
AMOU-KUN?
HUH?
OH, SORRY.
WHAT'D YOU SAY?
WE WANTED TO KNOW WHERE YOU WENT TO GRADE SCHOOL.
YOU KNOW, KIRIHARA WAS HERE UNTIL 4TH GRADE, SO...
SORRY, BUT...
...THAT'S NOT SOMETHING I CAN TALK ABOUT.
WHAT? WHY NOT?
HOW RUDE.
WHAT'S HIS PROBLEM?
OH NO!
WHAT IS IT, NAT-CHAN?
OOPS, I TOTALLY FORGOT.

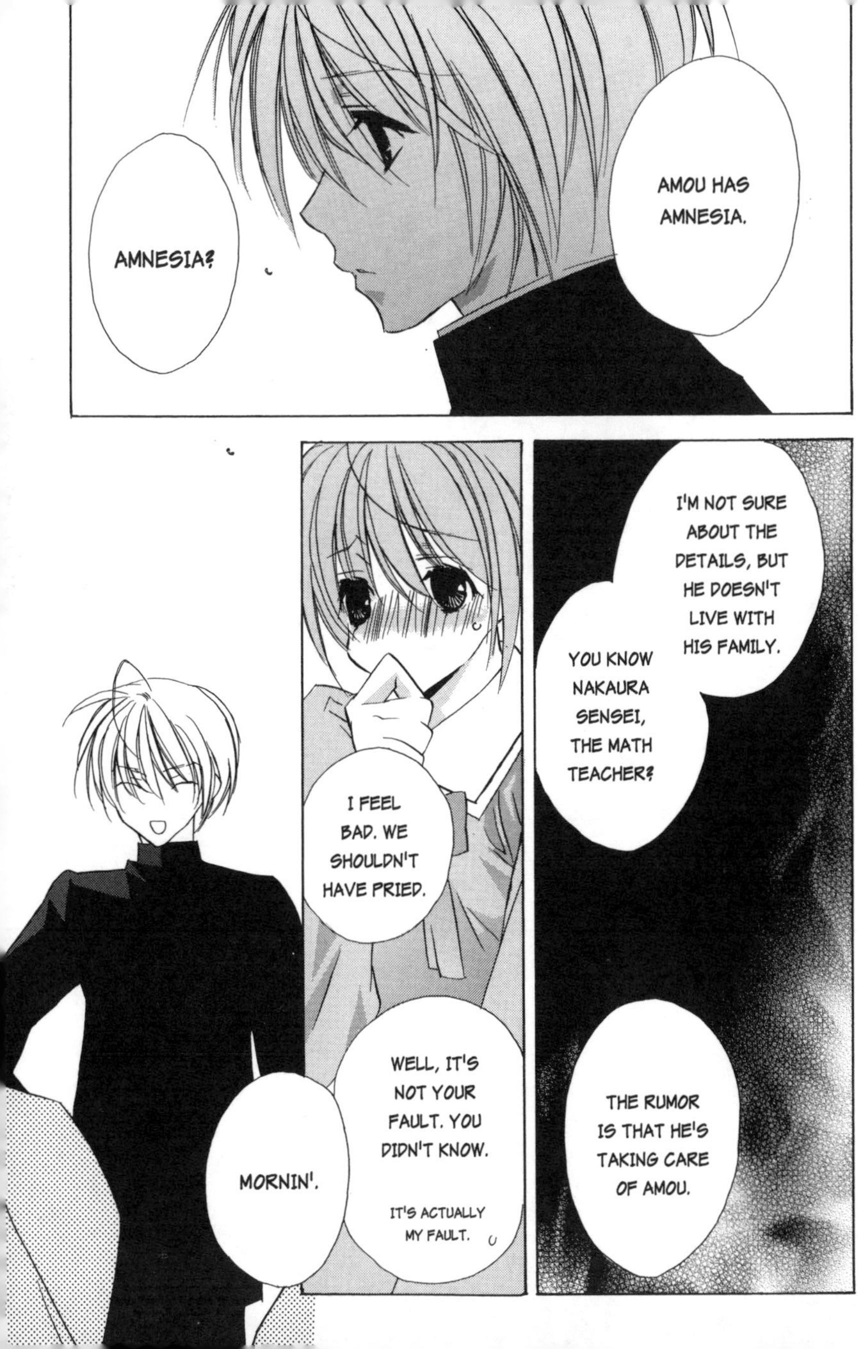
AMOU HAS AMNESIA.
AMNESIA?
I'M NOT SURE ABOUT THE DETAILS, BUT HE DOESN'T LIVE WITH HIS FAMILY.
YOU KNOW NAKAURA SENSEI, THE MATH TEACHER?
THE RUMOR IS THAT HE'S TAKING CARE OF AMOU.
I FEEL BAD. WE SHOULDN'T HAVE PRIED.
WELL, IT'S NOT YOUR FAULT. YOU DIDN'T KNOW.
IT'S ACTUALLY MY FAULT.
MORNIN'.

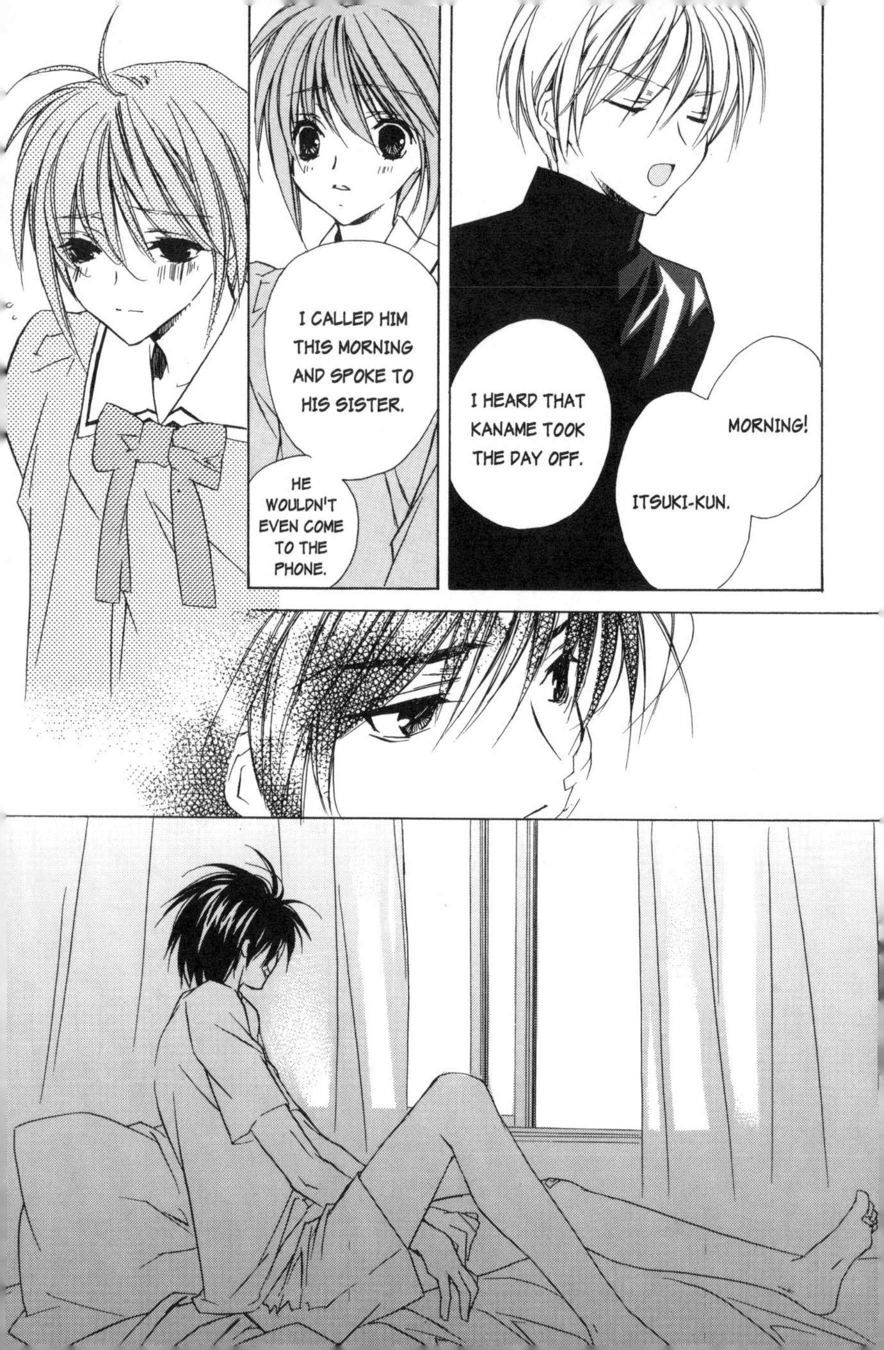
MORNING! ITSUKI-KUN.
I HEARD THAT KANAME TOOK THE DAY OFF.
I CALLED HIM THIS MORNING AND SPOKE TO HIS SISTER.
HE WOULDN'T EVEN COME TO THE PHONE.

turn.6

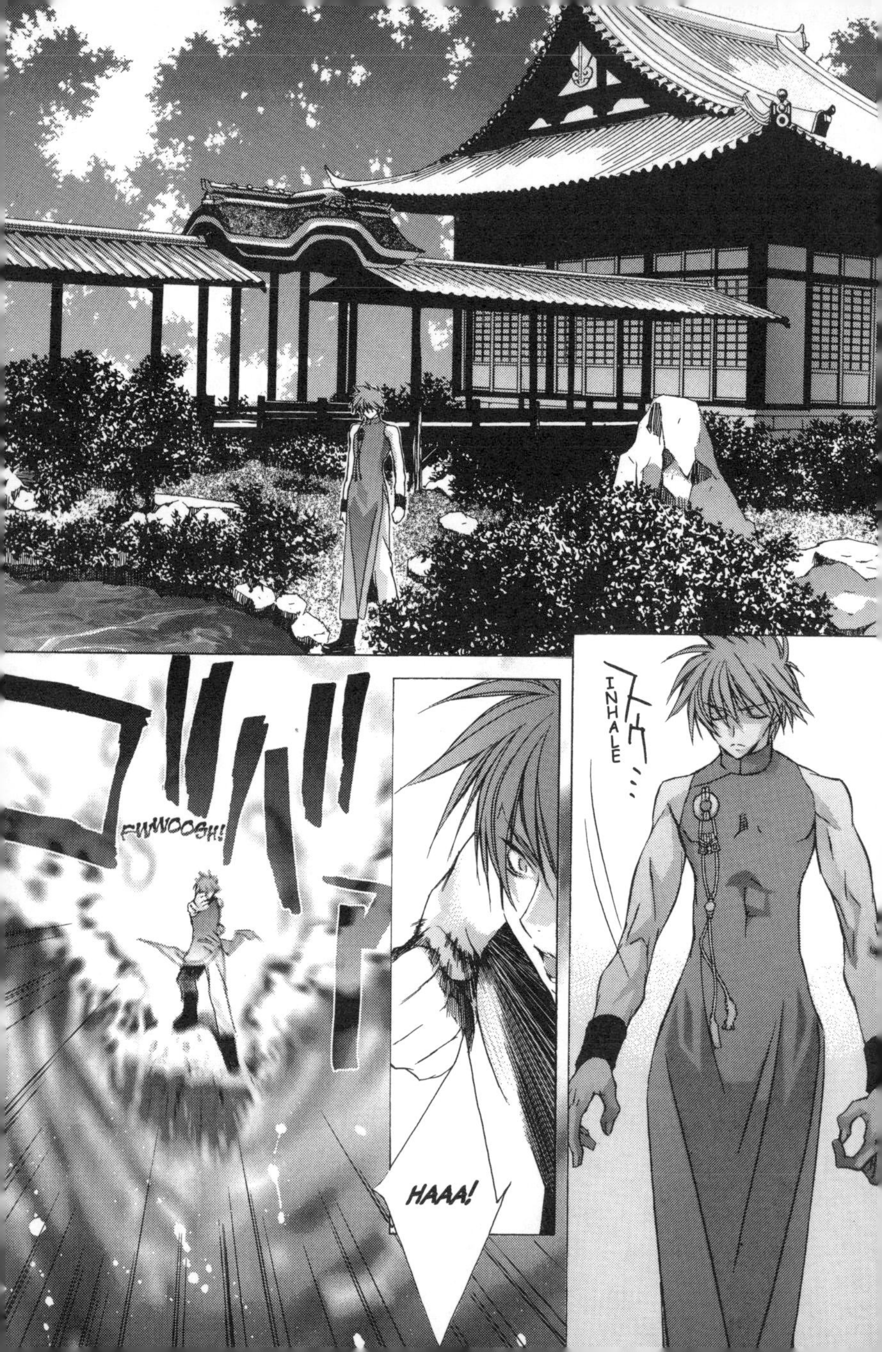
INHALE
HAAA!
FWWOOSH!

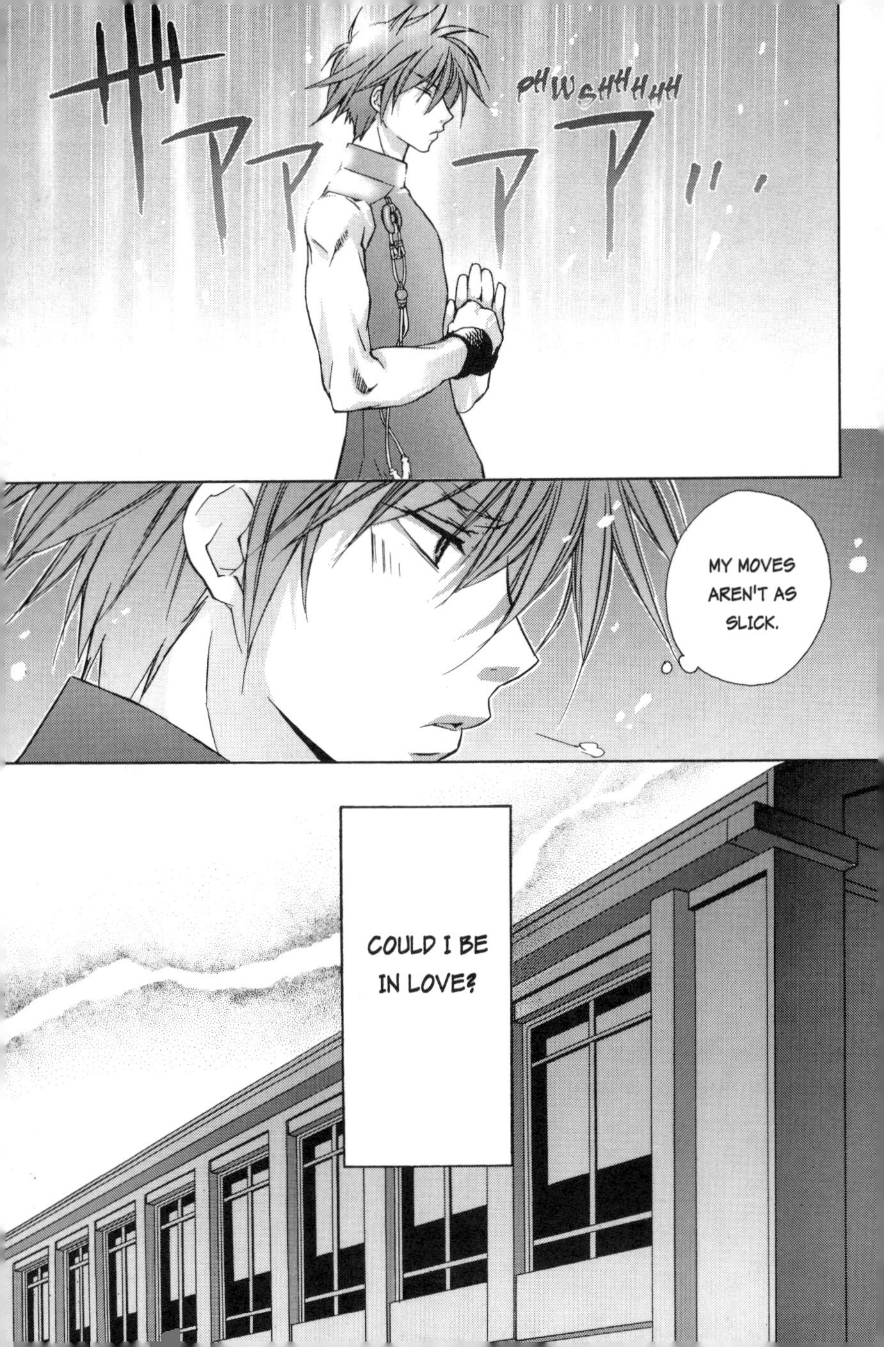
PHWSHHHHH
MY MOVES AREN'T AS SLICK.
COULD I BE IN LOVE?

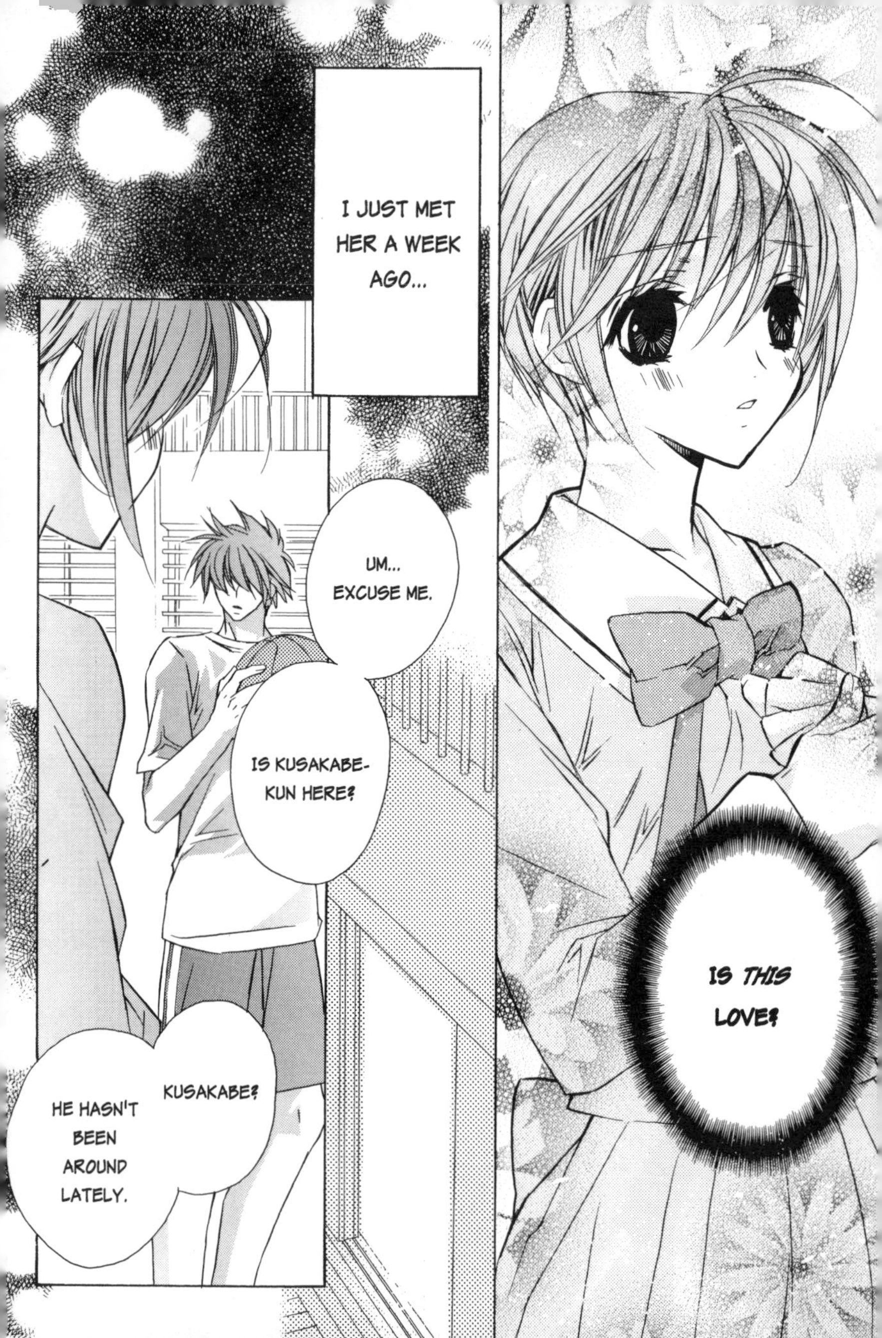
IS THIS LOVE?
I JUST MET HER A WEEK AGO...
UM... EXCUSE ME.
IS KUSAKABE-KUN HERE?
KUSAKABE?
HE HASN'T BEEN AROUND LATELY.

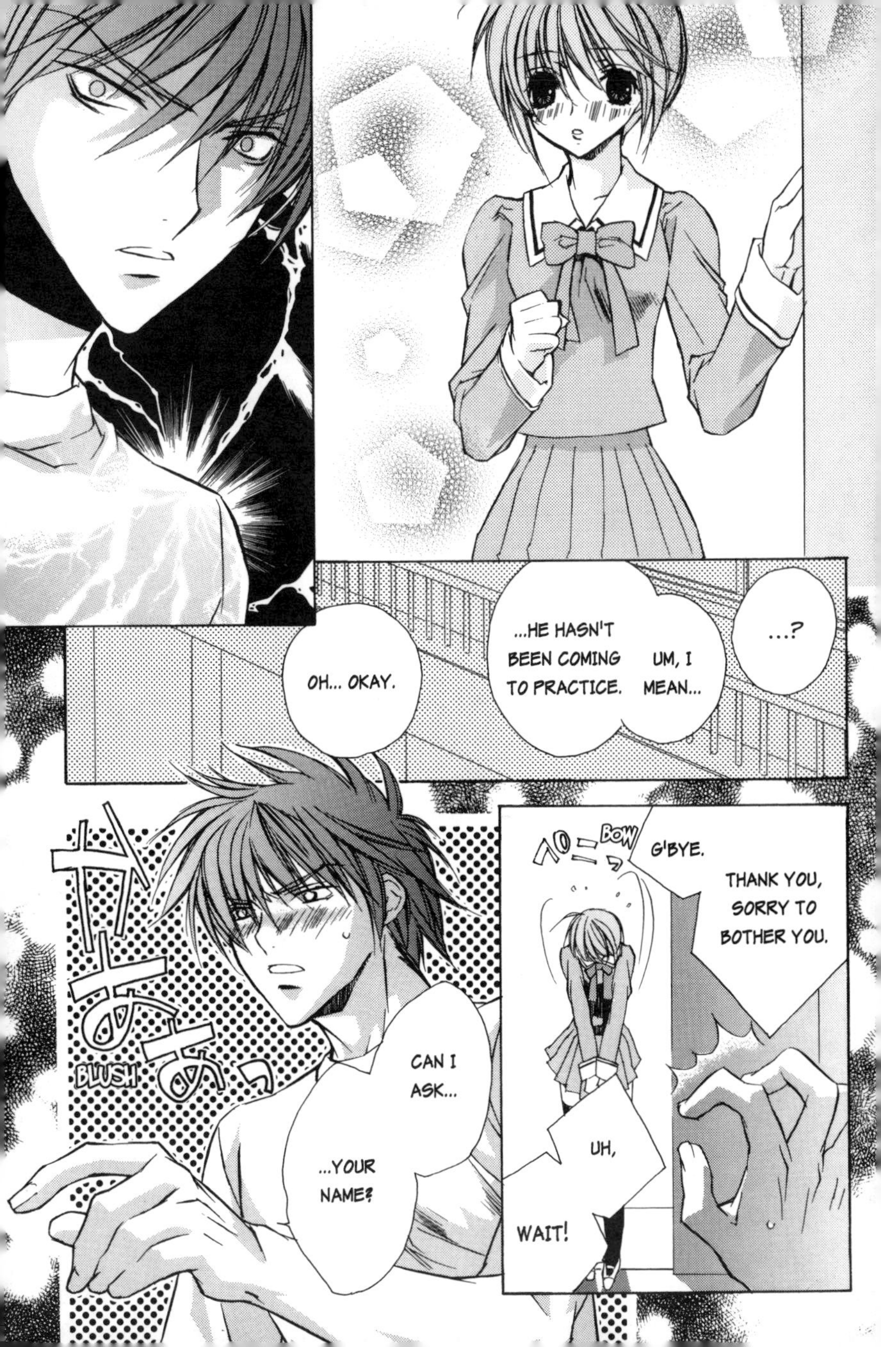
...?
UM, I MEAN...
...HE HASN'T BEEN COMING TO PRACTICE.
OH... OKAY.
THANK YOU, SORRY TO BOTHER YOU.
G'BYE.
BOW
UH,
WAIT!
BLUSH
CAN I ASK...
...YOUR NAME?

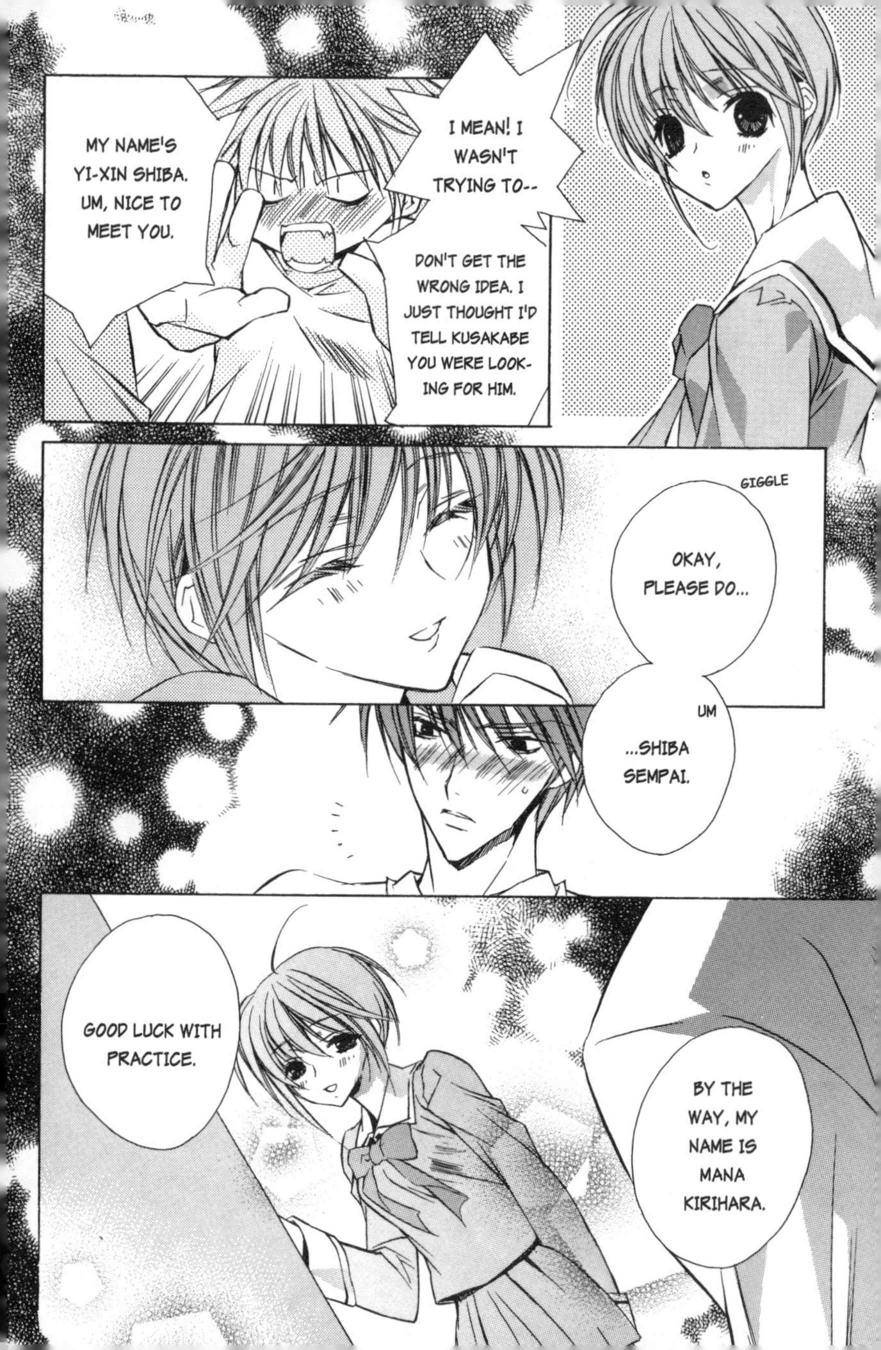
I MEAN! I WASN'T TRYING TO--
DON'T GET THE WRONG IDEA. I JUST THOUGHT I'D TELL KUSAKABE YOU WERE LOOKING FOR HIM.
MY NAME'S YI-XIN SHIBA. UM, NICE TO MEET YOU.
GIGGLE
OKAY, PLEASE DO...
UM
...SHIBA SEMPAI.
BY THE WAY, MY NAME IS MANA KIRIHARA.
GOOD LUCK WITH PRACTICE.

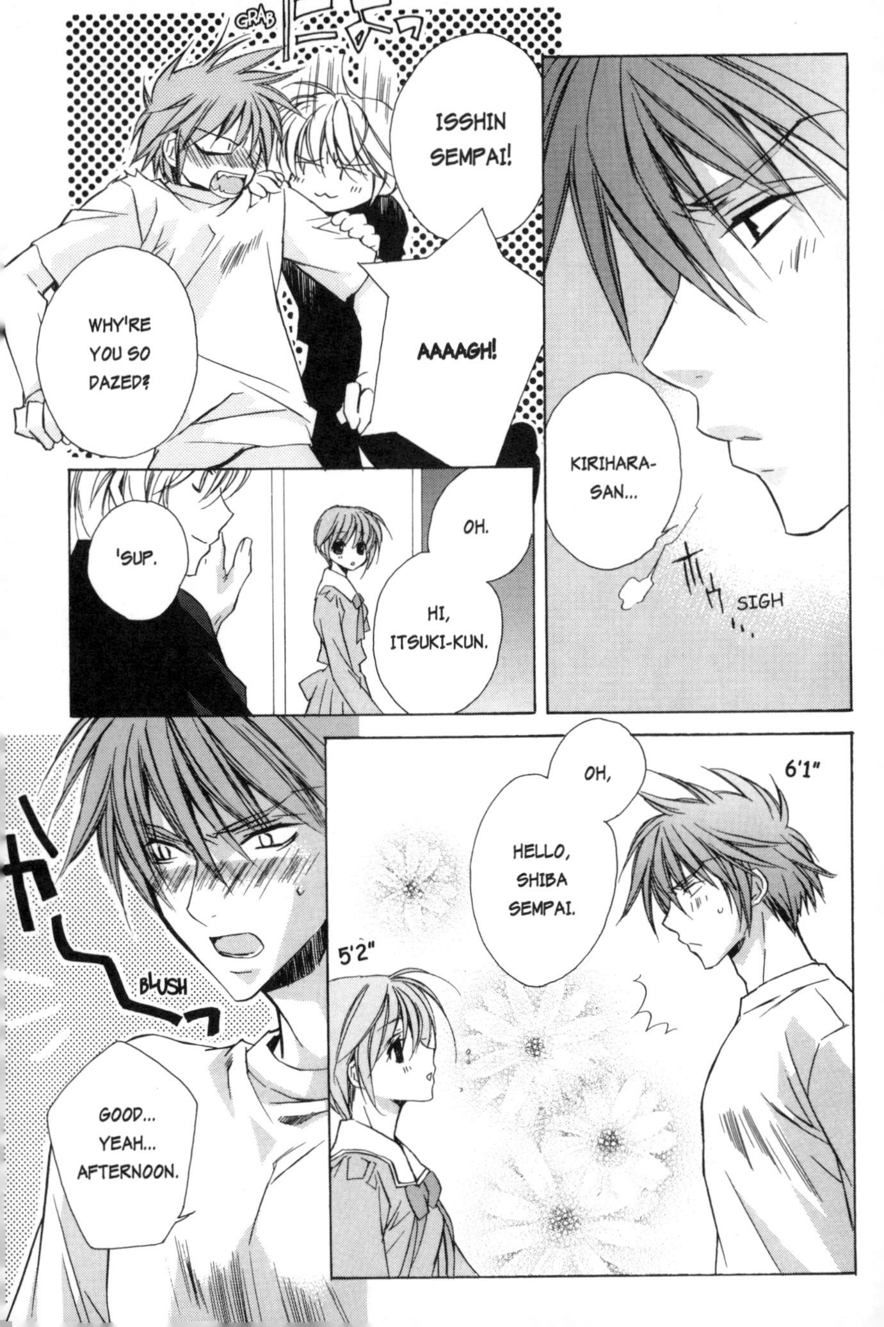
KIRIHARA-SAN...
SIGH
GRAB
ISSHIN SEMPAI!
AAAAGH!
WHY'RE YOU SO DAZED?
OH.
HI, ITSUKI-KUN.
'SUP.
6'1"
OH,
HELLO, SHIBA SEMPAI.
5'2"
BLUSH
GOOD... YEAH... AFTERNOON.

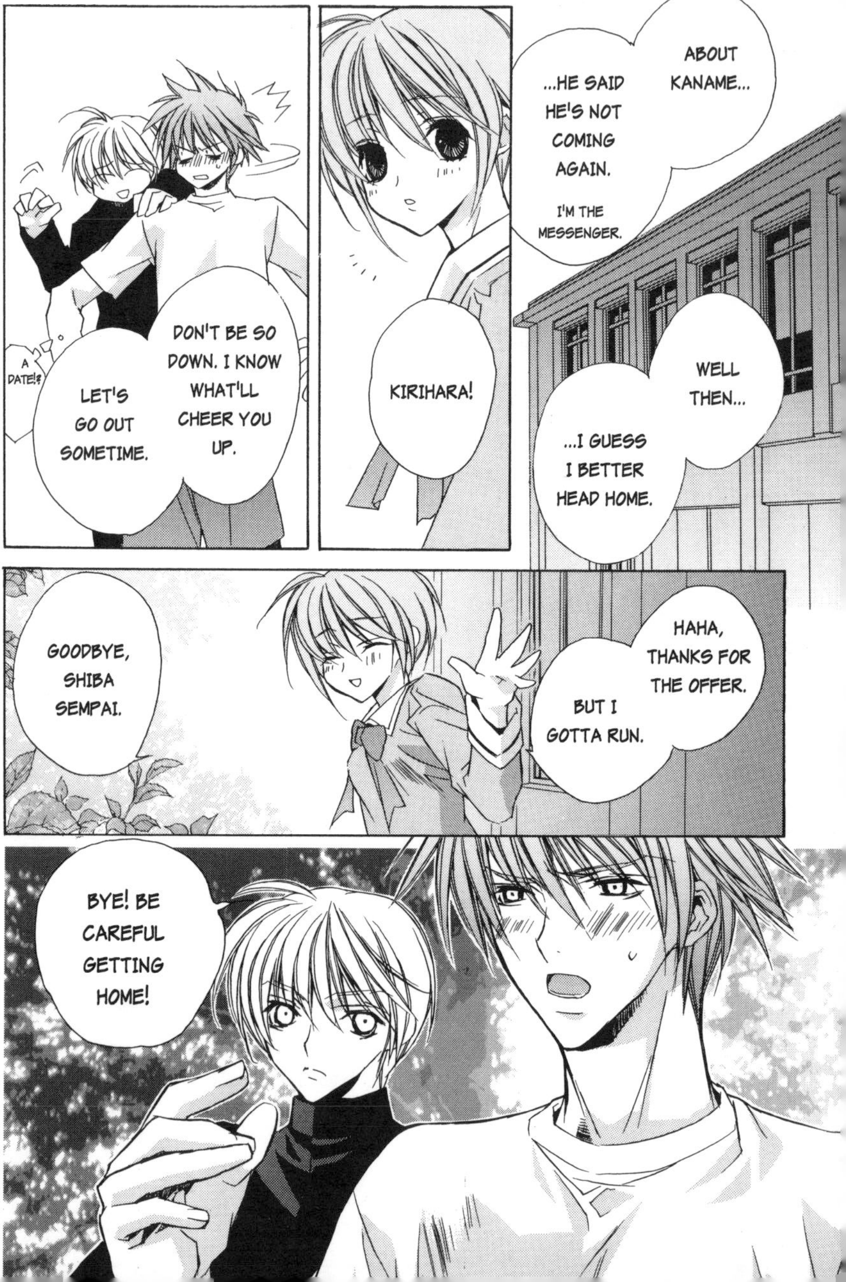
ABOUT KANAME...
...HE SAID HE'S NOT COMING AGAIN.
I'M THE MESSENGER.
WELL THEN...
...I GUESS I BETTER HEAD HOME.
KIRIHARA!
DON'T BE SO DOWN. I KNOW WHAT'LL CHEER YOU UP.
LET'S GO OUT SOMETIME.
A DATE!?
HAHA, THANKS FOR THE OFFER.
BUT I GOTTA RUN.
GOODBYE, SHIBA SEMPAI.
BYE! BE CAREFUL GETTING HOME!

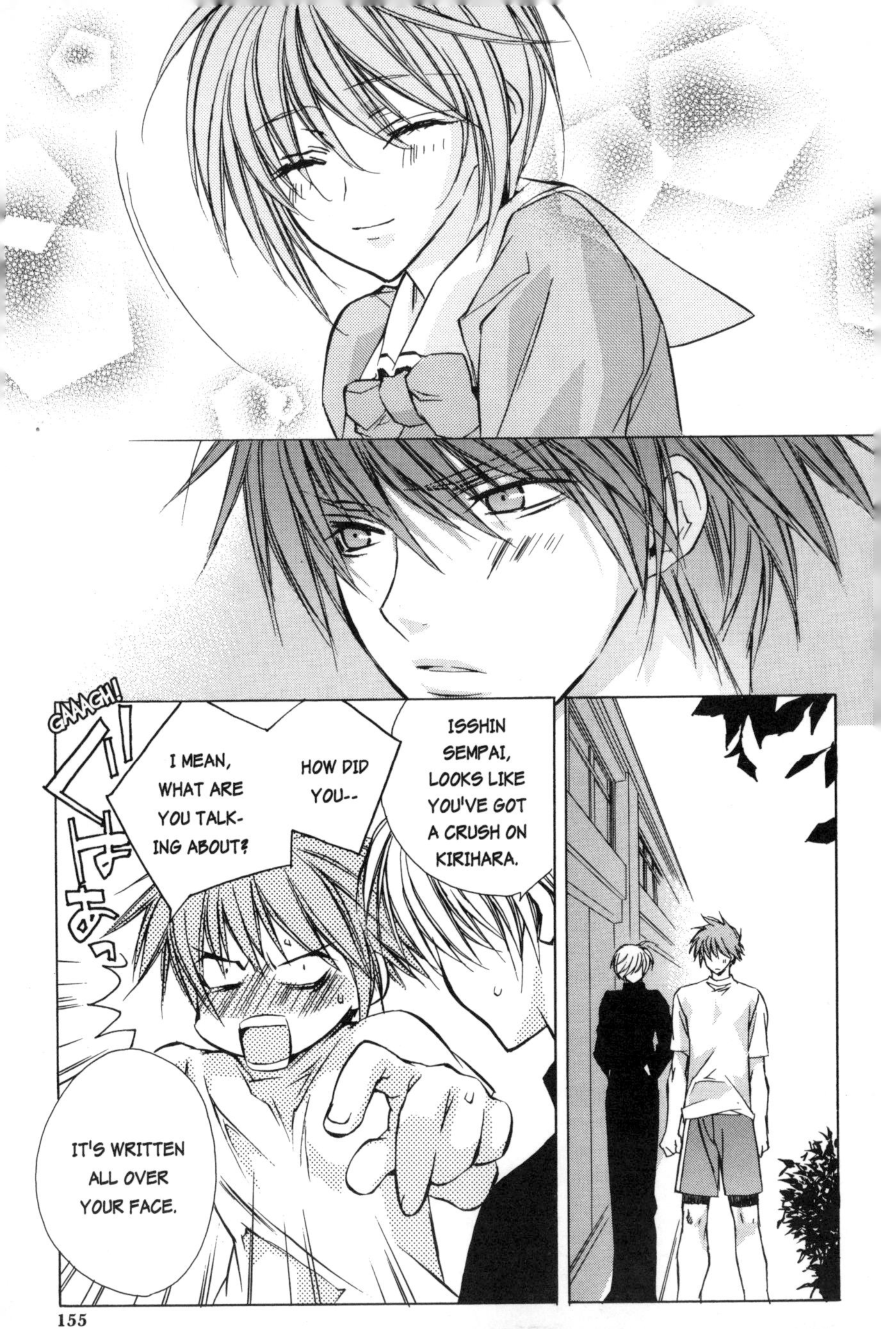
ISSHIN SEMPAI, LOOKS LIKE YOU'VE GOT A CRUSH ON KIRIHARA.
HOW DID YOU--
I MEAN, WHAT ARE YOU TALK-ING ABOUT?
GAAACH!
IT'S WRITTEN ALL OVER YOUR FACE.

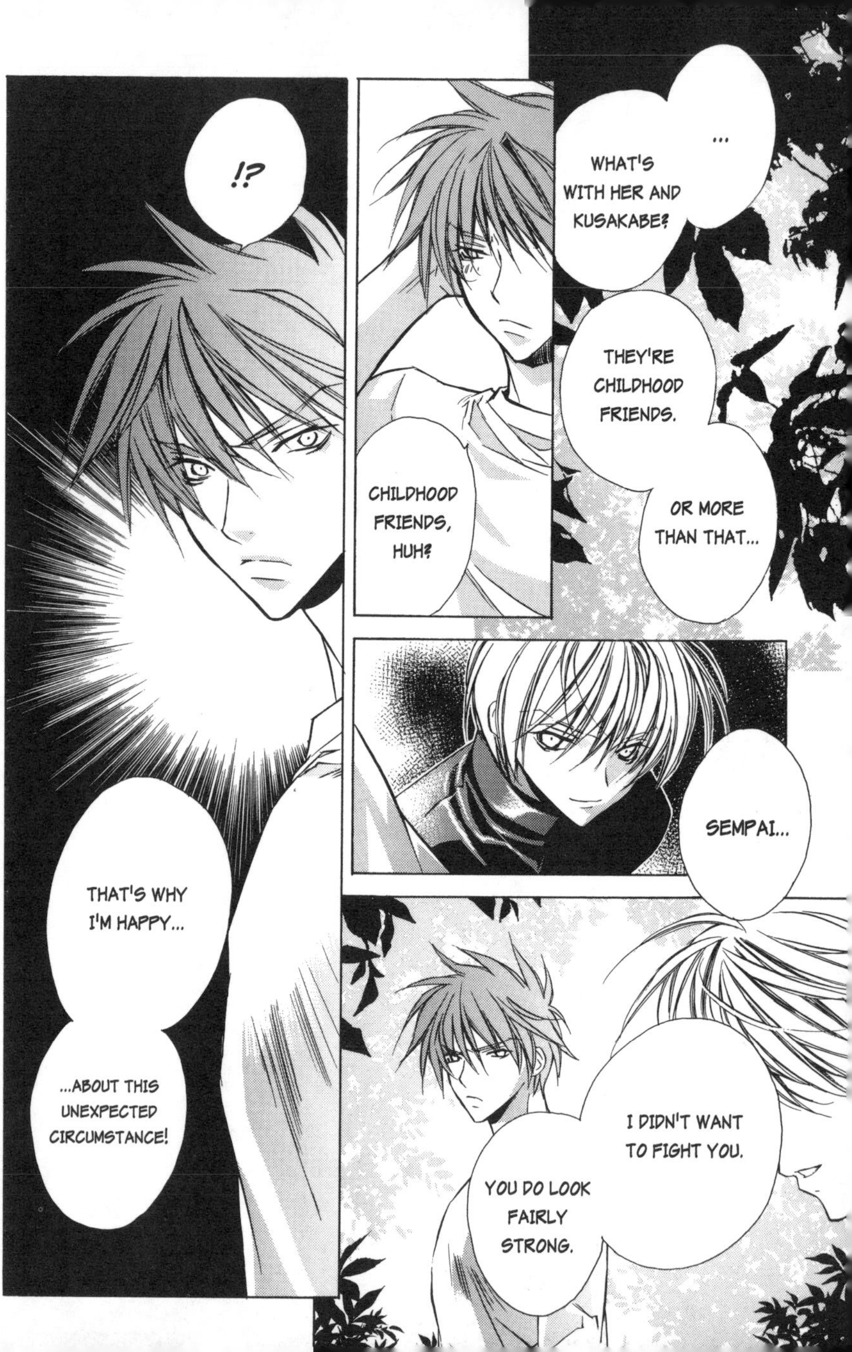
...
WHAT'S WITH HER AND KUSAKABE?
THEY'RE CHILDHOOD FRIENDS.
OR MORE THAN THAT...
CHILDHOOD FRIENDS, HUH?
SEMPAI...
I DIDN'T WANT TO FIGHT YOU.
YOU DO LOOK FAIRLY STRONG.
!?
THAT'S WHY I'M HAPPY...
...ABOUT THIS UNEXPECTED CIRCUMSTANCE!

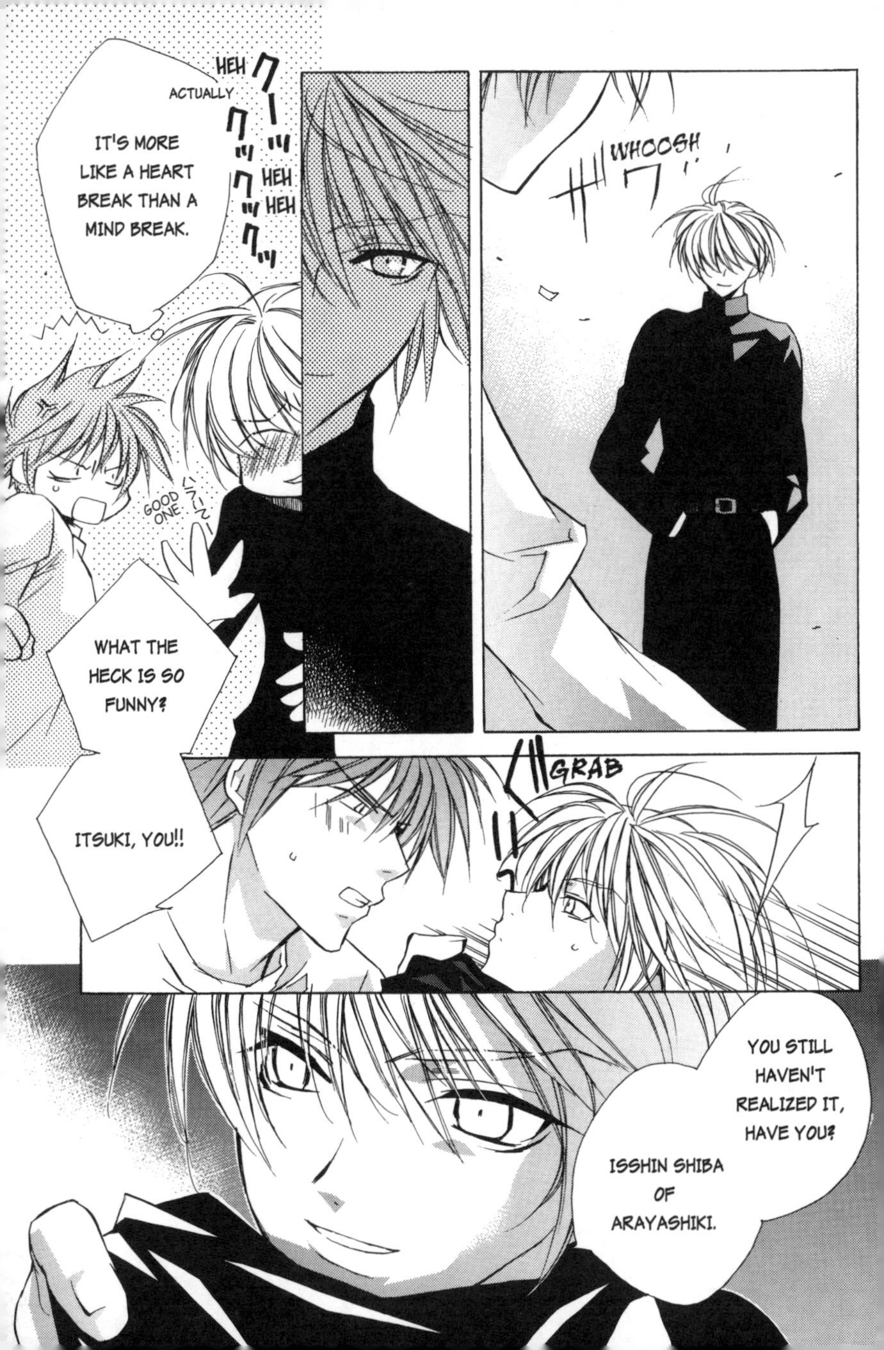
WHOOSH
ACTUALLY
IT'S MORE LIKE A HEART BREAK THAN A MIND BREAK.
HEH HEH HEH
GOOD ONE
WHAT THE HECK IS SO FUNNY?
ITSUKI, YOU!!
GRAB
YOU STILL HAVEN'T REALIZED IT, HAVE YOU?
ISSHIN SHIBA OF ARAYASHIKI.

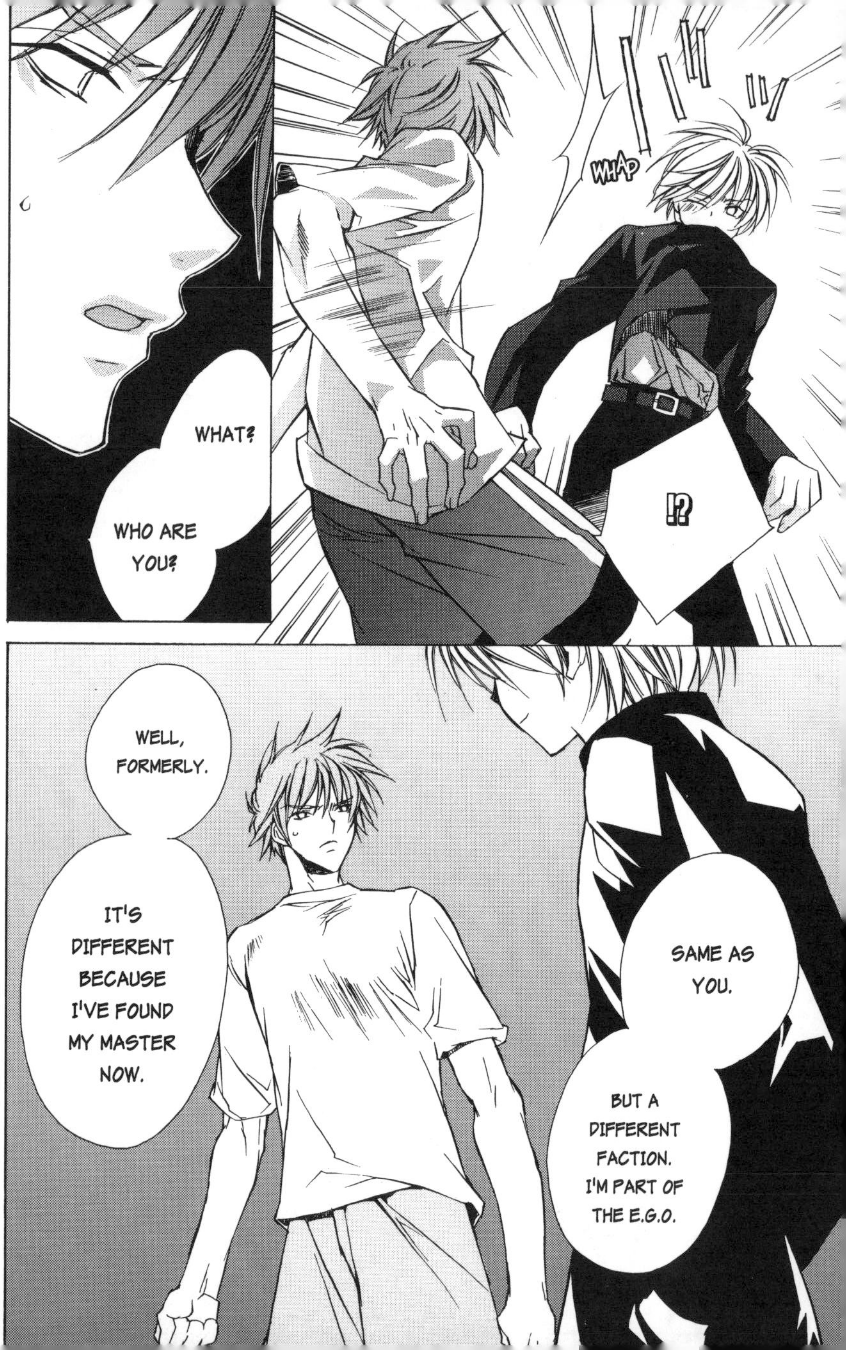
WHAP
!?
WHAT?
WHO ARE YOU?
SAME AS YOU.
BUT A DIFFERENT FACTION. I'M PART OF THE E.G.O.
WELL, FORMERLY.
IT'S DIFFERENT BECAUSE I'VE FOUND MY MASTER NOW.

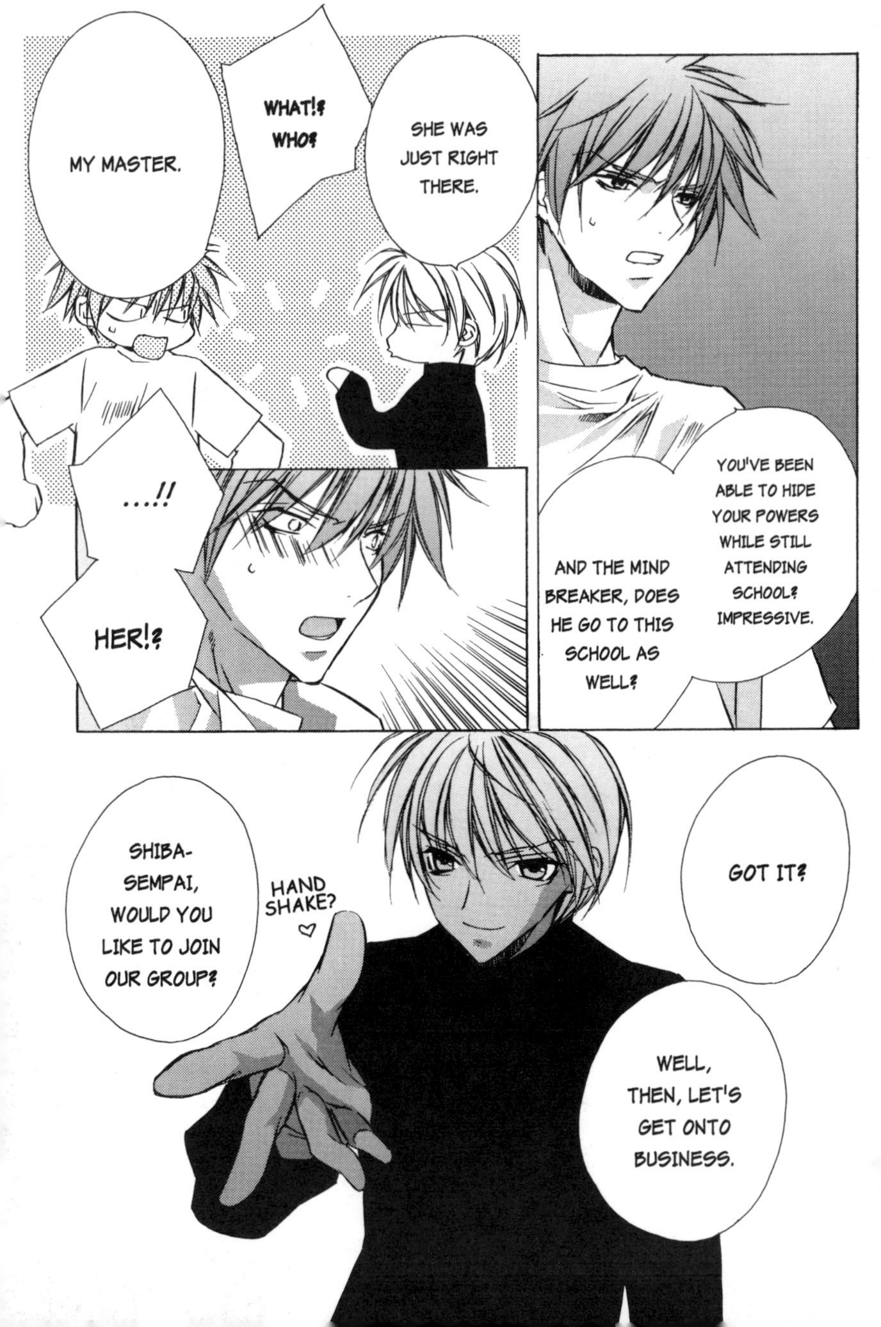
YOU'VE BEEN ABLE TO HIDE YOUR POWERS WHILE STILL ATTENDING SCHOOL? IMPRESSIVE.
AND THE MIND BREAKER, DOES HE GO TO THIS SCHOOL AS WELL?
SHE WAS JUST RIGHT THERE.
WHAT!? WHO?
MY MASTER.
...!!
HER!?
GOT IT?
WELL, THEN, LET'S GET ONTO BUSINESS.
SHIBA-SEMPAI, WOULD YOU LIKE TO JOIN OUR GROUP?
HAND SHAKE? ♡

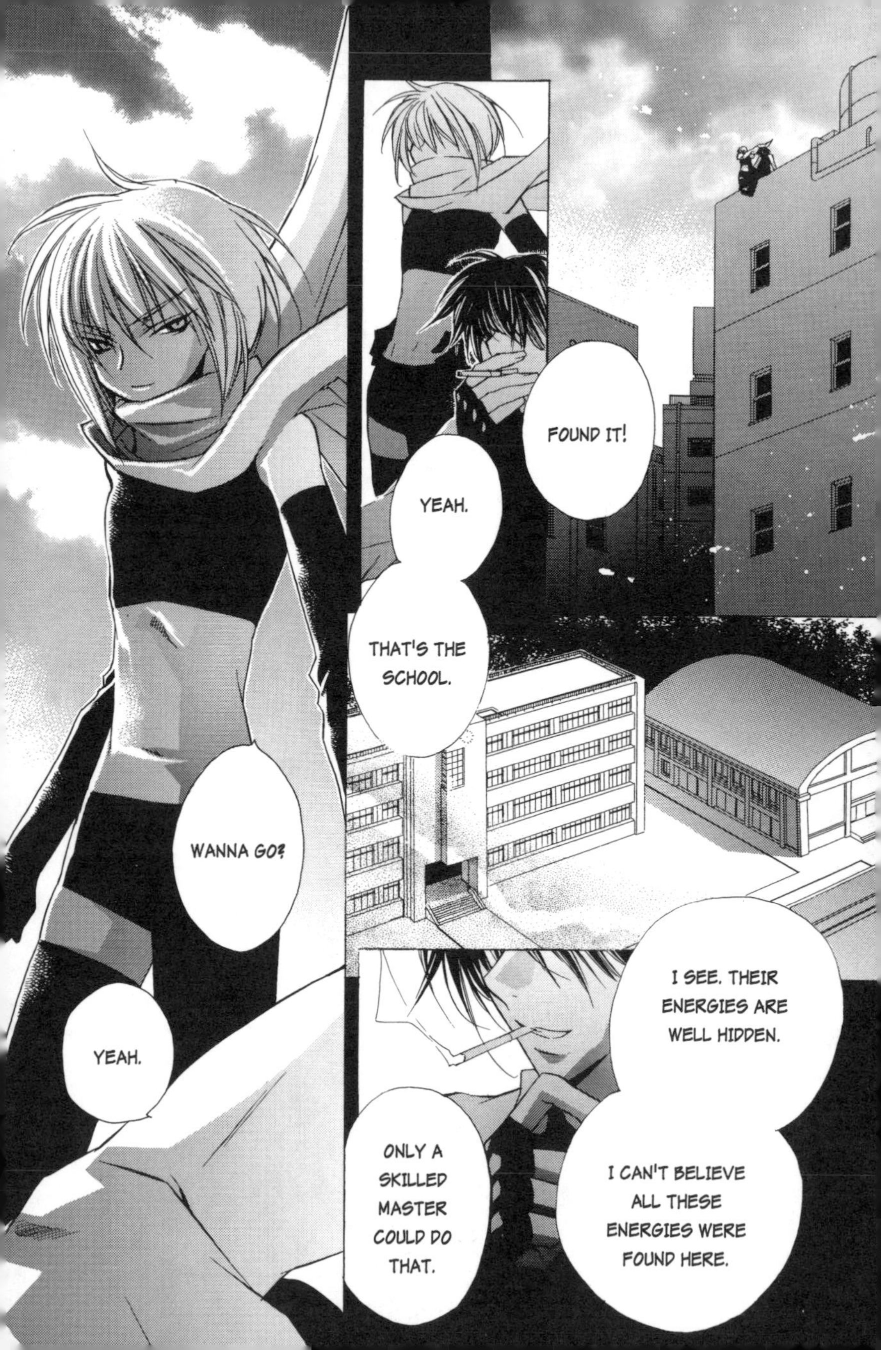
FOUND IT!
YEAH.
THAT'S THE SCHOOL.
I SEE. THEIR ENERGIES ARE WELL HIDDEN.
I CAN'T BELIEVE ALL THESE ENERGIES WERE FOUND HERE.
ONLY A SKILLED MASTER COULD DO THAT.
WANNA GO?
YEAH.

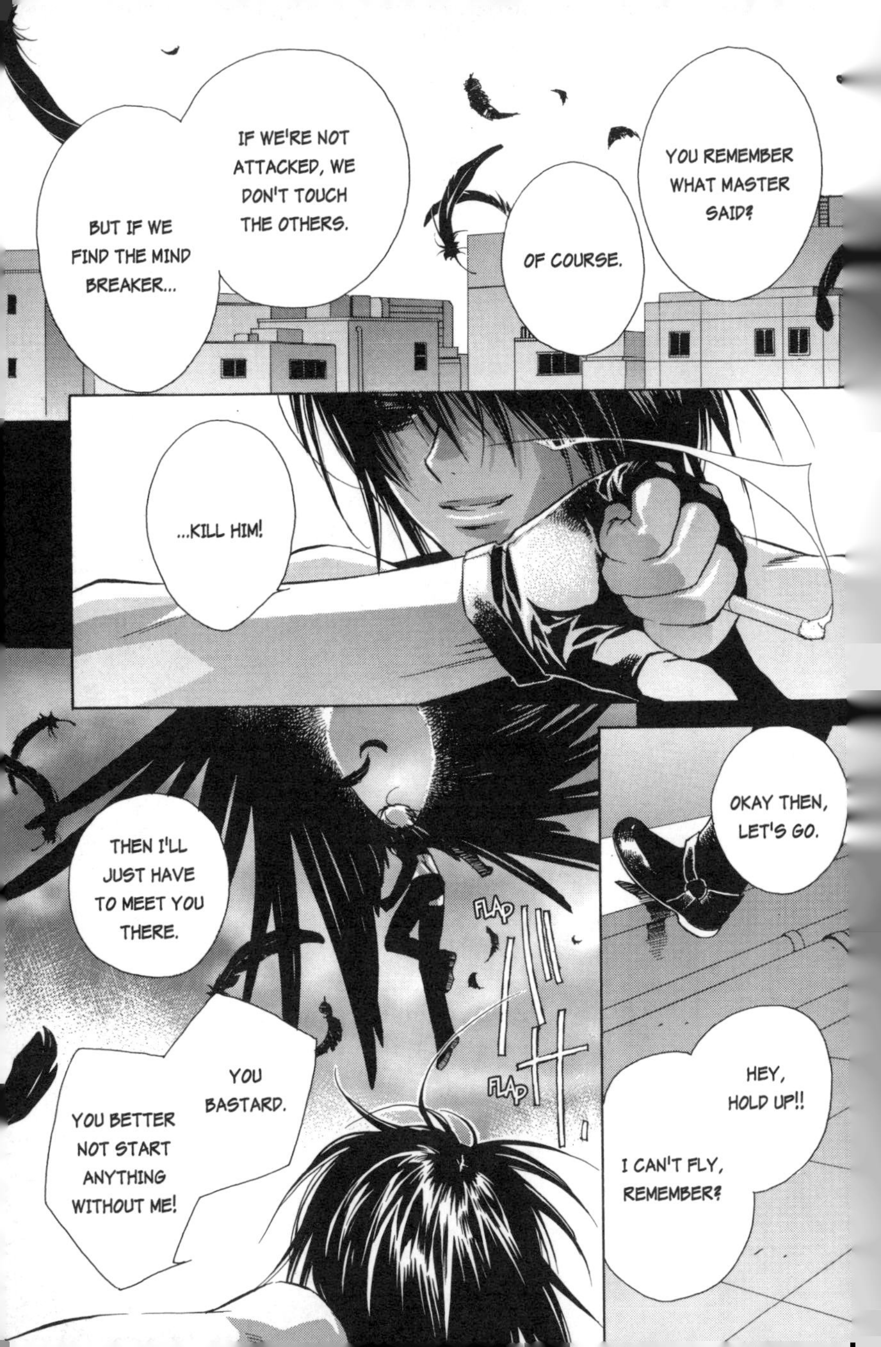
YOU REMEMBER WHAT MASTER SAID?
OF COURSE.
IF WE'RE NOT ATTACKED, WE DON'T TOUCH THE OTHERS.
BUT IF WE FIND THE MIND BREAKER...
...KILL HIM!
OKAY THEN, LET'S GO.
THEN I'LL JUST HAVE TO MEET YOU THERE.
FLAP
FLAP
HEY, HOLD UP!!
I CAN'T FLY, REMEMBER?
YOU BASTARD.
YOU BETTER NOT START ANYTHING WITHOUT ME!

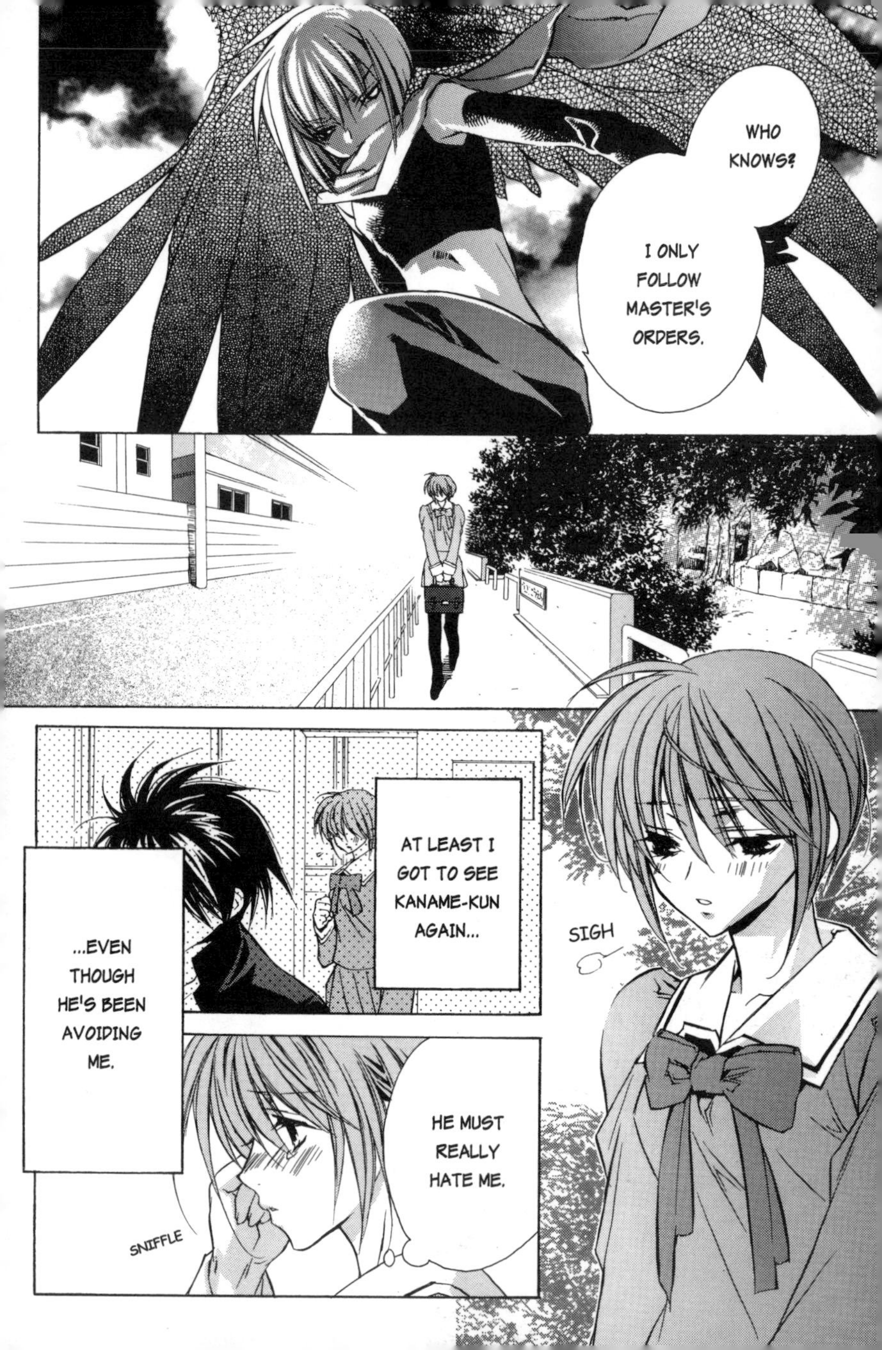
WHO KNOWS?
I ONLY FOLLOW MASTER'S ORDERS.
SIGH
AT LEAST I GOT TO SEE KANAME-KUN AGAIN...
...EVEN THOUGH HE'S BEEN AVOIDING ME.
HE MUST REALLY HATE ME.
SNIFFLE

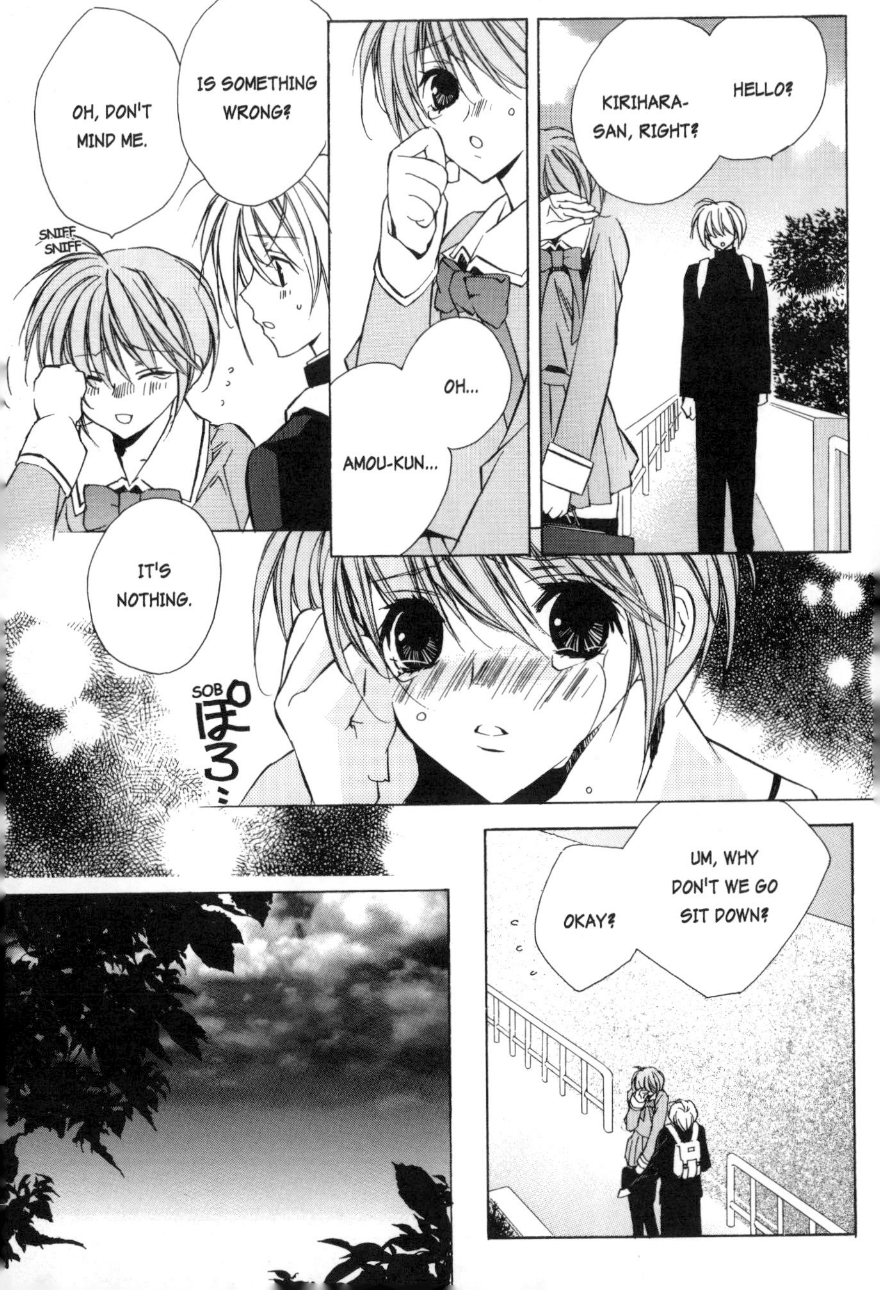
HELLO?
KIRIHARA-SAN, RIGHT?
OH...
AMOU-KUN...
IS SOMETHING WRONG?
OH, DON'T MIND ME.
SNIFF SNIFF
IT'S NOTHING.
SOB ぽろ
UM, WHY DON'T WE GO SIT DOWN?
OKAY?

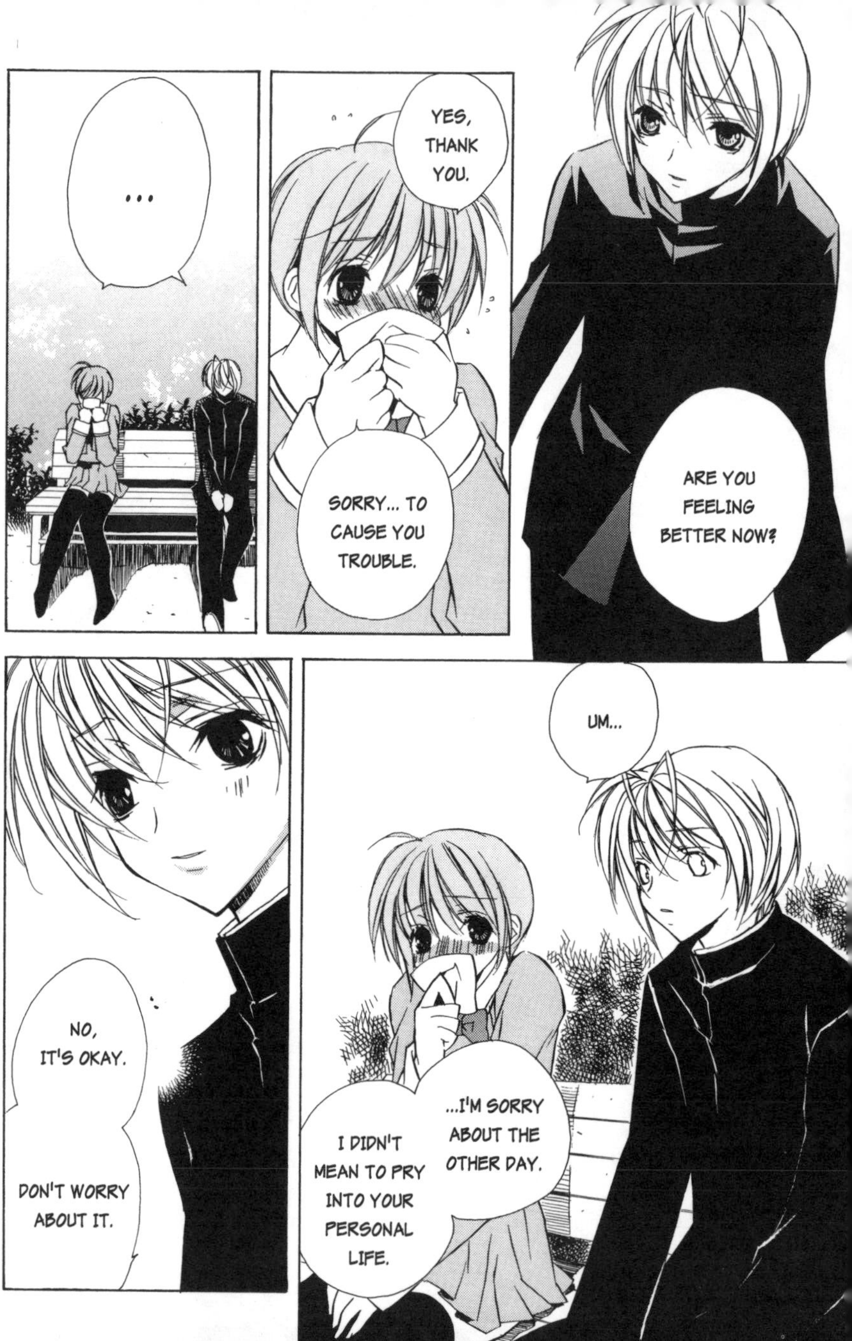
ARE YOU FEELING BETTER NOW?
YES, THANK YOU.
SORRY... TO CAUSE YOU TROUBLE.
...
UM...
...I'M SORRY ABOUT THE OTHER DAY.
I DIDN'T MEAN TO PRY INTO YOUR PERSONAL LIFE.
NO, IT'S OKAY.
DON'T WORRY ABOUT IT.

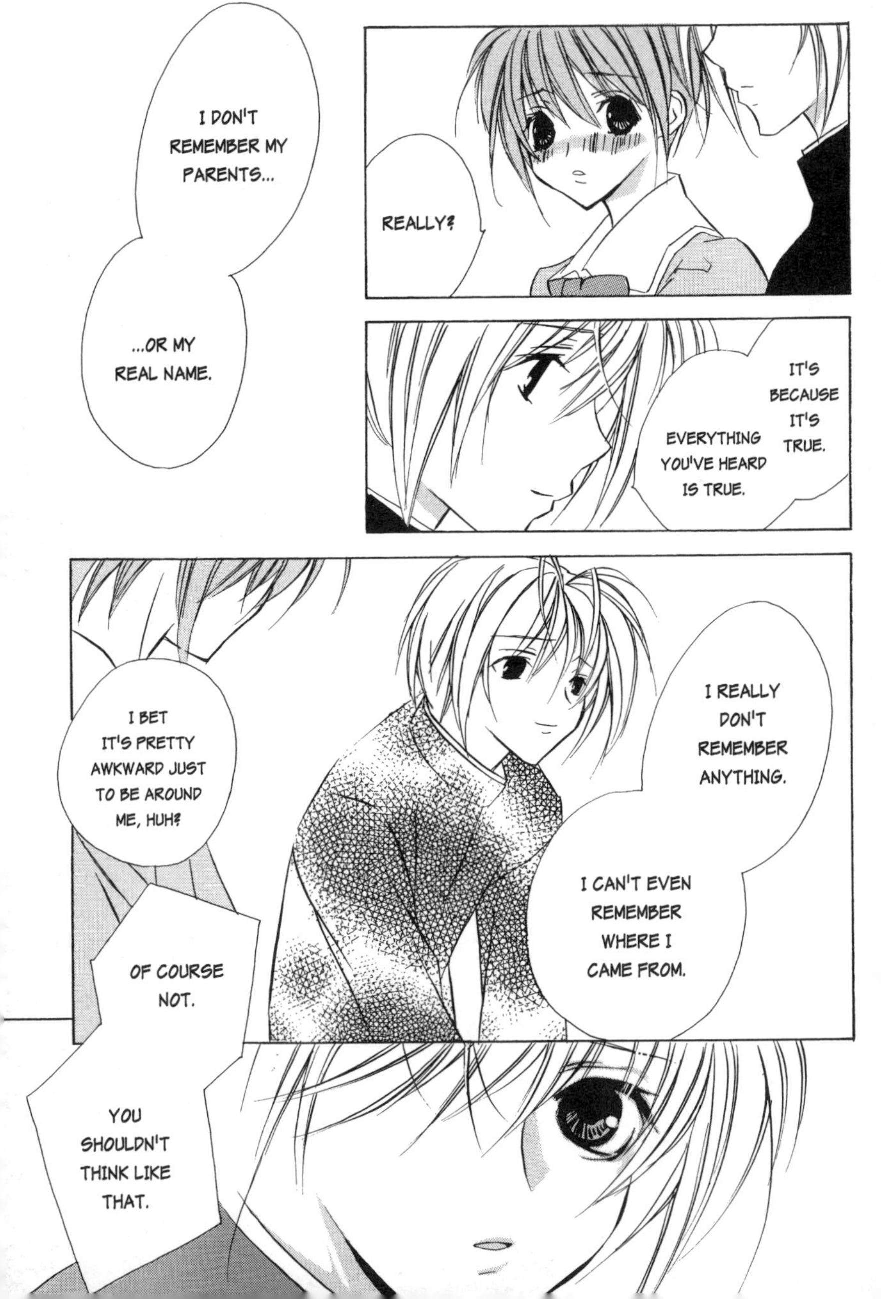
REALLY?
IT'S BECAUSE IT'S TRUE.
EVERYTHING YOU'VE HEARD IS TRUE.
I DON'T REMEMBER MY PARENTS...
...OR MY REAL NAME.
I REALLY DON'T REMEMBER ANYTHING.
I CAN'T EVEN REMEMBER WHERE I CAME FROM.
I BET IT'S PRETTY AWKWARD JUST TO BE AROUND ME, HUH?
OF COURSE NOT.
YOU SHOULDN'T THINK LIKE THAT.

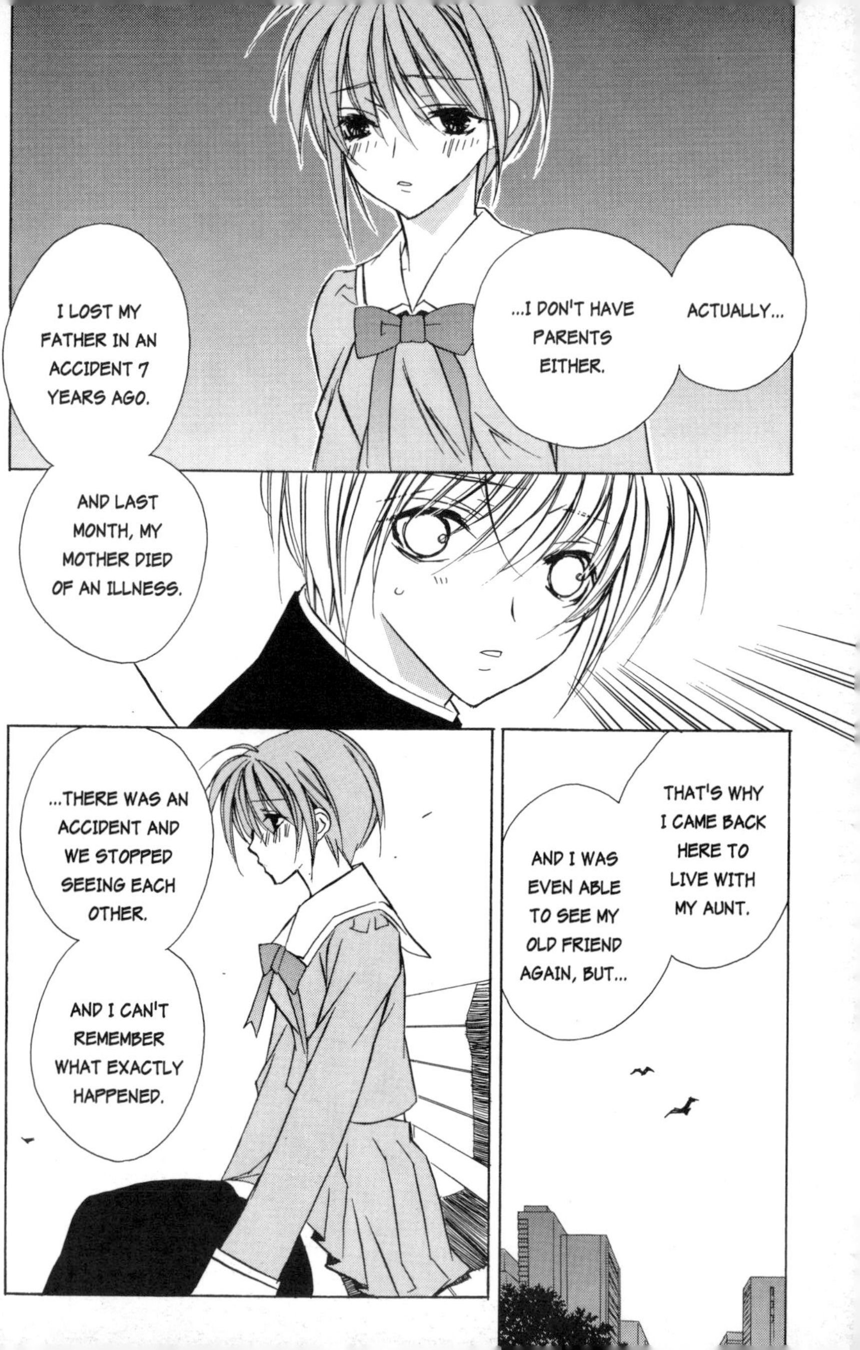
ACTUALLY...
...I DON'T HAVE PARENTS EITHER.
I LOST MY FATHER IN AN ACCIDENT 7 YEARS AGO.
AND LAST MONTH, MY MOTHER DIED OF AN ILLNESS.
THAT'S WHY I CAME BACK HERE TO LIVE WITH MY AUNT.
AND I WAS EVEN ABLE TO SEE MY OLD FRIEND AGAIN, BUT...
...THERE WAS AN ACCIDENT AND WE STOPPED SEEING EACH OTHER.
AND I CAN'T REMEMBER WHAT EXACTLY HAPPENED.

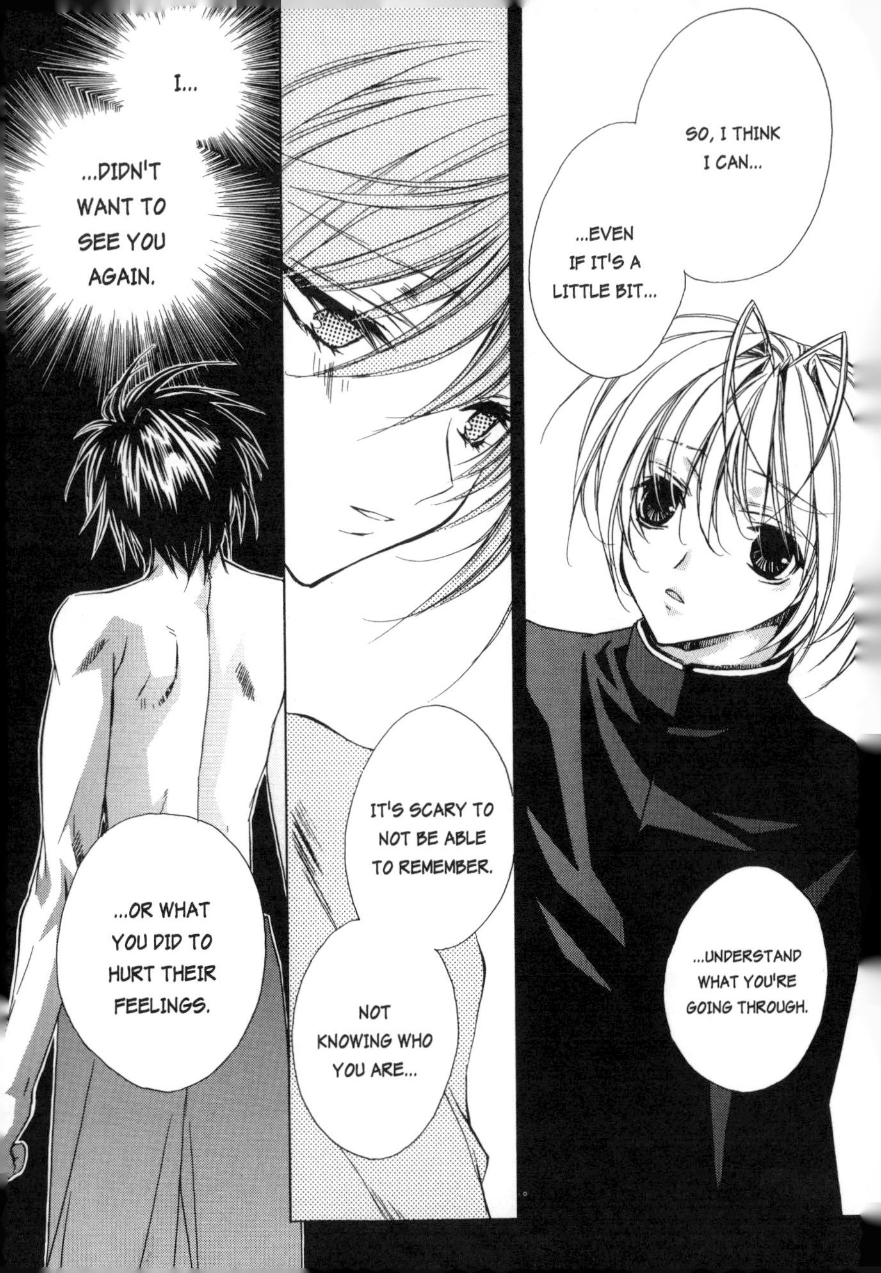
SO, I THINK I CAN...
...EVEN IF IT'S A LITTLE BIT...
...UNDERSTAND WHAT YOU'RE GOING THROUGH.
IT'S SCARY TO NOT BE ABLE TO REMEMBER.
NOT KNOWING WHO YOU ARE...
I...
...DIDN'T WANT TO SEE YOU AGAIN.
...OR WHAT YOU DID TO HURT THEIR FEELINGS.

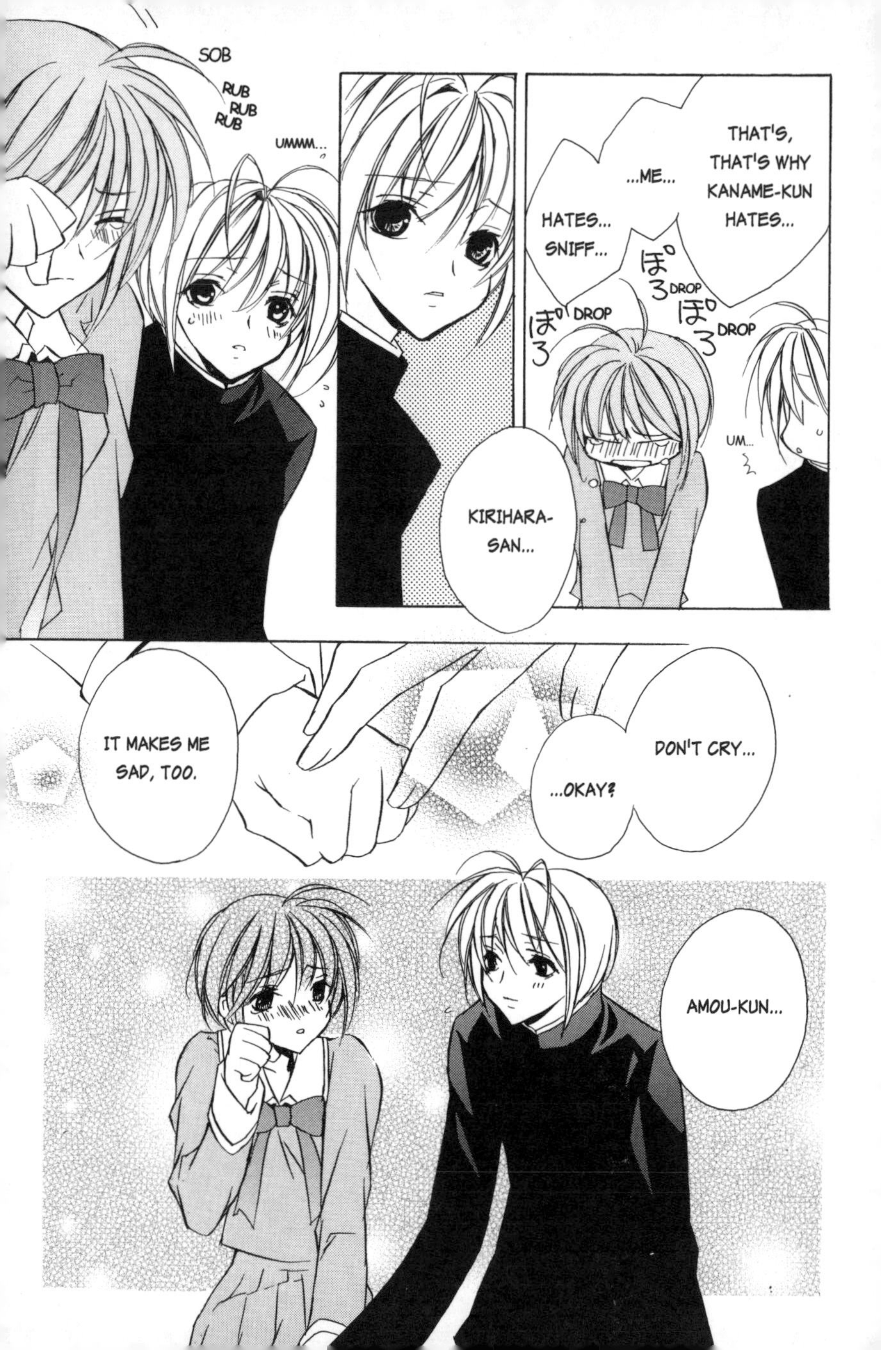
THAT'S, THAT'S WHY KANAME-KUN HATES...
...ME...
HATES... SNIFF...
ぽろ DROP
ぽろ DROP
ぽろ DROP
UM...
KIRIHARA-SAN...
SOB
RUB RUB RUB
UMMM...
DON'T CRY...
...OKAY?
IT MAKES ME SAD, TOO.
AMOU-KUN...

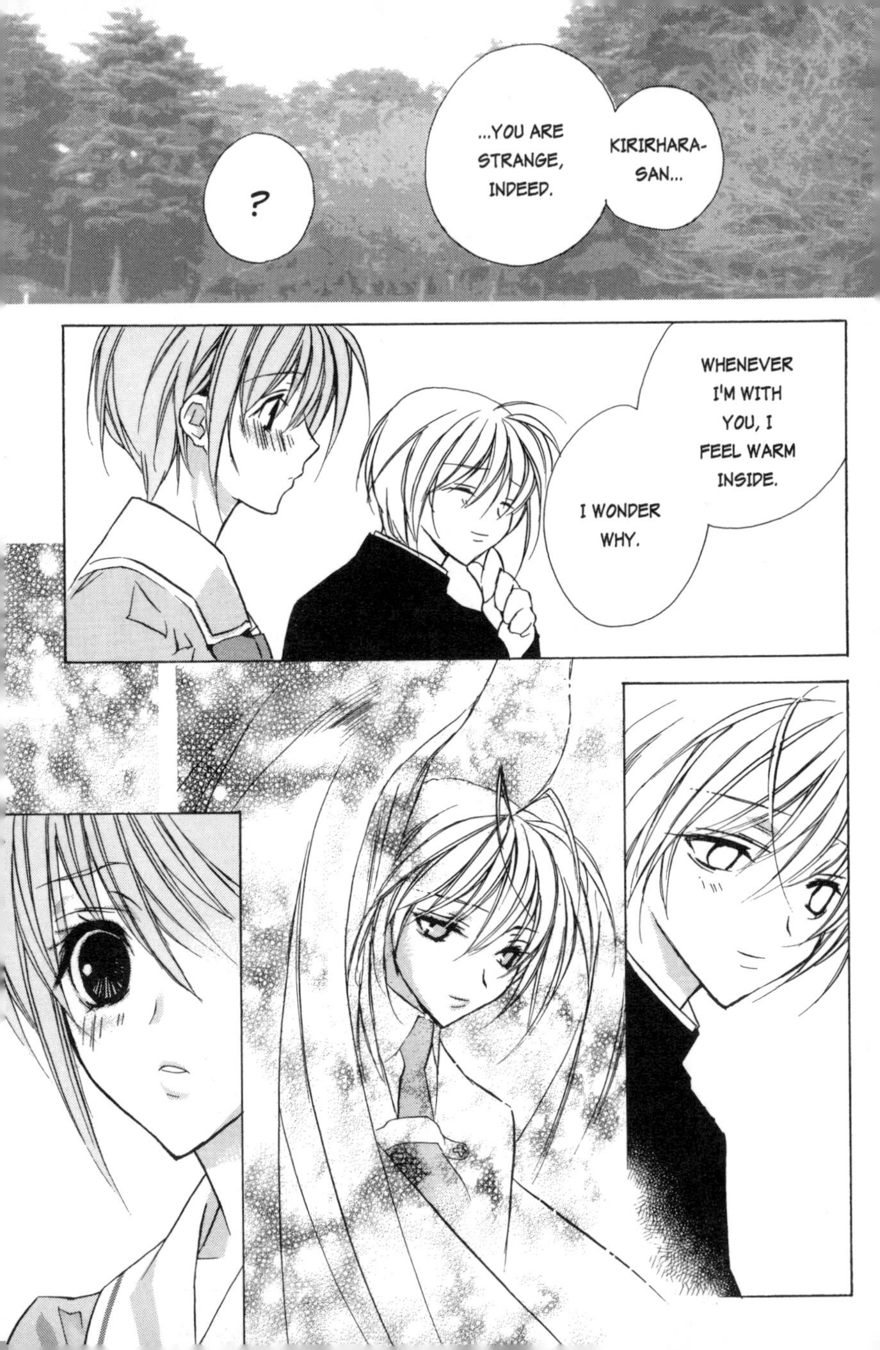
KIRIRHARA-SAN...
...YOU ARE STRANGE, INDEED.
?
WHENEVER I'M WITH YOU, I FEEL WARM INSIDE.
I WONDER WHY.

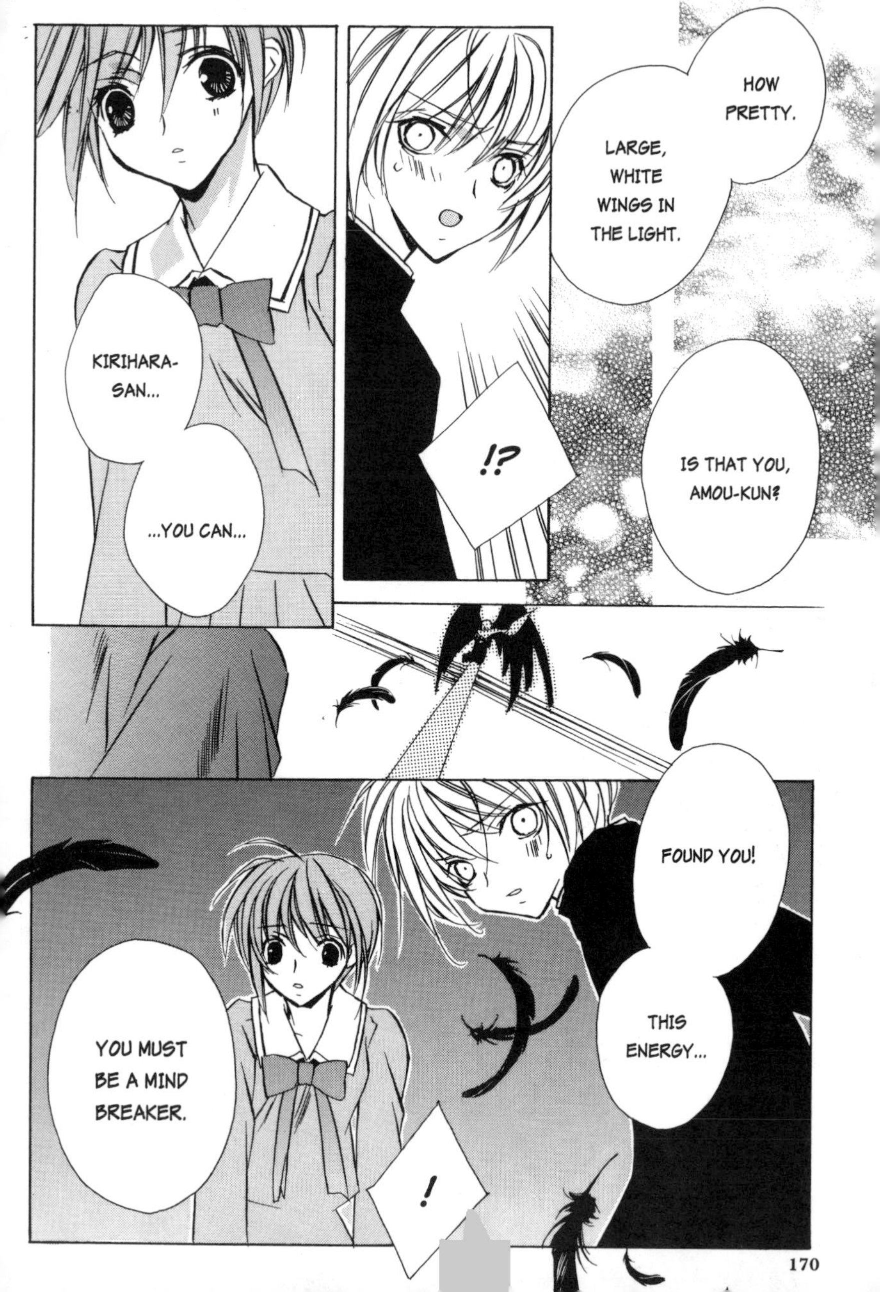
HOW PRETTY.
LARGE, WHITE WINGS IN THE LIGHT.
IS THAT YOU, AMOU-KUN?
!?
KIRIHARA-SAN...
...YOU CAN...
FOUND YOU!
THIS ENERGY...
YOU MUST BE A MIND BREAKER.
!

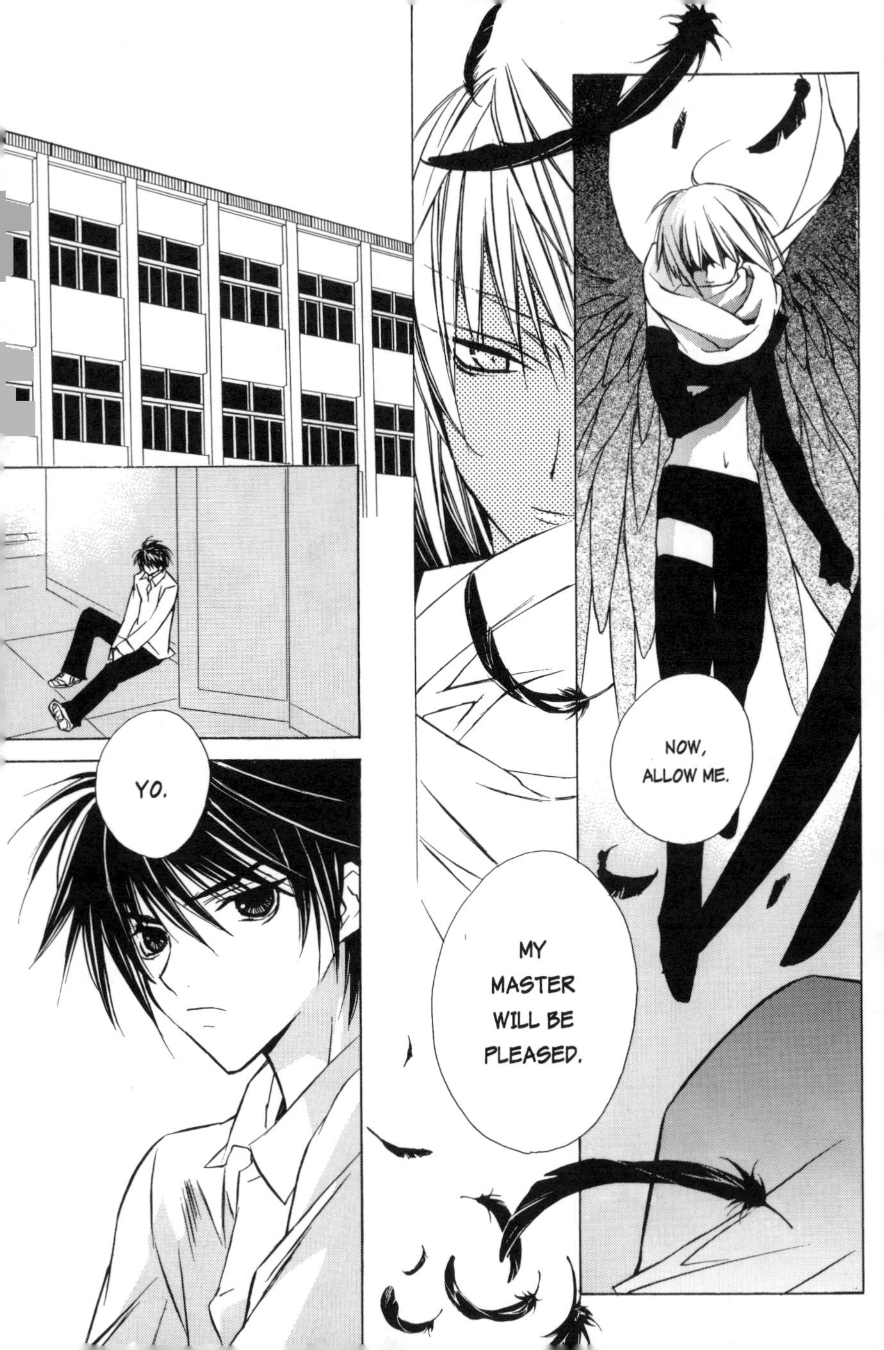
NOW, ALLOW ME.
MY MASTER WILL BE PLEASED.
YO.

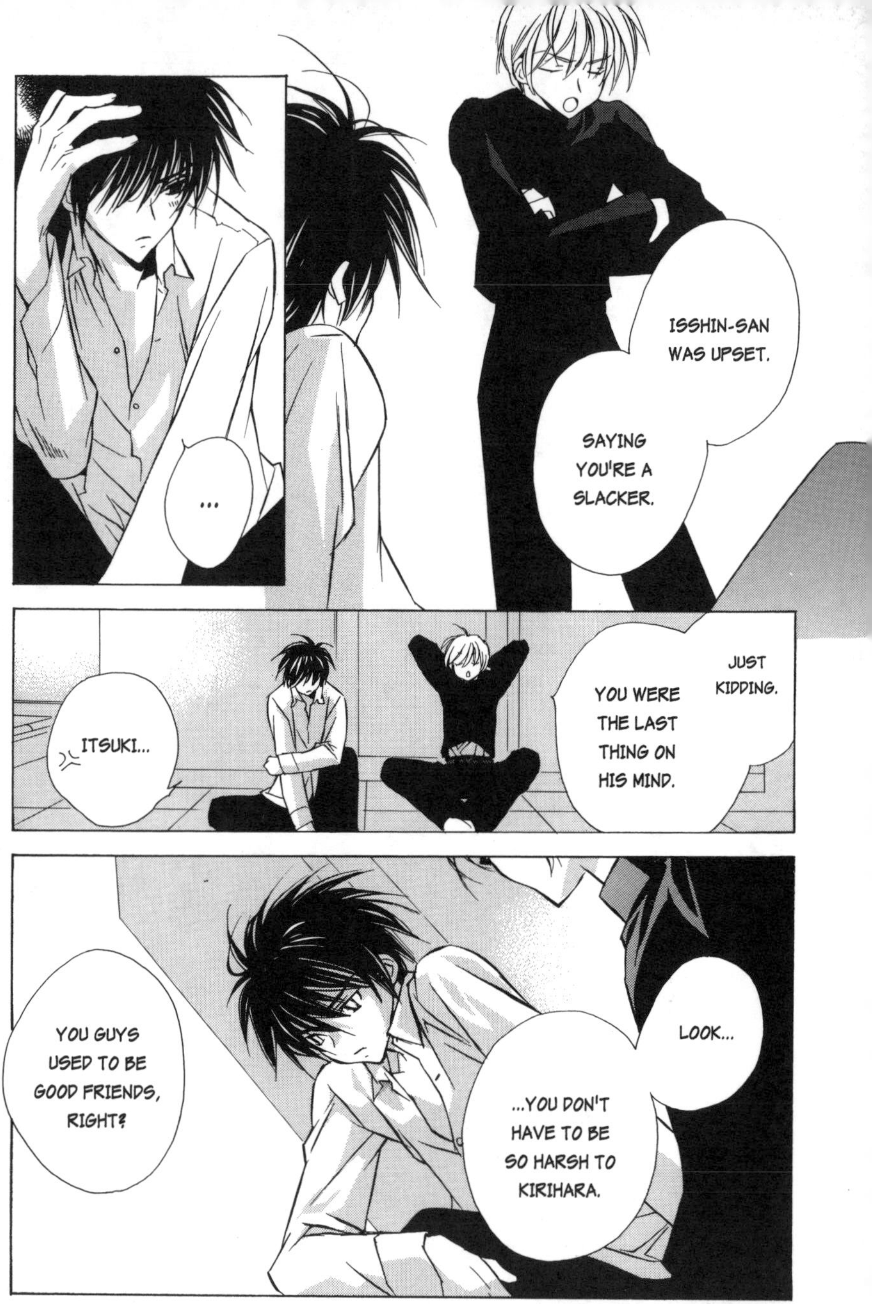
ISSHIN-SAN WAS UPSET.
SAYING YOU'RE A SLACKER.
...
YOU WERE THE LAST THING ON HIS MIND.
JUST KIDDING.
ITSUKI...
LOOK...
...YOU DON'T HAVE TO BE SO HARSH TO KIRIHARA.
YOU GUYS USED TO BE GOOD FRIENDS, RIGHT?

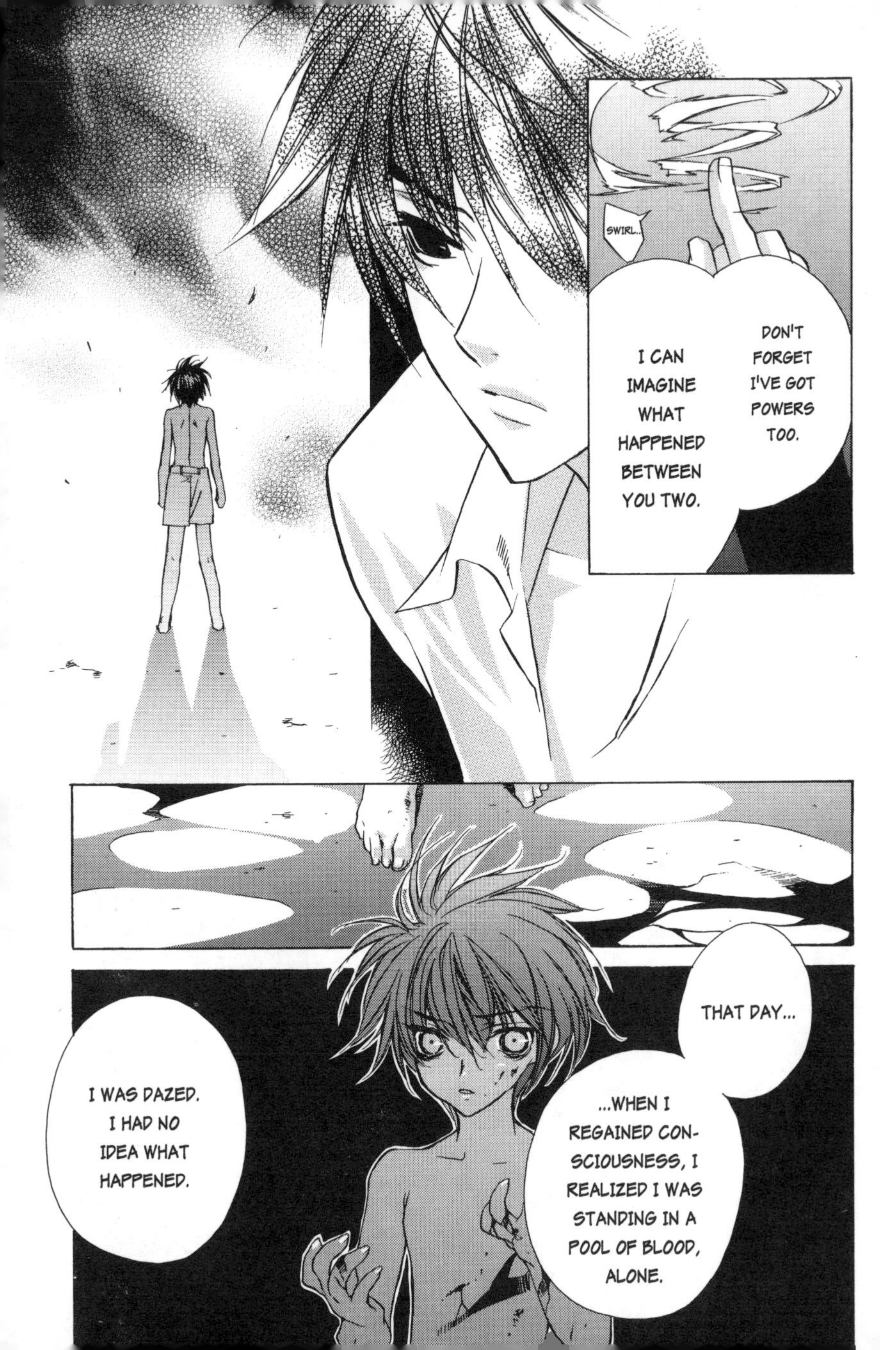
SWIRL...
DON'T FORGET I'VE GOT POWERS TOO.
I CAN IMAGINE WHAT HAPPENED BETWEEN YOU TWO.
THAT DAY...
...WHEN I REGAINED CON-SCIOUSNESS, I REALIZED I WAS STANDING IN A POOL OF BLOOD, ALONE.
I WAS DAZED. I HAD NO IDEA WHAT HAPPENED.

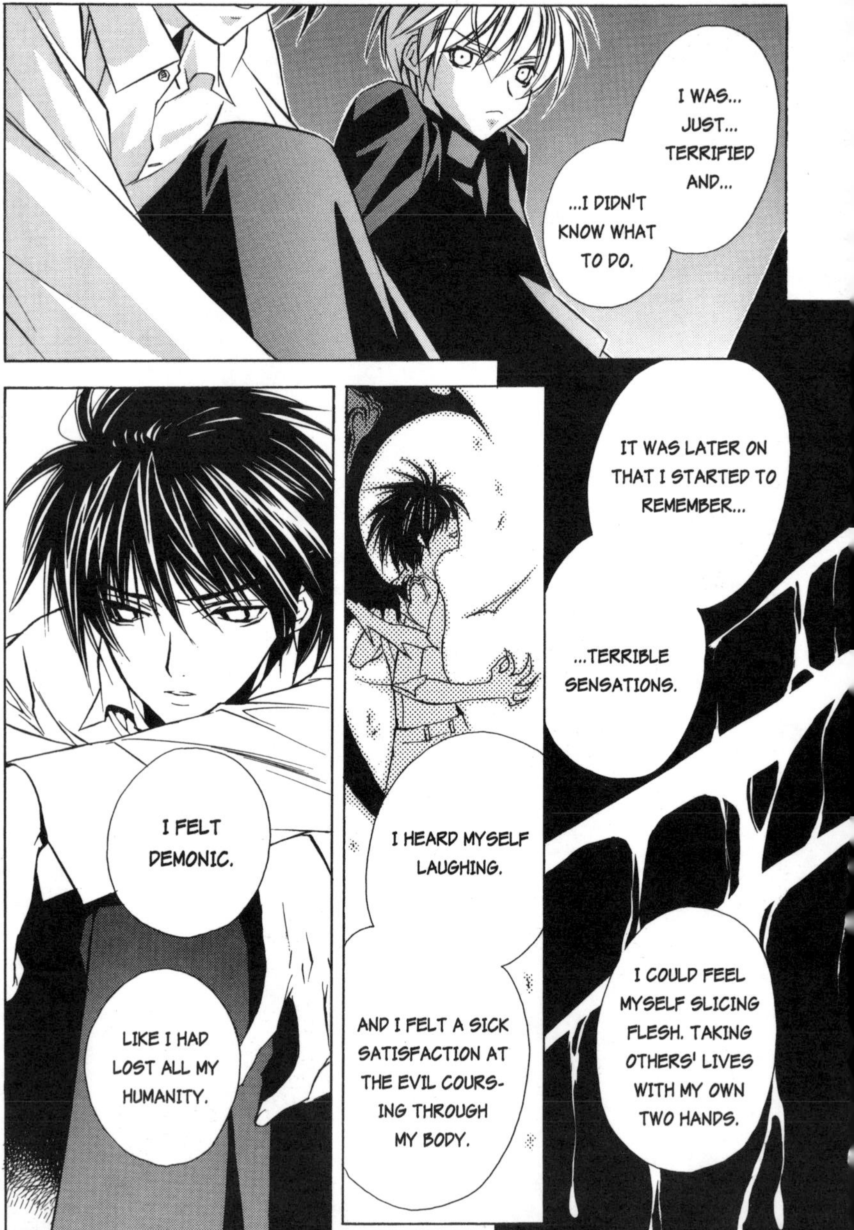
I WAS... JUST... TERRIFIED AND...
...I DIDN'T KNOW WHAT TO DO.
IT WAS LATER ON THAT I STARTED TO REMEMBER...
...TERRIBLE SENSATIONS.
I COULD FEEL MYSELF SLICING FLESH. TAKING OTHERS' LIVES WITH MY OWN TWO HANDS.
I HEARD MYSELF LAUGHING.
AND I FELT A SICK SATISFACTION AT THE EVIL COURSING THROUGH MY BODY.
I FELT DEMONIC.
LIKE I HAD LOST ALL MY HUMANITY.

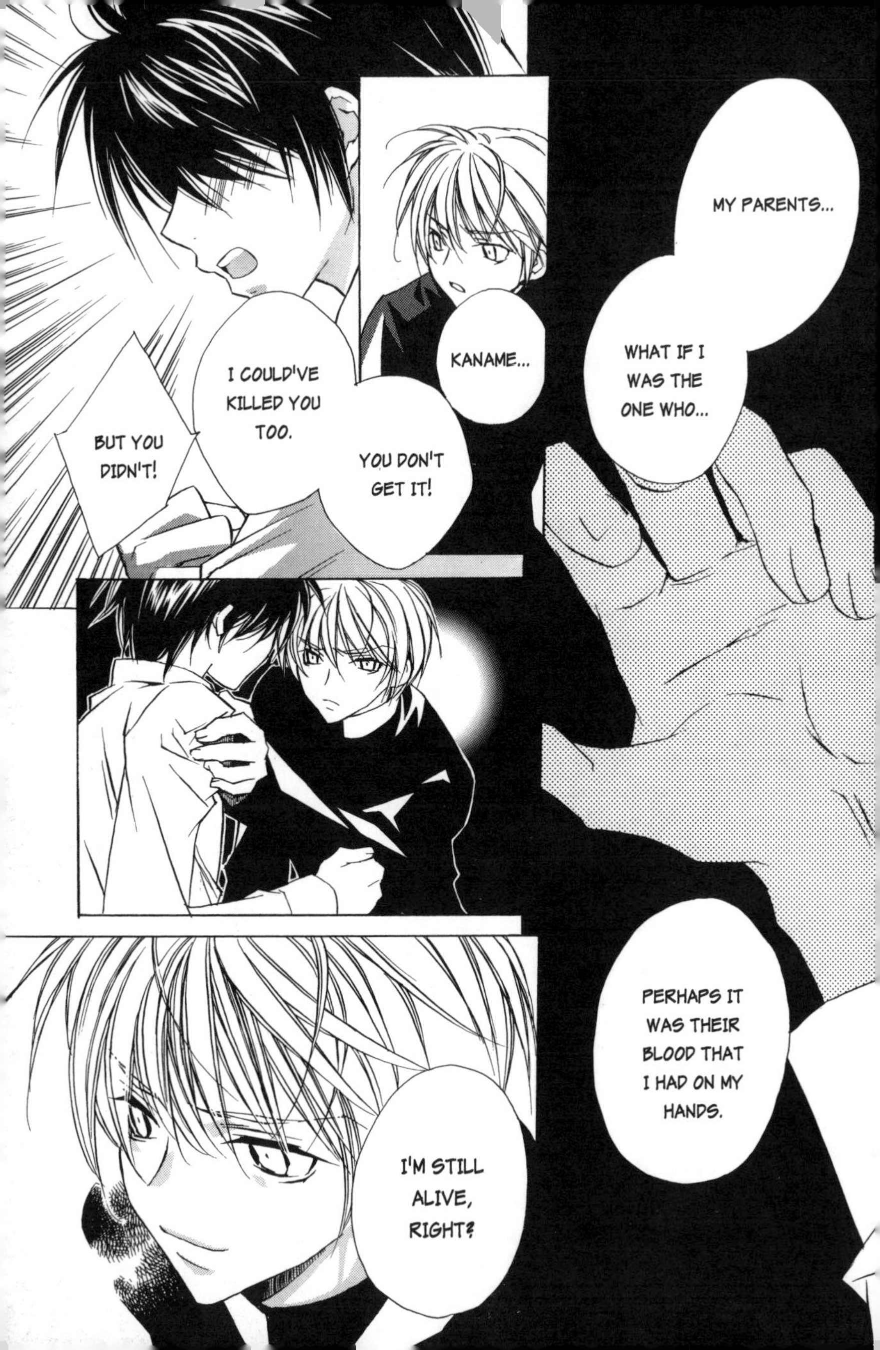
MY PARENTS...
WHAT IF I WAS THE ONE WHO...
PERHAPS IT WAS THEIR BLOOD THAT I HAD ON MY HANDS.
KANAME...
I COULD'VE KILLED YOU TOO.
YOU DON'T GET IT!
BUT YOU DIDN'T!
I'M STILL ALIVE, RIGHT?

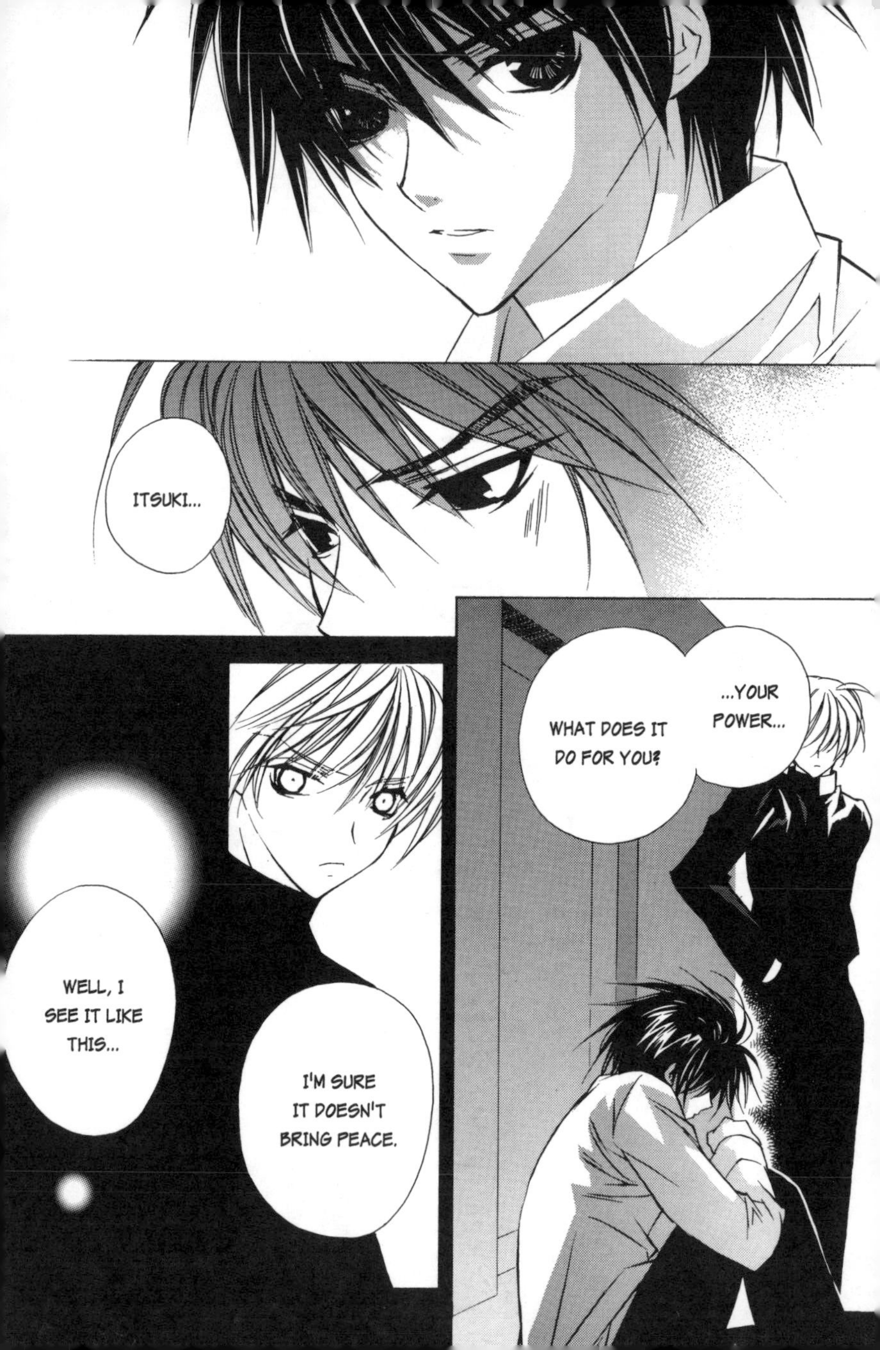
ITSUKI...
...YOUR POWER...
WHAT DOES IT DO FOR YOU?
WELL, I SEE IT LIKE THIS...
I'M SURE IT DOESN'T BRING PEACE.

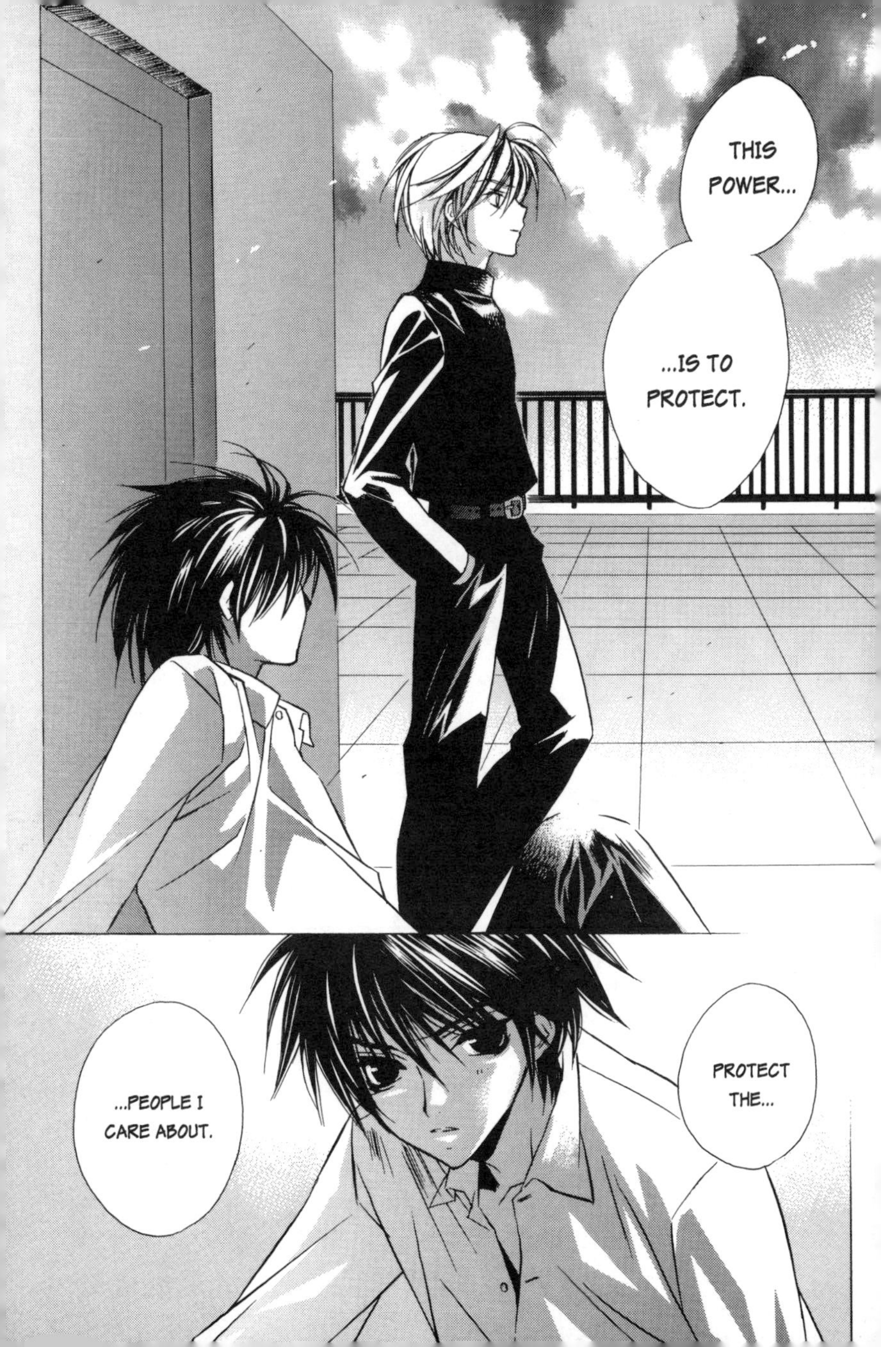
THIS POWER...
...IS TO PROTECT.
PROTECT THE...
...PEOPLE I CARE ABOUT.

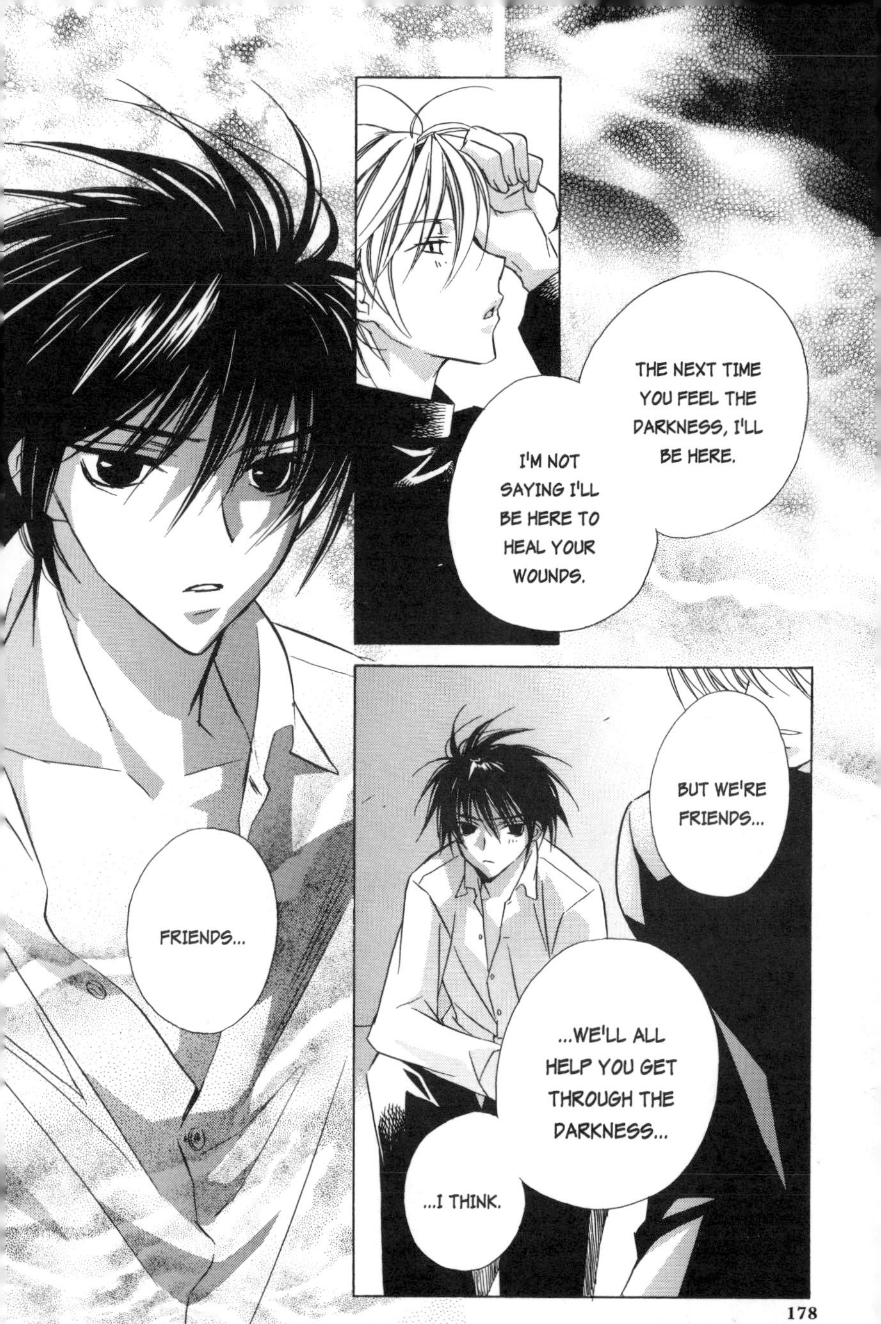
THE NEXT TIME YOU FEEL THE DARKNESS, I'LL BE HERE.
I'M NOT SAYING I'LL BE HERE TO HEAL YOUR WOUNDS.
BUT WE'RE FRIENDS...
...WE'LL ALL HELP YOU GET THROUGH THE DARKNESS...
...I THINK.
FRIENDS...

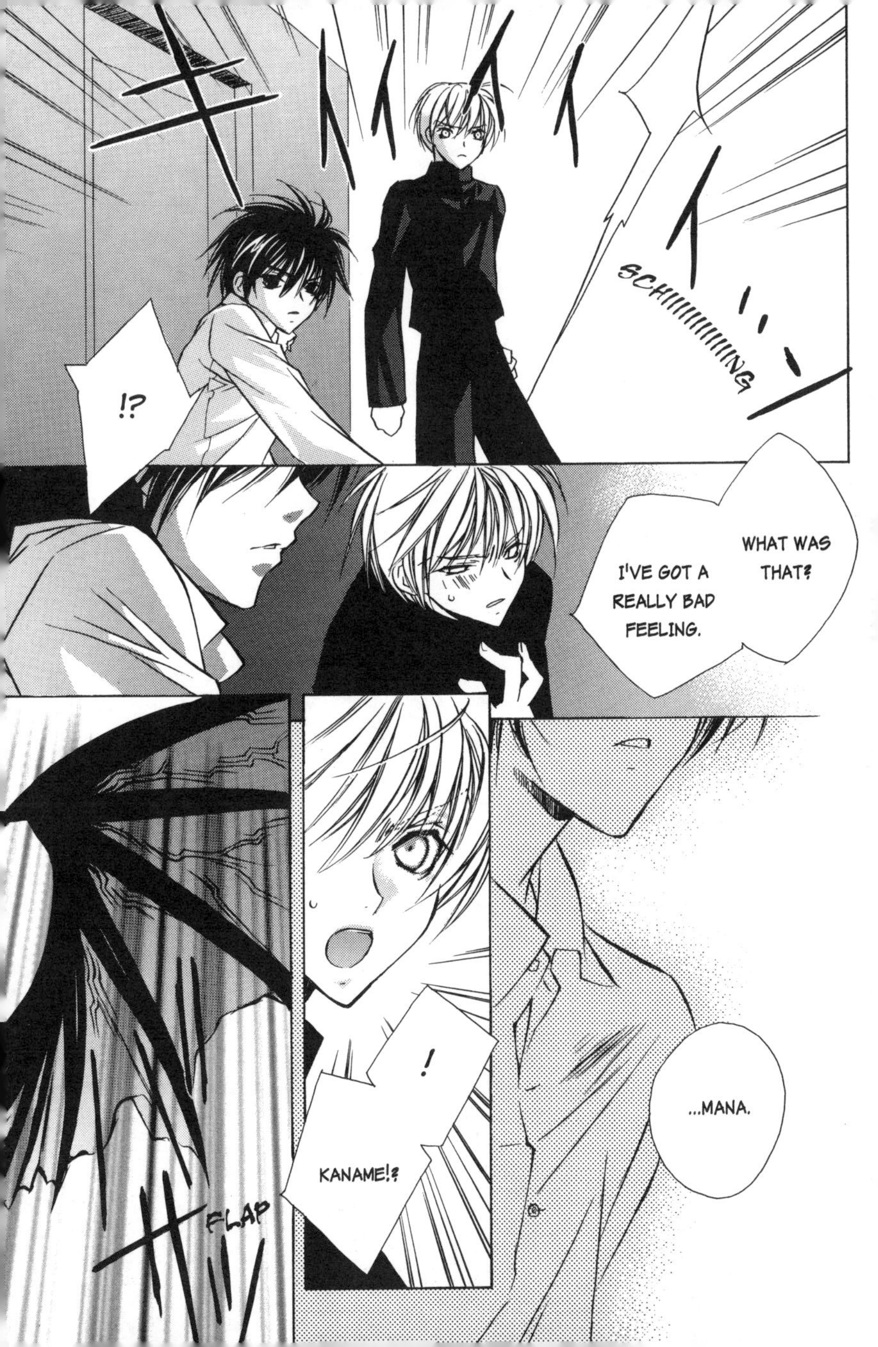
SCHIIIIIIIIIING
!?
WHAT WAS THAT?
I'VE GOT A REALLY BAD FEELING.
...MANA.
!
KANAME!?
FLAP

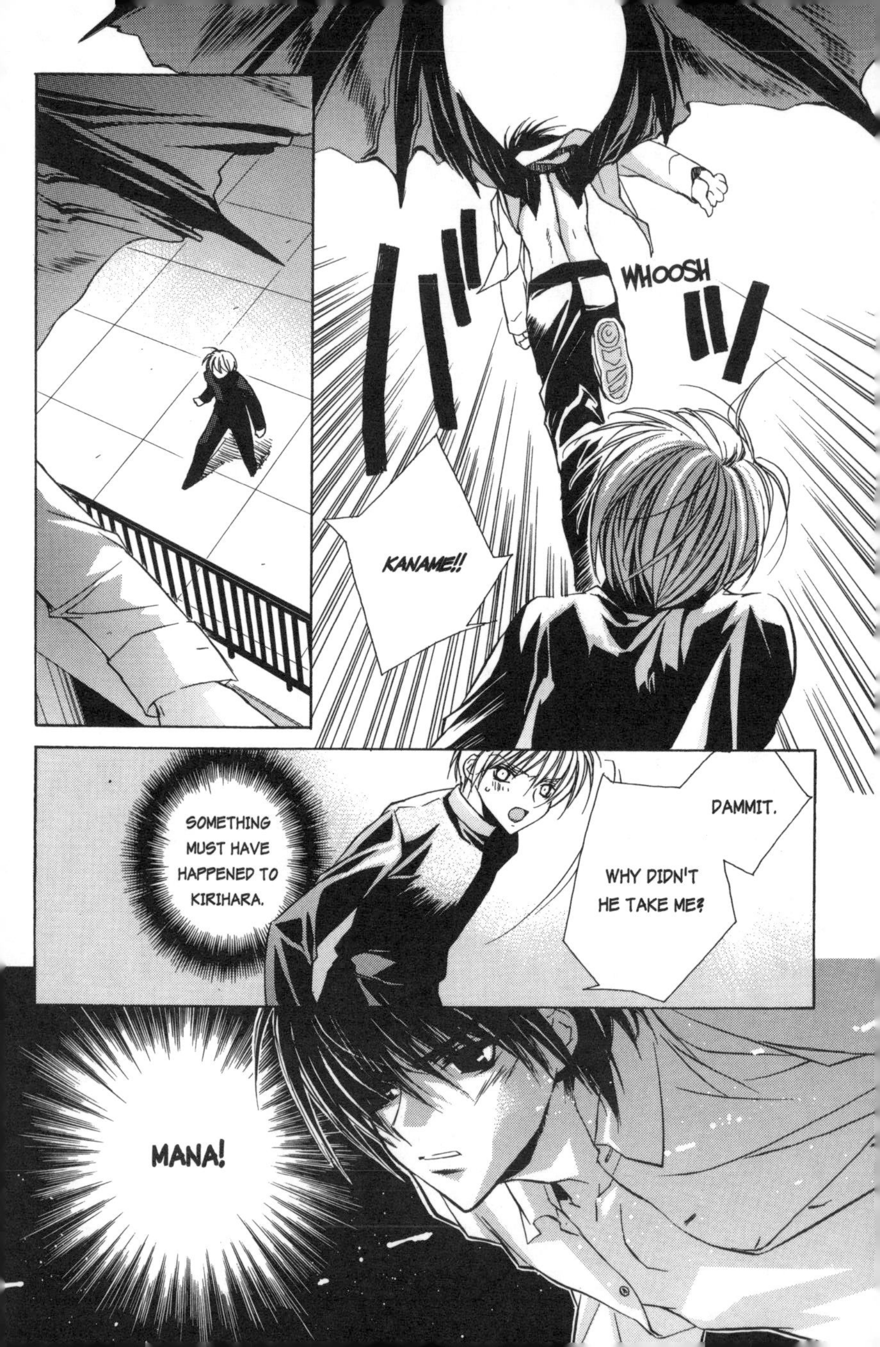
WHOOSH
KANAME!!
DAMMIT.
WHY DIDN'T HE TAKE ME?
SOMETHING MUST HAVE HAPPENED TO KIRIHARA.
MANA!

THE MORE I DRAW THIS
LONGER AND LONGER THEY GET
WHITE WINGS OF AMOU

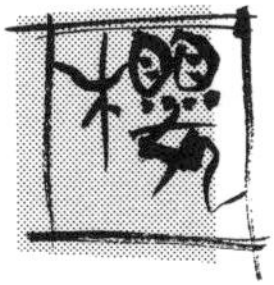

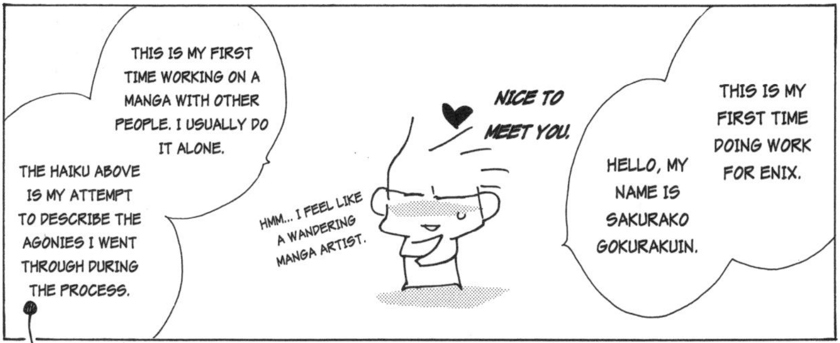
THIS IS MY FIRST TIME DOING WORK FOR ENIX.
HELLO, MY NAME IS SAKURAKO GOKURAKUIN.
NICE TO MEET YOU.
HMM... I FEEL LIKE A WANDERING MANGA ARTIST.
THIS IS MY FIRST TIME WORKING ON A MANGA WITH OTHER PEOPLE. I USUALLY DO IT ALONE.
THE HAIKU ABOVE IS MY ATTEMPT TO DESCRIBE THE AGONIES I WENT THROUGH DURING THE PROCESS.

THESE CHARACTERS WERE ACTUALLY CREATED FOR A POSTER. BUT BEFORE I REALIZED WHAT WAS HAPPENING, THEY STARTED DEVELOPING AND IT TURNED INTO AN IDEA FOR A CD DRAMA AND MANGA. SO BY THE TIME I'D GOTTEN USED TO WORKING ON THE PROJECT AMOU'S WINGS HAD CHANGED DRAMATICALLY. THEY WERE EVIDENCE OF HOW TIME HAD JUST FLOWN BY.

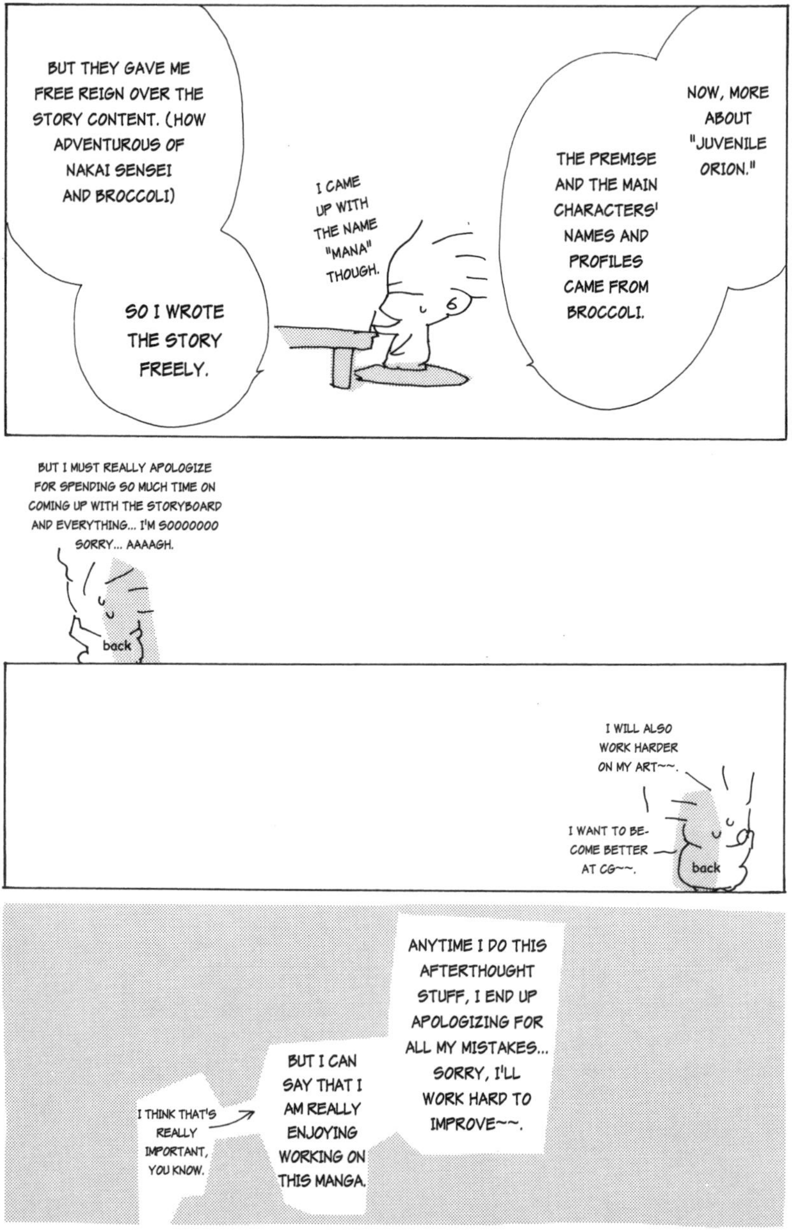
NOW, MORE ABOUT "JUVENILE ORION."
THE PREMISE AND THE MAIN CHARACTERS' NAMES AND PROFILES CAME FROM BROCCOLI.
I CAME UP WITH THE NAME "MANA" THOUGH.
BUT THEY GAVE ME FREE REIGN OVER THE STORY CONTENT. (HOW ADVENTUROUS OF NAKAI SENSEI AND BROCCOLI)
SO I WROTE THE STORY FREELY.
BUT I MUST REALLY APOLOGIZE FOR SPENDING SO MUCH TIME ON COMING UP WITH THE STORYBOARD AND EVERYTHING... I'M SOOOOOOO SORRY... AAAAGH.
back
I WILL ALSO WORK HARDER ON MY ART~~.
I WANT TO BECOME BETTER AT CG~~.
back
ANYTIME I DO THIS AFTERTHOUGHT STUFF, I END UP APOLOGIZING FOR ALL MY MISTAKES... SORRY, I'LL WORK HARD TO IMPROVE~~.
BUT I CAN SAY THAT I AM REALLY ENJOYING WORKING ON THIS MANGA.
I THINK THAT'S REALLY IMPORTANT, YOU KNOW.

NOW WHERE WAS I? I KEEP TALKING IN CIRCLES.

DON'T WORRY, I'M GONNA KEEP GOING WITH THIS STORY.

YOU'RE PROBABLY WONDERING WHY TSUKASA AND THE PRIEST ARE SO LOVEY DOVEY AND WHY ITSUKI IS SOOOOO INTO KANAME.

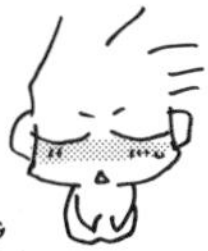

AND EVERYTHING SEEMS FISHY, BUT I STILL LIKE TO THINK OF IT AS A LOVE STORY. (I'M REFERRING TO THE ROMANCE BETWEEN MANA AND KANAME, OF COURSE.)

PLEASE PICK UP VOLUME 2 IF YOU ENJOYED THIS VOLUME.

NEXT TIME I PROMISE NOT TO DWELL ON MY STUPID SELF, BUT INSTEAD GIVE SOME CHARACTER SKETCHES OR SOMETHING...

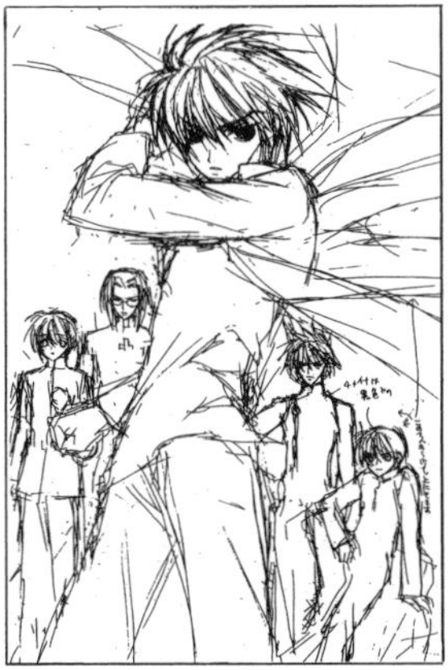

◎ Special thanks ◎

◎

A.K

S.T

◎

PREVIOUS EDITOR H-SAMA

CURRENT EDITOR M-SAMA

M-SAMA FROM BROCCOLI

SEND FANMAIL TO
GOKURAKUIN SENSEI AT
FANMAIL@BROCCOLIBOOKS.COM

AQUARIAN AGE

JUVENILE ORION 2™

オリオンの少年

Mana and Tsukasa are attacked by Lafayel,
who knows about Tsukasa's past.

And finally, "the enemy" reveal themselves...
Will Kaname and the others be able to protect Mana?

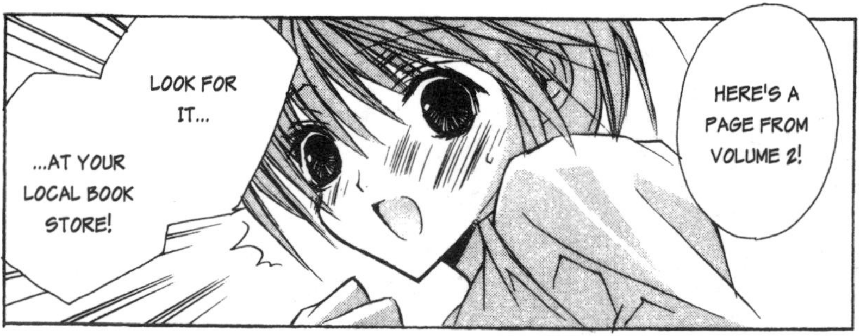

HERE'S A PAGE FROM VOLUME 2!
LOOK FOR IT...
...AT YOUR LOCAL BOOK STORE!

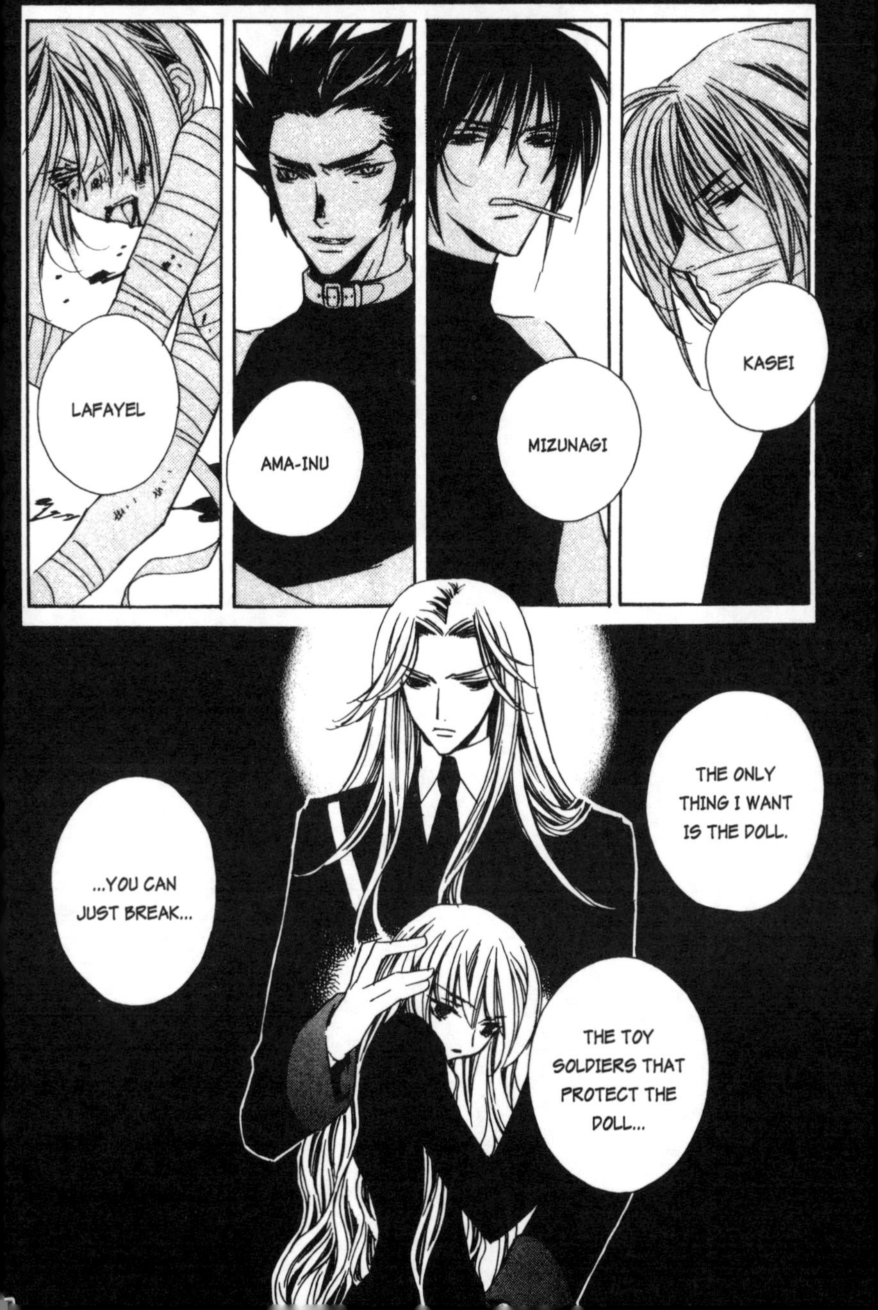
KASEI
MIZUNAGI
AMA-INU
LAFAYEL
THE ONLY THING I WANT IS THE DOLL.
THE TOY SOLDIERS THAT PROTECT THE DOLL...
...YOU CAN JUST BREAK...

JUVENILE ORION
TRANSLATION NOTES

A Note About First and Last Names

The characters in this story call each other by different names, sometimes using first names and sometimes using last names. Usually in Japan, classmates and teachers would call each other by their last names. Friends who are close call each other by their first names or nicknames.

pg. 6-7 Tsukasa is an "early-born." Kids who are born from January through March are put in school with kids who are born between April through December of the previous year. The cut-off date is March 31/April 1, because the school year starts in April in Japan. That is why Tsukasa is 16, even though Naoya is 17.

pg. 20 Kun - A suffix, usually goes after a boy's name.

pg. 31 Sama - A suffix indicating respect.

pg. 32 Sempai - The Japanese word for "senior." The direct translation is "you who came first." Kaname and Naoya call Isshin "sempai" because Isshin is older than them.

pg. 32 There is actually a real temple by this name, Isshin Temple, located in Osaka, Japan.

pg. 35 San - A suffix; can be put after any name indicating respect.

pg. 135 Sensei - Means "teacher" in Japan.

pg. 144 Chan - A suffix; can be put after any name. It is often used for children, good friends or those younger than oneself.

pg. 181 Haiku - A type of Japanese poetry that is composed of seventeen syllables, and has a seasonal theme.

pg. 181 Juvenile Orion poster - Sakurako Gokurakuin drew the promotional poster for Broccoli's original trading card game *Aquarian Age - Juvenile Orion*.

pg. 181 Enix - Enix is now known as Square Enix.

pg. 182 Broccoli - The company who created the original card game Aquarian Age. The characters in Juvenile Orion are characters in the card game.

pg. 182 Nakai Sensei - Referring to Marekatsu Nakai, who came up with the game play of Aquarian Age.

pg. 190 Five Factions - As of Aquarian Age Saga II, there are now six factions. ERASER is replaced by a new faction.

Chart of what the characters call each other

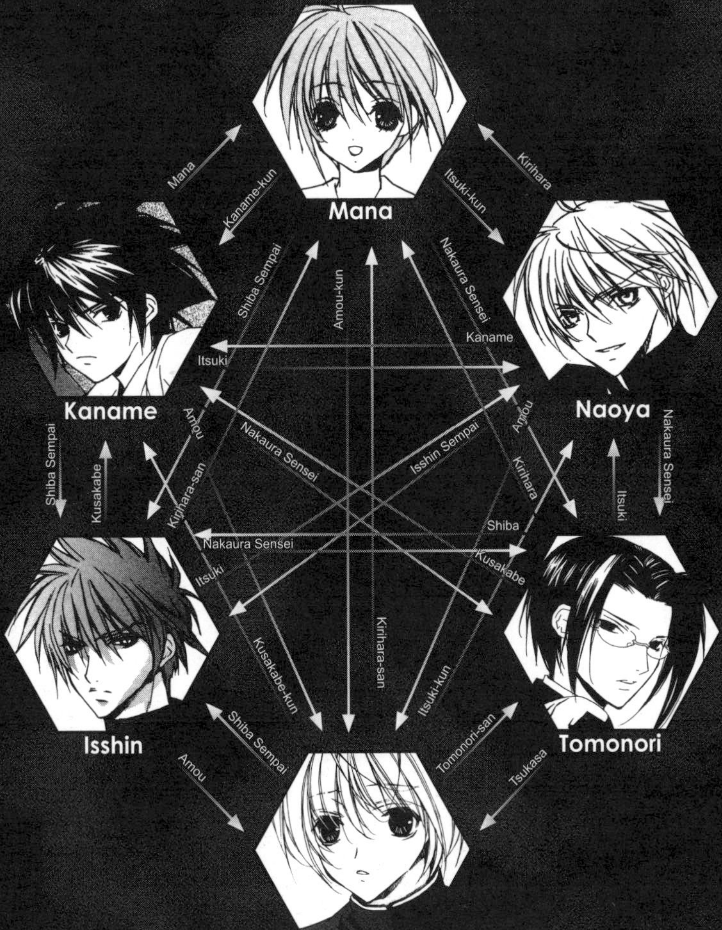
Mana
Kaname-kun
Kirihara
Itsuki-kun
Mana
Shiba Sempai
Amou-kun
Nakaura Sensei
Kaname
Itsuki
Kaname
Naoya
Amou
Nakaura Sensei
Isshin Sempai
Amou
Nakaura Sensei
Shiba Sempai
Kusakabe
Kirihara-san
Kirihara
Itsuki
Shiba
Nakaura Sensei
Kusakabe
Itsuki
Kusakabe-kun
Kirihara-san
Itsuki-kun
Isshin
Shiba Sempai
Tomonori-san
Tomonori
Amou
Tsukasa
Tsukasa

JUVENILE ORION
THE CARD GAME

Aquarian Age is an original trading card game created by Broccoli that was first introduced in July of 1999. The unique game system and the illustrations featuring many talented artists in Japan have fascinated card game players of all kinds.

The Rules

Objective
In this game, the players are Mind Breakers who control various characters in order to beat their opponent.

Getting Started
Preparing your deck
• The deck should contain a minimum of 40 cards and not exceed 60 cards.
• The deck cannot contain more than 4 copies of the same card title. A starter deck will give you all the cards you need to challenge an opponent. By adding cards from expansion packs, your deck can become stronger with various combinations.

Game Space
Every card you play will be placed or discarded in your Territory. The diagram on the next page shows where to place your deck and cards during a match.

Your Territory is divided into two main areas known as the Control Area and the Faction Area. The Control Area is the area closer to you, the player.

Each Territory has an area on the right where you can place your cards. It is divided into the Discard Area, the Deck Area, and the Damage Area.

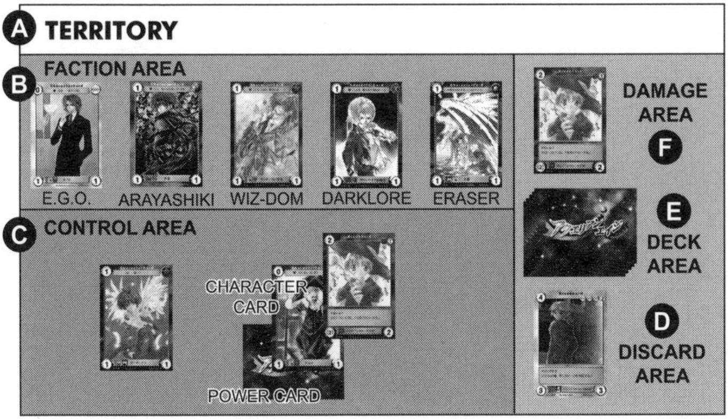
A TERRITORY
B FACTION AREA
E.G.O.
ARAYASHIKI
WIZ-DOM
DARKLORE
ERASER
C CONTROL AREA
CHARACTER CARD
POWER CARD
DAMAGE AREA
F
E
DECK AREA
D
DISCARD AREA

A. *Territory*: Where you place your cards.
B. *Faction Area*: Where your uncontrolled character cards go. By controlling the characters you place here, you can increase your battle potential.
C. *Control Area*: Where your controlled character cards go. You can use these characters for battle.
D. *Discard Area*: Where you put the cards you discard.
E. *Deck Area*: Where you put your deck.
F. *Damage Area*: This area shows how much damage you have. When a player has 10 cards in this area, the player loses.

How To Win
A player loses when:

1. By the end of the player's turn, there are 10 or more cards in the Damage Area.

2. There are no more cards in the player's Deck when the player needs to draw a card.

The Cards
In Juvenile Orion, there are 2 main types of cards that are split in 5 factions: E.G.O., ARAYASHIKI, WIZ-DOM, DARKLORE, and ERASER.

Card Types
Character Cards
Each character card has a different character in it. Character cards are placed in the Faction Area during the Main Phase.

1) *Mental Strength*
This number shows how much "mental strength" this character has.

2) *Attack Power*
This number shows how much attack power this character has.

3) *Defense Power*
This number shows how much defense power this character has.

4) *Classification*
These symbol or symbols describe what attributes the character has.

5) *Title*
This is the name of the card.

6) *Faction*
This symbol describes which faction this character is from.

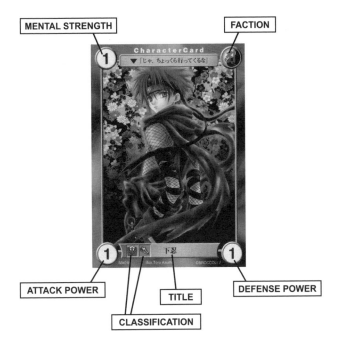

MENTAL STRENGTH
FACTION
CharacterCard
1
「じゃ、ちょっくら行ってくるな」
1
下忍
1
ATTACK POWER
TITLE
DEFENSE POWER
CLASSIFICATION

Illustration by Toru Azumi

Break Cards

Break Cards cause characters to awaken and become stronger characters. They are placed on top of Character Cards that have a same Classification icon. Once placed, the character's powers are replaced by the Break Card. The original character's powers cannot be used. As long as the requirements are met, multiple Break Cards can be placed on a Character Card. Multiple Break Cards are counted as one character.

Power Cards

A Power Card is any card that is face down and placed under a Character Card or Break Card.

Power Cards show a character's mental strength and energy, and for most actions the player needs to "pay" a Power Card. Power Cards can only be placed during the Power Card Phase.

*Note: There are more card types in the original Aquarian Age card game. Juvenile Orion uses a "Limited Style" rule and therefore, simpler.

Factions

There are five factions in Aquarian Age.

E.G.O.
ARAYASHIKI
WIZ-DOM
DARKLORE
ERASER

Discarding Cards

When discarding cards, they are placed faced up and placed in the Discard Area.

Using Cards

When Character Cards and Break Cards are placed in the Territory, these cards remain in the Territory.

In order to place a Break Card, you will need to fulfill the factor and cost requirements. Factor requirements are indicated by how many faction marks there are on the card. You will need to have that many Character Cards in your Control Area to place the Break Card. The cost requirement is the number indicated next to the faction mark. You will need to "pay" the number of Power Cards in your Control Area. The Power Cards can be taken from any character in your Control Area, and can be taken from multiple characters.

Starting the Game

1. Both players shuffle their respective Decks and hand them to their opponent to shuffle. The Decks are then returned to their owners.
2. The players then place their Decks faced down on the Deck Area.
3. The players choose who will go first.

Game Flow

Turn

Your Turn is broken up into smaller units called Phases. The match proceeds with each player taking Turns until one player wins.

Phase

One Turn is made up of 5 Phases.

1. Draw Phase
2. Faction Phase
3. Main Phase
4. Power Card Phase
5. Discard Phase

After the Discard Phase is over, that Turn is over.
Once the Turn is over, it is the opponent's Turn, which begins with the Draw Phase.

The Five Different Factions

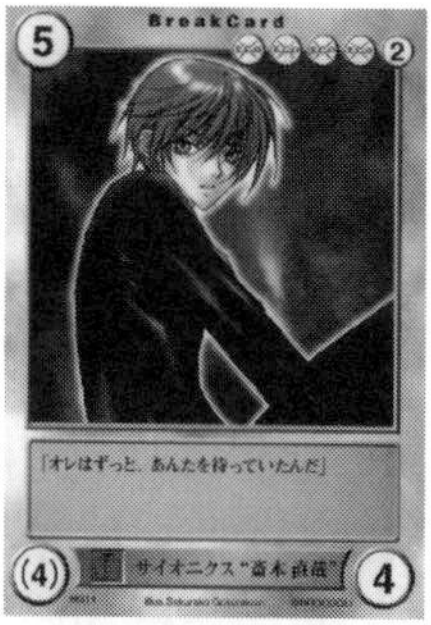
BreakCard
5
2
(4)
4

E.G.O.
Officially named the "Evolutional Girls Organization," they claim to be a new kind of race with special psychic abilities. They rose to unite the other three factions on earth.

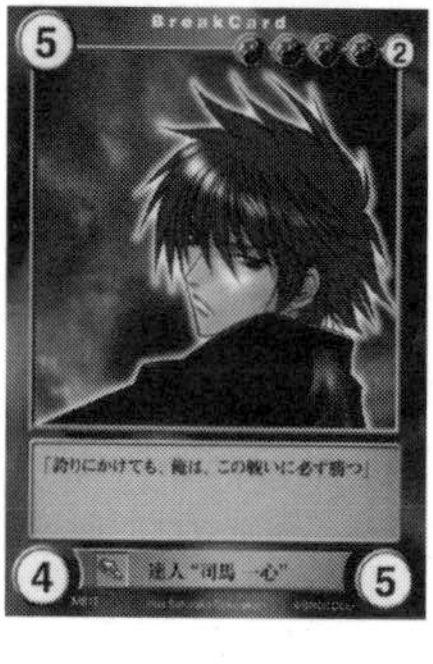
BreakCard
5
2
4
5

ARAYASHIKI
With the power of the gods and nature on their side, they use their own spiritual powers as a catalyst for their spells. ARAYASHIKI is the federation that the Eastern spell casters created.

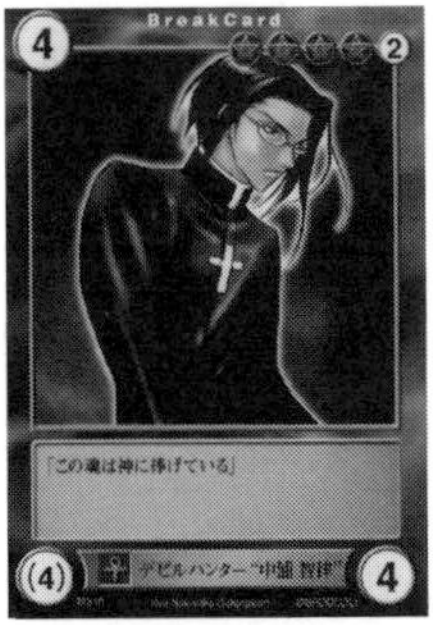
BreakCard
4
2
(4)
4

WIZ-DOM

Born in the West, the forbidden art of "magic" has been passed down through generations despite facing much persecution. The secret organization created by these magic users is WIZ-DOM.

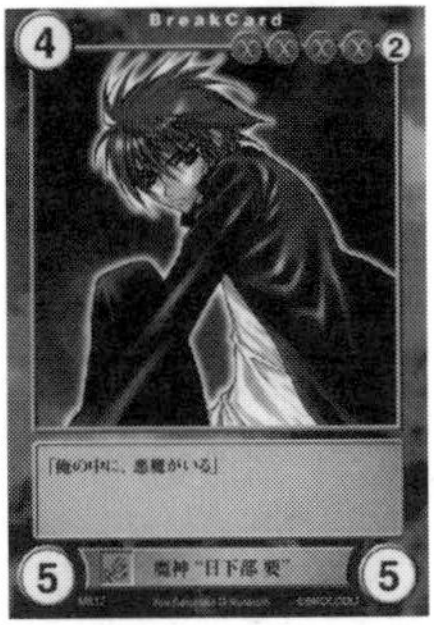
BreakCard
4
2
5
5

DARKLORE

They are the descendants of various legendary species that ruled the earth during ancient times.

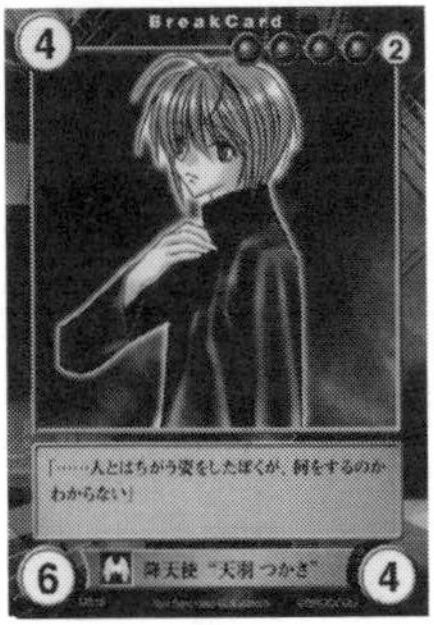
BreakCard
4
2
6
4

ERASER

This space crew of aliens suddenly appeared from the outer world. Their merciless attacks on the Earth's four powers earned them the name "ERASER."

MORE RULES TO COME IN VOLUME 2!

JUVENILE ORION
SERIES 1 CARD LIST

No.	Faction	Rarity	Card Name	Artist
MA001	E.G.O.		Private Elementary School Student	Gureko Nankin
MA002	E.G.O.		Businessman	Kaoru Yaezaki
MA003	E.G.O.		Band Member	Kazuki Shu
MA004	E.G.O.		Intern	Reiichi Hiiro
MA005	E.G.O.	★	Basketball Player	Kazuki Shu
MA006	E.G.O.	★	Delinquent	Koge-Donbo
MA007	E.G.O.	★★	Private Investigator	Denki Akiba
MA008	E.G.O.	★	Police Captain	Kairi Yura
MA009	E.G.O.	★	Class President	Fubito Mikanagi
MA010	E.G.O.	★★	Vocalist	Kasumi Ryowa
MA011	E.G.O.	★★	Surgeon "Kengo Ashihara"	Reiichi Hiiro
MA012	E.G.O.	★★	Lightning Striker "Tsubasa Shouji"	Koge-Donbo
MA013	E.G.O.	★★★	Surgeon "Kengo Ashihara"	Reiichi Hiiro
MA014	E.G.O.	★★★	Lightning Striker "Tsubasa Shouji"	Koge-Donbo
MA015	ARAYASHIKI		Martial Artist	Gureko Nankin
MA016	ARAYASHIKI		Shinto Priest	Towa Oozora
MA017	ARAYASHIKI		Psychic	Fubito Mikanagi
MA018	ARAYASHIKI		Lower Ninja	Toru Azumi
MA019	ARAYASHIKI	★	Kendou Student	Toru Azumi
MA020	ARAYASHIKI	★	Doushi	Haruhiko Mikimoto
MA021	ARAYASHIKI	★★	Kannagi	J-ta Yamada
MA022	ARAYASHIKI	★	Japanese Exorcist	Kohu
MA023	ARAYASHIKI	★	Student	Koge-Donbo
MA024	ARAYASHIKI	★★	Page	Kaoru Yaezaki
MA025	ARAYASHIKI	★★	Onmyouji "Seimei Tsuchimikado"	Fubito Mikanagi
MA026	ARAYASHIKI	★★	Tennen Rishin Ryu "Souji Okita"	Toru Azumi
MA027	ARAYASHIKI	★★★	Onmyouji "Seimei Tsuchimikado"	Fubito Mikanagi
MA028	ARAYASHIKI	★★★	Tennen Rishin Ryu "Souji Okita"	Toru Azumi
MA029	WIZ-DOM		Prophet	Gobanjima
MA030	WIZ-DOM		Warlock	Kazuki Shu
MA031	WIZ-DOM		High Schooler Wizard	J-ta Yamada
MA032	WIZ-DOM		Gymnasium Student	Kanan
MA033	WIZ-DOM	★	Loyal Subject	Mako Takahashi
MA034	WIZ-DOM	★	Psychic Medium	Towa Oozora
MA035	WIZ-DOM	★★	Priest	Shibuko Ebara

JUVENILE ORION
SERIES 1 CARD LIST

No.	Faction	Rarity	Card Name	Artist
MA036	WIZ-DOM	★	Netzach	Aya Shouoto
MA037	WIZ-DOM	★	Officer	Toru Azumi
MA038	WIZ-DOM	★★	Bishop	Kohu
MA039	WIZ-DOM	★★	Prince "Ludwig van Schattenburg"	Kanan
MA040	WIZ-DOM	★★	Wizard "Merlin"	J-ta Yamada
MA041	WIZ-DOM	★★★	Prince "Ludwig van Schattenburg"	Kanan
MA042	WIZ-DOM	★★★	Wizard "Merlin"	J-ta Yamada
MA043	DARKLORE		Little Demon	Kanan
MA044	DARKLORE		Devil Boy	Banri Sendou
MA045	DARKLORE		Nosferatu	Chata Tachibana
MA046	DARKLORE		Puppy Boy	Hina.
MA047	DARKLORE	★	Vampire Student	Narumi Kakinouchi
MA048	DARKLORE	★★	Imp	Towa Oozora
MA049	DARKLORE	★★	Red Branch Knight "Cu Chulainn"	Kiriko Yumeji
MA050	DARKLORE	★	Delinquent Vampire	Banri Sendou
MA051	DARKLORE	★	Werewolf	Denki Akiba
MA052	DARKLORE	★	Demon	Gureko Nankin
MA053	DARKLORE	★★	Demon God "Shuten Douji"	Makoto Sajima
MA054	DARKLORE	★★	Vampire Lord "Ray Arucard"	Chata Tachibana
MA055	DARKLORE	★★★	Demon God "Shuten Douji"	Makoto Sajima
MA056	DARKLORE	★★★	Vampire Lord "Ray Arucard"	Chata Tachibana
MA057	ERASER		Android Servant	Kanan
MA058	ERASER		Student Angel	Aya Shouoto
MA059	ERASER		Prototype Android	Lala Takemiya
MA060	ERASER		Angel	Sakurako Gokurakuin
MA061	ERASER	★	Cherubim	Nobita Nobi
MA062	ERASER	★	Dragon Warrior "Zunag"	Hirotaka Kisaragi
MA063	ERASER	★★	Principality	Gobanjima
MA064	ERASER	★	Ghost Shelled Android	Gobanjima
MA065	ERASER	★	Scrapped Android	Lala Takemiya
MA066	ERASER	★★	Dominion	Kiriko Yumeji
MA067	ERASER	★★	Archangel "Gabriel"	Sakurako Gokurakuin
MA068	ERASER	★★	Angel of Death "Azrael"	Aya Shouoto
MA069	ERASER	★★★	Archangel "Gabriel"	Sakurako Gokurakuin
MA070	ERASER	★★★	Angel of Death "Azrael"	Aya Shouoto

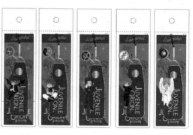

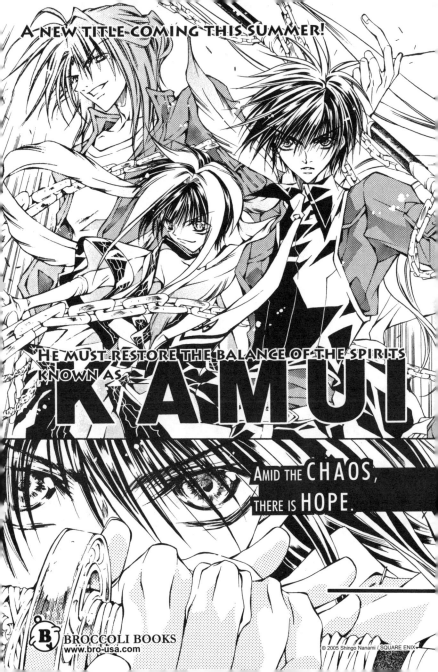

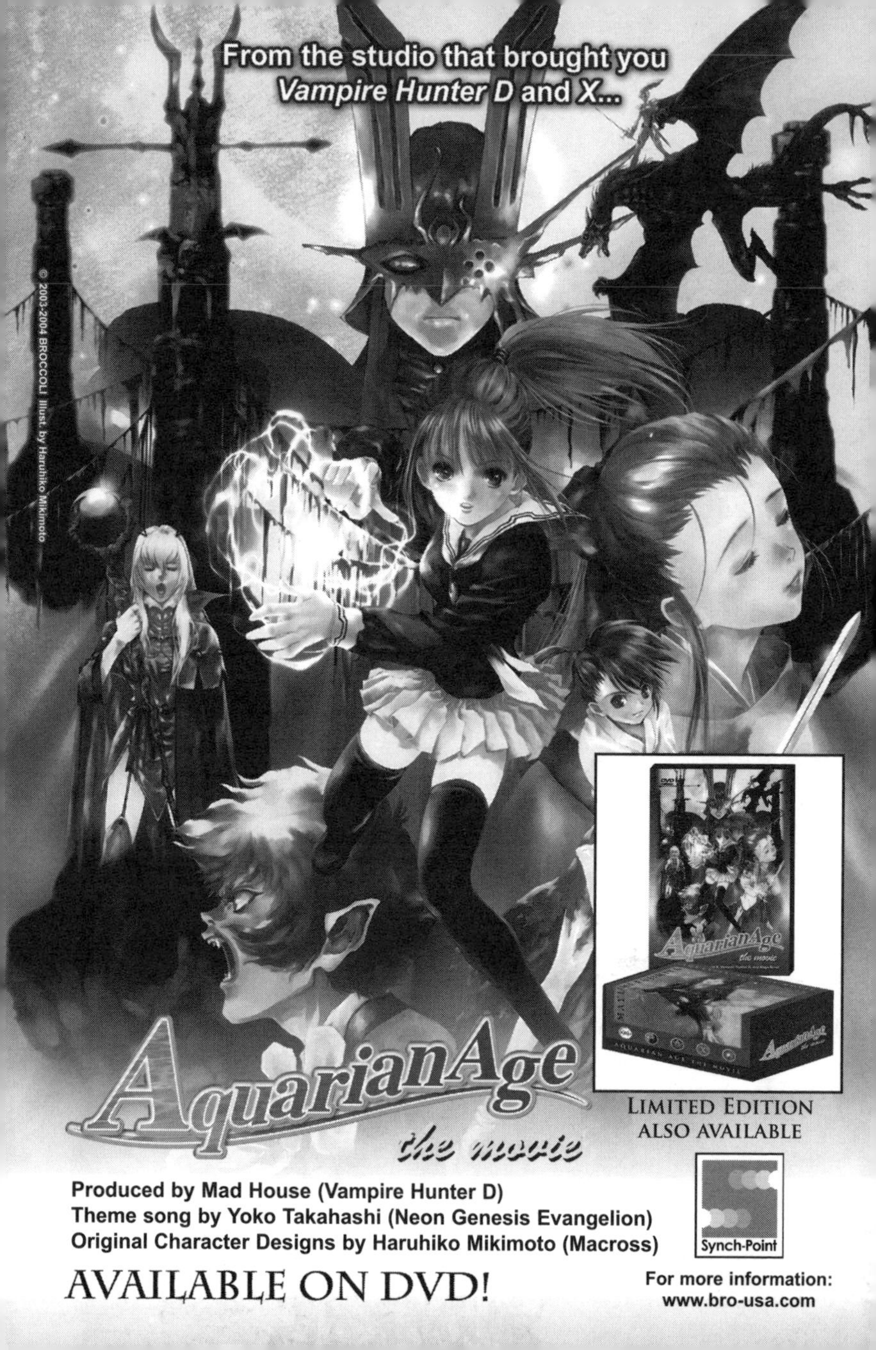

From the studio that brought you
Vampire Hunter D and X...
© 2003-2004 BROCCOLI Illust. by Haruhiko Mikimoto
AquarianAge
the movie
LIMITED EDITION
ALSO AVAILABLE
Produced by Mad House (Vampire Hunter D)
Theme song by Yoko Takahashi (Neon Genesis Evangelion)
Original Character Designs by Haruhiko Mikimoto (Macross)
AVAILABLE ON DVD!
Synch-Point
For more information:
www.bro-usa.com

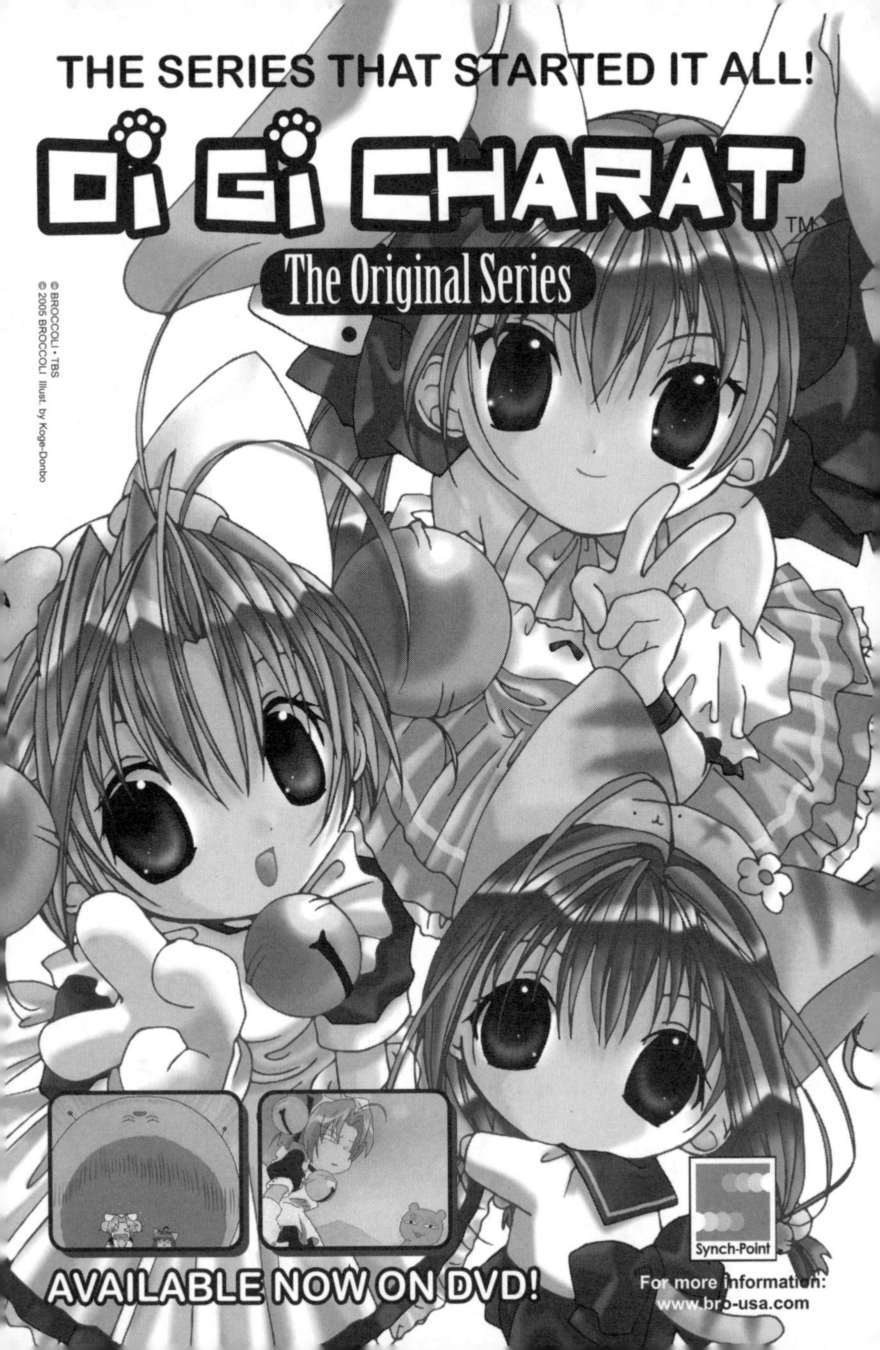
THE SERIES THAT STARTED IT ALL!
DI GI CHARAT™
The Original Series
© BROCCOLI • TBS
© 2005 BROCCOLI Illust. by Koge-Donbo
Synch-Point
AVAILABLE NOW ON DVD!
For more information:
www.bro-usa.com

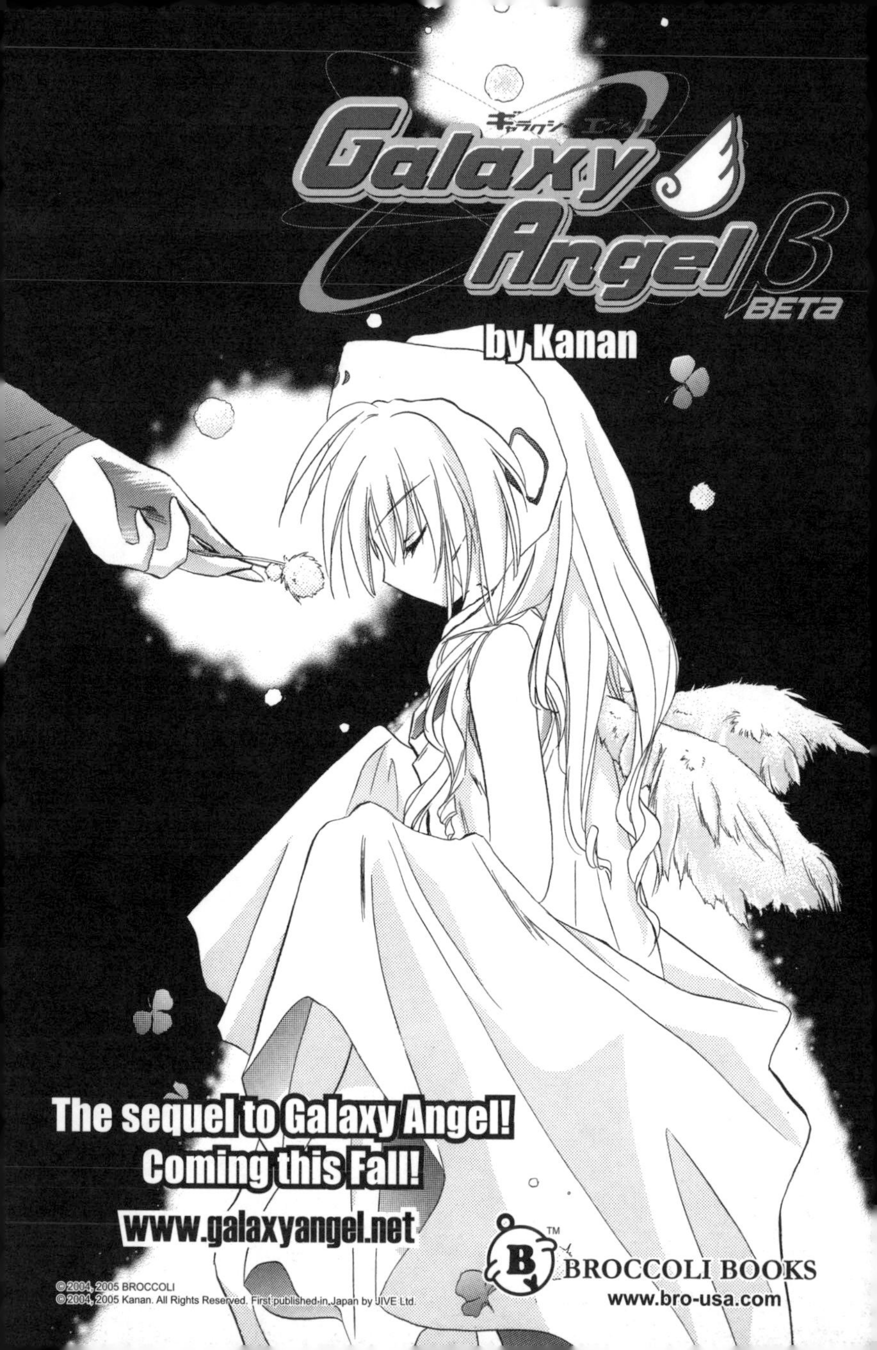
Galaxy Angel β BETA
by Kanan
The sequel to Galaxy Angel!
Coming this Fall!
www.galaxyangel.net
BROCCOLI BOOKS
www.bro-usa.com
© 2004, 2005 BROCCOLI
© 2004, 2005 Kanan. All Rights Reserved. First published in Japan by JIVE Ltd.

By the best selling author of FAKE!

Until the **FULL MooN**

Marlo has a problem. On the night of the full moon, this half-werewolf, half-vampire undergoes a mysterious and terrifying transformation:

He turns into a girl.

But when his parents turn to Doctor Vincent for help, Vincent's son, the vampire playboy David, develops an interest in Marlo's female form. If a remedy can't be found, their parents believe the next best solution is marriage—a marriage between Marlo and David!

A two volume series out now from Broccoli Books!

BROCCOLI BOOKS

READ: POINT: CLICK.:

www.bro-usa.com

After reading some Broccoli Books manga, why not look for more on the web? Check out the latest news, upcoming releases, character profiles, synopses, manga previews, production blog and fan art!